# Warner Mifflin

EARLY AMERICAN STUDIES

Series editors:
Daniel K. Richter, Kathleen M. Brown,
Max Cavitch, and David Waldstreicher

Exploring neglected aspects of our colonial,
revolutionary, and early national history and culture,
Early American Studies reinterprets familiar themes and
events in fresh ways. Interdisciplinary in character, and
with a special emphasis on the period from about 1600
to 1850, the series is published in partnership with the
McNeil Center for Early American Studies.

A complete list of books in the series
is available from the publisher.

# Warner Mifflin

## Unflinching Quaker Abolitionist

Gary B. Nash

**PENN**

UNIVERSITY OF PENNSYLVANIA PRESS

PHILADELPHIA

Published by
University of Pennsylvania Press
Philadelphia, Pennsylvania 19104-4112
www.upenn.edu/pennpress

Printed in the United States of America on acid-free paper
1 3 5 7 9 10 8 6 4 2

Library of Congress Cataloging-in-Publication Data

Names: Nash, Gary B., author.
Title: Warner Mifflin : unflinching Quaker abolitionist / Gary B. Nash.
Other titles: Early American studies.
Description: 1st edition. | Philadelphia : University of Pennsylvania Press, [2017] |
Series: Early American studies | Includes bibliographical references and index.
Identifiers: LCCN 2017016851 | ISBN 978-0-8122-4949-1 (hardcover)
Subjects: LCSH: Mifflin, Warner, 1745–1798. | Quakers—Delaware—Camden—Biography.
Classification: LCC BX7795.M48 N37 2017 | DDC 289.6092 [B] —dc23
LC record available at https://lccn.loc.gov/2017016851

Nothing which ought to be done, should be deemed impracticable; a few noble spirits may excite a whole nation to action . . . and finally triumph over evils the most enormous and appalling which have ever afflicted mankind.

—R. R. Gurley, Introduction to *Abolition of the African Slave-trade by the British Parliament Abridged from Clarkson [History of the Abolition of the Slave-trade] with a Brief View of the Present State of the Slave-trade and Slavery* (Augusta, Maine: P. A. Brinsmade, 1830), v.

The one thing that doesn't abide by majority rule is a person's conscience.

—Atticus Finch in Harper Lee, *To Kill a Mockingbird* (1960)

# Contents

# Abbreviations

| | |
|---|---|
| ALC | American Loyalist Claims, Public Record Office, UK, Ancestry.com |
| C-P-W | Coxe-Parrish-Wharton Papers, HSP |
| DCMB | Duck Creek Manumission Book, HSP transcribed version |
| DCMMM | Duck Creek Monthly Meeting Minutes, HSP transcribed version |
| DCWMMM | Duck Creek Women's Monthly Meeting Minutes |
| DHFFC | *Documentary History of the First Federal Congress*, Linda Grant DePauw et al., eds., 21 vols. (Baltimore: Johns Hopkins University Press, 1974–2017) |
| DHS | Delaware Historical Society, Wilmington |
| DPA | Delaware Public Archives, Dover |
| *Drinker Diary* | Elaine Forman, ed., *The Diary of Elizabeth Drinker*, 3 vols. (Boston: Northeastern University Press, 1991) |
| FHLSC | Friends Historical Library, Swarthmore College, Swarthmore, Pennsylvania |
| FMCSC | Franklin and Marshall College Archives and Special Collections, Lancaster, Pennsylvania |
| HSP | Historical Society of Pennsylvania, Philadelphia |
| *KCDLR* | *Kent County Delaware Land Records*, 12 vols.; various compilers (Millsboro, Delaware: Colonial Roots) |
| LC | Library of Congress, Washington, D.C. |
| LCMMM | Little Creek Monthly Meeting Minutes |
| LCP | Library Company of Philadelphia |
| PAS | Papers of the Pennsylvania Abolition Society, Microfilm edition, HSP |
| *PMHB* | *Pennsylvania Magazine of History and Biography* |
| PMMMM | Philadelphia Men's Monthly Meeting Minutes |
| PPAS | Papers of the Pennsylvania Abolition Society, HSP |

| | |
|---|---|
| PQMM | Philadelphia Quarterly Meeting Minutes |
| PWMMM | Philadelphia Women's Monthly Meeting Minutes |
| PYMIC | Philadelphia Yearly Meeting Indian Committee Records, QCHC |
| PYMM | Philadelphia Yearly Meeting Minutes |
| PYM-MME | Philadelphia Yearly Meeting Minutes of Ministers and Elders |
| PYM-MS | Philadelphia Yearly Meeting Minutes for Sufferings |
| QCHC | Quaker Collection, Haverford College, Haverford, Pennsylvania |
| RIHS | Rhode Island Historical Society, Providence |
| SQMM | Southern Quarterly Meeting Minutes |
| WCLUM | William Clements Library, University of Michigan, Ann Arbor |
| *WMQ* | *William and Mary Quarterly* 3rd Series |
| WQMM | Western Quarterly Meeting Minutes |

# Introduction

*At a time when questions* about race, equality, and social justice flood the media, it is fitting to bring out of the shadows one of the most unflinching friends of black Americans who strode through the boisterous Revolutionary era. In a notice of his death, at the end of the eighteenth century, the new nation's foremost newspaper wrote that "The number, difficulties, and success of his labours in the cause of the enslaved Africans in the United States would furnish materials for a volume."[1] But such a volume has never been written, more than two centuries after the death of a man named Warner Mifflin. Today, his name is known to hardly anyone.

That was not true in the time of Franklin, Washington, Hamilton, Adams, Jefferson, and Madison. All these celebrated founders knew Warner Mifflin well, and some of them did not like what they saw in the man. Some of the luminaries of the European Enlightenment—especially St. John de Crèvecoeur, Jacques-Pierre Brissot de Warville, and Thomas Clarkson—communed with Mifflin, and they very much liked what he said, what he did, and what he stood for. There was no such thing as a mid-Atlantic Quaker who couldn't recognize the man, not just for his unusual height, little short of seven feet, but for his moral intensity that was exceeded only by his haunting fear that he would displease his God with inadequate efforts on behalf of black Americans. He was, in fact, the key bridge figure in the early abolitionist movement, connecting the first wave of antislavery spokesmen in the decades leading up to the American Revolution with another wave of emancipationists awakened in the third decade of the nineteenth century.[2] Operating between these two cohorts was a small but determined band of abolitionists whom historians only recently have begun to disinter from history's graveyard. Among them, Mifflin was the most energetic, the most uncompromising, and the most reviled.

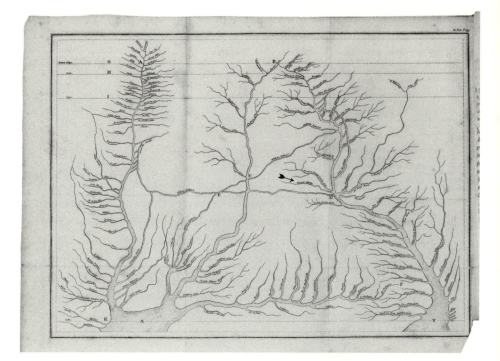

***Figure 1.*** Thomas Clarkson's eye-catching depicture of rivulets flowing into streams and streams joining to form rivers, followed a time line. Ralph Sandiford, Benjamin Lay, John Woolman, and Anthony Benezet preceded Mifflin (see arrow), with James Pemberton and Benjamin Rush falling in just behind him. Clarkson provided commentary explaining his map, at pains to show the prominent role of the Society of Friends while scanting the contributions of other denominations. From Clarkson's *History of the Rise, Progress, and Accomplishments of the Abolition of the African Slave Trade*, 1808. Courtesy Library Company of Philadelphia.

Among that first wave, none was more important than Anthony Benezet, school teacher of poor black and white children in Philadelphia and the most prolific author of letters and pamphlets denouncing the scourge of slavery disfiguring societies everywhere around the Atlantic rim. By the end of the American Revolution, when his body was beginning to fail him, his thoughts turned to Mifflin and two Philadelphia Friends as those most likely to help him get the approval of the Quaker Overseers of the Press to publish what might be his last stroke against slavery—a radical essay proposing immediate universal emancipation of enslaved Africans.[3] On May 3, 1784, with his essay unendorsed and unpublished, Benezet died at seventy. Black Philadelphians turned out by the hundreds to follow the casket to the grave, and all asked who would succeed the man who had led the way in creating an Atlantic-wide phalanx of those committed to ridding the world of the curse of enslaving fellow humans. The school teacher's demise, wrote James Pemberton, the city's prominent Quaker leader, "necessarily occasions a chasm in many respects not easily supplied and an additional weight which few will be disposed to bear."[4]

Few even tried to fill the vacuum. But Mifflin *was* so disposed. No one else in the 1780s and 1790s walked so unswervingly in the footsteps of Benezet. Nobody else was as ready to bear the slings and arrows ready to rain down on any postrevolutionary advocate of summarily ending the slave trade and dismantling the slave system. Remarkably, only a few years before Benezet's death he had been one of the largest slaveholders in Kent County, Delaware, living a life of affluence through inheritance, a propitious marriage, and the fruits of his slaves' labor. As of 1775, when an epiphany turned him into a tribune of the natural rights of all humans, black as well as white, the enslaved as well as the free, he could not have had the slightest inkling that he would soon join an international movement to abolish the African slavery that powered plantation societies in much of the Americas. Nor could he have had a hint that he would develop skills as a political lobbyist, drawing on his outsized stature and a disarming, sweetly reasonable person-to-person approach that made him a savvy and admirable antislavery advocate to those of his persuasion and, in the eyes of proslavery stalwarts, a disturber of the peace, an unhinged fanatic, a man who minded everyone's business but his own. At his death, seaboard newspapers celebrated him as the man who "begat hope in the minds of the miserable," while slaveholders "(by some of whom he was grossly insulted) trembled at his name." For one of his Kent County neighbors, appointed by President Jefferson to be the figurehead of law in the new Mississippi Territory, his unalloyed embrace of black Americans "disturbed society more than any other person in it."[5]

Forgotten for his leading role as a part of the postrevolutionary Atlantic-wide abolitionist network, Mifflin has also been overlooked as the pioneer of reparations for enslaved Africans—the radical idea, with roots in Old Testament scripture, that those carried across the Atlantic in chains and consigned to lifelong, uncompensated labor had the right not only to their freedom as fellow humans but also to some form of restitution for the unchristian pillaging of their bodies and minds. Since the civil rights movement of the post-World War II era, the idea of reparations has entered political discourse, but its origins in the conscience of a handful of mid-Atlantic Quakers, as the revolutionary era unfolded, have been almost entirely forgotten. Though he was not the first to propose what Quakers called "restitution," Mifflin was perhaps the first to move from idea to action, providing reparations through cash payments and land as well as shared crop arrangements for his liberated adult male slaves. That much done, he led the way in preaching "restitution" for those restored to the natural rights that Enlightenment thinkers declared the birthright of all humankind. This marks him as the forgotten trail blazer of a movement that attracts attention to the present day.

As the key abolitionist in the waning years of the eighteenth century, Mifflin wrote much less for publication than Benezet had done, and this may partly account for why he has receded into the mists of history. But distinct from Benezet, Mifflin became the premier legislative lobbyist of his generation, introducing methods of reaching those with power that became the hallmark of modern politicking. Amid many contemporaries who broadcast antislavery *sentiments*, Mifflin strode into state and national capitals to promote antislavery *action*. Many southerners regarded him as a menace to the new republic. Some thought he was the most dangerous man in America. They detested his repeated exercise of the right of petition, interrupting what they regarded as the legislative work on their agenda with memorials regarding the slave trade and slavery. They also hated his argument that an all-seeing and affronted God would punish Americans for "national sins" and that the republic would not survive the betrayal of its Enlightenment natural rights founding principles. He was welcome to keep his own conscience, they complained, and they needed none of his help to keep theirs.

## Measuring the Man

Restoring Warner Mifflin to public memory—perhaps even gaining him recognition in the history schoolbooks from which young people learn about the shaping of the American state, about cycles of reform, and about the long struggle for racial equality and social justice—requires mediating between his private and public lives. The latter is the easier of the two to document, for his words and actions can readily be seen in legislative papers and proceedings, court records, political correspondence, published and unpublished political memoirs and diaries, and pleading essays he put before the public in the 1790s. His message to fellow countrymen and fellow humans abroad is clear. His inner life, however, is more difficult to fathom, only partly understood by consulting more opaque sources: his private correspondence to friends and family, autobiographical fragments, notations in Quaker meeting records, descriptions of him by St. John de Crèvecoeur and J.-P. Brissot de Warville, heart-wrenching reflections on his life and dying days by his second wife, and memorials penned after his death.

In searching for that interaction between his interior life and his outward behavior, this much can be said at the outset. Mifflin's early years gave few clues to how his life would change. But by his late twenties, he experienced out-of-body visitations that shook him so severely that he soon became fiercely determined to live out the Golden Rule and devote himself to God's work. Frightened that he would disappoint the God who gave meaning to his life, he internalized the belief that if he was to save himself, he must save others.[6] Those others were fellow Quakers, oppressed Africans, and the nation at large. From 1775 forward, after he acquired a clear sense of purpose, his moral compass never failed him.

That moral compass directed him in two ways. First, he was drawn deeply into the campaign to revitalize American Quakerism that first swept through the colonies in the years before the American Revolution. Centered in Philadelphia, a band of determined reformers aimed to cleanse the Society of Friends of its materialistic ways and return it to the self-denial, simplicity, and purity of their seventeenth-century English ancestors. Deeply embedded in this effort was gradual withdrawal from slave trading and slaveholding, for it was love of material things that corroded Quaker rectitude and the enslaving of fellow humans that provided the wherewithal of such things of the world. By the time Mifflin had undergone a religious awakening in 1774, Quakers had moved away from trading in human flesh to purifying the Society from slaveholding altogether. Mifflin was not one of the leaders of this reform movement; rather, he became one of its faithful followers, earnestly committed to completing the work of self-purification as he traveled thousands of miles to visit Friends' meetings from New England to the Carolinas. That was his work *within* the ranks of American Quakerdom.

The needle of his moral compass directed him in a second way: in moving *outside* the Society of Friends to save the afflicted enslaved Africans and, in the process, to save the souls of those who practiced violence against them. In time, this became his crusade to save the soul of America. Filling the shoes of Anthony Benezet, he became a leader in the growing ranks of Atlantic basin emancipationists who looked beyond sectarian purification to governmental action on ending the slave trade and slavery. For Mifflin, this was a holy war—with words, not weapons. This idea frightened some who shared his belief that the new United States would drown in its own blood and corrupt the principles they boasted would usher in a new epoch of enlightened humanity but who thought he was moving too fast. Among those who tried to put a brake on his boldness were leading Philadelphia Friends. Mifflin sometimes bowed in submission to warnings that he should temper his intensity and curb his impatience, but he never surrendered the belief that he could change the arc of history.

Mifflin became broodingly devout, poring over his Bible and littering his letters and appeals to legislative bodies with scripture. But he never claimed a special channel of communication with God—the posture of a prophet. Nor did he feel that he was in possession of revealed truth, touched on the shoulder to enlighten the unenlightened. Rather, he abased himself before the omnipresent God and hoped he was worthy of a place in the Celestial Heaven. Twin sources, the Bible and the history of "antient Friends" witnessing for nonviolence, were the animating sources of his lifelong crusade against slavery. He worshiped Christ the Redeemer, and the moral pivot of his outlook on boisterous postrevolutionary America was no more complicated than the Golden Rule, for Friends a core guiding principle. He invoked it—"whatsoever ye would that men should do to you, do ye even so to them" (Matthew 7:12)—with variant wordings over and over again.

Mifflin's intense religious and moral commitment brought him up against a dilemma that he never fully acknowledged. His absorption with God's plans convinced him that without divine intervention no change was possible in a unruly and sinful world. Yet he spent his adult life acting on the belief that nothing would change without human will put into play. The helpless individual in providential history, putty in God's hands, had to be reconciled with the man of action who could make a difference. It was a reconciliation that he never resolved.

Mifflin was tenacious, hyper-earnest, singleminded, made of stronger stuff than most of his contemporaries. This came at a cost. More than once, he frightened himself, falling into periods of self-doubt and fits of remorse at pushing too far for conducting what seemed at times a one-man assault on the bastions of the slaveowners' republic. Agony of his spirit was sometimes produced by thoughts that he was not doing enough to root out the cancer of

***Figure 2.*** Brought from seventeenth-century County Wiltshire in England by Warner Mifflin's great-great-grandfather, the family coat of arms bore the motto "*nil desperandum*" (never despair). This characterized Mifflin's life. From Hilda Justice, *Life and Ancestry of Warner Mifflin*, 1905.

slavery but even more because of the condition of his country after the Revolution. It is likely that this intense introspection brought on recurrent "bodily indispositions," the general term Friends used to describe the gamut of maladies. Debilitating illnesses plagued him from his mid-twenties to his end at fifty-three. He almost willed his death in trying to convince an unbending nation that it was a fatal mistake to accommodate the growth of slavery rather than putting it on the road to extinction.

The other side of Warner Mifflin was a man who matched his steely pronouncements on slavery with sweet reasonableness in his dealings with fellow

Friends. After his death, remembrances of him spoke approvingly of his "amiable character," his "affable disposition," his "open, sociable behaviour towards all," and his qualifications "as a peacemaker, being frequently made use of in settling differences."[7] Even in his most fervent lobbying efforts with combative southerners, he insisted that he loved them as fellow humans, whatever their faults. Through all of it, never flinching, Mifflin insisted that he was a lover of his country, a well-wisher to all his fellow Americans, a brother at heart even with those who excoriated him, a servant of the Christian God, and a friend of all humankind. He was compassionate, he was forgiving, he was self-deprecating—and he was utterly impossible to intimidate.

That he could not fetter himself in his antislavery campaign exacted a toll on his family. He was too much away from his first and second wives and his many children, who needed him, especially in times of recurrent sicknesses, more than he was willing to concede. Ever restless, he was constantly in motion, leaving behind overtaxed spouses to manage his plantation properties in mid-Delaware. This left his finances shaky at best. Twice, he married women who bore up under his lengthy absences, gave birth between them to a dozen children, and treated his frequent maladies. His first wife, Elizabeth Johns, after gladly participating in the life of a self-indulgent Kent County planter-gentleman, followed him with reservations about his efforts at self-purification. His second wife, Ann Emlen, after her own teenage conversion experience, outdid him in "bearing the cross" while managing a household of stepchildren and children.

## The Light Within

For all but a few wayward years in his early manhood, Mifflin defined himself and governed his day-to-day life as a devout member of the Society of Friends, who lived by the doctrine of the Inward Light, that all believers—every man, woman, and child—could find divine light and the spark of redemption within themselves. For this leveling notion that reduced everyone to a simple community of worshipers, their Puritan enemies called them "the chokeweed of Christianity." Thomas Hobbes scoffed that in this demolition of class distinctions "every boy or wench thought he spoke with God Almighty." Early Friends fended off such attacks with a strength flowing from participation in a common religious experience that made them all "Children of the Light."[8] Fired by this egalitarian ethos, the Friends stripped their worship of liturgy, religious statuary, and other churchly apparatus. In Quaker eyes, salaried clergy delivering sermons from a carved pulpit were nothing but "a hireling ministry." In their bare, severely functional meeting houses, barren of pulpit, organ, choir, or communion table, silent meditation took up most of the service, broken only by a man or woman moved to speak spontaneously or sometimes by a divine message presented without script by someone recognized as a "Public Friend," or minister, for his or her spiritual warmth and inspiration. From their founding in mid-seventeenth-century England, Friends trusted that an uncluttered simplicity of belief and manner of worship would return believers to the purer days of the early apostles of the Christian church.

Likewise, the ideal of simplicity governed speech and dress. Founder George Fox had told his followers that "ye that dwell in the light and walk in the light use plainness of speech and plain words." Thus, the singular and familiar "thee" and "thou" replaced the plural and deferentially formal "you," in effect, a form of social leveling. Likewise, refusing "hat honour," doffing one's hat at the approach of a social superior, was to reject a customary form of deference. In dress, plain clothing signified a distaste for apparel advertising one's wealth or social classification. Hence the woman's dove gray or dull brown gown and plain shawl and bonnet, the avoidance of lace and silver buckles and buttons, the man's drab coat and broad-brimmed black hat all followed the counsel of Pennsylvania's Quaker founder William Penn: "If thou art clean and warm it is sufficient; for more doth but rob the poor." For Friends, everyone was equal in the sight of God. Such a commitment to equality, like water flowing downhill, led naturally to the Quaker concern for social justice.[9]

Though they disdained trained, salaried ministers, from their beginnings Friends put great stock in identifying men and women, some as young as sixteen, who exhibited special gifts in preaching the word of the Lord and in serving as counselors in their local areas. Such a man was Warner Mifflin, designated as an elder in his twenties, charged with counseling the young (and sometimes backsliding adults) and visiting families in neighboring or regional meetings to offer advice for walking the true path.[10] Equally important were "Public Friends," either resident or itinerant, whose "gifts" of inspired speaking were acknowledged by their local meetings for worship. These apostles, often traveling thousands of miles on foot or by horse and usually enduring extraordinary deprivations, served "almost the same function as the circulation of the blood in the animal organism," as Quaker historian Frederick Tolles has put it, "giving Friends at the remotest extremities of the Atlantic world a sense of belonging to a single body."[11] On his own prolonged horse journeys, not as a traveling minister but as an elder and political lobbyist, Mifflin was often accompanied by such Public Friends, as often female as male.[12] Mifflin was never acknowledged as a minister, and this hobbled his effort to spread the "truth," as he understood it, across the Atlantic. The reason is clear: though steeped in biblical knowledge and passionate in his campaign on behalf of a universal brotherhood endowed with natural rights, he was too political and insufficiently spiritual in his eloquence. Public Friends, speaking extemporaneously out of divine inspiration, nurtured the Light Within in other Quakers, but they did not haunt legislative chambers and importune congressmen and presidents.

## Fanaticism

Like radical activists in any age, Mifflin did not lack for critics. "Fanatic" was a favorite term hurled at him by his southern contemporaries, and the word can be found in the evaluation of some modern-day historians who harshly assay Quakers and others who dared to raise the issue of abolition after ratification of the Constitution. But who is a fanatic? And what is fanaticism? Much depends on place, time, and, circumstances; and much hinges on who deploys the word and in what context.

The word "fanatic" was familiar to Quakers from the moment of their founding in the midst of the fabric-rending English Civil War of the 1640s and 1650s. When the followers of Quaker founders George Fox and Elizabeth Fell broke up Anglican church services, inspired young women to go naked in the streets as a sign of the nakedness of supposed Christians, motivated followers to ride through villages backward on an ass, refused to report for militia duty and make war, denounced authorities in public places, and insisted on the spiritual equality of women, the charge of fanaticism clung to their simple clothes like mud—and they paid for it dearly. Massachusetts Puritans in the 1650s were sure the Quakers were fanatical—the "chokeweed" that threatened religious uniformity at the city on the hill. But who were the fanatics when four Quaker preachers, two of them women, ventured into the Bay Colony to preach the "inward light" available to every human seeking eternal peace, and died on the gallows on the Boston Commons, quickly to be lowered into an unmarked grave? Was it the Puritans or was it the Quakers? Stephen Crane, famous for his *Red Badge of Courage*, was sure in 1848 that it was the Puritans who were the fanatics and the Quakers the tolerationists.[13]

Quakers never suffered such charges of fanaticism when they flocked to the shores of the Delaware to build prospering colonies in Pennsylvania, New Jersey, and Delaware. Nor did their peace testimony occasion such an opprobrious label when they would not fight during the Seven Years' War and then during the colonial struggle for independence. Even Thomas Paine's sledge-hammer attack on the Quakers in the appendix to his *Common Sense* (1776) never charged Friends with fanaticism, only for "inconsistency," for "mingling religion with politics," and for misplaced logic. Pinning the badge of fanaticism on Quakers came only *after* the victorious fight for independence brought peace in its wake. And it came only from a handful of South Carolina and Georgia Congressmen. Postwar Quaker emancipationists, particularly Warner Mifflin, who hovered over the conscience of the nation with calls for ending the slave trade and gradually abolishing slavery, became the fanatics of America, even if ending slavery had emerged as a key element of a revolutionary reform agenda and indeed had grown "from a strange belief held by some dissenting Protestant Quakers into a secular idea that pervaded revolutionary societies."[14]

To call someone a fanatic is to alert the reader that this person's ideas or behavior are not to be considered seriously, except as they pose a mortal threat to the community or nation. But if we turn our angle of repose, as did historian Robert McColley a half-century ago, we can appreciate that people such as Warner Mifflin "had faith in the power of moral energy to create beneficial change, while the statesmen, supposedly some of the most liberal in American history, held to a gloomy set of immutable principles which man, it appeared, could have no power to alter."[15] Mifflin's critics charged that his work for ending the slave trade and beginning the gradual abolition of slavery would fracture if not dissolve the new nation. But was he wrong in contending that the union could never be other than fractured and fragile while slavery continued? Or was Mifflin right in regarding the defenders of slavery as the fanatics, those who defiled the bedrock principles of natural rights and universal freedom on which the nation was founded and defied the biblical pronouncement that all humans sprang from Adam's seed? So how do we take the measure of such a man, who never called for immediate abolition but only for gradual emancipation? In the main, historians have agreed with a small number of hardcore southerners, representing a tiny fraction of postwar white Americans, that Quaker idealism had to yield to political pragmatism, that slavery could *not* have been abolished by the revolutionary generation. It is an argument that reeks of the odious concept of historical inevitability, almost always in historical writing a subterfuge advanced to excuse mistakes and virtually never employed by those writing on behalf of the victims of a supposedly inevitable decision.[16]

Whether we judge Warner Mifflin's crusade as fanatical, or, alternatively, see it as a shrewdly calculated, strenuously uphill battle against severe odds, it is clear that his struggle on behalf of black Americans was all but encoded in his genes. So far as he was concerned, it mattered little how often he was publicly denounced as a fanatic in the halls of Congress, for he took his cues not from external events but from inward promptings. John Woolman and Anthony Benezet were not charged with fanaticism because they wrote at a time when even those most heavily invested in chattel bondage regretted the cruel, coercive system, even agreeing they were corrupting themselves as they exploited the enslaved. But Mifflin's antislavery activism centered not on penning screeds deploring slavery but rather on lobbying legislatures and pelting them with memorials. Woolman went from house to house on his foot journeys into the slaveholding South to soften the hearts of slaveowners. Benezet kept to his schoolhouse and his modest dwelling, scripting his arresting essays. Mifflin was different, raising the bar of antislavery commitment. On horse journeys carrying him from mid-Delaware northward as far as New England and southward to North Carolina, he challenged the centers of state and national political power, transforming antislavery sentiments into antislavery action. His life's purpose was not to imperil the fragile state of the new republic, but to save it by excising the cancer of slavery that ate at its vitals.

In recent years, as the abolitionists of Mifflin's generation have earned some respect, along with a revival of Quaker studies, this has begun to put the charge of fanaticism at bay. Once dismissed as hopelessly naïve or clinically unhinged for insisting that slavery was the new nation's Achilles heel and that the republic would not survive slavery's continuation without massive bloodshed, the postrevolutionary activists are gaining greater appreciation.[17] Still, students in the schools learn, if postwar abolitionists are treated at all, that they were dreamy, unrealistic, meddling fanatics who threatened to tear apart the fragile new nation. This puts young readers on the side of Deep South Congressmen in the 1790s who heaped abuse on Quaker petitions—some drafted by

Mifflin—that drew on the Constitution's general welfare clause to lobby for ending the slave trade and the gradual abolition of slavery.

It is the goal of this book to restore to memory the man known to Deep South Congressmen as "a meddling fanatic" who kept stirring the embers of sectionalism after the ratification of the Constitution of 1787. In effect, he all but stitched a target on the back of the simple, undyed clothes he wore. Yet he inspired those who believed that America had betrayed its founding principles of natural and inalienable rights by allowing slavery and the dispossession of Indian lands to spread in the new nation. Mifflin understood that the arc of history bends slowly; but he believed that testifying for the dispossessed, even if his efforts appeared unsuccessful on the surface, would move the arc in the direction of universal freedom and racial justice and the belief that humankind was indivisible.

# Chapter 1

## The Making of a Quaker Reformer

*"I was born, and chiefly raised* on the Eastern Shore of Virginia." Thus began the memoir of Warner Mifflin, written in the year the new nation was waging war with native peoples in the trans-Appalachian territory and negotiating touchy relations with revolutionary France. "Although my parents were of the religious society called Quaker," he continued, "and exemplary in their lives, yet I witnessed great incitements to a departure from the principles held by that people, there being none of that profession, except our family, within sixty miles."[1]

To be more precise, Mifflin entered the world on August 21, 1745, in Accomack County, on the ocean side of Virginia's Eastern Shore, just below the Maryland border. Here at Pharsalia, his parents' plantation worked by scores of enslaved Africans, he received his early home schooling as much in the fields and barns and seaside as in the spacious house. "My associates," he wrote in a memoir of his life, "were those who tenaciously held the prevailing sentiments in favor of slavery," and he, like his father, "was in great danger of becoming blinded by the influence of custom, the bias of education, and the delusions of self-interest." From these beginnings, where enslaved blacks outnumbered the small Mifflin family more than ten to one, emerged the new American republic's most outspoken antislavery advocate and a man unusually devoted to helping free black men and women obtain justice in an unfriendly white world.

Though raised in Virginia, Mifflin would make Philadelphia, the Delaware River capital of William Penn's "Holy Experiment," the city where he was anchored, religiously, ideologically, and politically. He never resided in Philadelphia, but he was a familiar figure for many years as he walked the streets in his drab collarless overcoat and brimmed black hat, standing half a foot or more over his fellow countrymen.[2]

Understanding how Mifflin became a radical abolitionist requires some backtracking to his Quaker roots. Almost all the early Quaker antislavery spokesmen—Daniel Francis Pastorius, William Southeby, John Hepburn, Ralph Sandiford, Benjamin Lay, John Woolman, and Anthony Benezet—were Philadelphia area Quakers, and only Lay had ever been involved in the dirty business of enslaving fellow humans. But Mifflin's maternal and paternal grandparents, as well as those of his first wife and her parents and grandparents, were among the Chesapeake Bay peninsula's largest prerevolutionary slaveowners. Chews, Galloways, Littletons, Eyres, Warners, Maxfields, Parrishes, and Johns were all branches of Warner Mifflin's elaborate family tree. All were well known among the slave- and land-rich patriarchs of the tobacco, corn, and wheat producing plantations that connected them with the wider Atlantic world. All were Quakers except the Littletons. This tangled ancestry, as we will see, was an inspiration for Mifflin to rescue the victims of a long lineage of slaveowners, but also a thorny problem threatening to trip him up at awkward moments.

## A Philadelphia Quaker on the Eastern Shore

Warner Mifflin's great-great-grandfather, John Mifflin, had preceded William Penn to Pennsylvania, arriving with his wife and teenage son from Wiltshire, England, in 1677 as part of a small flotilla of ships laden with hardy Quakers numbering in the hundreds. Landing in what became Burlington, West New Jersey, they were the second group of Quakers planting themselves on the east side of the Delaware River in a sparsely populated territory contested by the English and Dutch since 1664. The Lenape people for years had jockeyed with European newcomers, as was now the case. On the other side of the Delaware were about one hundred Swedish, Finnish, and English families—the Swedes most numerous among them—who had clung to their log cabin outpost at Wicaco, on the Delaware River in present-day South Philadelphia, for two generations.[3] Unique along the Atlantic seaboard, this mosaic of Europeans mingling with little bloodshed among native people prefigured Penn's open-door policy.

Good fortune accompanied John Mifflin and his Quaker friends. In reaching the mid-Atlantic seaboard region, they were spared the horrific English-Indian bloodbath that just a few years before had scourged the Chesapeake region to the south and New England to the north. For many years, the Lenape people had maintained steady trading and political relationships with the Swedish and Finnish settlers, marred only by occasional low-grade violence. Edmund Andros, the duke of York's governor, operating from Manhattan but extending his authority to the Delaware region in 1675, meant to keep it that way, though the arrival of the English Quakers began to complicate the multiparty relationships. All the more to the arriving Quakers' advantage, smallpox and other European diseases had reduced the Lenape people severely over recent decades, easing the competition for land on both sides of the Delaware. To their dismay, the Quakers triggered another smallpox epidemic, which by one Quaker account swept through the Lenape villages so hard that "they could not bury all the dead."[4]

Early accounts of the Burlington settlement tell of how the Quakers hastily constructed wigwams, patterned after those of the Lenape, to get through the winter of 1677–1678, and how the Friends relied on the "very serviceable" natives who provided provisions until crop regimens could be established the next year. From this modest beginning, Mifflin and his farming family might well have secured a foothold in West New Jersey, where working the porous, relatively flat land seemed favorable. Yet difficulties in securing clear title to land led some of the Quaker newcomers, including John Mifflin's family, to think that their New Jerusalem on the banks of the Delaware lay elsewhere. As summer heat rose in late June 1679, the Mifflins, father and son, were among thirteen Quakers who reconnoitered the other side of the Delaware River, liked what they saw, and petitioned Governor Andros for land near the falls of present-day Morristown.[5]

Andros approved the grant, but with unexpected results. When the "old settlers"—Swedish, Finnish, and a few English—joined their allies, the Lenape, in opposing this land grant, the Mifflins wavered. It was a wise choice. Within a year, their Quaker friends relocating across the Delaware were beset by angry Lenape and soon were crying that they were "in great danger of our lives, of houses burning, of our goods stealing, and of our wives and children affrighting."[6]

Meanwhile, the Mifflins stayed put. But, seeking more secure land amid the tangle of claims—and perhaps ruffled by a criminal charge against John Mifflin—they moved across the Delaware, not upriver to the falls but downriver to the mostly Swedish settlement at Wicaco. "They lived some time among the Swedes' settlements on the banks of the Delaware and Schuylkill," wrote a

**Figure 3.** When William Russell Birch painted Fountain Green for his *Country Seats of North America* (1808), he limned a much improved and extended version of the one-story stone building, without wings or parapet, built by Warner Mifflin's great-grandfather and where his grandfather was born. Courtesy Library Company of Philadelphia.

grandson of John Mifflin, embedding themselves, even if briefly, amid the Swedes and Finns.[7] This sojourn lasted less than a year. In October 1680 the duke of York's court at Upland (now Chester) granted John Mifflin and his son 300 acres—later remeasured at 270 acres—on the east bank of the Schuylkill River. Partly meadow, partly loamy land tilled for generations by the Lenape people, and partly forest, it became the homestead for six generations of Mifflins. With the help of his son, John Mifflin began the construction of Fountain Green, a stone farmhouse in what is now Philadelphia's Fairmount Park.

If this was a lonely life, it would not remain so very long. John Mifflin and his son John Mifflin II were among those witnessing the arrival of the Quaker settlers recruited by William Penn, who clambered ashore just fourteen months later. It was the first wave of a human groundswell washing up on Philadelphia's shores between December 1681 and December 1682—twenty-three ships carrying some two thousand settlers. Six thousand more arrived, including William Penn and his family, in the next three years, driving up the

price of land and proving a windfall for those like John Mifflin who had preceded them.

Along with a preponderance of yeoman farmers and skilled artisans came
indentured servants. Then came Africans—150 directly from West Africa in
late 1684 in a Bristol-based slave ship. The Mifflins were probably among the
Philadelphia pioneers who eagerly parted with precious gold and silver to
obtain strong hands and backs. That enslaved Africans were involved in erect-
ing additional buildings at Fountain Green is indicated by John Mifflin's will
in 1713 that included "all the messuage, tenement, plantation and tract of land
... with the other buildings and improvements, with all the negroes and other
servants and all the stock and creatures remaining on and belonging to the
plantation."[8] Continuing to own slaves and indentured servants like so many
other prospering Quakers, Mifflin cast aside the warnings of the nearby Germantown Quakers, who in 1688, led by Francis Daniel Pastorius, the learned
and lawyerly leader of German immigrants, warned that Pennsylvania's
Quaker-run "Holy Experiment" would lose its reputation in Europe if it continued to participate in the stealing of unoffending people in Africa and "here
handle men as they handle their cattle."[9] Two generations later this branch of
the Mifflin family would begin to reckon with these warnings.

In 1683, just a year after William Penn's arrival, John Mifflin II married at
twenty-one. His wife, Elizabeth Hardy, another recent English Quaker immigrant, bore nine children and outlived her husband by twenty-two years. John
II took possession of Fountain Green after his parents transferred the title to
him in 1693, and soon became part of Penn's inner circle, prospering as a merchant in the blossoming city. He died in 1714, leaving Fountain Green to his
widow during her lifetime and then to be divided among the surviving children.
Among them was their firstborn, Edward Mifflin, the grandfather of Warner
Mifflin.

Born in 1685, the year after William Penn returned to London, Edward
Mifflin had a bright future ahead of him in Philadelphia. Bearing the name of
one of the city's founding Quaker families, he nimbly took his place in the
ranks of merchants securing a foothold in the thickening commercial network
of the Atlantic basin. But suddenly, in the spring of 1714, he abandoned the
budding port city, making his way to Magothy Bay at the southernmost tip of
Northampton County on Virginia's remote Eastern Shore, probably by horse,
in a day of only the most primitive carriage travel. The reason has been shrouded

by the keepers of Quaker records and unknowingly by historians of the Quaker adventure in North America.

Why would the eldest son of John Mifflin II withdraw from the political, economic, and social life of Penn's "green countrie town" for a region of the Eastern Seaboard where Quakers had suffered severe persecution and where their rude meetinghouses were hardly functioning? Certainly it was not that Edward Mifflin was without prospects in Philadelphia. He was anything but poor and knew that after his father's death, which the family realized must come very soon, he would receive a valuable lot on High Street (now Market Street), a share of Fountain Green after his mother's death, and an insider's lane on the Atlantic world commerce in which Philadelphia was a fast growing partner.

The answer to why he put Philadelphia behind him is the simplest of all: he had fallen in love. The magnet was the fetching twenty-year-old Mary Eyre Littleton (c. 1694–1775) of Northampton County and very likely she was pregnant. Buried in the minutes of the Philadelphia Monthly Meeting that administered the preparative meeting for worship at Second and High Streets was this brief request: "John Mifflin on behalf of his son Edward Mifflin informs this meeting that he intends to take a wife in Virginia and desires a certificate [of removal]."[10] This was the standard practice of the tightly organized Society of Friends—to issue their kind of passport to departing members seeking admission to a preparative meeting at their new destination. That his father was the one requesting the certificate is explained by the fact that Edward had already hurried southward, where he had witnessed the will of a certain Susanna Browne two months before.[11] Within months, after an inconveniently short period of marriage, Edward Mifflin became the father of a baby girl. They named her Ann after his wife's mother. We will see in the chapters below how this daughter lived a sadly short life, long enough only to bear a daughter whose long and harrowing life unspooled during an era of revolution in recurrent intersections with Warner Mifflin, her second cousin.[12]

Edward Mifflin's wedding to Mary Eyre Littleton at windswept Magothy Bay must have been an unusual mix of sober reflection and joyous celebration because the bride, now or nearing twenty-one, had been widowed little more than a year before. Even in an age when death was a constant presence, it was unusual that her young husband had died in their first year of marriage. No records reveal the cause of death, but in penning his will on the last day of 1712,

Southey Littleton (1692–1713) described himself as "sick and weak of body." Within two months of setting his signature to the will, he slipped away.

From the beginning, it was a fraught marriage. On the positive side, Southey Littleton came land-rich to the marriage in 1712 and traced his lineage back to England's medieval nobility. In Virginia, his grandfather had been a trusted member of the council of William Berkeley, the royal governor of the colony in the 1670s when Nathaniel Bacon led an insurrection of indentured servants, slaves, and land-poor settlers. Southey's father, Nathaniel Littleton (1665–1703), left extensive landholdings to his adolescent son.[13]

On the downside, the Littletons were staunch Anglicans, and this must have troubled the family of his betrothed young Quaker woman. But to secure the heart of the young Mary Eyre, Southey had promised to become a "convinced Quaker." Local Friends had admitted him to the Society of Friends— or so the legend goes—on a pledge to live a Quaker life. His will shows that he kept his pledge, providing a substantial sum to build a Quaker meetinghouse in the Magothy Bay area.[14]

If shaken by the demise of her young husband, Mary Eyre Littleton could at least face the future with enviable resources. Apart from the fortune she inherited, she also was the daughter of one of Northampton County's wealthiest land and slaveowners. Her father, Daniel Eyre, was the son of one of the Eastern Shore's first Quaker residents—a man who had settled there when the Virginia legislature was passing laws in 1659 that prohibited Quakers from assembling for worship or even remaining in the colony, on the grounds that they were "an unreasonable and turbulent sort of people . . . attempting to destroy religion, lawes, communities, and all bonds of civil societie."[15] Rivaling that of the Puritan campaign to proscribe Quakerism in Massachusetts, this persecution drove most Virginia Quakers north to Maryland's Eastern Shore. There they established Maryland meetinghouses that continue to the present day. But some Virginia Eastern Shore Quakers, the Eyres among them, held on, hoping for better days.[16]

If affluence was of concern, the marriage of Edward Mifflin and Mary Eyre Littleton had little to lack. Still, it was doubtless a sober, Quaker marriage, almost certainly a "home wedding," because the decayed local meetinghouse many miles to the north had not gathered Friends for several years.[17]

Mifflin's abrupt relocation, trading northern Quaker urbanism for southern Quaker-adverse ruralism, plunged him into large-scale slave dealing at a time when the calcifying system of enslavement was shutting down chances for enslaved Africans to obtain freedom.[18] At twenty-nine, Edward had moved some 240 miles south, traveling through the fertile Chester County Quaker farms south of Philadelphia, across the head of Chesapeake Bay, through the Eastern Shore of Maryland where several Quaker meetinghouses had been established, and finally through Accomack and Northampton Counties of Virginia's Eastern Shore. There, just north of the tip of the peninsula he alit at Magothy Bay, where the scent of salt water was always in the air. Taking up life on his wife's dowry land, the displaced Philadelphia Quaker became master of a slave labor force working a 4,050-acre plantation. Known as the Golden Quarter, the plantation embraced forested wetlands and salt marshes—home to shorebirds and waterfowl that were so prolific that they could blacken the sky when in flight. All of it looked eastward toward the Atlantic.[19]

For some fourteen years, Warner Mifflin's grandparents lived at their remote, windswept plantation at Magothy Bay, attended by many slaves. Three children came in the early years of the marriage, all dying young.[20] At the Chesapeake peninsula's tip, only the occasional visit of a traveling Quaker minister from England allowed them to cling to their Quaker ties, though family lore maintains that they practiced their Quaker faith in their home setting. John Fothergill, a tough English farmer-turned-minister, capable of enduring the most strenuous Quaker traveling ministries, reached the Mifflins in 1721.[21] The next year brought them their first child to survive infancy. They named the boy Daniel (who would become Warner Mifflin's father). Six years later, in 1728, Samuel Bownas, another English "messenger of the truth," found the Mifflins at Magothy Bay. This was the kind of occasion for the handful of Quakers in Northampton County to gather from great distances to commune with a traveling minister who could relate his foot journeys and fortify their spirits.[22]

In the same year, perhaps seeking Quaker fellowship and favored with several options accrued through a dower-rich marriage, Edward Mifflin and his wife moved their family north to the Virginia-Maryland border to take up life at Pharsalia, another plantation his wife had inherited from her first tragic marriage.[23] Here in Accomack County, on 840 acres on the northern side of Great Mattapony Creek where Swansgutt Creek emptied into Chincoteague Bay, John Fothergill found them on a return trip to the Eastern Shore in 1736. An enterprising man, Edward began assembling additional plantations, including one in 1735 with a water mill just a few miles from Pharsalia across the Maryland boundary in Somerset County. Now one of Accomack County's largest cultivators of tobacco and corn, Mifflin had reached the top layer of the Eastern Shore's planter aristocracy. In an ironic twist of history, Warner Mifflin's Quaker grandfather from Philadelphia had become lord of large tracts of land long possessed by those who had persecuted Quakers, even refusing to recognize their marriages, a few decades before.[24]

It was here at Pharsalia that Warner Mifflin's father, Daniel Mifflin, reached adulthood, surrounded by the plantation's enslaved men and women. At twenty-one, after his father Edward died in 1743 at fifty-eight, Daniel became the master of Pharsalia, along with the water mill property just across the Maryland line. For many years his mother would remain with him at Pharsalia, guaranteed her place in her husband's will. To Samuel, his second son, Edward bequeathed the old Fountain Green homestead in Philadelphia. To the youngest son, Southey, went the valuable lot on High Street. The rest of the estate was bequeathed in equal parts to his widow and his three sons. Included were thirty-three slaves (leaving "a young Negro woman" named Nan to his granddaughter, Ann Eyre); hundreds of cattle, sheep, pigs, oxen, horses; plantation tools; spinning and weaving apparatus; and an immensity of furniture, housewares, bolts of various cloths, guns, barreled beverages, Bibles, and Quaker literature.[25]

A year after his father's death, Daniel Mifflin, staying within the fold of the Society of Friends, found the marriageable seventeen-year-old Mary Warner nearly one hundred miles to the northwest in Kent County, Maryland. Still a sliver of the population, Quakers could be counted on to flock to a marriage within one or two days' ride of their meetinghouse, and this case was no different. Forty-five Quakers gathered at the Cecil Meetinghouse, in Lynch, Maryland, close to the Pennsylvania boundary, to witness the marriage of Warner Mifflin's mother and father, she the daughter of the Cecil Monthly Meeting clerk—the most important leadership position in the region. After "some time of solitidy and waiting upon the Lord," as the marriage certificate solemnized it, the marriage partners stood, taking each other by the hand and pledging their troth.[26]

## Boyhood at Pharsalia

Returning to Pharsalia, the young Mifflin couple, still distant from the nearest Quaker meeting, kept faith within their own household, fortified by the books in his father's small library from which Daniel had absorbed his Quaker faith.[27] They named their first child Warner, after his mother's family name. Born a year after his parents' marriage when his mother was eighteen, Warner, like his father, received his Quaker upbringing at Pharsalia without the company of Quaker friends or regular weekly worship. His mother saw to that. "Being a lively witness of the benefit of silent retirement in families," recalled one of Warner's best friends after his death, she "maintained a godly zeal in promoting opportunities of quietude with her children and servants, often several times in a week."[28] To judge by Warner Mifflin's highly literate torrent of letters, memorials to state and federal legislatures, and published pamphlets, it was a rigorous home schooling, at least equal to that available at the hands of private tutors. Only an occasional Quaker home marriage at Pharsalia netted together the scattered Eastern Shore families, whose limited marital choices led to frequent second cousin marriages.[29]

Growing up at Pharsalia, Warner learned a lot about life cycles and the precariousness of life. Before he turned six, he saw his parents bury his brother and two sisters who died as infants. Early deaths were common in an area regarded as unhealthy, but this was unusual. Then in 1754, when Warner was almost nine, a robust brother, Daniel, arrived. Two years later death again hovered over Pharsalia when his mother died before her thirtieth birthday. Though the Quaker records give no hint of the cause, it is possible that malaria bred in the mosquito-infested tidal salt marshes at Pharsalia had claimed another victim.[30]

A widower at thirty-five, Warner's father within a year found a new wife, Ann Walker of nearby Mattapony Hundred. She brought to the marriage a 200-acre plantation that had once belonged to Phillip Mongon, one of Accomack County's free black men and one of the casualties of the clamping down on free black independence in the late seventeenth century.[31] Eager to solidify his Quaker commitment, Warner's father, "not having opportunity of being joined to any monthly meeting of Friends more convenient to him," applied to the Little Creek meeting, two days by horse to the north, a month before his proposed wedding.[32] Was this move triggered by ripples of the Friends' reform movement centered in Philadelphia that was gathering momentum during the Seven Years' War, leading Daniel Mifflin partially to conquer the distance between Pharsalia and the nearest Quaker meetinghouse? Or was he concerned, after burying three of his first four children and then his young wife, that he needed to anchor his uncertain life through a more regular connection to

Quaker worship? Whatever the reason, his father's acceptance into the Little Creek meeting was soon to have an important bearing on Warner Mifflin's life.

Twelve-year-old Warner, tall for his age, was present at the wedding in October 1757. In his autobiographical accounts, he never mentioned his mother's death or that of his stepmother, who joined his grandmother in raising him as a teenager. But taken far north of Pharsalia to witness the Quaker wedding joining his father and stepmother, he surely understood that his father was striving to strengthen his Quaker faith. Rather than holding the wedding at Pharsalia, the decision had been made to tie the marriage bonds at the small, framed, Little Creek Meetinghouse five miles east of the village of Dover, Delaware, but almost one hundred miles by a primitive road from Pharsalia to Lewes at the southern boundary of Delaware and then by the King's Highway north to Dover.

It was probably the first Quaker meetinghouse Warner had seen. We can only imagine what the boy might have thought, quietly peering at the plainly dressed men and women, shorn of the finery seen at most Christian weddings, who came to bear witness to the simple Quaker ceremony. Stripped of the music, Bible readings, exchange of rings, and officiating of a priest or minister that were customary in other Christian churches, the ceremony Warner looked upon was over almost before it began.

As practiced by Quakers since their inception more than a century before in England, the Friends filed into the simple clapboard meetinghouse, took their rough-hewn seats, and sat silently with a few minutes of solitude and "waiting upon the Lord." Then Warner watched his father stand. "Taking Ann by the hand, did in a solemn manner openly declare that he took her to be his wife, promising through divine assistance, to be unto her a faithful and loving husband until the Lord is pleased by death to separate them." The boy then saw his new mother repeat the same words with the roles reversed but adding that "according to the custom of marriage assumed the surname of her husband."

That was it. Only remaining was the signing of the marriage document— "to these present set their hands and we whose names are hereunder subscribed being among others present at the solemnization of their said marriage and subscription." The spirit of George Fox was almost palpable in the modest room, for the ceremony, only a few minutes long, conformed to Fox's advice: "The right joining in marriage is the work of the Lord only, and not the priests' or the magistrates'; for it is God's ordinance and not man's; . . . we marry none;

*Figure 4.* Little Creek Meetinghouse. Marriages, like First Day (Sunday) worship, were based in silence. The Quaker marriage ceremony, unchanged over nearly four centuries, is available on many websites. Library of Congress.

it is the Lord's work, and we are but witnesses." What Warner saw that day would be repeated down the generations to the present day.[33]

As Warner passed through his teens, he watched his father steadily acquire new tracts of land to be worked by many enslaved Africans. When he was six, his father purchased one hundred acres on the barrier Assateague Island, where today wild ponies that have evolved into a subspecies of their own are the delight of visitors roaming the 37-mile-long Assateague Island National Seashore. Mifflin augmented his Assateague holdings near the end of his life: 163 acres across the channel from Piney Island and another 358 acres at Ragged Point. How the young Warner might have skiffed across the inland waterway to gambol along the beaches of the island we can only imagine. But the importance of the island to his father is indicated by how the first third of his long will, penned in 1795, at seventy-three, spelled out in detail his Assateague Island purchases and the sales of some portions of it.[34]

A man ever working to provide for his growing family, Warner's father secured more land in 1750 upstream from Pharsalia, where he could build a dam to provide water power for another grist mill. Here, the wheat and corn bounties, harvested by slaves, were milled and sent by shallop or wagon to the grain-hungry markets in Wilmington and Philadelphia. The purchases continued in the 1760s, as Warner entered his twenties, at a pace that made his father a land baron on the Virginia-Maryland border. Acquisitions continued in the early 1770s until the Revolution shut down his appetite for extending his plantations. By the time the tax assessor came around in 1783, Warner Mifflin's father had stitched together 2,943 acres of Eastern Shore property worked by about one hundred enslaved Africans.[35]

Meanwhile, Warner saw his stepmother bring a succession of babies into the world. The first, born in 1758 just ten months after her marriage, presented Warner with his first half-brother. Four more half-siblings, all girls, came regularly at intervals of two years before Warner was twenty. Two of them died early, before he left home, and the other two, Mary and Patience, became his playmates. Four more half-sisters would follow, but that was in the future. With a prolific father, the Pharsalia homestead was aquiver with three generations of Mifflins and their black servants.

Warner's companions, other than a brother eight years his junior and two younger half-sisters, were almost entirely young enslaved Africans—and there were many of them, since his father was one of the largest slaveowners on Virginia's Eastern Shore.[36] Writing many years later, Ezekiel, one of the slaves toiling at Pharsalia, remembered how "we were brought up children together, slept together, and eat at the same table, and never quarreled." "Oh!" he exclaimed as an old man, "How it comforts me to believe that after suffering a few more pains, I shall live with him [Warner], forever, in sweet communion." Ezekiel's remembrances of his slave past may have been tinctured by his gratefulness for Warner's kindnesses after freeing him in 1775. But we have no reason to doubt that closeness developed between the adolescent boys, one white and free, the other black and enslaved.[37]

Though Warner Mifflin's grandmother and parents were devoted Quakers, they were largely untouched by the stirrings of abolitionism emanating from Philadelphia in the years when Warner was coming of age at Pharsalia. New Jersey's John Woolman and Philadelphia's Anthony Benezet were mounting the first sustained Quaker crusade against slaveholding in the early 1750s, and Woolman had made the first three of his walking ministries to the Eastern Shore peninsula by 1757 to soften the hearts of slaveowners. However, Warner's family was not among them. In two autobiographical accounts, he wrote how

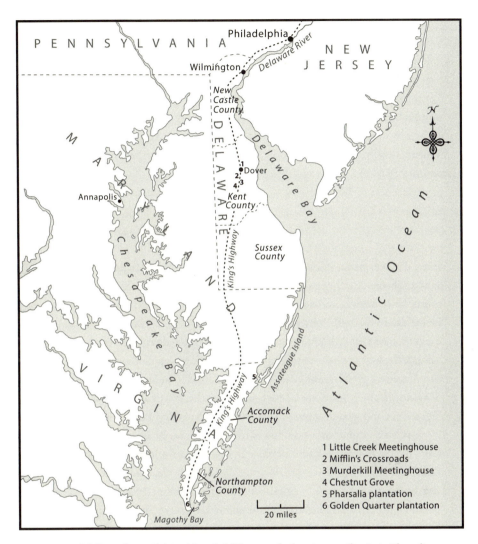

*Figure 5.* Mifflin, often with his wife and children, made the ninety-mile trip to Pharsalia dozens of times to visit Daniel Mifflin, his father, and his three sequential wives.

"I had no opportunity of having my heart and views enlarged ... by conversing with such of my brethren in profession, who had come to see the necessity of an impartial inquiry into the nature and tendency of [the] atrocious practice [of] slavery." Nor did his parents have qualms. "I don't remember while I lived with my father ever to have heard him say he believed it was wrong to hold slaves," he related to the Archbishop of Canterbury many years later.[38]

Then in 1759, at fourteen, he was moved to tears by hearing "from the relation given by some Guinea Negroes in the family of the manner of their being
taken and treated . . . , together with a general account . . . how that business
was carried on." Soon a young slave toiling beside him in his father's fields
"questioned me, whether I thought it could be right, that they [the slaves]
should be toiling in order to raise me, and that I might be sent to school; and
by and by, their children must do so for mine." Though flustered and irritated,
Warner held his tongue. But soon, he later remembered, the slave's "reasoning
so impressed me, as never to be erased [from my mind]."[39]

## Marriage

Even if it was never completely erased from his mind, Mifflin put aside the
matter of slaveholding as he reached adulthood. What was very much on his
mind, however, was marriage. In 1767, at twenty-one, star-struck and impulsive,
he courted Elizabeth Johns, the beautiful teenage daughter of wealthy slaveowners in Murderkill Hundred, Kent County, two days by horse from Pharsalia.[40] Though she had no shortage of suitors, Betsy, as she was called, fell for
the affable, ruggedly built Warner. They married in unusual circumstances in
May, not in the Little Creek Meetinghouse where Warner had witnessed his
father's second wedding ten years before, but in far-off Philadelphia.

Mifflin descendants and Quaker historians have been coy about this marriage or, for reasons we will explore below, have chosen to misrepresent it.
Elizabeth Johns (c. 1749–1786), Warner's bride, was a "descendant of a respectable friend of that name, one of the first settlers in Maryland," wrote Warner's
second wife, Ann Emlen Mifflin.[41] That much was true. While Ann was silent
on the parents of Warner's first wife, only that they were of the Johns family,
Mifflin descendants have maintained that young Elizabeth's parents were
Kensey Johns II (1722–1763) and Susanna Galloway Johns (c. 1726–after 1790).
For several centuries, the story was passed down in the family's lore.[42] If that
lineage had been true, Warner's bride would have had as her only brother a
certain Kensey Johns, III (1759–1848), who became a notable postrevolutionary Delaware statesman and state Supreme Court justice—and thus a pillar
of the new American republic. In this mistaken lineage, Elizabeth's brother
would have survived her death in 1786 by 62 years. But in fact, Elizabeth was

the daughter of Samuel Johns (1717–1758), Kensey Johns's older brother.[43] And that, we shall see, made all the difference.

This confusion of brothers would usually be a matter of detail only for genealogists to sort out. But for historians it is essential to unpacking Warner Mifflin's career trajectory and his complicated involvement in the American Revolution. Both Johns brothers, Samuel the elder by five years, were part of the migration of Talbot County and Anne Arundel County, Maryland, Quakers who had traveled eastward across the Delmarva Peninsula in the early 1730s. Included in this migration were branches of now famous families— Chews, Dickinsons, and Galloways—who would play important roles in the American Revolution. Both Johns brothers died at forty-one, during the Seven Years' War. But when Samuel Johns married the teenage Elizabeth Galloway (c. 1729–1790) in about 1745, he would acquire a brother-in-law, Joseph Galloway (1731–1803), who would eventually become a prominent legislator in colonial Pennsylvania, a close associate of Benjamin Franklin, and then a hated and exiled Philadelphia Loyalist. This would complicate Warner Mifflin's life almost from the day of his marriage until his death thirty-one years later, but he never distanced himself from the Galloway connection.[44]

Joseph and Elizabeth Galloway were the offspring of Peter Galloway (1696–1752), whose transplantation from Anne Arundel County, near Annapolis on Maryland's shore looking eastward toward the vast Chesapeake Bay, established the Galloway family in Kent County as large landowners and important office holders. Peter Galloway almost immediately became a justice of the peace, land surveyor, attorney, and extensive proprietor of slave-based plantations, sending his son to Philadelphia in 1747 for legal training that launched Joseph Galloway on a luminous political career. Contentious and prideful, he was Franklin's steadfast ally in opposing the proprietary party, served as the speaker of the Pennsylvania Assembly from 1766 to 1774, and represented Pennsylvania as a delegate to the first Continental Congress. The Galloways in Delaware had drifted away from the Society of Friends, and the bonds seem to have been completely severed by the time of Peter Galloway's death in 1752.[45] The Quaker records for Kent County are silent on the marriage of Peter Galloway's daughter Elizabeth to Samuel Johns and the birth of their second child, also Elizabeth, who was to become Warner Mifflin's wife. But the Duck Creek Monthly Meeting records show that Elizabeth Johns was a member in good standing of the Murderkill Meeting and raised her daughter as a Quaker. That would change abruptly when, widowed, she took a second husband.

What the exuberant young Warner Mifflin also knew as he courted the daughter of Joseph Galloway's sister was that the father of his wife-to-be had died intestate in 1758, when Elizabeth was about nine. Her mother, widowed at twenty-nine, inherited much of her husband's extensive estate, some of it in Maryland but most of it in Kent County.[46] Warner also knew that two years after becoming a widow, his intended bride's mother had married Charles Hilliard, another land- and slave-rich Kent County plantation owner. Descended from one of William Penn's intimate friends and an early investor in Delaware lands, the Hilliard family had also drifted away from the Society of Friends. Quakerism long behind him, Hilliard became a county militia captain, a justice of the peace, and a pillar of the Dover Anglican church.[47]

While courting the comely young Elizabeth Johns, Warner no doubt heard what was common knowledge among Kent County Quakers—that her mother had been disowned by her meeting for violating Quaker discipline by marrying an Anglican. At eleven, Elizabeth must have suffered in bearing witness to the painful collision between her mother's faith and her marriage choice. A few years before, marrying Charles Hilliard would not have caused a problem, for Quakers in the mid-Atlantic region had been overlooking exogenous marriages for decades. But as part of the campaign to reverse the Society's slackness in discipline, the Philadelphia Yearly Meeting in 1761 took up the question of "mixed and clandestine" marriages that reformers argued promoted "libertinism and a manifest deviation from the purity of our profession." A year later, the yearly meeting urged all the monthly meetings under its purview promptly to disown peccant members and readmit them only when convinced the ousted Friend had made an acknowledgment of error that "proceed[ed] from a true ground of conviction."[48]

Elizabeth Johns Hilliard was one of the first Kent County Quakers to fall under the reenforced marriage discipline. Women of the Duck Creek Monthly Meeting had cautioned her against this marriage, and when she brushed them aside, they solicited help from the men's meeting in "drawing a testimony" against her for "marrying out of the approved way of Friends."[49] The testimony was read "publickly at the close of a first day meeting" and then given to her in a personal visit. That is how matters stood as her daughter Elizabeth progressed through her teenage years.

With her mother worshiping at Christ Church, her second husband's Anglican church in Dover, the young Elizabeth could hardly do otherwise. Indeed, she fell easily into the circle of young Anglicans for whom dances, hunts, and shore jaunts were the pleasures of life in Dover's wealthy coterie. Knowing this in courting the dazzling Betsy Johns, Warner knew the price he would pay, disappointing his family and taking vows without his grandmother, father, stepmother, siblings, and many relatives in attendance. Yet, Betsy had a dowry of a thousand pounds or more, tagging her as one of the half-dozen "ladies of fortune" in Kent County.[50] The headstrong and ebullient young Warner, not yet listening to the strictures of the Philadelphia-based reformers calling for a more austere Society of Friends, slipped his moorings in the spring of 1767.

The decision made, the young couple stole away to Philadelphia to be married by a "hireling Priest"—the Quaker term for a salaried minister.[51] As Warner's second wife explained to their sons many years later, their father had "married Elizabeth Johns and from circumstances of supposed difficulty in their proceeding by meeting, in a fit of youthful inconsideration, they went out of the order of Society in accomplishing their marriage."[52] The price for this "youthful inconsideration" could not have been in doubt: disownment from the Murderkill meeting. Within months of his marriage, Warner and his wife were religiously adrift, after the meeting issued a complaint against him for marrying a woman not "of our discipline."[53]

It did not take long, however, for Warner and his wife to repair the damage. His second wife recalled that "no sooner was the [marriage] ceremony [in Philadelphia] past than he became deeply smitten with remorse for his precipitation," and in later years "frequently expressed apprehensions that this misstep might be suffered to have a crippling effect on him all his days."[54] Perhaps adding urgency to regain their Quaker standing was the pregnancy of Elizabeth Johns Mifflin that began two months into her marriage. Moreover, her mother had already tried to pave the way, penitently presenting a paper to the Duck Creek Monthly Meeting "condemning her outgoing in marriage" to Charles Hilliard. When it was "received as satisfactory," restoring her to unity with the Murderkill meeting, Warner and Elizabeth saw a clear path forward.[55] Two months after his ejection from the Society, and just after welcoming his first child, Warner humbled himself in 1768 before the Duck Creek Monthly Meeting "desirous to make satisfaction." His wife did the same three months later. The Duck Creek Monthly Meeting elders put them on the watch list for ten months, and then surveyed the young couple again when Warner and Elizabeth appeared a second time to condemn themselves for this "outgoing in marriage." Finally, in 1769, they were accepted into the fold "as long as their future conduct shall correspond with the Rules of our Discipline."[56]

## Moving to Delaware

Duly repentant and thus reprieved, Warner and Elizabeth Mifflin set about establishing themselves in Murderkill Hundred. That in itself had required a decision as they prepared to marry, one involving both opportunities and perils. They might have taken up married life in Accomack County on Virginia's Eastern Shore, where Warner had been born and raised and where his extended family still lived. But the young couple rejected this option. Mifflin never told the world in his autobiographical essays how they decided in favor of Kent County, Delaware. But genealogical research, combined with land and tax records that registered property transfers, makes the decision abundantly clear. At the heart of the matter, Elizabeth Johns had a lavish dowry of land and slaves in Kent County's Murderkill Hundred. Yet the young couple had to balance two considerations, one positive and the other ominous.

On the positive side, Kent County was a prime place to grow corn and grain at a time when the world market for cereals was booming. Discerning Chesapeake-area planters had begun to see that Delaware was a hidden jewel, possessing a web of interconnected factors—soil, waterways, climate, labor supply, and markets—ready to be exploited.[57] Even before Warner Mifflin's birth, some Maryland Eastern Shore bayside plantation owners had figured this out. Seeking new land for a growing number of sons, they had moved eastward in the 1730s and 1740s, lured by the relatively inexpensive land in one of the least populated pockets of the Eastern Seaboard. Among them were the Galloways, Chews, Johns, and Dickinsons—all Quakers, all large slaveowners, all quickly assuming leading roles in politics, and all people whose lives became entangled with Warner Mifflin's. Non-Quakers such as the Rodneys and Ridgelys had also staked out their family's future in Kent County. By the 1760s, when Warner Mifflin arrived, they had dotted the landscape in Dover and its outlying districts with genteel houses. The Anglican church, built in Dover in 1733, quickly became their focal point.[58]

Another incentive for Warner to leave Accomack County behind was the labor factor. As every planter knew, land without labor was useless. In Kent County, as everywhere on the eastern and western shores of Chesapeake Bay, landowners large and small prized coerced labor; indeed, they thought they could not do without it. Quakers were no exception. All those rising to the top of Kent County society owned slaves, with the largest plantations worked by as many as fifty. Mifflin needed no army of black bound laborers for growing wheat, corn, and other crops, and he found his needs readily supplied by the slaves brought to the marriage by his wife, seventeen transferred from his father's Accomack County plantation, and a slave family sent from his maternal grandmother in Kent County, Maryland.[59]

Moreover, tapping into the grain-hungry Atlantic market was facilitated by the numerous navigable creeks and rivers flowing from Kent County's interior to the coastal water route leading north to Philadelphia through Delaware Bay. Mifflin's timing couldn't have been better. When the overseas hunger for wheat and corn surged at mid-century, with southern Europe and the West Indies providing the sharpest increases in demand, by the 1760s the Delaware bread basket provided unusually favorable opportunities.[60]

Other factors added to the advantages of taking up life in Delaware. Every farmer needed meat and fowl as well as grain, and Kent County easily accommodated these demands. The horned beasts, wrote James Tilton, a Philadelphia-trained doctor and agronomist, are "bred in the greatest number of the marshes & forest of the two lower counties from whence they are driven in large droves to the county of New Castle, where the most cultivated meadows abound and they are grazed and stall-fed for the markets of Wilmington and Philadelphia." All this made for a healthy diet with meat, milk, bread, vegetables, and fruit found on nearly every table. "Even the meanest slaves have this indulgence," observed Tilton, including a breakfast with some meat and a full meal at noon with meat, bread, and vegetables.[61]

Finally, another indispensable commodity was plentiful in Kent County. Wood—for fences, for constructing houses, churches, stores, and barns; for cooking and heating; and for fashioning wagons, plows, barrels, and hoes—was close at hand. In 1739, George Whitefield, spreading his Methodist message on the Eastern Shore, rode his horse twenty-seven miles entirely through forest on his way from Lewes in Sussex County to Kent County's Dover.[62] Forty years later, the depletion of wood was still in the early stages. Traveling through Dover in 1778 as part of a troop of French officers coming to fight with

Washington's army, Count Louis Segur found the small town still "surrounded by thick woods." A few years later, the authoritative James Tilton reported, "This state abounds with wood, the most lofty & fine. We have no such thing as barren hills or plains. The most common trees are oaks, hic[k]ory, poplar, walnut, maple, ash &c."[63]

Yet for all these advantages, one frightening dimension of life's rhythms loomed in mid-Delaware. If Kent County was almost incomparable for raising corn and wheat, it was frightful for raising children. In fact, it was the disease capital of the Delmarva Peninsula and one of the most unhealthful places on the Atlantic seaboard. Topography and climate conspired to make this so.

The problem began with mosquitos. As early as 1710, Jacob Henderson, the young Irish missionary sent to establish an Anglican church in the tiny village of Dover, wrote within months to the Society for the Propagation of the Gospel for a transfer, unstrung by the mosquitos' insatiable taste for human blood. "There are in that place Bugs and Mascatoes, the one a Vermine in beds and the other a fly that infests always in the heat of Summer," he wrote plaintively, "and so troublesome that it is impossible for a Stranger to Continue there without Extreme Danger."[64] Breeding fiendishly in Kent County's vast marshes fronting the Delaware River, they feasted on humans without regard for gender, age, religion, or skin color, leaving malaria in their wake. Eight decades later, Dr. Nathaniel Luff, who had served as a battalion surgeon with the Continental Army in Washington's crossing of the Delaware to attack the British at Trenton and Princeton, was still warning about mosquitos swarming in Kent County.[65]

It was more than mosquitos—a lot more. Tilton wrote at length about the peculiar lethality that had been devastating human life in Kent County for years. Working from his long years practicing medicine in Delaware, he explained that "the medical history of Delaware . . . is peculiar" considering its territorial smallness—about one hundred miles in length and, on average, about twenty-four miles in breadth from the Delaware Bay to the Maryland border. Within the small state, healthy conditions prevailed in the hilly New Castle County, north of Kent, which was "as healthful a district of country as any in America." South of Kent stood Sussex County, where the town of Lewes, fanned with ocean breezes, was even more salubrious, "as healthful as Bermudas." But in between lay almost hill-less Kent County—the highest elevation is twenty-five feet—where the Mifflins staked out a plantation. "Kent," wrote Tilton, though "blessed with the most fertile soil, is the most sickly of the three counties of Delaware." As for Dover, just north of the Mifflins' new home, Tilton called it "truly unhealthful." Situated eight miles from Delaware Bay "and shut off from all water communication by high timbered woods, the air of this district in the hot season of the years suffers exceedingly from stagnation." *Cholera infantum* was particularly lethal. Tilton claimed he never heard of one case of this in Lewes, "while at Dover it has for years past swept off our children in manner that is scarcely credible elsewhere." It showed in the faces of old and young alike. If the Mifflins had consulted Tilton, they would have known exactly what he meant when he wrote that "In the highlands of New-Castle, a man thinks himself quite unfortunate to be overtaken by epidemic sickness, even in the fall of the year; whereas an inhabitant of the inland districts of Kent and Sussex thinks himself lucky to escape a year or two together."[66]

Elizabeth and Warner Mifflin paid dearly for the home they made in insalubrious Murderkill Hundred. Six of the twelve children Warner fathered did not live long enough to see their fourth birthday, and he buried his first wife in the Murderkill Quaker cemetery before she reached forty. He himself fought fevers and other congestive ailments nearly every year through his forties and fifties.

Did Mifflin know he was steering his life toward a life-sapping pocket of the Atlantic seaboard? Perhaps not at first. But after several decades he knew it all too well. When it became known that he was courting Ann Emlen for his second wife, one of her closest friends in Philadelphia opposed the marriage on the grounds that she was taking a terrible health risk.[67] But by then Mifflin believed he had a God-directed mission in life and that if God called his children, his wife, or himself across the river, then that was not his right to dispute.

Whatever the dangers, Elizabeth Johns's dowry crowded out all other options. Her father Samuel Johns had died without a will nine years before, and the time had come to divide his extensive properties. First on the list was Gainsborough, the 676-acre home plantation of the Johns family strategically bordering King's Highway. When Elizabeth divulged her intention to marry Warner in 1766, the husband of her older sister Ann, Richard Holliday, an upstanding Kent County Quaker, petitioned the Orphans Court to survey the property in order to effect a convenient three-part split: Elizabeth got 288 acres of Gainsborough "without any building thereon," while her sister and mother split the other 388 acres with the dividing line passing neatly through the stately four-bay brick and framed house. In a silent agreement, Elizabeth and Warner agreed to buy out her mother and sister, already settled in their husbands' homesteads in St. Jones and Duck Creek Hundreds.[68] Though in disease-ridden Murderkill Hundred, Gainsborough was the home of Warner's bride, where she had been born and raised. To put their own stamp on it, they renamed it Chestnut Grove.

Once settled in at Chestnut Grove and restored to Murderkill Meeting in 1769, Mifflin worked hard to earn the respect and affection of his fellow worshipers, among Kent County civil leaders, and within the broad network of Quakers encompassed by the Philadelphia Yearly Meeting. Handsome, tall, and sweet-tempered as he was, his rise was meteoric. Remembered after his death as a gentle and persuasive mediator—his second wife recalled "his peculiar talent at reconciling differences"—Mifflin was soon tasked as a representative of his local Quaker meeting to the Duck Creek Monthly Meeting.

By 1770, he began attending meetings of the Western Quarterly Meeting, which required him to travel some eighty miles from his Delaware plantation to London Grove and Kennett Square in Chester County, Pennsylvania, where policy issues were discussed and implemented. In 1773 his local meeting appointed him to "take charge of the Book of Discipline," which inquired into missteps of its members. Two years later, the Duck Creek Monthly Meeting approved him as an elder. That in turn led to his appointment as delegate from the Western Quarterly Meeting to the spring and fall meetings of the Ministers and Elders of the Philadelphia Yearly Meeting.[69] By the time the colonies were declaring independence, Mifflin's reputation was firmly established as one of the most dedicated Friends on the peninsula working to strengthen Quaker discipline.[70]

While earning respect among nearby Quakers, Mifflin began to cut a figure in Kent County civil affairs, though this would soon put him in an untenable position. "His manners [were] affable and conversation cheerful and pleasing," his second wife later remembered, and this made him "an object of attention by people in gay and high life."[71] By 1770, still a newcomer to Kent County and not yet twenty-five, he was appointed a justice of the peace by John Penn, the governor of Pennsylvania and the Lower Counties. Among his fellow justices on the bench, the appointment that paved the way to higher office and rural gentility, were the sons of the county's most prominent slave-owning families—Charles Ridgely, Thomas Rodney, Samuel Chew, and John Chew.[72] Several decades later Mifflin admitted he relished these appointments, regretting in retrospect that such a "thirst for preferment in government . . . much impeded the progress of my testimony against slavery, as it furnished an idea of additional necessity for slaves to support me in that mode of life."[73]

Furthering his reputation as a man on the make, Mifflin plunged into acquiring additional tracts of land, some near Chestnut Grove, others in Little Creek Hundred to the north, and still others in Mispillion Hundred to the south.[74] By the eve of the American Revolution, in a county with a population about one-fourth that of Philadelphia, Mifflin had become a country squire.[75] So much a squire, in fact, that on the eve of the revolution, he stood in the top 1 percent of Murderkill Hundred's property owners.[76]

What might Elizabeth have thought of her husband's almost frenetic engagement in civil and religious affairs in the early years of their marriage? Given the frailty of the sources, this can be only a matter of speculation. What can be said with assurance is that she was consumed with pregnancies, childbirths, and infant care. For the first seven years of their marriage Elizabeth was pregnant or nursing a newborn child more or less continuously. Discounting possible miscarriages, she gave birth to four children, all females, between 1768 and 1774. Their first child, Mary, born in 1768, survived infancy (though she died at fifteen). Baby Elizabeth died in 1770 after only fifteen days. Sarah, born in 1773, went to her grave after three months. A second Elizabeth, born in 1771, was the only one of the four to live to marriageable age. During these same years, enslaved women at Chestnut Grove birthed six babies, adding to the responsibilities of a planter's wife, as well as those of the slave mothers.[77] Grief was never far from Chestnut Grove in the years leading up to the American Revolution.


## Resisting Abolition

Despite their "out of meeting" marriage, Warner Mifflin and his wife were well aware they were establishing themselves in an area heavily populated by Friends. Nor could they have been unconscious that upper Delaware was becoming a forcing ground for Quaker efforts to quit the dirty business of enslaving fellow humans. Moving northward from Accomack County, Virginia, to Kent County, Delaware, placed Mifflin much closer to the pulse of Philadelphia-centered antislavery directives and firmly within the orbit of the Philadelphia Yearly Meeting. Thus began seven conflicted years after their marriage in 1767, when the young couple brushed aside Mifflin's troubled conscience while brooding about the currents of Quaker antislavery sentiment swirling around them.

Even in Accomack County, where Mifflin had come of age, word had been spreading since the 1750s about how a small number of redoubtable Quakers had unseated the conservative leaders of Philadelphia Yearly Meeting, in one of the most remarkable examples of bottom-up reform in Early American history. In Mifflin's youth, the yearly meeting had kept a tight lid on the occasional cry against slavery and the slave trade, even sanctioning Benjamin Lay, the outspoken and demonstrative radical, as a "disorderly person." But the tide turned in 1754, when younger Quakers gained control of the yearly meeting and agreed to publish *An Epistle of Caution and Advice Concerning the Buying and Keeping of Slaves*, written by John Woolman and edited by Anthony Benezet. In searing language, they argued that holding fellow humans in bondage was an offense against God and civilized society. "To live in ease and plenty by the toil of those whom violence and cruelty have put in our power," they wrote, "is neither consistent with Christianity nor common justice.... How then can we who have been concerned to publish the gospel of universal love and peace among mankind, be so inconsistent with ourselves, as to purchase such who are prisoners of war; and thereby encourage this antichristian practice?"[78]

In this same year, New Jersey's John Woolman, called by one historian "perhaps the most Christ-like individual that Quakerism has ever produced," published *Some Considerations on the Keeping of Negroes.*[79] As the Seven Years' War broke out, the twin efforts of the young Quaker reformers broke through the resistance of the wealthy, slaveowning leadership. That slaveholding was sinful was no longer the question; rather, the question became, what was to be done about such iniquities? In 1755, the PYM issued a directive against the slave trade, but it was not yet a censurable offense. Three years later, in 1758, the yearly meeting approved another advisory against dealing with slaves and banned from leadership roles any owners who continued to buy or sell slaves. It was the next year, at age fourteen, that Mifflin decided "that when I was of age to act for myself I never would hold a slave."[80] It was a promise unkept.

While passing through adolescence, Mifflin may not have heard that antislavery commitment was taking hold among younger Quakers in the mid-Atlantic region and that the emancipation of enslaved Africans was becoming the touchstone of their religion. But this is unlikely. Monthly meetings from Delaware, Maryland, and Virginia's Eastern Shore were sending delegates to the Western Quarterly Meetings convened in Chester County, and to yearly meetings in Philadelphia, so the advices were not unheard by them. Yet some meetings "flatly refused to enforce the ban against buying and selling slaves for a number of years," and some of these were in the Chesapeake peninsula, where Mifflin was coming of age.[81] Was he disingenuous in claiming he never heard his father say a word against slaveholding?

By the time Mifflin had made his decision to marry the Quaker-born Elizabeth Johns, Kent County Friends were fitfully joining the antislavery campaign. Much earlier, six years before they exchanged vows, the Western Quarterly Meeting was reminding the Duck Creek Monthly Meeting, to which the Murderkill meeting reported, to implement the 1758 decision that Friends buying or selling slaves should be banned from leadership roles and that visiting committees should start urging slaveowning Friends to consider the sin of owning fellow humans. Members of the preparative meeting Warner would shortly join moved forward, cudgeling balky members to comply. The Wilmington Monthly Meeting in New Castle County went farther by moving to disown any member found guilty of buying and selling slaves. Led by David Ferris, born into the Presbyterian faith but later a fearless convinced Quaker, Wilmington Friends began freeing slaves as early as 1761, with the manumissions recorded dutifully by Ferris in a book of manumissions, the first of its kind.[82] Describing slaveowners as "Leprous persons" hindering "Israel's march," Ferris overshadowed even the most stalwart Philadelphia antislavery leaders.[83]

Then, in 1765, Western Quarterly Meeting delegates read the yearly meeting's testimony against "importing, buying, selling, or keeping slaves; [and] that all may acquit themselves with justice and equity towards a people, who by an unwarrantable custom are unjustly deprived of the common privileges of mankind." The next year brought the bearded traveling plainspoken tailor-minister John Woolman, clad in undyed homespun, through the Duck Creek and Murderkill area further to prepare the ground for antislavery activity. "The Lord moved me," Woolman wrote in his journal, "to travel on foot amongst them, that by so travelling I might have a more lively feeling of the condition of the oppressed slaves [and] set an example of lowliness before the eyes of their masters."[84] Just three months before Mifflin married Elizabeth Johns, the Duck Creek Monthly Meeting, convening just north of the plantation they would take up, received copies of Anthony Benezet's *A Caution and Warning of the Calamitous State of the Enslaved Negroes* (1767), the hard-hitting pamphlet where Benezet had asked, in the midst of the Stamp Act furor over the English

abridgment of American liberties, "how many of those who distinguish themselves as the Advocates of Liberty, remain insensible and inattentive to the
treatment of thousands and tens of thousands of our fellow men"—enslaved
Africans.[85] By this time, the Wilmington Monthly Meeting reported that "few
members still owned slaves," an accomplishment matched by almost no other
monthly meeting within the jurisdiction of the Philadelphia Yearly Meeting.
Soon, the Wilmington meeting was requiring members to seek out slaves they
had bought or sold and secure freedom for them.[86]

All this while, Warner and Elizabeth acted much like their neighboring
landowners, exploiting slave labor to farm wheat, corn, hay, flax, and orchard
fruit. Regarding himself as a kindly master, young Warner "became almost
persuaded I could not do without them" and "was glad to embrace" the "prevailing opinion . . . that negroes were such thieves that they would not do to be
free." The lures of a comfortable, indeed affluent marriage had swamped
Warner's mind. He had been "debating, resolving, and re-resolving" the matter of slavery, he recorded in an autobiographical fragment, but "on settling in
a married life commenced the proving of my faith on this head. . . . I concluded
I should never be able to support my family without them"; that "the whole
mass of people was against" freeing slaves; and that Delaware laws required a
master to post sixty pounds security for each manumitted person. And so
Warner closed his ears to "what I held was my religious duty."[87]

As Warner and Elizabeth Mifflin established themselves in the late 1760s,
the Duck Creek Monthly Meeting and the Western Quarterly Meeting continued to take up the issue of freeing enslaved Africans, urging that they be
unshackled "as fellow creatures entitled to freedom." At the same time they
called for feeding and clothing those as yet enslaved and providing them with
"a Christian education." Yet in 1770, and again in 1772, the quarterly meeting
regretfully reported that most Friends were not yet of "a mind disposed to set
them free."[88] Warner and Elizabeth were among these.

Closing one's ears and eyes became more difficult as the movement against
British imperial regulations intensified. Drifting southward from Philadelphia,
a succession of pamphlets reached Kent County, arguing that slavery must be
extinguished if the American calls for protection of their natural rights—the
shrill argument levied against British taxes and new regulations—were to be
taken seriously.[89] By 1773–1774, some progress had been made, with visiting
committees cudgeling foot-dragging slaveholding families one by one.[90] Still,
Mifflin ignored the calls for manumission, even in 1772 when his grandmother,

who had shared in raising him at Pharsalia, penned a will at age eighty-six, freeing one female slave and her children, while naming Warner and his father as executors.[91]

## Revelation

For Mifflin, the moment of truth came after attending the Western Quarterly Meeting in August 1774. Appointed as a delegate to the yearly meeting, a singular mark of respect, he was poised to present the quarterly meeting report that, with the exception of one monthly meeting, no Friends were guilty of "uncleanness" in buying or selling slaves and that the work of freeing slaves "from their unreasonable bondage" was proceeding apace. That phrasing would surely have occasioned moments of chagrin, if not embarrassment, because his many slaves at Chestnut Grove were still toiling in "unreasonable bondage."[92]

Mifflin had time to think hard about this because, as fate would have it, his "very great desire to be at the [yearly] meeting" was thwarted by near disaster at Chestnut Grove. Returning home from the quarterly meeting, he was laid low by the dreaded autumn "bilious fever" for eight days; then his daughter, also struck by fever, "fell into a convulsion fit." His distraught wife, on the eve of the yearly meeting's first sessions, prematurely delivered for the fifth time. Wife, newborn Ann, and Warner recovered, but he was homebound, "resigned to the will of Him that knows what is best for us," as he wrote John Pemberton in Philadelphia two days after the birth.[93] Shortly after that, news reached him of a historic decision reached by the yearly meeting.

The late September 1774 yearly meeting is celebrated in the annals of the antislavery movement, because it was then that mid-Atlantic Quaker leaders made the crucial decision that slave *owning*, as opposed to buying and selling slaves, was inconsistent with the principles of the Society of Friends, that monthly meeting committees should fan out in "a speedy and close labour" to convince Friends to free their enslaved fellow creatures, and that Friends who would not comply should be banned from business meetings and possibly disowned. It was the first time in the history of the Western world that a constitutive body had sounded such a trumpet call disavowing slaveholding. The final stroke came in September 1776, when the yearly meeting agreed to disown those who refused to free their chattel property.

On October 22, 1774, less than four weeks after the yearly meeting declared slaveowning an iniquitous practice and an offense against humanity and the Christian God, Mifflin cut through the confused feelings and guiltiness that had plagued him since his adolescence. Snared since marriage between the trappings of a comfortable life and the crescendo of moral promptings all around him, he lifted his pen to inscribe his first deed of manumission. It gave freedom to the three Africans his wife brought to the marriage and to two small girls birthed at Chestnut Grove by one of them. The five slaves were twenty-seven-year-old James, twenty-three-year-old Mariah, her two daughters aged six and three, and twelve-year-old Melissa. All three female minors would receive their freedom when they reached eighteen. The perfunctory wording of the deed perhaps hinted at his hesitation. Without a single word expressing sentiments about the evil of slaveholding, Mifflin simply listed the five manu-mitted slaves.[94] Left unmentioned were seventeen others.

If he said little about what pushed him in late 1774 past several years of procrastination, Mifflin said plenty about it later in three accounts. The first, in 1779, was spilled out in a confessional letter to his neighbor Alexander Huston, a College of New Jersey graduate who ministered in Kent County's first Presbyterian church. In urging Huston to free his own slaves, Mifflin recounted in detail how a "spell of sickness" severe enough to make him fear for his demise pushed him close to "set[ting] them free" in the early 1770s, lest he die a sinner. But recovering his health and calculating the worth of his slaves, he went "back to the old road." Subsequent bouts of fever led him prayerfully to "enter into solemn covenants with my Maker that if he would be pleased to spare me, I would comply" with what he recognized as his duty. Still, he tarried. Finally, came the awful autumn of 1774, when a life-threatening fever and a fevered, convulsive child pushed him to the moment of resolution.[95]

When he recounted this decision at length eight years later in a letter to the Archbishop of Canterbury and again in 1796 in his *Defence of Warner Mifflin Against Aspersions Cast on Him on Account of his Endeavours to promote Righteousness, Mercy, and Peace among Mankind*, Mifflin altered the narrative, where thunder and lightning replaced prolonged severe fevers as the catalyst. "He who hath his way in the clouds, in the whirlwind, the earthquake, and thick darkness, was pleased to arouse me to greater vigilance by his terrors for sin." Explaining that "I could get no rest or peace of mind, day or night," he trembled in the midst of "a violent storm with thunder and lightning" when "every flash appeared as though it might be the instrument to dispatch me into a state of fixedness." Now he was certain he could only expect "an eternal separation from heavenly enjoyment . . . , that I should indeed be excluded from happiness if I continued in this breach of the Divine law, written upon my heart, as by the finger of Heaven." Either way—by contemplating his death during a raging fever or by crashing thunder and lightning in the dark of night—it was his fear of a hellish afterlife that finally broke through his cost-benefit calculations. "My fig leaf covering of excuse [for not freeing his slaves] was stripped off," he wrote. It was not the last time he would confess that the spring of action was as much to save his own soul as the lives of the enslaved.[96]

God and the yearly meeting had joined hands to force the decision in October 1774. But not yet fully. Mifflin admitted that, having freed his wife's dowry slaves, he entertained the fiction for some weeks that he might retain those "who came from their own accord," that is seventeen others from his father and his maternal grandmother.[97] Then God spoke to him again, tormenting him with the prospect of "an awful eternity" that would be his lot for "the abominable practice of enslaving fellow-men."[98] Mifflin's God was a God of love and comfort but also a harsh and vengeful God.

Mifflin acted accordingly. Three months after the first deed of manumission, he freed the slaves sent to him by his father and maternal grandmother. This time the language in the document was impassioned, contrasting sharply with the bare-bones first deed:

> I, Warner Mifflin, of Kent County, Delaware, Merchant, fully persuaded in my conscience that it is a sin of a deep dye to make slaves of my fellow creatures, or to continue them in slavery, and believing it to be impossible to obtain that peace my soul desires while my hands are found full of injustice, as by unjustly detaining in bondage, those that have as just and equitable right to their freedom and liberty of their persons as myself, . . . I declare all the Negroes I have hereafter . . . named, absolutely free, them and their posterity forever.[99]

Here, finally, came the melding of religious commitment, moral rectitude, and the natural rights philosophy that was becoming the master message of the American colonists' case against what they conceived as English oppression. Such phrases—"fellow creatures," "my . . . hands full of injustice," "a sin of deep dye," "[an] equitable right to their freedom and liberty to their persons as myself"—were not recycled from deeds of manumission in currency at the time.

These were the words of a man who had reached a crossroads where he could not live a double life—the ambitious Kent County planter-merchant and the Quaker caught in the throes of the Society of Friends' self-cleansing return to ancient principles. After much backing and filling, he had cast the die.

Close upon freeing the remainder of his slaves, in what surely was a coordinated move, Mifflin traveled the ninety miles to his birthplace at Pharsalia to witness a mass emancipation unmatched anywhere in Virginia for many decades. "Not long behind me in espousing the cause of liberty," Mifflin wrote autobiographically, his father liberated "about a hundred slaves" in April 1775. The language of the deeds—one for adults, the other for minors—was inscribed a week before the Minutemen at Concord and Lexington engaged the English army. It echoed his son's self-admonitions: "Being convinced of the inequity and injustice of detaining my fellow creatures in bondage (it being contrary to the standing and perpetual command injoined by our blessed lord to his followers, to do unto others as we would they should do by us)," Daniel Mifflin provided them "their natural, just, and inherent right and privilege, the liberty of their persons (which they are intitled to by nature)." Since the deed of manumission was technically illegal in Virginia—the colony did not allow manumissions without legislative approval—Warner recorded the deeds in the Duck Creek Manumission Book to guarantee their safekeeping. Inspired by his son, Daniel Mifflin soon became a fervid abolitionist. Encouraging Eastern Shore planters to free their slaves, he witnessed many Accomack County deeds of manumission, and, "as nowhere else in Virginia," a recent historian avers, became a leader of "a true culture of manumission."[100]

Within four months of Warner Mifflin's release of all his chattel property, the Duck Creek Monthly Meeting proposed him as an elder. This was a position signifying respect for probity and leadership qualities, one rarely conferred upon someone as young as Mifflin. Not yet thirty, he must have cherished this trust. It was reinforced a month later when his Murderkill Preparative Meeting installed him as clerk, a time-consuming position as presiding officer that required diplomacy combined with firmness.[101] From this moment on, as if the floodgates of commitment to antislavery had been opened, he became an unflinching champion of abolitionism and a leader in working to improve the lives of those recently released from slavery. Consistent with this transformation, Mifflin stepped down from his civil position as a Kent County justice of the peace.

Yet even after penning his deeds of liberation, Warner found his conscience still not washed clean. Troubled about several slaves he had sold before 1774, including one brought by his wife to their marriage and another he had inherited while still a minor, Warner decided he was obligated to seek them out, purchase them "to a considerable amount," and then free them. For several, he made what he considered "reasonable offers." When the owners declined, he bound his estate to rescue them from slavery "should I not live to see [this] accomplished."[102] In still another case, in 1777, he rid "an uneasiness in my mind" about Ned, a male slave his father had previously sold, giving the sale price to Warner. "I purchased, [him]," Mifflin wrote in the freedom deed, "to manumit and set him at liberty."[103]

This bone in his throat clogged his conscience as late as 1784, when he was troubled about "the occasion of a Negro being sent to the West Indies many years back that I have sometimes thought whether it would not lye on me to go in quest of [him], although I had account years back that he was hanged." Still, the matter "appears the greatest tye on me," Mifflin murmured. But finding that the man had died, Mifflin put the matter at rest.[104]

## To Be Free at Chestnut Grove

What did it mean to be manumitted at Chestnut Grove and Pharsalia in 1774–1775, as the storm clouds of revolution gathered? In an era long before slave narratives began to tell first-hand stories of the Day of Jubilee and its bittersweet ambiguities, the historical record is thin and fragile. But the unusually detailed record of Warner and Daniel Mifflin's deeds of manumission and the oral testimony of several freedmen yield insights into what freedom meant, both for the manumitted and the manumitter.

Among the twenty-two blacks in Warner's two deeds of manumission were Hannah, "an ancient Negroe woman" whose age nobody could determine; five adult males—James, Solomon, Ezekiel, Beniah, and Paul—ranging from twenty to about forty, and three adult women of thirty, twenty-seven, and twenty-three. All the others were children, ranging from thirteen to a babe of ten months. Mifflin did not identify the fathers, but he specified that all but one of the twelve children were birthed by three women. Nancy, about thirty, bore Hannah (14), Daniel (10), Jenny (5), Nanny (3), and Abram (10 months). Grace, about 27, was mother to Betty (13), Henny (11), Richard (almost 10), and

Rebecca (3); and Mariah with her husband parented Lydia (6) and Ann (3). Only twelve-year-old Melissa was parentless.[105]

From this composite picture, we can glimpse the lives of the enslaved and discern the strategies pursued by their master to preserve his plantation work-force. It does not diminish Mifflin's conviction that it was sinful to hold fellow humans in perpetual bondage by saying that he surrendered little in deploying labor at Chestnut Grove by freeing his slaves. It is only to say that working out wage labor agreements kept his workforce intact, though he had to reckon with a net loss of income by dispensing wages or shares of the crop. Balancing this was the incentive for the freed people to work harder and more efficiently at Chestnut Grove. From the black point of view, living as free men and women— this was the great hope of enslaved Americans—was coupled with the prospect of wages and the chance to lay up a reserve for striking out on their own when their children matured.

A second matter concerned the children. Twelve of the twenty-two enslaved people at Chestnut Grove were fourteen or younger, and at his father's Phar-salia the pattern was much the same, except for many "ancient" men and women. By conforming to the standard practice of delaying the complete freedom of the minor children until they reached the legal age of adulthood—eighteen for females and twenty-one for males—the Mifflins, both son and father, kept the black youngsters closely enfolded. This also answered to the strictures from the Quaker leadership in Philadelphia that slaveowners, after freeing their slaves, should protect them, support them, and educate the young. Since the mid-1760s, the Western Quarterly Meeting had instructed all Friends "under their verge" to provide a "Christian education to all blacks in their possession or under their care."[106] Since no schools had been established in rural Delaware, this instruction was done primarily within individual households, though reports from monthly meetings produced complaints from the quarterly meet-ing that manumitters were neglecting the education of the people they had liberated. Mifflin was not one of them. "Considering himself their guardian and protector," he later told a friend, he "took care that they [the adult freed people] were taught some useful employment, and their children instructed in the principles of the religion that had influenced him to set their parents at liberty."[107]

What of the three mothers of the twelve children who would remain at Chestnut Grove, most for more than a decade? Though plantation day books have not survived to track their presence, it is almost unthinkable that the three mothers would strike out on their own, leaving their children behind. To stay within the household of Elizabeth and Warner Mifflin was the logical choice. As household and field wage laborers, they could raise their children, have adequate food, clothing, and shelter, and otherwise be advantaged by the Mifflins' protective cloak.

As for the fathers, the case was the same. Granted, they could have left Chestnut Grove to seek complete independence. However, the fathers' love of wife and children was usually more than enough for them to work out a waged labor arrangement, if the manumitting master agreed. Moreover, the alternatives were few and none were very attractive. Without land and housing, and without free black churches and communities to join, the world away from the plantation probably seemed cold and forbidding.

Fortunately, we have testimony from Ezekiel and James, two of the five adult males released by Mifflin, to fill in the story and confirm these speculations. Ezekiel, about twenty-five years of age, was the first male Mifflin listed in his second deed of manumission. More than fifty years later, he related his story to Samuel Canby, a Wilmington, Delaware, Quaker abolitionist. Sent by Warner's father in the late 1760s from Virginia's Eastern Shore to serve Warner and his wife at Chestnut Grove, he married one of the slaves Elizabeth Johns had brought to the marriage. After eighteen months, Warner sent him to work at another of his plantations, six miles from Chestnut Grove, and there he labored for "about four years." It was here that Mifflin came in 1775, "calling Ezekiel from the field where he was ploughing." Told that he was to be free, Ezekiel protested that he was "so well satisfied with his situation that . . . he could not leave" his master. "Their conversation on the subject produced such feelings of tenderness," Ezekiel related, "that they both wept much." Mifflin insisted that his conscience would no longer permit slaveholding but that he would give Ezekiel land to work, apparently on shares. For fourteen years, until 1789, Ezekiel fulfilled this "mutual agreement." Then, as Washington was assuming the presidency, Mifflin gave Ezekiel "a piece of land upon which he built a house, where he remained until he came to reside in the neighborhood of Wilmington."[108]

Ezekiel's success must have given Warner Mifflin much satisfaction, while confirming his belief that freed blacks, if given a chance to succeed, would become valuable citizens. At some point after gaining freedom, Ezekiel took the surname Coston, most likely before he became a property owner. Mifflin may not have lived to learn of Ezekiel's move northward to Wilmington, where he worshiped at the Asbury Methodist Episcopal Church. If not, Mifflin's kinfolk probably took satisfaction that Coston became one of the followers of Peter Spencer, the self-educated black preacher, who, insulted by relegation to a segregated gallery, stormed from Asbury in 1805 to found Ezion Methodist Episcopal Church. When white Methodists contested Ezion's ownership of their church in 1813, Coston was among those who established Wilmington's African Union Methodist Protestant Church ("Old Union" or African Union Church), aided by Quaker support.[109]

James, the first enslaved male released by Mifflin, gave his story of the freedom experience—with particulars and a moving dialogue—that was first related ten years later by St. John de Crèvecoeur.[110] Calling James to his side to announce his freedom, Mifflin asked, "Well, friend James, how old is thee?" When James answered twenty-nine and a half, Mifflin replied that "Thee ought to have been free, as our white brothers are, at twenty-one," and explained that "religion and humanity enjoin me to give thee today thy liberty; and justice commands me to pay thee for eight and a half years' labor." "Astonished by a scene so novel so touching and so unexpected," the story related, James "burst into tears as though he had been accused of some great wrong." But recovering, he protested, "Ah, master, what shall I do with my liberty?" He had been well treated, had gone to worship by horse, was treated gently when sick, had "Saturdays to ourselves," and "wished for nothing." Freedom would only be a burden, he protested. "When I am free, where shall I go? What shall I do?" Mifflin answered: "Thee will do as the whites, go and hire thyself to those who pay thee the highest wages. In a few years thee can buy thyself some land; thee will marry a girl who is good and industrious like thyself, thee will bring up thy children as I have brought thee up, in the fear of God, and the love of work." But James would not hear of it. "Ah, master, how good you are! That is why I can never leave you. . . . Pay me what you like each year, call me freeman or slave, it matters little to me, as I can only be happy with you. I shall never leave you." Bowing to James's pleas that he remain with him, Mifflin, the narrative continues, consented to hire him by the year. The dialogue ends with James accepting his freedom and pledging that his "devotion and gratitude will only cease when [my heart] ceases to beat."[111]

Almost certainly the dialogue between Mifflin and James was a broth of historical and romantic ingredients. But the basic outline of the event was confirmed by Ezekiel Coston. When the dialogue between Mifflin and James was read to Coston many years later, he wept and said, "It is just so, poor Jim and I lived together with master [Mifflin] and worked together in harmony."[112]

## Lighting the Torch

Once he decided to free his slaves, Mifflin never turned back. If Philadelphia stood as the center of northern emancipationism, Mifflin's Duck Creek Monthly Meeting now became the most important wellspring of abolitionist activity south of the nation's capital. Assuming a pivotal role, Mifflin worked within his local preparative meeting and then throughout the Eastern Shore.[113]

His work began with the Duck Creek Monthly Meeting and radiated out from there. Previously lagging behind Wilmington Monthly Meeting, the Duck Creek meeting now made up for lost time.[114] With visiting committees carrying the conscience question from home to home, the Duck Creek meeting reported that by January 26, 1775, less than three weeks after Mifflin freed the last of his slaves, "a visit had been made to all or nearly all [slaveowners]" and "found in many places the minds of Friends engaged under an exercise to their duty to the poor slaves in their possession." But many "still need the encouragement and assistance of Friends," and many others still appeared "to be too unthoughtful of their duty."[115] Such work required persistence larded with persuasion, and sometimes the efforts involved Mifflin's close relatives. Ann Holliday, his wife's sister, was readily convinced after her husband died, freeing her dowry slaves in March 1775. But convincing his mother-in-law must have caused considerable anguish. Though Elizabeth Johns Hilliard had been restored to membership in the Murderkill meeting, she and her Anglican husband were among Kent County's last Quaker holdouts. Only many earnest pleadings convinced the Hilliards to free their twenty-two slaves in April 1778. By the next year, "only one member of the meeting house . . . still held slaves."[116]

In other cases, only the threat of disownment brought them around. Such was the effort to persuade Samuel Hanson, the grandson of one of Philadelphia's pioneering families, to free his slaves. When first visited by Mifflin's committee in October 1776, Hanson did not "see it to be his duty" to free his five slaves. When repeated efforts failed, Duck Creek Monthly Meeting disowned Hanson and his wife. With their faith on the line, they relented, freeing their slaves sixteen months later and gaining prompt reinstatement to their meeting. Such was the rod of chastisement.[117]

Into the mid-1780s, the Duck Creek Monthly Meeting continued its efforts to put slaveholding to an end. For a small number of Friends who would not relinquish their slaves, despite repeated mixed-gender visiting committees, disownment proceedings were approved, bringing the decades-long effort to a conclusion.[118]

Beyond Duck Creek, it was a different matter, especially across the Chesapeake Bay in Maryland, where Friends had many settlements. As might be expected, those with the greatest investment in coerced labor were particularly resistant. Among them was Mary Mifflin, the widow of Warner's uncle Southey, his father's younger brother. Not until 1781 would she free her twenty-five slaves. It took another five years before the Western Quarterly meeting, which extended to Maryland on both sides of the Chesapeake Bay, could report that the work of ending slaveholding had been accomplished. That this resulted in the disownment of most of Chesapeake Bay's large slaveowners belonging to the Society of Friends testified to the price Quakers enlisting in the abolitionist cause were willing to pay.[119]

Outside Friends' fellowship lay a world of non-Quaker slaveholders. Though he had commercial relations with many of them, Mifflin was able to penetrate the armor of only a few in Kent County. Many of them—the Chews, Rodneys, and Ridgelys, for example—managed large cereal-growing plantations, secured high political offices, worshiped at the Anglican Church, and became staunch defenders of slavery.[120] Thomas Rodney, brother of Caesar Rodney, one of Delaware's signers of the Declaration of Independence, spoke for many of them. When in their mid-twenties, he and Mifflin had served together as Kent County justices of the peace. But Rodney and Mifflin were poles apart on the issue of slavery and the character of enslaved Africans. Sounding much like Georgia or South Carolina slaveowners, Rodney argued that Africans were born to be slaves, inherently disposed as "hewers of wood and drawers of water." It was "impossible for them to rise above it." In an essay written after Mifflin had made antislavery his life's mission, he put restraint aside: "You may ask perhaps why the Negroes were born slaves to be hewers of wood and drawers of water more than others? And may you not as well ask why the buzzards are obliged to eat nothing but carrion, and the tumble bugs to work continually among excrements? Nature answers by saying it was necessary and therefore she has fitted them for it and made it their delight."[121]

Another of those who spurned Mifflin's visitations to inoculate non-Quakers with the virus of emancipationism was Benjamin Chew, a second cousin of Mifflin's wife. While pursuing a highly successful political and legal career in Philadelphia, Chew maintained Kent County's largest slave plantation. Here at Whitehall and at Cliveden, his stately mansion six miles from Philadelphia, Chew was master of two enslaved workforces. But neither the appeals of Quaker reformers such as Mifflin nor revolutionary pamphleteers could soften the heart of the man who became the presiding judge of Pennsylvania's supreme court.[122]

While Mifflin failed to reach Anglican slaveowners such as Rodney and Chew, his example does seem to have influenced John Dickinson. Raised as a Quaker on Maryland's western shore and married to Mary ("Polly") Norris, the immensely wealthy daughter of one of Philadelphia's most eminent Quaker families, Dickinson had drifted from the Society of Friends, though his wife remained a devout Quaker. There was more than a little irony that while his *Letters from a Farmer in Pennsylvania* (1767–1768) became an essential part of the protests against British tyranny—pamphleteers often charged that the mother country was trying to *enslave* their American subjects—he was one of the largest slaveowners north of Maryland.[123]

Yet Dickinson was troubled by owning a captive labor force. As a delegate to the Continental Congress, he asked a committee drafting the Articles of Confederation to consider "an article to prevent those who are hereafter brought into these colonies from being held to slavery?"[124] A year later, in 1777, he scratched out a deed of manumission for thirty-seven slaves at his Kent County Poplar Hall.[125] It was more a first-step gesture rather than a full antislavery commitment, since the deed of release provided that the twenty-two adults would serve as indentured servants for twenty-one years—nearly a life sentence for adult slaves—while the children would remain in bonds for as long as their mothers remained indentured. Yet it was a beginning.

In 1781, Dickinson freed six slaves unconditionally; five years later he freed the other fifty-nine.[126] This brought a heartfelt letter from Mifflin that contained a revealing admission. "It gave me satisfaction when I heard that thee had recorded a manumission for thy blacks more on thy account than theirs, for however people may think I favour black people I think I am more in the white interest than the other when laboring to have them freed from oppression, which if rightly done is certainly in my view of more advantage to the master than [the] slave." At first glance, one might think that Mifflin had qualms about freedom for the enslaved. But understanding his convictions about heavenly punishments and rewards leads to a different interpretation: enslaved Africans had never offended God and needed no redemption by gaining their freedom; but holding other humans in bondage was a cardinal sin that doomed his white countrymen—and the nation—from ever receiving saving grace. Reminding Dickinson of his Quaker background, he pointed to the favor he would gain in the eyes of God for "unfettering thyself from the delusive entanglements of temporal and uncertain riches."[127]

With Presbyterians, Mifflin made little headway. When he scolded the slaveholding minister of Kent County's first Presbyterian church for "unjustly depriving them of their natural right of liberty," all the more surprising "with a professed Minister of the Gospel and a great advocate of liberty," he got only a cold reply from Alexander Huston, who justified slaveowning with biblical passages. Mifflin pressed the case of "my African brethren" with no success. With their clerical leader defending slavery, why would parishioners do otherwise?[128]

Where Mifflin's antislavery appeals did resonate was with the Methodists. Since before the Revolution, they had made Delaware the mid-Atlantic heartland of their faith, and Kent Countians had especially warmed to their evangelical message. With their traveling ministers—Freeborn Garretson, black freeman Harry Hosier, Francis Asbury, and others—the Methodists had saturated the state, gaining momentum after the war and erasing some of the animus against them for their lukewarm support of the "glorious cause." When Asbury, their first bishop, memorably lectured their annual conference in Baltimore in 1780 that slavery was "contrary to the laws of God, man, and nature, and hurtful to society, contrary to the dictates of conscience and pure religion," they began to follow the Quakers in manumitting their slaves. Five years later the Methodist conference's antislavery plank cautioned that slavery was "contrary to the Golden Law of God . . . and the unalienable rights of mankind as well as every principle of the Revolution to hold in the deepest debasement in a more abject slavery than is perhaps to be found in any part of the world except America." Crucial to hearkening to such stern language in Kent County was the example provided by Methodist ministers such as Garretson, who freed his own slaves, and political leaders with wartime reputations such as Richard Bassett and Allen McLane, who did the same. Analysis of Delaware deeds of manumission awaits further research to estimate the number of Methodist manumitters, but the best estimates put the number at several thousand by the end of the century, with those in Kent County leading the way.[129]

A comparison of the composition of black inhabitants in Delaware's three counties in 1790 shows how effectively Quakers and Methodists altered the social landscape. Home to 38 percent of the state's black residents in 1790, Kent County counted two-thirds of Delaware's free blacks. More than half of the county's African Americans were free at the time of the first federal census in 1790, while in New Castle and Sussex counties, where resistance to abolitionist appeals ran high and no outspoken antislavery leaders such as Mifflin and Bassett emerged, 80 and 85 percent respectively were still in bondage.

From the vantage point of black Delawareans, the general outlines of the ratio of free to enslaved could have been no secret, for Delaware was a small state with travel by creek, river, and bay putting everyone in close touch. By 1790, Kent County's 2,570 free blacks almost doubled those in Sussex and Newcastle counties combined. By the time the federal government was moving from New York City to Philadelphia in 1791, Kent County's slaves had enjoyed one chance in two of becoming free—more than two and a half times as great as in New Castle County and six times as great in Sussex County. What became clear after the first federal census was published in 1790 was that nowhere in New York, New Jersey, or Delaware had a pathway to freedom been blazed more rapidly than in Mifflin's Kent County.

# Chapter 2

## Trial by Fire

"*What can be said in extenuation* of the guilt of those who set others on to war, who never saw each other's faces nor ever had any possible occasion for hatred or animosity? At an early period of that calamity [the American Revolution], I had been convinced that it would not do for me, even in idea, to wander without [outside] the boundaries of my professed principles; [otherwise] I could not expect to be sustained by the secret aid of the God of the faithful, whose everlasting arm of help, with humble gratitude, I may acknowledge."[1] This is how Warner Mifflin, writing two years before his death, with his health failing, recalled his unwavering pacifism during the long war with Great Britain. He and the Society of Friends would pay dearly for this.

Among the legions of Revolutionary War historians, few have had anything good to say about Quaker pacifism and noninvolvement, and many have called it cynical opportunism—a chance to avoid war taxes and blood sacrifices while profiting in a stressed economy in which they had vital foodstuffs to market and trading networks to maintain. In this view, it is the fervor of dedicated revolutionists and the loftiness of their cause that deserve our attention. If Quakers were vilified by Patriots, these were self-inflicted wounds earned by a fanatical pacifism that jeopardized the independence movement. From the Quaker perspective, both at the time and by historians since, maltreatment was to be expected, even courted, for suffering had been "an integral part of church history," in fact, "almost a prerequisite to religious virtue" and "a sure passport to an eternal reward."[2]

Now, in an era when Americans are weary of massively expensive wars and casualties greater than those of the American Revolution, Quaker war resistance is getting a second look. While the American and British armies during the revolution fought seasonally, withdrawing each year to winter encampments for as much as four months, strict Quakers such as Warner Mifflin enlisted in their religion-bound "nation militant" for year-round service. Throughout the long war, Mifflin made no compromises in defending the peace testimony, seeing it as an essential part of returning the Society of Friends to its primitive roots. Indeed, he was willing to journey for weeks on horseback during the latter stages of the war to hold wavering Quakers as far north as Nantucket Island to the peace testimony, while hectoring them for yielding to materialistic urges. Other American revolutionaries had their agendas for reform; Quakers had theirs. In their two-pronged campaign to secure their own virtue and salvation while pointing American society at large toward living up to its vaunted principles of universal freedom and social justice for all, Mifflin proved to be an exemplar, though at the expense of responsibility to his large and sickly family.

## Testing His Mettle

By early July 1776, when bells and bonfires were rocking a tumultuous Philadelphia after the Declaration of Independence, Mifflin had opened a new chapter of his life. From an office-hungry, comfort-seeking, prospering slaveowner and merchant-farmer, he was becoming the voice of antislavery in mid-Delaware, a member of the Philadelphia Yearly Meeting leadership cadre, a Quaker emissary of the Friends peace testimony in the midst of a blood-filled war for independence, and the father of three young daughters in a household where he and his wife were beginning to practice plain living and strict moral rectitude.[3]

The American Revolution went hard with Friends, especially in the midAtlantic region. In the stormy years leading toward independence, most Philadelphia-area Quakers tried to stay on the sidelines, committing to neither side, or, in small numbers, remaining loyal to King George III. Either way, they often refused to join the boycotts of English imports, deplored the democratic surge that culminated in the radical Pennsylvania constitution of July 1776, abjured service in the militia, and discouraged the use of Continental Congress-issued currency.

Professing allegiance to the founding principle of nonviolence did little to rescue Quakers from charges of loyalism and therefore of being enemies of the "Glorious Cause." For most Patriots, "disaffected" and "neutral" were simply code words for "toryism." Though he had rivals for cynicism, no one exceeded John Adams in flaying the Friends: "We have been obliged to attempt to humble the pride of some Jesuits, who call themselves Quakers, but who love money and land better than liberty or religion," he wrote his wife from Philadelphia when the war was going badly for the Patriots. "The hypocrites are endeavoring to raise the cry of persecution and to give this matter a religious turn, but they cant succeed," he continued.[4] But Quaker loyalty was not to George III but "to their core theological principles and their own uniquely Quaker constitution in Pennsylvania," which, among other important features, emphatically protected religious liberty.[5] Whether they were passive Loyalists or passive Patriots—the latter far outnumbered the former—the peace testimony required that they give support to neither side. Strict neutrality, therefore, was the rule. That decided, Friends nervously sat out the war while adopting a siege mentality and hoping for a quick end to the clash of arms.

No amount of revulsion and physical abuse convinced more than a fraction of Friends to abandon their code of nonviolence. Those who did took the name Free Quakers in 1780 and formed their own meetings for worship.[6] But this was unthinkable for most Quakers, especially since the yearly meeting, two months after the delegates to the Continental Congress signed the Declaration of Independence, had mandated a withdrawal from all connection with government, even to the lowest level of office holding. This completed the disengagement from public life initiated during the Seven Years' War, when Quakers in the Pennsylvania Assembly had relinquished their seats rather than support the bloodshed drenching the land.[7]

Mifflin had anticipated the Philadelphia Yearly Meeting when he withdrew from his commissions to the Kent County courts in late 1774. For several years he had been stewing about this. "I was solemnly impressed with the importance of the trust," he wrote, and "endeavoured to perform this to the best of my understanding." But he "never felt that peace of soul I desired during my continuance in office," leading to "a strict scrutiny" that brought him to "the truth of our great master's declaration—My Kingdom is not of this world." Instrumental to this scrutiny was the remarkable Rachel Wilson. Born in Westmoreland County, England, appointed minister at eighteen, and the mother of ten, Wilson had transfixed outpourings of Quakers and non-Quakers from Charleston, South Carolina, to Boston in an American trip in 1768–1769. Described by George Whitefield, the spellbinding leader of the Great Awakening, as "this very extraordinary woman," Wilson had met with Mifflin as she journeyed northward through Delaware on her way to preach to the students of the College of New Jersey. By the account of George Churchman, Mifflin's "intimate friend," it was the "powerful ministry" of Wilson that moved Mifflin to quit "a busy engagement in affairs that belong to the laws of outward government."[8]

Meanwhile, most Friends watched in dismay as a fraction of their fellow Quakers joined the Patriot cause, agreeing to shoulder arms, pay war taxes, and swear oaths of allegiance to Pennsylvania's revolutionary government.[9] Included among those abandoning the Quaker faith was Warner's second cousin, Thomas Mifflin, soon to become a Quarter-Master General in Washington's Continental Army and eventually governor of Pennsylvania. This brought immediate disownment from the Society of Friends. Yet, as one historian of Quaker pacifism has written, "the Society on the whole . . . emerged strengthened from the rather painful process of eliminating its nonpacifists."[10]

As the war grew more intense in 1775 and 1776, most Patriots begrudgingly accepted Friends' refusal to bear arms as a conscience-driven, indissoluble tenet of Quaker faith. But they drew the line at their refusal to pay fines in lieu of military service or war taxes levied against everyone. Philadelphia's Committee of Safety, populated by fervid revolutionaries, argued that "where the liberty of all is at stake, every man should assist in its support, and where the cause is common, and the benefits derived from an opposition are universal, it is not consonant to justice or equity that the burdens should be partial."[11] This was common sense to a vast majority of Patriots.

Resistance to war taxes divided Quakers and brought scorn and abuse down upon the shoulders of those who turned their faces against the tax collectors. Equally troubling to the Patriots was the Quakers' refusal to recognize the authority of revolutionary state governments (though they tacitly agreed to this by 1780). Strict pacifists, including Mifflin, paid heavily for this. Adhering to core principles, they stood helplessly while a sheriff seized their property—a horse, a cow, a wagon, bushels of grain, bolts of cloth, a chair, or any moveable possession. If this was to be their lot, then the war fulfilled the Friends' darkest prophecies of suffering. Yet, this became for Mifflin and most of the Meeting for Sufferings, the activist arm of Philadelphia Yearly Meeting and recorder of persecutions against its members, an opportunity to purify their sect while heightening a sense of their identity as a people. However small and lonely, it was they who must become the conscience of the nation.[12]

Through these dark days, Warner Mifflin willingly accepted the mantle of suffering. His resolve was strengthened as winter snow melted in Kent County in the late winter of 1777, when he suffered a serious leg injury that pained him severely each time the wound was dressed. Likening this agony to the travails of the common soldier "whose leg being fractured [and] . . . left without help in the field of battle," he disclosed how this deepened his pacifism. "Even since arriving to years capable of judging, I have had a testimony against war; but never so powerfully as at that time." Turning to his wife, he vowed that "if every farthing we were possessed of was seized for the purpose of supporting war, and I was informed it should all go, except [unless] I gave voluntarily one shilling . . . that I was satisfied I should not so redeem it."[13]

Knowing him as an uncompromising pacifist, the Western Quarterly Meeting often sent Mifflin during the war years as a representative to the annual Philadelphia Yearly Meeting and Meeting for Sufferings.[14] This marked his entry into the Philadelphia-dominated Quaker policy-making elite. Here he served on committees to write epistles to the London Yearly Meeting and other American yearly meetings—in New England, Rhode Island, New York, Virginia, and North Carolina—in the effort to create a united front. All were passionate cries about the sufferings of Friends under attack as unpatriotic, if not treasonous, in the long war with England. But along with accounts of suffering came principled statements about what was required for a new nation in the making if it intended to make good on its founding principles. Thus, as a delegate to the yearly meeting, Mifflin signed his name to the peace testimony delivered to the Continental Congress that had cast the die to win independence through force of arms.[15]

Even to leave his Kent County home to attend the yearly meeting, traditionally held during the last week in September, Mifflin was taking chances. Managing the trip of sixty miles, usually on horseback, he risked detention by Pennsylvania authorities, who by 1776 had required taking a test oath renouncing "allegiance to the king and a statement of loyalty to the Continental cause." This Quakers refused to do on the basis of their century-old conviction that oath-taking violated the biblical injunction not "to swear at all."[16] But each year, as the war swept through the mid-Atlantic region, Mifflin found a way to reach Philadelphia.[17]

Mifflin's problem of reaching Philadelphia became especially parlous in 1777, when the British were poised to capture the city in a knockout blow that would cripple Washington's army and send the Continental Congress scurrying for safety. This strategy unfolded that summer, when General William Howe led the largest part of his army of some 16,000, composed of well-trained and heavily equipped British and Hessian professional soldiers, to splash ashore on August 25 at the top of Chesapeake Bay. One day earlier, Washington had paraded his army of about 8,000 through the streets of Philadelphia on his way south to meet the anticipated redcoat attack. To give some sign of his army's professionalism, despite their tattered uniforms and boots, Washington had the baggage train and women camp followers bypass the city, meeting his troops after crossing the Schuylkill River. At Washington's side was the newly arrived nineteen-year-old Marquis de Lafayette, the French boy-general just commissioned by Congress.[18]

Meanwhile, after marching to the Head of Elk, a small upriver village, the British force moved eastward into Delaware to present-day Glasgow, only about thirty-five miles from Mifflin's home. On September 3, the Americans contested the British advance, but only briefly. Then the British marched northward to Kennett Square, Chester County, a village where Quakers had predominated since the days of William Penn and where Mifflin often joined Friends for their Western Quarterly meetings.

On September 11, just east of Kennett Square, the armies clashed in the Battle of Brandywine, remembered in sadness in the annals of the American Revolution as a blood-filled defeat. Much of the action occurred around the Birmingham Meeting House, the vital Quaker center of Chester County farmers, artisans, and millers. In one of the most lethal engagements of the entire war, Brandywine Creek ran red with blood. The small fieldstone Quaker meetinghouse itself was commandeered by the American forces for use as a field hospital. Ripping the doors from their hinges, the Continentals turned them into crude operating tables for the amputation of arms and legs of soldiers carried off the battlefield. The day after the battle both American and British dead were buried within the walls of the meetinghouse yard, along with amputated limbs.

Though the Americans fought bravely, with the Polish Casimir Pulaski and Lafayette leading several of the American units, they were shattered by the more disciplined and experienced British and Hessian forces. The British casualties of 93 killed and 488 wounded were doubled by the American losses, with hundreds more taken prisoner by the British. While the Quakers would not bear arms, they suffered greatly from the fierce battle. Penn's peaceable kingdom lay in ruins with trampled fields, destroyed fences, shattered trees, wrecked wagons, maimed horses, and plundered crops confirming the Quakers' worst visions about the brutalities of war. For Warner Mifflin, who knew the area well, it only intensified his pacifist convictions.

After the Americans retreated on September 12 to Chester, southwest of Philadelphia on the Delaware River, the British veered southeast without opposition to capture Wilmington, dragging with them 315 American prisoners and nabbing by surprise the state's president, John McKinly.[19] By reaching Wilmington, Howe was able to join the Royal Navy to replenish his supplies, while cutting off access to Philadelphia from Kent County farmers, shallopmen, and merchants.

None of this carnage stopped Mifflin from what had become a nearly annual autumn religious routine—attending the Western Quarterly Meeting in Chester County in the third week of August, visiting other monthly meetings, and then journeying to Philadelphia for the late September yearly meeting, which ordinarily drew more than a thousand Quakers, some traveling for several days to reach the city.[20] By early September he had already reached Nottingham on the Maryland-Pennsylvania border, where he usually stayed with George Churchman, the farmer, surveyor, and much respected elder in his local meeting.[21]

While the contest between the American and British armies continued its course, Mifflin, Churchman, and a dozen other delegates from as far south as Virginia awaited Philadelphia's fate as the time neared for their yearly meeting. On September 26, three days before the scheduled meeting, Mifflin learned that General Lord Charles Cornwallis and Hessian Lieutenant General Wilhelm Knyphausen, a sixty-year-old starchy veteran of many European campaigns and ranking officer of the German mercenaries, had jubilantly led the Crown forces into the city without a single shot being fired. By their sides were leading Philadelphia Loyalists, including Joseph Galloway, once Speaker of the Pennsylvania Assembly, a steadfast friend and political ally of Benjamin Franklin, a delegate to the First Continental Congress, but now a hard-bitten Loyalist.

With Philadelphia in British hands, what were Mifflin, Churchman, and their fellow delegates to do? Taking counsel among themselves, they decided they must not swerve from their mission. "Even in times of outward commotions and bloodshedding," Churchman confided to his diary, they could "not shrink from upright endeavors to hold our yearly meeting as a public testimony in the face of our country of an unshaken zeal for the cause of righteousness even where difficulties abound."[22] It was only the first of many times that Mifflin decided he could not disappoint his God by taking action to save himself.

To their surprise, the Friends were allowed to cross the Schuylkill at the Middle Ferry "without any molestation from the British Army," although American units blocked Quakers coming from north of Philadelphia or across the river from New Jersey.[23] Entering the city, Mifflin found that most of the Patriots had fled, leaving behind several thousand Quakers. Most Friends had pleaded neutrality, but many were suspected of loyalism and some were indeed out-and-out Tories. One of the latter, Mifflin's uncle by marriage, presented a delicate problem, for Joseph Galloway had accepted appointment as superintendent general of police. Nobody would have faulted Mifflin for keeping his distance from his wife's uncle. In fact, it would have been prudent for him to stay away entirely from occupied Philadelphia after Galloway accepted the position as civil overlord of the city.[24] But for Mifflin, blood was thicker than politics. The sources do not reveal whether Mifflin actually visited Galloway and his family during the British occupation, but he made no disavowal of his family connections. In the walking city, where Mifflin lodged within a few blocks of Galloway's house, it would have been almost impossible not to encounter the civil ruler.[25]

Of immediate concern to Mifflin and all those attending the Philadelphia Yearly Meeting was the forcible banishment from the city of twenty-two men, seventeen of them Quakers, just a few days before. Knowing that Philadelphia was defenseless against British occupation, the state's revolutionary council, backed by the Continental Congress, had sprung a dragnet to confine dozens of Philadelphians suspected of actively supporting the British.[26] Breaking into their houses in search of evidence, they quickly boiled down the number of prime suspects. Without hearings or trials, and ignoring a writ of habeas corpus from Chief Justice Thomas McKean, the president and executive council of Pennsylvania ordered the men marched from the city on September 10 through territory already pawed over by the contending armies, to live in exile for an indeterminate time in faraway Winchester, Virginia, tucked in the Shenandoah Valley. The Friends included the brothers Israel, John, and James Pemberton; Thomas Wharton; Thomas Gilpin; Henry Drinker; Miers Fisher; Samuel Rowland Fisher; John Hunt (a traveling minister from London); Samuel Emlen; and Samuel Pleasants, thus stripping the city of some of its most important merchants and a sizeable fraction of the yearly meeting leadership. As in most wars, one of the first casualties was civil liberties.[27]

Spread before Mifflin's eyes were the cold realities of the British occupation. Those faithful to the American cause bristled as the British appropriated the

Pennsylvania Hospital for the Sick Poor, the almshouse, and many of the churches for barracks. Owners of the best houses, many belonging to Quaker merchants, had to quarter the officers, including Hessians speaking only German. As cold weather set in, the occupying army tore up fences and church pews for firewood and requisitioned supplies to feed some 3,000 troops—about one-quarter of General Howe's forces (with the others garrisoned six miles to the northwest in Germantown). For Patriots remaining in the city, it was the beginning of a long winter of discontent. But Loyalist Philadelphians and some ostensibly neutral Quakers welcomed the chance to do brisk business with thousands of soldiers preparing to winter down in relative comfort.[28]

Mifflin's arrival at the yearly meeting brought prompt appointment to the key Oversight Committee of the Meeting for Sufferings.[29] Among their tasks was to draft a peace testimony and a protest—they called it an Epistle—to be presented to the ranking generals of the contending armies. The Epistle not only called for a halt to the violence but strove to dispel the charges that refusing to bear arms on behalf of American independence was equivalent to opposing "the cause of America." It also denied that Friends "maintain a correspondence [with the British] highly prejudicial to the public safety." But faithful to their peace testimony, they refused to join either side of the war. Meanwhile, they prayed only that men of Christian faith "may beat their swords into plowshares & their spears into Pruning Hooks, & nation not lift up sword against Nation, neither learn war any more" (Isaiah 2:4). Furthermore, they protested the banishment of the seventeen Philadelphia Quakers—an egregious affront to Pennsylvania's long tradition of protecting freedom of conscience. Without a trial, or even a chance to answer the charges made against them, "they have done nothing to forfeit their just right to liberty."[30]

## Across the Bloodied Ground

Eager to avenge the punishing defeats at Brandywine and Paoli and humiliated by the uncontested British occupation of Philadelphia, Washington had decided to throw the dice. Bivouacked at Pennypacker Mills, twenty-five miles north of Germantown, he made the fateful decision on October 2, 1779, to launch a four-pronged attack on the part of Howe's army encamped at Germantown. Marching in silence through the night on October 3, they vectored in on the village at dawn on the fourth.

**Figure 6.** *The Battle of Germantown* by Edward Lamson Henry (1875). The attack on the mansion of Loyalist Benjamin Chew, a relative by marriage of Warner Mifflin, was painted a century later. The artist portrayed the assault of the Americans on the British unit that had retreated to the most defensible structure in the village of Germantown. Among the American units launching an earsplitting artillery barrage were those from New Jersey, Pennsylvania, and North Carolina. Courtesy Art Institute of Chicago.

Little went as planned. A pea soup fog conspired with faulty communications and the exhaustion of men who had marched some twenty miles through the night before entering the fray. In fierce close combat, the British repelled Washington's dawn attacks, bloodying both sides badly. Though most of the American units fought with courage—one was led by the Rhode Island Quaker Nathanael Greene, who had put aside his pacifism—their casualties were heavy: 650 dead and wounded and another 438 captured or missing, compared with British and Hessian losses of 537. The entire Virginia 9th Regiment, mostly recruited from Accomack County where Warner Mifflin had grown up, surrendered after penetrating too deeply into the British lines.[31] After four hours of fierce combat, often hand-to-hand, Washington ordered a withdrawal. Carrying as many of the dead and wounded as they could off the blood-soaked field of battle, most of the exhausted troops reached Pennypacker Mills by nightfall.

As the Battle of Germantown raged on the morning of October 4, leaders of the yearly meeting were wrapping up their six days of sessions, with the sound of cannon fire six miles away rending the air.[32] Two days earlier, they had composed their peace testimony and protest about the exiled Friends now in Virginia, and on October 3 had appointed six delegates to carry the epistle to the commanders of the contending armies.[33] Not knowing fully the outcome of the battle, the mounted delegation left Philadelphia on the morning of October 5.

The peace delegation was a remarkable group. One was Nicholas Waln (1742–1813), a brilliant lawyer who a few years before had given up a luxurious lifestyle to devote himself to spreading the Quaker "messages of truth." Another was Samuel Emlen (1730–1799), a diminutive traveling minister with command of many languages and known as "the seer" for his remarkable ability to predict events. A third was Joshua Morris, who had resigned from the Pennsylvania Assembly in 1755 when Quakers withdrew from government rather than support the Seven Years' War. Fourth was James Thornton (1727–1794), a farmer living just north of Philadelphia, who had been recognized at twenty as a divinely inspired minister noted for radiating the inward light so prized by Friends. Fifth was William Brown, a Chester County Quaker farmer, who had served the Meeting for Sufferings since 1756. Completing the group was Mifflin. At thirty-two, he was the youngest and the only out-of-stater, signifying the respect for him that had grown in the few years since he had been restored to good standing.

On horseback, the delegation set out first for the headquarters of General Howe at Stenton, the fieldstone country seat built a half-century before by James Logan, William Penn's trusted secretary. Two miles east of Germantown and set back several hundred yards from the road, it was heavily guarded by Hessian Jägers.

It is remarkable that Howe received the Quaker delegation at all, for the British regiments were still tending the wounded, burying the dead, and preparing to pursue the retreating Americans. One can imagine the surprise of the pickets guarding the perimeter of the British encampment when out of the morning fog appeared six men, clad in somber gray greatcoats and black broad-brimmed hats. In the lead was a man of unusual height, by one account almost seven feet tall.[34] This was Mifflin, who wrote it was "a proving time—to pass through opposing armies most of whose minds were perhaps agitated, and many of them afresh fired by the spirit of war from their recent engagement— and with no passport or shield to protect us from any merciless attack but our own innocence, sheltered by the wing of divine preservation."[35] Six years later, in a letter to Nathanael Greene, who commanded two brigades at the Battle of Germantown, Mifflin recalled how he felt "terror removed from me when from an apprehension of duty to him who rules above the kingdoms of men, I had to travel through the contending armies and to observe the brutal revenge that appeared in the countenances of the soldiery against each other."[36]

Reaching Howe's headquarters, the delegation chose Mifflin to present the peace testimony and protest. Though much junior in years to the others, his great height and handsome visage may have been part of this; perhaps also figuring in the choice was the respect and admiration Mifflin had been gaining for his steady negotiating skills. But negotiations were really not the point. The chances that the English commanding general would conduct a peace initiative with the American general he had just defeated—this he could do only with instructions from the king and Parliament—were nil. But Mifflin and his fellow delegates, all ultra-strict Friends, were answering to a higher authority, conscience-bound to uphold founding Quaker principles and as sure as the revolutionaries that their cause was sacred.[37]

Perhaps to their surprise, Howe provided "a seasonable opportunity of a conference" at which he accepted the testimonials and listened to the Quakers profess "the peaceable Doctrines of Christ to seek the Good of all." Living up to his reputation for congeniality, Howe bade them farewell and then allowed the delegation to travel northward, where Washington's shredded army had fled in disarray.

Staying overnight somewhere north of Germantown, probably at the home of a welcoming Quaker, Mifflin and the others reached Washington's encampment at Pennypacker Mills (near present-day Schwenksville) on October 7. They passed through the line of pickets with only their graveness and drab civilian garb to vouch for them, knowing they might have been taken as British spies. Mifflin admitted that "I thought indeed it was like taking my life in my hands" when he went to Washington's bloodied encampment, considering "the exasperated situation of the minds of the American army & the inveteracy that had been let in against our Society."[38]

Though busy tending the wounds and buoying the spirits of their mangled troops, Washington and his officers gave the Friends "a very free opportunity of clearing the Society from some aspersions which had been invidiously raised against them." Then Mifflin and his group distributed the yearly meeting's epistle. General John Armstrong, commander of the Pennsylvania militia that had been nearly torn to pieces, grumbled that "We lost [a] great part of yesterday

[Oct. 7] with a deputation of Quakers from their yearly meeting." Though his officers shrugged off the Quaker delegates as though they were from a different planet, Washington ordered dinner prepared for them and then had them ushered out of the camp with orders to "do penance a few days at Pottsgrove until their beards are grown."[39]

Leaving Pottsgrove, Mifflin and his delegation made their way back to Philadelphia via the road that ran through Germantown and then south to the Ridge Road running along the Schuylkill River. At Vanderin's Mill, where the Wissahickon Creek joined the Schuylkill, they were detained by a Hessian Jäger unit and grilled by an angry officer looking for information on the condition of Washington's battered army.[40] Getting nothing of value, General Knyphausen, commander of Howe's German auxiliaries, permitted Mifflin and the others to return to Philadelphia on October 11. True to their belief that God was on their side (and sensitive to Patriot charges that Quakers to the last man were proto-Loyalists), the delegation reported that "no kind of intelligence was obtained from them, nor any departure from the language of the testimony they had delivered; we believe the Lord's Hand was in it in guarding us from improper compliances and bringing us through this weighty service though it was a time of close humbling baptism."[41]

We can only wonder what Mifflin felt as he urged his horse along the Ridge Road and passed Fountain Green, where his grandfather, Edward Mifflin, had been born and his uncle, John Mifflin, now lived. Perhaps he paused to think that almost a century before, his great-great-grandfather, who knew George Fox, had staked his family's future there to help establish the "seed of a nation," as William Penn imagined it. Now it had become a dark and bloody ground.[42] Whatever his thoughts, the harrowing mission stiffened Mifflin's spine, steeling him for work to come.

## Europe Meets Mifflin

Though Quakers circulated word of the 1777 peace testimony delegation down through their yearly, quarterly, and monthly meetings, the record is very thin on how widely it was reported within the swelling community of Atlantic-wide reformers who were seeing the American Revolution as ushering in a new epoch—in the words of Thomas Paine, the breathtaking effort "to begin the world anew." This changed seven years later when a highly embellished and sometimes laughably inaccurate account of the Mifflin mission came off the press in Paris from the hand of St. John de Crèvecoeur. If not in America, now in Europe the name of Warner Mifflin began to resonate.

Jefferson was among those in Paris in 1784, when Crèvecoeur published a much expanded French edition of his *Letters from an American Farmer*, titled *Lettres d'un cultivateur américain*. Mifflin (called Walter, not Warner) now gained international fame.[43] In a long account of the peace testimony mission, Crèvecoeur had Mifflin walking by himself into the British and American encampments, rather than as part of a Quaker committee of six. Risking his neck at the end of a rope as a spy in either camp, and disarming Generals Howe and Washington with his eloquence if not his arguments, Mifflin became the "good Quaker." Courting death, he advanced with the belief that without suffering there could be no spiritual progress. In an expanding republic of enlightened literature, this fed French readers, already well nourished by Voltaire, Montesquieu, Raynal, and others, with the belief that William Penn's "Holy Experiment" had come close to establishing a new world utopia.[44]

In Crèvecoeur's overheated account, Warner Mifflin barely escapes hanging. "Soldiers," bellows the first English officer he reaches, "take this hypocrite to the guard-house, till we can take him to the Sheriff, to be hung, when his turn comes. There you will see a great many rebels who tried, under the guise of humility and Quaker simplicity, to slip through the British lines and act as spies." Mifflin tries to ward off disaster. "In spite of all thee says, I am not a spy; perhaps I may be allowed to prove it." The red-coated British captain replies, "To prove it! Oh don't expect that! The trial of such a rebel as you is soon over—a rope, a nail, or a branch, and two good soldiers, to hoist it—that is all we need." The discourse goes on at length before the English officer tires of it and has Mifflin handcuffed and taken to the guard house. There, for seventeen days in a dark cell, he awaits his demise. But Quaker conscience trumps British militarism. Charmed with Mifflin after interrogating him, General Howe listens to Mifflin's plea to reach "an armistice, at least during the winter [and] that this armistice might lead to a friendly understanding [with the Americans] and the restoration of peace." Assuring Mifflin that "I approve of the idea of your Quakers; it seems a noble one, and may prove useful," Howe insists the intrepid Quaker share the general's dinner table and then offers passports to see Mifflin safely on his way. Mifflin demurs. "I will dine with thee since thee wishes it; but I cannot receive thy passports." "And why not?" asks the astounded Howe. "Because we should become guilty of the great crimes occasioned by war, in providing ourselves with passports and military privileges. I shall . . . pass out of thy lines as I entered them." The dialogue concludes with Howe expressing amazement at the Quaker's "strange principles . . . contrary to nature and the inner feelings which dictate self-preservation." General Howe then bids Mifflin goodbye, saying, "I have given orders for you to be allowed to pass. I wish you a pleasant journey."[45]

## Where Duty Lies

Threading his way in mid-October 1777 through the British lines controlling eastern Chester County, south of Philadelphia and then past Wilmington, still in British hands, Mifflin arrived home safely in Kent County, much to the relief of a loving wife and five children, the youngest, named Warner, Jr., only four months old. But another good office to perform still beckoned.

Everyone at the time knew the pitiable story of the Virginia 9th Regiment, officered by slaveowners from the Eastern Shore. Pushing rapidly ahead directly into the center of Germantown in the fog-shrouded dawn of October 4, the Virginians found themselves enveloped by British units. Facing annihilation, they surrendered. First holding them in the Quaker school house, the British marched them the day after the battle to the Walnut Street gaol in Philadelphia. Here they joined another 600 American prisoners suffering under atrocious conditions. Reduced to a quarter pound of salt pork and six biscuits each eight-day period, the prisoners, or so Washington was told, "have lately been obliged to enlist [with the British] or starve." One man, driven "to the last extreme by the rage of hunger" (and probably suffering post-traumatic stress) "ate his own fingers up to the first joint . . . before he died."[46] Before the year ended, one prisoner related, jail fever "swept off four hundred men who were all buried in one continuous grave without coffins. Death was so frequent it ceased to terrify."[47]

Philadelphia Quakers, out of basic humanitarian concern—and keenly aware of the opportunity to shed some of the animus against them for nonsupport of "the Glorious Cause"—took tea, coffee, bread, and other small comforts to some 400 Virginians thrown into the unheated Walnut Street gaol.[48] To this effort, Mifflin added his mite. After returning to Kent County, he journeyed to Virginia's Eastern Shore "for the special purpose of visiting the several families of the prisoners, procuring money, linen, blankets, &c. as well

GOAL, in Walnut Street PHILADELPHIA.

*Figure 7.* Built just before the revolution and often referred to as the "new gaol," Walnut Street Gaol appears in this 1798 lithograph as a model institution. However, it became a chamber of horrors for the hundreds of Americans captured by the British in the Philadelphia campaign in the fall of 1777. Efforts of Philadelphia Quakers to help the prisoners with basic needs—food, drink, blankets—were curbed by the shortages everyone suffered during the British occupation of the city.

as cheering news." Shortly after this, returning to Philadelphia, he completed his task. As this event was narrated many years later, "Both officers and men were astounded when the two brothers arrived . . . with so many comforts for them."[49] One of the grateful officers was to figure the next year in a most ungrateful way.

Like a moth drawn to flame, Mifflin could not stay away from the volatile war around Philadelphia. Dismayed, if not disheartened, Elizabeth and his children watched him prepare his horse on October 30 for an extended foray back into the battle zone on both sides of the Delaware River. They would not see him again for more than five weeks. Mifflin left no record of this seemingly reckless jaunt, but almost every day of the mission was detailed in the diary of

George Churchman, his friend and traveling partner through the late fall and early winter.[50]

Inspiring this dangerous trip was the conviction that Friends' pacifist commitment was wavering. Those who had completely abandoned the peace testimony by signing up for armed training and combat were a dead loss to the Society. But still at risk were a great many others, particularly the farmers in the agriculturally rich area outside Philadelphia who were willing to sell produce to either the American or the British army, understanding that if they did not sell to one army or another, their crops would simply be seized. To strict Friends such as Churchman and Mifflin, this was nonetheless blood on their hands and a crumbling of allegiance to the ancient pacifist testimony. The task at hand, therefore, was to meet quarterly, monthly, and preparative meetings in the war zone to stiffen the spines of backsliding Friends. Both Washington's bruised Continental Army encamped at Whitemarsh, sixteen miles west of Philadelphia, and Howe's army snugly billeted in Philadelphia were ready to pounce on any suspicious civilians.

Heading first for the Philadelphia Quarterly Meeting, Churchman, his wife, and others in the party met Mifflin in Wilmington on October 31. This involved crossing the American lines, where Mifflin had to persuade General William Smallwood, who commanded a garrison after the British withdrew to Philadelphia, to let him pass through toward the city.[51] From Wilmington, they headed north, only to be stopped at Darby by American militiamen, who forbade them from proceeding farther. With that option foreclosed, they spent two weeks combing Chester County meetings—at Concord, Bradford, Kennett Square, Birmingham, London Grove, and Nottingham—alternating between business meetings, meetings of ministers and elders, and meetings for worship.

Forbidden to enter Philadelphia from the south, they decided to swing northwest and then east in a long arc to reach the city from the north. Though it cost them several weeks, it provided a chance to canvass Quaker meetings in Bucks County and New Jersey. By mid-November, with winter closing in, they passed east of Valley Forge into the area, northwest of the city, where they encountered Washington's patrols "passing and repassing" from their encampment at Whitemarsh. After going from one meeting to another in Bucks County, they crossed the Delaware to reach Trenton. Carrying their cause to Freehold, Crosswicks, and Burlington, they asked, "how many within the pale of our Society are in a mixture with the world and too much in affinity with the

**Figure 8.** Washington made his headquarters for most of November and December 1777 in the country house built by George Emlen (1718–1776), father of Warner Mifflin's second wife, Ann Emlen. Her brother George Emlen, Jr. (1741–1812) occupied the house when it was requisitioned by Washington. Emlen importuned Washington for reimbursement for the fences that "were of great service for fires to the army" (Emlen to Washington, Nov. 20, 1778, in editorial notes to Washington to Emlen, Dec. 13, 1778, Founders Online). Courtesy New-York Historical Society Museum and Library.

military party spirit now prevalent?" By the end of the month, with stormy days presaging the onset of winter, they contemplated "having to pass through armed forces of two different parties" while moving south to reach Philadelphia. Six miles north of the city, Mifflin was chosen to negotiate with the American captain at Frankford.[52]

Once in Philadelphia by December 1, 1777, with the permission of the British—the good word of the Superintendent of Police Joseph Galloway may have cleared the way—they were not content with reiterating the peace testimony at all three meetinghouses. As Churchman confided in his diary, he and Mifflin went from house to house, day after day, to urge Friends "to pay closer attention to the pure principle [of pacifism] in order to purchase the smiles of heaven in this day of adversity." One can easily imagine that many urban Friends bristled at two rural Friends pushing the boundaries of officiousness, even if their hectoring was gently delivered.[53]

Leaving the city on December 6, Mifflin and Churchman feared they would be seized by American patrols on the other side of the Middle Ferry, "not having what they might term regular permission." After one more visit, this time to New Garden meeting, the men returned home. Mifflin had been gone five weeks and three days by the time he reached Chestnut Grove on December 8.

This much done, there was more to do. Mifflin, like all mid-Atlantic Quakers, was tortured by the plight of their Quaker friends sequestered in Winchester, Virginia. As expected, he answered the call of the Western Quarterly Meeting at London Grove to travel to Lancaster, where Pennsylvania's Executive Council and president had retreated after the British swept into Philadelphia. It was to that village that Mifflin and five others rode in the severe winter of 1778, steering clear of Valley Forge, where Washington's army now huddled in the snow. Asking to make their case on behalf of the banished Quakers on February 23, 1778, the delegation was told to submit their plea in writing. This done, they waited. But their pleas that the Winchester exiles "may be heard in their own vindication," before either the Pennsylvania state government or the Continental Congress, giving them the basic right of self-defense, fell on deaf ears. Neither would the president and council respond to the plea to halt the "exorbitant fines" imposed on Quakers who "because of our conscience sake . . . cannot yield our personal service in war." Nor would they commute to house arrest the imprisonment in the Lancaster jail of four other Quakers who had been incarcerated for an indeterminate time and without due process.

Almost before Mifflin returned home, two of the Winchester exiles had perished and been buried far from home. Israel Pemberton, his constitution badly compromised, would die shortly after his return to Philadelphia.[54]

Mifflin's problem of living on a knife's edge, trying to remain neutral yet harboring sympathy for the Loyalist position, came into play as winter began to wane in occupied Philadelphia. Again and again, he returned to the city as if believing that courting danger was what God wanted of him. How he was able to return there, in company with his wife, in February and March for meetings of the Ministers and Elders and the Meeting for Sufferings is something of a mystery, since Washington had ordered his officers, whose troops had encircled the occupying army, to prohibit Friends from entering the city.[55] But come he did. After visiting assembled Friends at all three of the city's Quaker meetinghouses, Mifflin helped construct the Meeting for Sufferings' advice to all monthly meetings that "those who become true Christians . . . will be kept out of all bustles & noises & tumults & parties and be enabled to exalt the Pure Standard of him, the Prince of Peace . . . seeking the good of all men." Knowing the importance of Quaker women in monitoring waywardness from doctrine in husbands, sons, and brothers, Mifflin and Churchman sat at the Women's Meeting the next day—inspiring a minute in the record expressing the women's appreciation of the men's "labor of love amongst us," which they hoped "will be impressed on the minds of all present."[56]

Returning to Kent County for spring plowing and seedtime, Mifflin found himself entangled in other awkward situations. As before, he had to walk a tightrope in striking a delicate balance between Patriots and Loyalists in Delaware. Never a hotspot in the long war, the state had been spared full engagements between the contending armies, for only Wilmington, a grain-exporting port on the Delaware Bay, was a worthy prize, with the rest of Delaware of little strategic importance. Yet the state was still a place where Loyalist sympathies ran high. In fact, up and down the Atlantic seaboard nowhere was loyalism more the majority position than in Delaware with the possible exceptions of western Long Island, pockets of northern New Jersey, and portions of lower New York. Thomas McKean, the state's most important political leader, believed that Sussex County was three-quarters Loyalist and Kent County five-eighths.[57] Nonetheless, Patriot and Loyalist partisans mostly kept armed clashes to a minimum, at least compared to the open civil war that tore New Jersey and New York apart.

But the lid came off the pot just after Warner returned to Chestnut Grove in April 1778. Across Delaware's narrow waist, on Kent County's Maryland border, twenty miles west of his home, an insurrection of poor farmers rose in defiance of the state's revolutionary government. Allied to the British and led by Cheney Clow, sometimes known as China Clow, several hundred alienated yeomen vowed to march to Dover to demand justice from the legislature they believed never represented them. Much like down-and-out insurrectionists of the previous year on Maryland's Eastern Shore, they were more eager to tend to local grievances than to defend the patriots' "liberty," which for them was an abstraction.[58] Entrenched in a hastily constructed fort, Clow's followers exchanged fire with state militia and pursued hit-and-run tactics against the patriots for several more years, until Clow was finally captured in 1782.[59]

Mifflin stayed clear of the insurrection, but when Clow's trial for treason began in Dover's courthouse in May 1783, he was there to witness the jury conviction and hear the sentence that Clow must die on the gallows. Mifflin took up the case, hoping to intervene with the president of Delaware to stay the execution, arguing that although he believed Clow "to be a very bad man," the jury was tainted and public opinion was sharply divided on whether capital punishment was justified.[60]

While China Clow was trying to liberate himself from what he regarded as Patriot oppression, another figure, black rather than white, was hearing God speak to him as he toiled in the fields of one of Kent County's slaveowners living just north of Dover, only a dozen miles from Warner Mifflin's home. Known only as Richard, the boy of seventeen was later to become a Philadelphia black leader who would eulogize Warner two decades later. Long before that, Richard had become the self-named Richard Allen, founder of Mother Bethel, Philadelphia's African Methodist Episcopal Church. In 1778, itinerant Methodist ministers began to work the Dover region with their revivalist messages, reaching out to blacks as well as whites. Freeborn Garretson, a martyrdom-bound English immigrant who ignited audiences with his golden voice, had been ranging through Maryland and Virginia before crossing the Chesapeake to preach in Delaware's Kent County. Small in stature but huge in voice, he was soon preaching in the neighborhood of Stokeley Sturgis, where Richard and his enslaved family lived. Whereas Warner Mifflin's antislavery trumpet had limited effect on Methodists, Garretson's was tremendous. Moved by Garretson's promise of what an angry God had in mind for evil slaveowners—"Thou art weighed in the balance," Garretson cried at Richard's master, "and found wanting"—Sturgis allowed Allen and his brother to purchase their freedom in installments. Convinced that Methodism was his deliverer, Allen directed his life toward that faith.[61] He probably had never encountered Warner Mifflin until this time, but soon he would do so in Philadelphia.[62]

While Methodism was sweeping through Kent County in 1778, Mifflin resumed his shuttling between Chestnut Grove and points northward, oblivious that the arrival of spring was bringing the British and American armies out of winter hibernation. Again with George Churchman as his traveling partner, Mifflin headed north for New Jersey in May 1778, leaving his wife, four children, and the mixed white and black workforce behind. Their mission, Churchman explained in his diary, was "a prospect of further attention to the yearly meeting's concern for searching out deficiencies." This time the American army would not let them cross the Delaware River south of Wilmington. But for men making the stewardship of Quaker meetings an almost full-time occupation, this was nothing more than an inconvenient obstacle put in front of them to test their mettle. Leaving their horses in pasture on the west side of the river, they borrowed a small boat, rowed their way below British ships "in military attire" that guarded the approaches to Philadelphia, and beached on the New Jersey shore. For two weeks they stiffened the spines of Quakers at Salem, Pilesgrove, Alloways Creek, and Greenwich, all in the sandy pinelands and small farms of southern New Jersey across the Delaware from New Castle County.[63]

Home by the end of May, Mifflin soon heard the long anticipated news that on June 18, 1778, the British army had evacuated Philadelphia and was marching north through New Jersey to engage Washington's refortified Continental Army that had decamped from Valley Forge. With the road now open to the Quaker city, Mifflin had to attend to unpleasant family business, occasioned by the decision of his wife's uncle to quit Philadelphia with his only surviving child, the beautiful Elizabeth Galloway. Left behind was Joseph Galloway's wife, Grace Growden Galloway, charged with protecting the vast Galloway properties, most of them hers through inheritance from her father. The result was pure pathos.

It was only a matter of time before Pennsylvania's revolutionary government attainted the Galloway properties and confiscated the Galloway mansion at Sixth and Chestnut Streets, with extensive properties in Bucks County scheduled for seizure. After Grace Galloway told the authorities that "nothing but force should get me out of my house," Charles Willson Peale, one of five Commissioners of Forfeited Estates, was deputed to do the forcing. Sputtering to Peale that she would not leave "unless by the force of a bayonet," she heard from him that "it was not the first time he had taken a Lady by the Hand." Escorted from the house, she was reduced to finding shelter with a friend, all the more humiliated by seeing upstart revolutionaries rolling around the city in the confiscated coach that for years had carried her through the streets. Warner heard all this—how she hurled insults at the Patriots, how she refused to "acknowledge their authority as I was an English woman and could not be a traitor" to the king; how she wrote pathetic letters to her husband and daughter, soon on their way from New York to England; how she nursed her emotional wounds as her health rapidly declined; how she tried to fight in the courts for the properties she had inherited from her father; and how she suffered spells of deep depression. "I am fled from as a pestilence," she confided to her diary, and that included all but a small group of wealthy Quaker Philadelphians with whom she had mingled for years.[64]

Mifflin did not waver in coming to Grace Galloway's side, one of the few Friends willing to be smeared by associating with the harassed, distraught, and deeply wounded wife of a notorious Loyalist. Mifflin came to sit with Aunt Grace only two weeks after the British left the city in a ruinous state, and he was back a month later when Grace scribbled in her diary that "Warner was very kind; I have a great love for him." He came again and again in her time of need. Also visiting her were Daniel Mifflin, Warner's younger brother; cousin Charles Mifflin, who tried to help Grace with her precarious financial situation; and Peggy and Betsy Johns, second or third cousins of Joseph Galloway and Warner Mifflin's as well. Again in September 1778 Warner and his wife visited her when in the city for the yearly meeting.[65]

Before she died in April 1782 at forty-nine, brokenhearted at the separation from her daughter and angry to the end with the husband who verbally bludgeoned her into submission and manipulated her dowry inheritance, the Mifflin kinfolk did their best to support her. Among them were Warner's future second wife, Ann Emlen, and her brother Samuel. Ann was one of the last to visit her on her deathbed and was among the Quakers who attended the funeral.[66] For Warner Mifflin, his contacts with the Galloway family were far from over.

## Enemy of the People

Mifflin escaped the wrath of Patriots while attending his Galloway Loyalist family. But at the height of the war in the mid-Atlantic region, he got an ample share of the attacks on Quakers for their neutralist (and sometimes proto-Loyalist) stances. At the center of this was the refusal of many Friends to accept Continental currency, regarding this as an indirect but still blood-stained way of supporting armed conflict. The Philadelphia Yearly Meeting had taken up this thorny issue in late 1775, deciding not to take a position on whether dealing in Continental currency was a violation of Quaker principles, leaving it to each individual to act according to his or her own conscience. Like many grain- and meat-producing farmers operating in a war zone, where both armies were bidding for horse forage and foodstuffs, Mifflin at first had traded in Continental currency, though with qualms. Similarly, many of his Philadelphia merchant friends, not daring to push their pacifism any farther, "had circulated [paper] money that it was alleged was made as much for war purposes" and had agreed to pay war taxes. On war taxes, Mifflin never wavered. "I refuse to pay taxes," he wrote Pennsylvania's Supreme Court justice in 1781, "believing it is the way pointed forth by the Captain General of the Lord of Hosts for us to wage war in righteousness [and] for the enlargement of his testimonies."[67] For this, Mifflin paid the same price as many other Quakers: a sheriff's seizure of anything that moved or could be moved. Even after the war ended, hefty taxes were imposed to retire the war debt. In 1784, for example, the tax collector left Chestnut Grove at planting time with what Mifflin calculated to be property worth eighty pounds.[68]

By 1779, Mifflin reached a critical point in dealing in Continental currency. The matter came to a head when he learned that his Quaker friend John Cowgill, who lived only a few miles from Chestnut Grove, had been ordered before the county Committee of Safety for refusing to deal in Continental currency. An early settler in Kent County, Cowgill was as deep-dyed a Quaker as could be found in Delaware. His grandfather had arrived as an indentured servant on the Lamb, one of the ships that carried William Penn and several thousand Quakers across the Atlantic to Philadelphia in 1682, so nobody questioned his Quaker credentials.[69] But in the heat of war that mattered little to the Patriots. Infuriated by Cowgill's refusal to back down, the committee ran notices in several newspapers, tarring him as an enemy to his country and warning that anyone doing business with him would be similarly labeled. Shortly after that, the Committee of Inspection interrogated Cowgill as an "enemy to the people" and gave him a choice: pay a heavy fine or expose himself "to the mercy of the mob." Choosing the latter, he was intercepted on his way to a Quaker meeting with his family by a mob that threw him unceremoniously into a cart and paraded him through the streets of Dover, with drums beating and a placard pinned to his back reading "On the Circulation of the Continental Currency Depends the Fate of America." Knowing that dealing with Cowgill would place them in danger, millers refused to grind his grain, while teachers were badgered to expel his children from their classrooms.[70]

Now it was Mifflin's turn. "Abundant threats were poured out," he wrote, "that my house should be pulled down over my head, that I should be shot, carted, &c." Thinking of Cowgill's harrowing experience, he thought, "my mind was almost overwhelmed, lest I should bring my family to want."[71] Mifflin searched his conscience for days, wandering at night through his plantation and looking for scriptural guidance. In five pages of rambling ruminations larded with biblical references he picked his way through the pros and cons, searching for a way to reconcile conscience with family security. "To me, it really appears to be a Lion's den," he wrote, "to be declared an enemy to the country and thrown out to the beastly nature in men now prevalent."[72]

Could he weather this storm? He doubted it. Then, "under this exercise and concern I walked about my plantation after night[fall], and seemed as if I never more should be able to make the stand. I thought if they took all my substance, I could give that up, but the fear for the poor body prevailed." Then, returning to his house, he grasped his Bible and "concluded to read the first Chapter I should open, which unthought for and providentially, I believe, was the 13th chapter of the Revelation." There he read that "all, both small and great, rich and poor, free and bond [are] to receive a mark in their right hand or in the forehead; and that no man might buy or sell save he that had the mark or the name of the Beast, or the number of his name." Here was a clear signal. He could not recall reading this passage and ones that followed. By candlelight he learned that anyone who received the mark of the Beast, that is from Satan, the Antichrist, "shall also drink the wine of God's fury, which has been poured full strength into the cup of his wrath [and] he will be tormented having sulfur in the presence of the holy angels. . . . There is no rest day or night for those who worship the Beast and his image."[73]

That decided it. With the Book of Revelation as his guide, Mifflin steeled himself for the result. "It clearly fixed in my mind if I received that [Continental] money I should receive the mark of the beast in my right hand." Now he had the strength "to appeal to Him who is the rightful dread of Nations . . . and felt a resignation to His Holy Will, if it was to the loss of all." Thus he decided he must refuse to "defile my hands with one of the engines of war."[74] It was costly. For several years, with only Continental currency in circulation, he was unable to market the produce from his farms, suffering "considerable pecuniary losses."[75]

A test of Mifflin's resistance to war taxes and use of Continental currency came not only from Kent County Patriots threatening to pour down havoc on his family and plantation, but from fellow Friends. Visiting the Evesham Monthly Meeting near John Woolman's New Jersey home, Mifflin "bore a very full plain clear and lively testimony against friends taking Congress money," recorded John Hunt, a New Jersey Quaker leader: "Some could hardly bear with" Mifflin's testimony, he sighed.[76] Other Quakers, including Nicholas Waln with whom Mifflin had crossed the battle lines at Germantown in 1777, saw themselves necessarily involved in dealing in the currency of the time (and trading profitably during the long war) rather than bring further opprobrium to the Society's doorstep.

When Waln chastised Mifflin for his purist position, probably during the yearly meeting of 1779, Mifflin held his tongue. But a few months later an astounding dream gave him the vindication he was looking for. Near the break of dawn, he dreamed he was attending Waln's funeral in Philadelphia.[77] Viewing the corpse at the home of a Friend, Mifflin was alarmed to see Waln's head turn. Then, to his amazement, "the upper part of his body moved." The corpse sedately climbed from the coffin and "shook hands with me in a very pleasant and friendly manner," admitting that Mifflin had "stood upright" in his wartime position on refusing to touch Continental currency. With such a self-justifying dream, the usually humble Mifflin could not resist sending Waln a letter describing his nighttime vision, reminding his friend how they had met with General Washington at his encampment north of Germantown three years before and how the American commander-in-chief had chastised Friends for depreciating the Continental currency by refusing to accept it in business transactions. But Waln, Mifflin recalled, had told the general he had large quantities of Continental dollars—something that "I have not mentioned but to very few."[78] Waln had crumbled when his feet were put to the fire; Mifflin had not.

After Washington moved his Continental Army south in late 1779, Quakers in the mid-Atlantic region hoped the cloud hovering over them would move south as well. This was not the case. They continued to suffer for their wartime neutrality, suspected Loyalism, and their opposition to Pennsylvania's radical revolutionary agenda that was yoked to the independence movement. Never friendly to the radical militiamen of Philadelphia, whose democratic aspirations took concrete form in the state's constitution of 1776, the Quakers found that the abuse heaped on them continued. In early October 1779, in the midst of furious arguments about price controls to relieve the lower classes from the fractured economy, the militiamen in Philadelphia turned on John Drinker, friend of Mifflin and brother of the exiled Henry Drinker, who had now been allowed to return to the city. Holding the key position as Clerk of the Philadelphia Meeting for Sufferings, John Drinker became the whipping boy of radical anger. Collaring him as he left the yearly meeting, militiamen paraded him around the city to the beat of the rogue's march. This quickly escalated into an attack on the house of James Wilson, not a Quaker and not a Tory but a conservative Patriot. On the second anniversary of the Battle of Germantown, the streets ran with blood as radical and conservative revolutionaries fought each other at "Fort Wilson." Before the melee was over, six lay dead in the streets, with more wounded and almost everyone's spirits depressed.[79]

Dark days for Quakers continued. Earlier, when Philadelphia Friends refused to illuminate their windows with candles on July 4 or the April and December days of fasting and thanksgiving sanctioned by the state's Supreme Executive Committee, they suffered shattered windows.[80] The epic American-French victory at Yorktown that brought the surrender of General Cornwallis's British and Hessian army on October 19, 1781, effectively ending the war for independence, brought another outburst of hatred. Philadelphians poured into the streets for a massive celebration on October 24, when all householders were asked to illuminate their windows with candles. But Quakers kept their windows dark. This brought havoc raining down on their houses from roaming mobs. From about 7 to 10 p.m., "scarcely one Friends House escaped," wrote diarist Elizabeth Drinker, describing how the "mob" shattered seventy panes of glass, splintered window sashes and front parlor panels, burst open the front door, and threw stones into their house. Other Quaker houses fared worse. After demolishing the doors, the crowd stormed in to destroy the furniture and frighten the women and children nearly out of their wits.[81]

Hearing of this from his Philadelphia friends, Mifflin exploded with uncus-
tomary heat. In a five-page letter to Thomas McKean, Pennsylvania Supreme
Court chief justice, he poured forth all the Quakers' accumulated grievances.
Mifflin had known McKean since Warner held office as a Kent County justice
of the peace. But his distrust of McKean had grown during the war, as the
volatile judge verbally abused Quakers brought before his court, especially
one who had refused to serve as a constable, though willing to hire a man in
his place.[82] Adding to Mifflin's simmering anger against McKean's role as
presiding judge was what most Friends regarded as the judicial murder of two
Philadelphia area Quakers tried for treason and executed in late 1778.[83]

Mifflin started temperately: "Notwithstanding the prejudices thou had let
in against the Society to which I belong, and the sentiments thou expressed
respecting myself, yet I did believe thou still retained something of that friendship that thou formerly manifested toward me and respect thou expressed to
my wife and mother." Then Mifflin unshackled his emotions. Referring to some
of McKean's harsh courtroom judgments against Quakers on trial for not
supporting the war, he charged that the chief justice apparently intended "to
crush and root out from the very earth . . . an innocent harmless people, who
are known to you to be such." Did McKean believe that Quakers who refused
to support the war did so out of a venal desire to curry favor with King George
in hopes of obtaining a salaried post? The king, Mifflin declared indignantly,
"had not a post of honor or profit to confer that I would give one bushel of
Indian corn for." His pacifism had its roots in no such motives, "nor do I believe
the thousandth part of our Society have." No, Mifflin protested, Quakers from
their founding moments had refused to make war. Now "we are called to the
support of a testimony against the spirit of war and bloodshed, for which we
are looked on as a people not worthy to live in the land, notwithstanding it
would be at the forfeiture of our Eternal All to forsake this testimony." Would
not a just God "who judgeth righteously and who taketh cognizance of the
actions of all men" punish a judge who abused those who "so far imitate their
pattern as to be sheep before their shearers, dumb, and not open their mouths
in their own defense"?

Mifflin wasn't done. Never one to hoard his words, now he used them to
excess. Charging the judge with gross inconsistency, he wrote: "You have
made a just stir in this land about liberty," but this had become a "licentious
liberty, even a liberty to endeavor to crush piety and virtue." As a prime
example, Mifflin reminded McKean of "the destruction of Quaker windows"

in Philadelphia on October 24, the place where Congress sat "to give laws to America." Meanwhile, while sitting as the president of the Continental Congress and chief justice of the state Supreme Court, McKean remained in stolid silence.[84]

Within a few days, the Philadelphia Meeting for Sufferings took the high road in responding to the attacks on Quaker houses: "the peaceable principle we profess is so opposite to the spirit of the world that it is no marvel if such an endeavor faithfully to maintain it have to partake in measure of that cup of affliction which Christ our holy parent so largely drank of . . . for it is through tribulation that the righteous in every age entered the Kingdom."[85] Broken windows and splintered doors were small prices to pay for showing what religious commitment was worth.

## Into the Jaws of the Lion

Several months before he unleashed his blistering letter to McKean, Mifflin, now thirty-six, embarked on a prolonged and dangerous mission to put his convictions on display and further the work of traveling ministers to renovate what one of them had called "the weak and almost ruined state of our discipline."[86] As recounted above, Mifflin had visited monthly and quarterly meetings in Chester, Bucks, and Philadelphia Counties in late 1779, logging 340 miles on what was becoming a lifelong quest: to follow decades of traveling Quaker elders and Public Friends to reawaken the divine spark in those who had become dull in their faith if not spiritually barren.[87] But that was a short jaunt compared to what he now embarked upon.

With the war for independence not yet over and his wife in her eighth pregnancy, the decision to set forth on a months-long journey northward to attend New York, Rhode Island, and New England yearly meetings, while dropping in on monthly and quarterly meetings in New Jersey and other states in his pathway, seems almost reckless. But reckless was not in Mifflin's vocabulary. The minutes of the Little Creek Monthly Meeting recorded that "Our friend Warner Mifflin having expressed at our last [meeting] some drawings in his mind to attend the ensuing Yearly Meetings of Long [New York] and Rhode Islands and some meetings of discipline within their verges as also of the Jersies . . . in company with some friends in his prospect having like concern."[88]

To put forward his "drawings in his mind," Mifflin was communicating in a way that would have been familiar to any Quaker, easily recognizable that he was speaking of inner promptings from God. Indeed, "drawings of the mind" was a phrase frequently used by Quakers seeking travel certificates from their local monthly meeting. From their inception Quakers had believed in the inward spark of divine inspiration, the corollary of which was the belief that no special training or formal education was necessary to equip a traveling "messenger of the truth." Yet, as Rebecca Larson explains, "distinguishing between one's own desires and 'divine instruction' was sometimes agonizingly difficult; but the ultimate test was within."[89] But not quite. Even the most erstwhile announcement of inward calling to spread the truth had to satisfy Friends in one's local meeting that the motives were pure and the goals of the traveling ministry were sound. Mifflin would have to reckon with this before long on another request for a traveling certificate.

Unlike other Protestant denominations, where elders and ministers who felt the call to preach outside their own jurisdiction were usually free to travel at their will, the Society of Friends strictly screened such desires, which indeed were sometimes impulsive. No meeting, whether preparative, monthly, quarterly, or yearly, would allow a self-designated emissary to appear before them without a certificate from his or her home monthly meeting endorsing such an endeavor. Rather, they cleaved to the dictum of the first yearly meeting in Philadelphia, even before William Penn reached the shores of the Delaware: "Agreed that if any Friend have it on his mind to travel in the service of Truth to any remote parts, that before they so do they first lay their intentions before the respective monthly meetings they do belong to in order to have approbation or consent thereof."[90] In this way, "traveling Friends" carried with them *bona fides* that would earn them respectful hearings and avoid the splintering that many Congregational and Presbyterian churches had suffered in the First Great Awakening of the 1720s to 1750s, when congregations had been by turns electrified and repulsed by itinerant and usually self-appointed dispensers of the "truth."

Mifflin was not undertaking this long journey by himself. In fact, that would have been unthinkable. A single man on a horse—the main means of transportation for Eastern Shore farmers—traveling through terrain still hotly contested by the American and British armies would hardly have lasted a week. Even proceeding in a group without military passes, Quaker pacifists were courting imprisonment or worse from either the British or the American forces.

For Mifflin, however, it was a test of bearing witness before his God. Though he could not know it at the time, this was a rehearsal for many traveling missions soon to come.

Leaving after spring planting on about May 4, 1781, Mifflin guided his horse along the familiar road northward from Chestnut Grove through New Castle and Chester Counties to Philadelphia. There he met his close friend George Churchman, the weather-worn veteran of scores of traveling ministries. Churchman would now be Mifflin's constant partner for the next three months.[91] They would have plenty to talk about while on the road, for both had been in the vanguard of reformers trying to put steel in the spines of Friends wavering on paying war taxes and using Continental currency.[92] They would also have plenty to worry about. Warner knew he would be away from his large family during the season of killing fevers in Kent County, while Churchman was leaving one of his sons hovering on the edge of death.

Arriving in Philadelphia, Mifflin and Churchman joined three other Friends, all mounted on their strongest horses for a trip they knew would be long and difficult. One of the Philadelphia traveling partners was James Thornton (1727–1794), the farmer from Byberry, just outside Philadelphia, who had ridden with Mifflin as part of the Quaker delegation carrying the peace testimony to Generals Howe and Washington four years before. The oldest in the group, Thornton was a Public Friend who radiated an inward light as a moving speaker as he traveled the long road ahead. Also joining the entourage was Samuel Smith (1737–1817), a prominent and hardy Philadelphia Quaker minister.[93]

Proceeding from Philadelphia across the Delaware River to Mount Holly, New Jersey, the group tarried to visit with John Woolman's widow. Then they rode on to Rahway, where they met David Cooper (1724–1795), a plain-spoken New Jersey farmer, acclaimed for his *A Mite Cast into the Treasury; or Observations on Slave Keeping* (1772), which helped spark the antislavery debate.[94] Having served in the New Jersey legislature for eight years in the 1760s, Cooper was schooled in political jockeying and was solidly in the pragmatic wing of the Society of Friends on the issue of resisting war taxes—a position that brought him in direct conflict with Mifflin. But on the issues of slavery and the refusal to bear arms, they were as one.

Now gathered, the group pointed their horses north. In ordinary times, embarking on such a long traveling ministry on horseback would have been strenuous, especially for the ailing Cooper at age fifty-seven and Thornton at fifty-four. But given what they were about to encounter, age was the least of their problems.

Churchman had warned at the outset they were "expecting to meet with difficulties in a perilous season for traveling [with] a military spirit predominating still in the Country." But how much did he know about the character of the "military spirit" in the region north of New York City, where the Quakers had plotted their route in order to reach the New York Yearly Meeting on Long Island? There is no reason to believe the Quaker contingent understood the details of strategic planning by either the British or American side in 1781. They certainly did not know that Washington's army, encamped in the Hudson Highlands for the winter of 1780–1781, was planning to rendezvous with the French troops stationed in Rhode Island for a long march south to Virginia. But surely they knew what had been publicized in newspapers up and down the seaboard, that ever since the British had seized Manhattan, Staten Island, and the western part of Long Island five years before, the zone they were entering was rife with Loyalists who had formed murderous quick-strike units that had desolated the region and driven most of its farmers for cover. Nonetheless, the group had set a goal and was not to be dissuaded.

Arriving in Elizabethtown (today's Elizabeth, New Jersey) to seek permission to proceed to British-occupied New York City, the most direct route to Long Island, the group ignored Cooper's advice that they were walking into the lion's mouth. Known for his ability to talk his way out of tight situations, Mifflin was deputized to approach the American commanding officer. Promptly arresting him, the officer sent for a justice of the peace to administer oaths of allegiance to the American revolutionary government. Told by Mifflin that Quakers on principle could not swear oaths, the officer released them with pointed advice to turn their horses southward and return home.

For committed Friends, this was simply another test of their service to their God. Soon, the sickened Cooper was "so unwell as to scarce be able to sit up [in the saddle]," believing he could not go on. But he prevailed. If not able to enter New York City and make an easy crossing to Long Island, the Quaker group was now obliged to plod northward up the west bank of the Hudson River in an arduous detour through Bergen County, New Jersey, and Orange County, New York, and thence into the rugged Hudson Highlands. From there they would have to cross the Hudson and circle back down through Dutchess and Westchester Counties to ferry over to Long Island. Along the way they would seek out Quaker households, where they could spend the night and

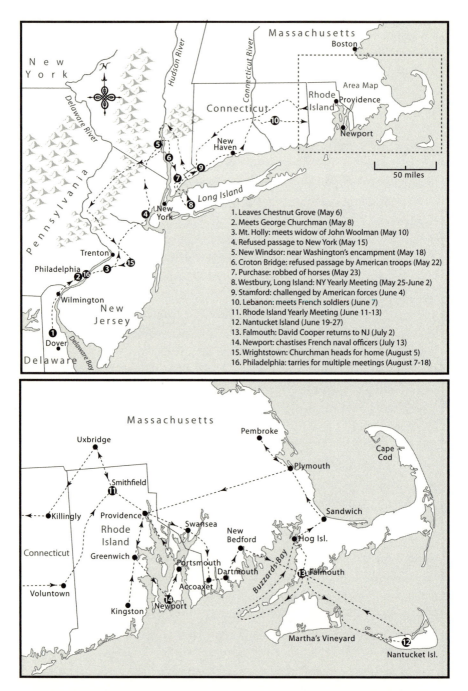

1. Leaves Chestnut Grove (May 6)
2. Meets George Churchman (May 8)
3. Mt. Holly: meets widow of John Woolman (May 10)
4. Refused passage to New York (May 15)
5. New Windsor: near Washington's encampment (May 18)
6. Croton Bridge: refused passage by American troops (May 22)
7. Purchase: robbed of horses (May 23)
8. Westbury, Long Island: NY Yearly Meeting (May 25-June 2)
9. Stamford: challenged by American forces (June 4)
10. Lebanon: meets French soldiers (June 7)
11. Rhode Island Yearly Meeting (June 11-13)
12. Nantucket Island (June 19-27)
13. Falmouth: David Cooper returns to NJ (July 2)
14. Newport: chastises French naval officers (July 13)
15. Wrightstown: Churchman heads for home (August 5)
16. Philadelphia: tarries for multiple meetings (August 7-18)

*Figure 9.* "Mission to the Northeast." The disposition of the British and American armies from northern New Jersey to the Hudson Highlands and Long Island contributed to the perilous weeks of travel undertaken by Mifflin and his Quaker friends.

grain their horses. As usual, they sniffed out backsliding: "Some serious hints were dropped," noted diarist Churchman, "on the subject of war, at which the women stopped their [spinning] wheels and listened attentively."

Riding up the west bank of the Hudson River for nearly seventy miles, Mifflin and his friends approached the ferry crossing at New Windsor, ten miles north of West Point, on May 19. Here Washington had made the Continental Army's last winter encampment in the winter and spring of 1780–1781. While awaiting permission to cross the Hudson, the Friends witnessed the pitiful state of the half-naked soldiers, most of them shoeless, who were preparing to march southward hundreds of miles in the now famous Washington-Rochambeau march for what Washington hoped would be the decisive victory over the enemy.[95]

Eager to visit Washington four years after his encounter with the general in the aftermath of the Battle of Germantown, Mifflin learned that though Martha Washington was several miles to the north, the general "was elsewhere."[96] Deciding to move on, the Quakers crossed the Hudson at the confluence of the Fishkill Creek and rode another twenty miles before evening set in. From there they turned their horses southward along a "rough and uneven road" through Dutchess County.

If David Cooper had earlier feared entering the lion's mouth when approaching New York City, the group now rode into the jaws of something far worse. Once across the swirling Hudson, full with spring tides, they left Dutchess County behind and entered Westchester County on May 22, knowing that they were attempting to pass through one of the most devastated areas of the Eastern Seaboard. "It seemed an awful undertaking to travel there in a country thus circumstanced," Churchman noted in his journal. Now they saw that civil government was all but destroyed. Known as the "Neutral Ground" because neither the British nor the Americans could control it, the country had been raked over, stripped of crops and cattle, its houses and barns plundered and scorched by roving irregular units, both British and American.[97] Among the American Loyalists most active in the area, the most famous were the DeLancey brothers, John and James, the latter the head of James DeLancey's Loyal Westchester Refugee Corps. The Quaker troop never met DeLancey, but they faced, to their regret, many of his "refugees."

The first taste of the viciousness of the "Neutral Ground" came when they reached the south bank of the Croton River where it emptied into the Hudson. Here, Christopher Greene commanded an American outpost. Like his third cousin Nathanael Greene, Christopher was a lapsed Quaker from Rhode Island. He drew most of his troops below the rank of corporal from the soon-to-be famous Rhode Island First Regiment (dubbed the Black Regiment many years later), composed of liberated slaves and a sprinkling of Native Americans.

Arriving at the Croton River bridge, the Quakers learned that nine days before DeLancey's Cowboys, so-called for their ability to rustle Patriot cattle to feed the occupying British army in New York City, had stormed Greene's outpost at dawn with sixty dragoons and one hundred forty foot soldiers, butchering Greene, other officers, and many of his troops. Of the thirty-three Americans taken prisoner, almost all were black, and DeLancey, a slaveowner himself, promptly sold them into slavery in the British West Indies.[98] Years later, William Nell, the Boston historian-abolitionist, set down with some exaggeration that Greene was "cut down and mortally wounded, but the sabers of the enemy only reached him through the bodies of his faithful guard of blacks, who hovered over him to protect him, and every one of whom was killed."[99]

When the American commander at the Croton River denied permission for the Quaker delegation to proceed across the "Neutral Ground," his decision probably spared the Quakers, at least for a moment, the wrath of "The Outlaw of the Bronx," as DeLancey was called. This forced the weary band to detour twenty miles in an arc swinging north, then east, and finally south to reach White Plains. Here, where another great battle early in the war had scarred the region, the Loyalists allowed them to pass through their lines, welcoming the weaponless Quakers as a predator, licking his chops, would lure defenseless prey.

By gathering other Friends intent on attending the New York Yearly Meeting, Mifflin and his friends only increased the bounty of the Loyalist marauders. Moving through the desolated Westchester terrain, described by Cooper as "almost uninhabited, houses empty, old grass of the last year's growth cover[ing] the fields, and the public roads grown up with grass," the Friends suffered the loss of several horses. Nonetheless, they pushed on, finally making it across Long Island Sound, where they spent a week at the New York Yearly Meeting at Westbury. On their return to the mainland on June 2, preparing to proceed north to Rhode Island's yearly meeting, they were again swarmed with the hit-and-run Loyalist Cowboys. Like so many vultures circling for fresh carrion, DeLancey's irregulars corralled many of the Quakers' horses, stripping them of the saddle bags, seizing the Quakers' greatcoats, and tearing "the cloathes off their backs and money out of their pockets." When Churchman lost his horse to the banditti, he gathered himself enough to put anger aside, finding "my mind enabled to submit & humbly rely on the care of my heavenly Father."

Leaving the "Neutral Ground"—it had been anything but that for the harassed but unswervable Friends—they made their way through Stamford, Norwalk, Fairfield, Old Milford, and New Haven, Connecticut, to arrive at Smithfield for the Rhode Island Yearly Meeting, where nearly a thousand Quakers gathered in mid-June. Over four days, they had pushed their horses 180 miles from Westchester to Smithfield. "Friends were put in mind," jotted Churchman, "to recollect that in [the] last century . . . divers worthy friends were suffered to be put [to] death by the Rulers of the Country as martyrs not far from this place."

For the next several weeks, the Quaker contingent combed Rhode Island to visit monthly and quarterly meetings at Woonsocket, Dartmouth, and Acushnet, accompanied by Moses Brown, Rhode Island's wealthiest merchant. All agreed that "it was manifest that weakness and defects abounded," and that only "strength and wisdom were afforded by our holy Head to treat in a close searching manner on serious subjects in the Spirit of Meekness and love."[100]

After the Rhode Island Yearly Meeting, Mifflin, Churchman, and the others made their way to New Bedford. There they embarked on an eight-hour trip across Buzzards Bay in rough water in late June to Nantucket Island, where St. John de Crèvecoeur, just a few years before, had found the Quakers prospering through hard work, love of family, mutual support, and relative equality. Here at last, on the windswept island breaching the Atlantic, Mifflin and his compatriots found solace from the war-ravaged northern states in the one place where Quakers dominated economic and cultural life.[101] For ten days, they spoke at large gatherings for public worship, with crowds over a thousand strong eager to hear the stalwart Quakers from the south. Though aggrieved that many had become "accustomed to lukewarmness" and thus became "irksome in our solemn assemblies," Churchman was mollified that "the dress of the females as they went out of the meeting was more uniform in regard to their heads [head coverings] and more in the moderation than I have observed in such a number anywhere heretofore."[102]

Returning to the mainland, the frail David Cooper took his leave from the others on July 1, 1781, to head home to New Jersey. His diary inspires awe at how a man near the end of his days could endure such a life-sapping journey on horseback. "I was out in this journey 9 weeks & 3 days, . . . having been at two Yearly, one Quarterly & four monthly meetings & rode about 1,000 miles & 120 by water."[103] But while Cooper made his way home, the others had many weeks ahead of them as they moved northward to visit meetings in Greenwich and Newport, Rhode Island, and then across the Massachusetts line to towns encircling Boston.

At almost every step, they encountered military units in a war reaching its climax. Attending Sunday worship in the Newport Quaker meetinghouse, which the French navy had commandeered as a provisions warehouse for feeding their 3,000-man army, they met French naval officers from the few ships left in the town after Rochambeau's army had headed south. Mifflin was pleased to see French officers attending a Quaker meeting, but was provoked by their less than sedate behavior. Ever ready to provide correction, he wrote that "I was pleased to see you come to our meeting, but sorry to notice so much whispering amongst you," then explaining that "any talk in our meetings" offends "that Great Being, whom we are concerned to know, and serve, agreeable to apostolic doctrine." God, he reminded them, is "not only omnipotent but omnipresent."[104]

Every disappointment had its reward. The next day, Mifflin and Churchman buttonholed the French commander to request that the meetinghouse be given back to the Friends for their undisturbed worship. The French officer, acknowledging that "we were a people who were known and revered throughout the world on account of our peaceable sentiments and conduct," ordered the military equipment and provisions removed.[105] With that small victory, Mifflin and Churchman resumed their tour of Quaker meetings in Rhode Island.

Not until late July did Mifflin and Churchman point their horses southward for the long journey home. Wherever they encountered backsliding Quakers— for example, a young woman sporting "a gay headdress"—they offered gentle reproof.[106] Making their way down the west side of the Hudson, the bone-tired party passed through Sussex County, New Jersey, where Mifflin, seeing black slaves at work, "gave some close admonition respecting slave holding" to their masters. A few days later, after crossing the Delaware River into Pennsylvania, Mifflin and Churchman parted, the exhausted Churchman intent on following "the nearest way home." The three-month perambulation had been enough.[107]

But not for Mifflin. Intent on spreading the word of their efforts to stiffen war resistance and encourage greater strictness in Quaker worship, he rode on to Philadelphia to visit meetings for several more weeks. Reaching the city, he learned that his wife, now in the seventh month of pregnancy, was danger- ously ill. But rather than spur his horse homeward, he felt he must "resign all [my family] I left behind into the keeping of him I desired to serve." In spite of the word of Elizabeth's precarious health and the sickness of his children, he "still . . . felt my mind engaged to continue round to some meetings in Pennsylvania, which I gave up to." And so, having visited several preparative and a monthly meeting in Philadelphia, he spent additional days in Chester County before finally turning his horse toward Kent County. From the time he had parted company with Churchman, it was more than two weeks before Mifflin got home.[108]

Finally, after fourteen weeks on his horse, covering some 1,400 miles, Warner Mifflin reached Chestnut Grove on about August 24. Yet his mind was still not at rest. "I found my wife very low," he wrote "[and] several of the children also had been ill." But he had been "mercifully favoured." From a man who knew the terrors of Kent County's infamous ill health, this was a way of thanking God for sparing his four children, aged thirteen, ten, seven, and four, after another of the fever seasons that had plagued Kent County for years. As for his wife, he could only say that "my dear companion bore our separation to my admiration."[109]

For Quakers enlisting in the root-and-branch reform crusade, complacency was never an option. But in the case of Warner Mifflin the intensity of his commitment was so great that it sometimes frightened others—and even himself on occasion. It seems clear from his letters to his closest confidants at the end of this fourteen-week journey that he was on the edge of a psycho- logical crisis. The men to whom he most candidly unburdened himself were John Pemberton, Henry Drinker, and Moses Brown. Arriving home from his trip to the Northeast, he wrote to each of them—of how he "found my dear companion [wife Elizabeth] . . . mercifully preserved in a state of resignation during the greatest part of the time of our separation." Thinking about how he had dodged death at several points of the journey and how his family had made it through another season of fevers, he saw this as "evident tokens of the heav- enly father's parental care." Yet he was frank that he knew "my family [had] wanted me very bad" and that it seemed "I never more might be allowed to see my dear companion." Surely he "should not have cause to repent" if he had "broke off from what I believed was my duty and gone home" to his dangerously sick family. But he did not. On and on in this long letter, he poured out to Pemberton how he "had like to sink under discouragement," but somehow pulled himself together with a resolve "for me daily to be endeavoring for a fresh supply of strength and support."[110]

Indeed, he found the renewed strength to go back on the road, even though his wife, in the ninth month of her eighth pregnancy, had another brush with death. After "I had been home some days," he wrote Moses Brown, "she was taken very ill and remained so thirteen days, more like to dye than to live." This troubled Mifflin sorely, because he was intent on attending the Philadelphia Yearly Meeting in late September. Then seeing Elizabeth "in such a brave way to recover," he decided, "I could not be easy to stay as the tryall was great."[111] If it was a trial for Warner, wrestling with himself to balance his family responsibilities with his dedication to meeting with Friends in Philadelphia, it was surely even more of a trial for the ailing Elizabeth with her brood of children.

Aside from psychological explanations of Mifflin's behavior, it is clear that his commitment to the yearly meeting trumped his regard for familial responsibilities. No doubt he wanted to relate his months-long journey. Beyond that, he had responded to his innermost thoughts that God, not family, was the pivot of his existence. And so he proceeded to Philadelphia for a yearly meeting he had rarely missed in recent years. It was a business meeting, a social gathering, and an opportunity to press one's point of view, particularly in 1781 on the doctrine of war resistance and the commitment to antislavery.

Something of his unrest—it would continue for the rest of his life—can be appreciated from Mifflin's missive to Moses Brown just after returning from the yearly meeting. Mulling over the trip to Long Island and New England, he found the results fell short of his hopes. In a delicate phrasing of self-justification, Mifflin allowed that "I have experienced in my small measure that nothing that we can part with or undergo is too much for his Great Namesake when this is the only object in our view; and he points our duty therein." Though only thirty-six years old, he peered into the future, sensing what lay ahead: "I feel a disposition of mind prevalent that I may not be pitied nor spared of anything that may conduce to my furtherance in that Holy Highway that leads to the Celestial Country."[112]

# Chapter 3

## To Reform a Nation

"*Being brought into deep feeling* for the oppressions of the poor Africans in the West Indies, [I] have never been easy with indulging in [using] the produce of their labour since, lest it should even in a small degree contribute towards the continued existence of a trade, which interests the planters in keeping up the numbers of their groaning labourers."[1] Such were Warner Mifflin's words as he reflected on the course of his life during the heat of the American Revolution. While armies clashed, Mifflin underwent a personal transformation within the larger revolution swirling around him. This reshaping of the way he and his family lived in their Kent County home required a suppression of materialistic urges in favor of a life of self-denial and simplicity. This in turn mingled with his intensifying antislavery stance; and from that abolitionist doctrine came his gospel of "restitution" for the injury suffered by enslaved Africans and their descendants. The man who had remained largely immune to the Quaker self-cleansing reformation that had gained momentum in the 1750s and 1760s now strode to the forefront of that campaign, as the unruly American Revolution captured international attention in its pursuit of universal freedom.

Closely braided to this reformation of fellow Friends was his vanguard performance in spreading the gospel of restitution for liberated slaves, so singular that he may fairly be called the father of American reparationism—the term used today to argue that the descendants of enslaved Africans and their progeny in the United States should receive compensation for unrequited labor and the assault on their humanity. From there Mifflin moved on to develop his skills as a legislative lobbyist. First achieving a victory in Virginia that would put thousands of slaves on the road to freedom, he joined the Quaker delegation that unleashed the first official assault on slavery before the national Congress.

This marked Mifflin's emergence as an important cog in the antislavery machine under construction by a determined fragment of the Society of Friends joining hands across the Atlantic. Most Quakers, intent on putting behind them their wartime pariah status earned by their pacifist noninvolvement, eschewed contest and confrontation as they worked to gain reacceptance into civil society by their forgiving countrymen. Mifflin was not among them. Rather, in his mid-thirties, he became an unapologetic, able, determined, and fearless figure, willing to wage war against the evil of slavery with an intensity that historians usually associate with the militant abolitionism of the antebellum decades.

## Seeding the Free Produce Movement

Just as they had blazed trails for the antislavery movement gaining ground during the advent of the American Revolution, John Woolman and Anthony Benezet were the standard-bearers of the sermon about the spiritually sapping effects of indulgent living and the accumulation of wealth.[2] Since the 1750s they had been preaching that the immodest displays of wealth on full view among the city's wealthiest merchants and landowners betrayed Quaker founding principles and choked off their inward communion with God.[3] It was not an easy sell. Many of the Quakers with whom Warner Mifflin associated at the Philadelphia Yearly Meetings—the Drinkers, Norrises, Logans, Emlens, Fishers, Pembertons, some of them Warner's Mifflin cousins—grimaced at the stern message of Woolman and Benezet, all the while retaining their stately city houses and country seats, their four-wheeled carriages, and their retinue of servants.[4] Like them, Mifflin in the early years of his marriage had resisted the reformers' strictures.

The run-up to the revolution heightened the tension within the affluent Quaker community on the issue of wealth and its twin brother avarice. In his *A Plea for the Poor: A Word of Remembrance and Caution to the Rich*, Woolman cautioned that Quakers were fencing themselves off from universal love and redemption through their worldly accumulative spirit. Spiritual dullness inescapably was the result. More than that, war, like slavery, had its origins in wealth-seeking and selfishness.[5] Benezet pushed the message, discomfiting many Quakers but reaching the hearts of others.[6] The wealthy Nicholas Waln, who would become Mifflin's good friend but sometimes a man with whom he

**Figure 10.** Averse to portraits as ostentatious and self-indulgent, many Quakers had their silhouettes taken as restrained side views of themselves. The four men pictured here (top: John Pemberton; Henry Drinker; middle, James Pemberton, John Parrish) give a sense of the heft and probity of Warner Mifflin's closest friends and advisors in Philadelphia. The bonneted Martha Routh, a well-traveled Public Friend from England, was one of the many female ministers who visited Mifflin at his Kent County home and worshipped with him at the Murderkill Meetinghouse. From Amelia Mott Gummere, *The Quaker: A Study in Costume*, 1901.

would tangle, was unusual in responding. Withdrawing from his lucrative legal practice, he scaled back his mode of living and refashioned himself as a Quaker traveling minister ready to endure all physical discomforts and fatiguing journeys. Only a few in Philadelphia's Quaker elite followed his lead. Among those ignoring Woolman and Benezet were the wealthy Quakers exiled to Winchester, Virginia, in the winter of 1777–1778. Sympathy for them was widespread; but in Benezet's eyes their "pride and indulgence so contrary to the low, humble, self-denying life of Christ & his immediate followers," so evident in the "the sumptuousness of our dwellings, our equipage, our dress; furniture & the luxury of our tables," had "become a snare to us," bringing God's retribution in the form of war-spawned attacks on Quaker property. Was it not time "to begin anew upon the true foundation of our principles"?[7]

Knotted to the Woolman-Benezet doctrine was an insistence that greed—the desire for material goods and a self-indulgent lifestyle—was at the root of slavery, for it was the unpaid labor of Africans that created the wealth supporting high living. Hence, in theory, the decision to free one's slaves went hand in hand with scaling back household furnishings and clothing—a return to the simplicity that anchored the faith of the early Quakers. Most of the slave-owning Quaker squirearchy reluctantly acceded to the abolitionist half of the equation but balked at returning to the plain living of their forefathers, finding that wage and indentured servants could serve as well as the enslaved and unwilling to give up Georgian grandeur.

Mifflin subscribed to both parts of this double cleansing, not at first but then with a vengeance. Modeling his life on John Woolman's and Anthony Benezet's, he moved by steps. Writing of his visit to Chestnut Grove, Crève-coeur, perhaps with exaggeration, noted that Elizabeth's dowry included "furniture, bureaus and closets . . . of mahogany and . . . of great beauty," as well as clothes, which "though simple, were rich and in large quantities." Then, adopting an austere life, Warner and Elizabeth had sold "everything which could be considered useless or superfluous," even including shoe buckles, which were to be replaced with laces. "She carried her scruples so far as even to have all the carving and ornaments on her furniture taken off, as being contrary to the simplicity of Friends."[8]

Changes in diet followed, as the Mifflins began to practice an early form of what would later become the Free Produce Movement. In the 1730s, the English immigrant Benjamin Lay, radical to the core in preaching his antislav-ery message, pledged not "to eat any food, nor wear any garment, no use any article which . . . was in the remotest degree the product of the labour of slaves."[9] Dismissed by Quaker leaders, though admired by many, Lay would be in his grave before other Quakers on the radical fringe of the Society's reformation and antislavery movement haltingly reinitiated the campaign in the early 1760s. Distressed "day and night" by the "cries of the slaves in the West-India Islands," Joshua Evans, a Public Friend from Haddonfield, New Jersey, forswore slave-produced sugar, rum, and molasses.[10] By the 1770s, Benezet was echoing Evans. The message was simple: just as enslaving Africans was a form of theft, consuming what slaves produced was to partake of stolen goods. But the remedy, to disengage from the consumer market, was not simple, and for all but a few ultra-strict Quakers this seemed impossible. Very few Friends fell into line.

For Mifflin the watershed moment came in the heat of revolution. As usual with him, dramatic events produced dramatic self-examination. In April 1777 news spread that the *Morris*, an American merchantman reportedly loaded with sugar from the West Indies, had been run aground by the English fleet at Lewes, Delaware, and blown up by its crew to prevent the British from plundering it.[11] With the explosion heard for sixty miles, Mifflin saw this as a "clear presentation" from above that he should consider forgoing "those sweets that I am so fond of," which came "in a time of national hostility . . . at the manifest risk of the lives of my fellow men." Invading his mind was the biblical account of "David's sensation, when his valiant men rushed through the Philistine army, to bring him water from a well, which he longed for." But David "was struck with sympathy for them; and because they went in jeopardy of their lives, he was not easy to gratify his palate therewith, but poured [the water] out in dedication to the Lord." Now it was clear to Mifflin: "In like manner, I felt a prohibition from using foreign imports."[12] Thereafter, well before the first English pamphlet arguing against the consumption of "blood-stained sugar," Mifflin banned the sweetener from his table, later replaced by maple sugar produced by free labor.

Knowing that sugar was the foundation of the rum trade, Mifflin turned his attention to that as well. In his memoir, he explained how "I frequently kept the bottle and the bowl on the table, from morning till night." But now he banished alcohol from his house, regarding it as another worldly luxury and sign of self-indulgence. By convincing those working his farm to give it up during work routines, he also hoped to gain labor efficiency. In these seeds of the nineteenth-century Free Produce movement, he also added indigo to the list of prohibited articles, while sharply limiting his use of salt.[13]

## Counseling the Liberated

From reforming himself, Mifflin turned to reforming others. As his life's mission began to revolve around tearing down the walls of slavery, he threw himself into the arduous business of home visits to free black families and drop-by consultations with Friends who retained the minor black children, who, though legally emancipated, served until they reached their majority. Mifflin's months-long trip to the Northeast was in the company of other male Friends, and the purpose was to repair fractured Quaker discipline and fortify war resistance. But for several years before this trip, and continuing into the 1780s, he became a key figure in mixed-gender visiting committees that scoured the area embraced by the Western Quarterly Meeting. Rather than war resistance, their purpose was tending to the needs of blacks, which necessarily meant holding former masters to account for the welfare of those they had unshackled. This allowed Mifflin to open up the contested terrain of reparations.

"Family visits," as they were called, had a long history in the Society of Friends.[14] Whether to urge closer attention to inculcating the youth in Quaker principles or enforcing rules against out-marriage, the visiting committees had gained greater importance when the reformation movement swept through Quakerdom before the American Revolution. Now, with the war raging, they reached new heights. By late 1777, Mifflin was participating in the call for monthly meetings to seek out Friends whose self-indulgent behavior imperiled their communion with God. This led to a nine-person committee, commissioned by the Duck Creek Monthly Meeting, where four female Friends joined five males to see how Friends, in the midst of war, could "carry forward a Reformation."[15]

This required "weighty work," as Quakers often called innovative or disputed practices. Constructing this gender-mixed committee demanded careful preparation. To be sure, women had long been engaged in Quaker affairs, as in no other denomination. Since the advent of the Society of Friends in mid-seventeenth-century England, they had been preaching and prophesying everywhere the Quakers went—in England, Scotland, and Ireland; in the West Indies; and in North America. Female Public Friends had criss-crossed the Delmarva Eastern Shore for generations, welcomed as much as male ministers for their spiritual gifts.[16] At the local level, their authority in Quaker meetings was firmly established, with their attention to the "clearness" of proposed marriages, breaches of Quaker discipline, and support of the poor especially valued.[17] New responsibilities for women now came when the Society's monthly meetings formed committees to visit families, one by one. Cudgeling foot draggers unwilling to give up slaveholding was one part of this reformation work.[18]

The Duck Creek reformation committee of nine agreed that before descending on the homes of other Friends they should "visit each other at our respective places of abode in order to strengthen [each other] herein and remove such things amongst ourselves as might obstruct our way and be likely to retard our service." Such oblique language suggests the novelty of such a mixed-gender deputation. Once they had "put away such things as we believed Truth's testimony was against," the committee sallied forth.[19] Leaving their families in the hands of their husbands, the four women traversed a large swath of Delaware. Traveling by horse in the dead of winter, they reported "unexpected openings regarding our service." Despite "slackness of discipline" and indifference to weekly worship among some, they found "a remnant in most meetings . . . to unite in this great and necessary work." In concluding their report, the committee made the conventional Quaker nod to Providence: "we hope to stand open to a further labor . . . being encouraged from a belief that the Master of our Assembly owns the work."[20]

That "further labor" came quickly. Building on the reformation committee's efforts, a second mixed-gender committee, appointed in spring 1778, embarked upon a protracted effort to reach out to the black people Friends had released from bondage. In taking this action, the Duck Creek Monthly Meeting took sides in an ongoing argument within the Philadelphia Yearly Meeting leadership. There, many Friends held that once they had cleansed their hands of slaveholding, their work was done. But some believed otherwise. For Warner Mifflin and the other men and women of the committee, the work of true Christians only began with the liberation of their human property. After that, they were morally obligated to provide for the education of the black children, to care for aged and disabled men and women coming out of thralldom, and to help freed people with legal assistance when white predators tried to drag them back into slavery. Far bolder was the idea promoted by Mifflin that manumitted fellow humans deserved compensation for the years of toil they performed after they had reached adulthood. It was a matter of simple justice.[21]

Limiting the activist reformers was the cloudy advisory of the yearly meeting. As far as it would go, in an epistle in late 1778 that went out to all quarterly and monthly meetings, was the advice that monthly meetings should "consider the circumstance of these poor [manumitted] people, and the obligation we are under to discharge a religious duty to them." But that duty consisted mainly in "promoting their instruction in the principles of the Christian religion and the pious education of their children."[22] This was hardly a clarion call for providing the means for a farming people to acquire land, tools, and livestock of their own as they emerged from slavery with little but the clothes on their backs. Most noticeably, the epistle avoided the word "restitution."

Venturing forth after spring planting in late April 1778, and acting well ahead of the Philadelphia Yearly Meeting advisory report, the Committee for Visiting Free Negroes, led by Mifflin, gathered about forty blacks at the Duck Creek meetinghouse in Smyrna. The next day, riding southward, they welcomed some seventy blacks, who flocked to the Little Creek meetinghouse to hear what the Quakers proposed. A day later, the committee met with nearly one hundred free blacks at Murderkill meetinghouse—a heartening turnout of those so recently liberated.[23] In the next two days, in southernmost Delaware, over forty freed men and women made their way to Three Runs and thirty to Cold Spring meetinghouses.[24]

Then, riding their saddle horses southward through Maryland's Eastern Shore to the Virginia border, five of the committee, joined by three other Friends, reached the home of Daniel Mifflin, Warner's father. What occurred in the next two days was memorable. First, on Saturday, the committee met with about fifty of the slaves Daniel Mifflin had liberated in 1775 who still lived at Pharsalia. On Sunday, the committee visited most of the other fifty blacks manumitted by Mifflin "at their different places of abode," most nearby and some perhaps settled on Mifflin's many parcels of land. Then, in what bears the appearance of a carefully staged event, the committee invited the former slaves to stay over and meet with other nearby blacks "who were still in a state of slavery." Surprisingly, some of Mifflin's neighbors, "most of them slave-holders," also came. The committee called this "a parting opportunity" to soften the hearts of those who still held slaves and show them that the gathered freed people were making a successful transition to freedom. The "nature of our errand was opened to advantage," the committee reported.[25]

Whether the First Day (Sunday) meeting included biracial worship is not disclosed in the visiting committee report. What is certain is that the visiting committee, "disposed to do justice and equity," pressed the necessity of education, both religious and secular. The Friends offered "gospel truths," "the way of life and salvation," "the fundamentals of the Christian faith," and "many hints of instruction, caution, and counsel, with respect to their present conduct and well-being." This was formulaic Quaker instruction, no different from that directed by many masters at the enslaved, and it was doubtless the daily fare proffered to the freed men and women remaining in Quaker households or living on the land of their former owners.[26]

How, we may ask, did the freed men and women who had struck out on their own receive the men and women dressed in Quaker drab, their heads bonneted or covered with broad-brimmed hats? Lacking direct testimony from the freed people themselves, we have only the Friends' observations faithfully recorded in the monthly and quarterly minute books. "They appeared glad of the visit[s], manifested by their conduct, [and] a nearness of affection to Friends," ran one account, "and we believe an open door is set for further fruitful labor." The former slaves "were cheerfully disposed to attend," and were "generally behaved soberly" and "solid in their countenances."[27] Though it might be suspected that this hopeful attitude of the visiting committee put too rosy a hue on what occurred, the fact remains that a large majority of the freed people, taking time from work regimens and weekend leisure, voluntarily chose to attend these meetings.

Still, the earnest Friends had little to offer concretely beyond words of moral support and advice. No schools for blacks existed in rural Delaware, and there was no likelihood that the kind of school established in Philadelphia by Anthony Benezet would find support or even attract black children dispersed over a large region.[28] Yet, having come to see what Friends were prepared to do for them, black families returned again after fall harvest in 1778. Few had horses, so most trudged on foot. The visiting committee kept coming, in February 1779 and again in May, to meet with them. If black families could not gather at the meetinghouses, which often meant traveling many miles, then the committee went to visit them in their homes.[29]

### Reparations Doctrine

In the course of the recurrent family visits and biracial meetings, the issue of "restitution" frequently came to the surface, often pushed forward by Mifflin. He had reached his own decision in 1775 about what he owed those enslaved to him, admitting that on liberating his slaves he at first "thought it best to put them from me, to manifest they were so." That provided an opening for some of his Kent County neighbors, who had little use for Quakers and no intention of freeing their slaves, to charge that "Mifflin had set free a parcel of lazy, worthless Negroes," that "he could make nothing by them [and] therefore had set them at liberty." Stung by these charges, "I found an engagement," he wrote, "to make restitution to those I had held in a state of bondage for the time so held [past the legal age of adulthood]," which was done "according to the judgment of indifferent [unbiased] men agreed on by myself and the blacks." That he would put such a matter before a committee where those being liberated had input was in itself extraordinary. When the committee "propose[d] their having land and teams; and in return, they should give me half their produce," the deal was struck "to their full satisfaction . . . and mostly to mine."[30]

Thus, Mifflin had pried open a thorny issue that has continued to the present: what is owed to the descendants of enslaved Africans whose uncompensated labor for two and a half centuries helped build America; what form would such compensation take; and who should pay for it?[31] In today's parlance, "reparations" is the operative term, and historians have followed suit in adopting it to cover a gamut of compensatory schemes proffered by a tiny minority of masters who freed their slaves: small grants of land or money by last will and testament; pensions awarded from the estate of a deceased slaveowner; share-cropping arrangements; living dispensations of land, tools, and seed; and outlays of cash for labor performed by slaves during their adult years.[32] In all these cases, "restitution" proceeded from the acknowledgment that slavery was profoundly unjust and that the injustice could be redressed only by some form of equitable compensation to the liberated fellow creature. Thus, in principle, restitution differed sharply from the "freedom dues"—a suit of clothes, a few tools, or a token cash payment—that were often given to indentured servants who had completed a contracted term of service. Far from "restitution," the master or mistress of an indentured servant admitted no injustice at all in negotiating a labor contract entered into freely by both parties.

Mifflin was not the first to raise the issue of reparations. For many years, a handful of Friends had freed slaves in wills that made small grants of land and money. As early as 1708, a Maryland Quaker provided two slaves to be liberated at his death with fifty acres of land, a house, and livestock.[33] In nearby Wilmington, Delaware, David Ferris had been strenuously pushing the idea of restitution since the year of Warner and Elizabeth's marriage. Ferris owned no slaves of his own, but he urged Quakers to do what he deemed as common justice. In 1767, he insisted that elderly slaves, beyond labor, should be supported after they were freed. As for younger men and women still of laboring age, they should be "not, by any means, sent away empty but should be liberally furnished out of your stock," an acknowledgment that since the slave's labor had increased the master's wealth, the liberated person, as a matter of equity, was entitled to a share of that bounty. Ferris went to the Old Testament for biblical commandment:

> And if thy brother, a Hebrew man, or a Hebrew woman, be sold unto thee, and serve thee six years; then in the seventh year thou shalt let him go free from thee. And when thou sendest him out free from thee, thou shalt not let him go away empty: thou shalt furnish him liberally out of thy flock, and out of thy floor, and out of thy winepress: of that wherewith the LORD thy God hath blessed thee thou shalt give unto him. And thou shalt remember that thou wast a bondman in the land of Egypt, and the LORD thy God redeemed thee: therefore I command thee this thing today. (Deuteronomy 15:14)

Then he used the example of a man who had served until he was forty. "That is 19 years more than is just," he advised, "and his service has been well worth £12 per annum, amounting to £228. Now to turn such a one away and give him nothing is unchristian, yea; it is dishonest! It shows that we would not pay a just debt unless compelled by the law."[34]

John Woolman and his younger brother Abner also raised this issue at about the same time in New Jersey. Abner went so far as to argue that if a man's estate was "advanced by the labor of slaves," then those slaves, when freed, should be repaid at least a share of the enhanced estate. This would have "equity put in practice." Woolman argued similarly, putting a fine point on the matter. Calculating the labor value of a man "violently taken from Guinea" at age forty and "labored hard till old age," he totted up what the man's children should be given, with interest added. "Where persons have been injured as to their outward substance and died without recompense, so that their children are kept out of that which was equitably due to their parents, here such children appear to be justly entitled to receive recompense from that civil society under which their parents suffered."[35] Granville Sharp, the engine of early English abolitionism, argued similarly in a letter to Anthony Benezet in 1775 that American slaveholders professing to be Christians should "divide what lands they can spare into compact little farms, with a small wooden cottage to each" for their liberated bonds people. "Let such negroes hold these small portions of land by leases for a certain number of years," Sharp continued, and "at equitable rents to be paid in such portions of the produce from time to time as shall be thought most reasonable, leaving the tenants a moderate gain . . . and yet so as to yield the landlords a due profit from each portion of their estates."[36] Farther north, a newly arrived English merchant served up the same Mosaic law from Deuteronomy to Boston slavekeepers, apparently with no effect.[37]

Circulating at the same time was a cruelly different notion of reparations. Eager to make gradual abolition palatable to slaveowners, Connecticut Congregational minister Levi Hart proposed that it was the manumitting masters who should not be left empty-handed. Every master should be rewarded with the equivalent of wages for each year of the liberated slave's majority. In the chilly world of market transactions and sanctity of property, reparations should go to the slave masters rather than to the freed people.[38]

None of these protagonists discussing reparations was a slaveholder with capital at stake. But Mifflin had a hefty pecuniary interest in slaveowning, and he did more than talk about it. A few Friends within the ambit of the Philadelphia Yearly Meeting followed his example for restitution, but the general view prevailed that slaveholding was "a sin to be banned from the Society, not as a condition from which Afro-Americans must be delivered."[39] As the American Revolution lurched from one crisis to another, Mifflin gently raised the issue of reparations. In fall 1778, he reported that most of the members of the Committee for Visiting Free Negroes "had been more or less concerned in the oppression of this people, some having many years back sold Negroes that were yet living and in a state of slavery, some having released them at an advanced age, and made no restitution, others had hired [out] slaves and paid the wages to their masters." In short, "justice had not enough been attended to."[40] In May 1779, the committee pushed again, recognizing "the necessity of restitution being made to those oppressed people for the injustice done them." Though admitting that repeated visitations to manumitting Quaker families had not produced the desired results, they hoped that "the divine blessing will attend our labours." Meanwhile, they called for a meeting of free blacks in June 1779 "to examine what remains to be done for, and towards, this people." Having embraced the doctrine of reparations, the committee reported that "the gospel net is spread [and] will, in Father's time, entangle the feet [and] the minds of many." It was not just the "welfare of individuals," Mifflin wrote for the committee, but "of society and of our country [that] is deeply interested."[41]

Prompted by these efforts, Mifflin now went even further in leading reparationist efforts. Years before, he had leased enslaved men from their nearby owners; but now, four years after freeing his own slaves, he "found myself bound in point of duty" to tell the masters that the wages agreed upon for hired men should go to the slaves themselves. Of course, this was business nonsense, for what slave master would lease his property only to benefit the slave? Nonetheless, Mifflin decided that "if they would not pay it, I must." By 1779 he had already paid one slave for his hired time and expected "many pounds more will be advanced." He had fully absorbed the lesson from Isaiah that only the one who "despiseth the gain of oppression" was to survive the "devouring fire" and "the everlasting burning."[42] Such was his evolving concept of reparations.

While Mifflin and other Duck Creek leaders staked out their justice doctrine of reparations, the Philadelphia Yearly Meeting equivocated. At the September meeting in 1779, deliberating on the report of the Western Quarter, the yearly meeting advised only that "the state of the oppressed people who have been held by any of us or our predecessors in captivity and slavery calls for a deep inquiry and close examination how far we are clear of withholding from them . . . their just right." The opaqueness of this advice continued with the entreaty "to bring this matter home, and that all who have let the oppressed go free may attend to the further openings of duty."[43] In effect, the matter was for each individual to decide.

After the yearly meeting advisory, far short of a sanction, Mifflin and likeminded Friends of his committee continued to press their "increasing concern to make restitution" into the 1780s.[44] If this "concern" needed reinforcement, it sometimes came from the freed men and women themselves who attended gatherings of the Committee for Visiting Free Negroes, held through the 1780s. In 1781, as Mifflin's committee continued to gather "collected bodies" of the freed black people throughout Kent and Sussex Counties, they reported to the yearly meeting that "a sense of injustice . . . remains in some of the Negroes' minds," and that this "appears to us to demand the further care of sympathy of friends."[45]

But Mifflin's cadre had only the power of persuasion to move fellow Quakers to provide former slaves with small land grants, cash, share-cropping arrangements, or other forms of support. Though many Friends crafted wills that left money or small amounts of land to former slaves, these were only end-of-life dispensations given to liberated men and women long after they had gained their freedom. How many manumitters provided cash, land, or tenancy arrangements at the time of liberation, as did Warner Mifflin and his father, is hidden to history, but monthly meeting records indicate that there were many.[46] If their efforts often went unrewarded, they were buoyed by heartening incidents. Three cases in 1780 and 1781, all involving collateral kin of Mifflin, set examples for others to follow.

The first case concerned Thomas and Joseph Nock, brothers from one of Delaware's earliest Quaker families. Kinsmen by marriage to Warner Mifflin, they were his neighbors and constant associates in Murderkill Hundred. The committee of men appointed by the Duck Creek Monthly Meeting, including Mifflin and his wife's brother-in-law Robert Holliday, was asked to investigate how the Nocks, in disposing of slaves left to them in their father's will, had sold them "for a term of years after they were of lawful age." For many months the committee wrestled with the case, meeting the Nock brothers and bringing them together with the five black adults—three men and two women—who were now free. In August 1780 the case was resolved. The "Negroes appeared in a forgiving disposition," the committee reported, "and not much to bear in mind the injury done them, nor did they appear anxiously desiring of recompense being made them." Yet the committee was eager to make a point. With the Nocks agreeing to abide by the committee's advice, the deal was struck: twenty pounds each to Palm, Esther, Eleanor, and Aaron; thirty pounds to Moses, precisely the amounts Thomas and Joseph Nock had sold them for.[47]

Then came the moment for cash settlement. In a day when a free agricultural worker earned less than twenty pounds a year, reparations in this amount were sufficient to purchase many acres. Mindful that anonymity was hardly possible in a county populated by only about 7,000 people, and that the future of freed men and women depended on good relations with former masters, the committee assured the Nocks' former slaves that they should speak their minds freely "without reserve or fear of offence." At the final meeting, two days before Christmas in 1780, the liberated blacks were "emboldened," the committee reported, announcing what the Nock brothers had little reason to expect: Palm "chose to accept the whole of his £20, likewise Esther her £20." But Aaron "would accept but £9," exclusive of three pounds he had been promised by another man for whom he had worked. Moses, entitled to £30, would accept only £12 and Eleanor only a third of what she could have received. It is impossible to know why Aaron, Moses, and Eleanor would accept less than offered, but it is likely they wanted to maintain a close connection with their former masters and mistresses and may even have remained in their households as wage workers. Their magnanimity might also be explained as an expression of their gratitude to the Quakers or to secure the patronage of their former owners.[48]

In the second case, Mifflin's committee moved aggressively, bringing a complaint against Jabez Jenkins, another of Mifflin's collateral kin. Jenkins condemned himself for hiring out a slave before freeing him and agreed to pay reparations as recommended by the committee.[49] In the third case, on the heels of this settlement, Mifflin's Committee for Visiting Free Negroes showed how far back it was willing to reach in extending reparations to slaves who had years before been freed. Jonathan Hunn, descended from another of Kent County's oldest Quaker families and near neighbor of Warner Mifflin, had purchased Caro, a male slave, several years after the Philadelphia Yearly Meeting "Rule of 1758" banned from meeting for business anyone purchasing an enslaved person. Dismissed from the Society, Hunn gave Caro his freedom but remained unrepentant about the purchase. "What may be in justice due to said Negro," asked the committee, for the time he was detained beyond 1758? After Hunn agreed to provide such reparations as the committee deemed appropriate, the committee brought Hunn and Caro together. Perhaps to the committee's surprise, Caro avowed that he was "fully satisfied and so far from expecting or desiring restitution . . . that he acknowledges himself under obligation to him and esteems him his benefactor."[50] Such was the disposition of a man freed by a Quaker, knowing the advantages of a white patron but also aware that most Anglican and Presbyterian Kent County slaveowners had rebuffed Quaker efforts to spread their emancipationist call to duty.

By 1783, another committee, appointed by the New Garden Monthly Meeting—the indefatigable Mifflin was on it—reported an increase in "a disposition to do them justice." In 1784 the report went out that some in the Western Quarter "have bound themselves to render justice to those formerly by them held."[51] The parallel work of obtaining restitution for freed people continued until about 1786, with mixed results. Disownment was never contemplated, so after more than seven years of such efforts, the "non-reparationists," as we might call them, were spared the arm-bending of visiting committees. By the end of the decade, the diminishing results led to abandoning the effort. Nonetheless, Mifflin had made restitution an issue and in the process produced a degree of reparationism in mid-Delaware exceeding that of any other part of seaboard Quakerdom.[52]

Additional cases involving Mifflin's personal intervention, sometimes occurring far from his Kent County home, shine a bright light on the depth of his commitment. One instructive case explains why freedmen and -women beat a path to Chestnut Grove to see a truly committed Friend. "I am just about to start for the dark land of Virginia," he wrote Henry Drinker in January 1781, "in order to see what can be done in the case of the Negro sold there for a demand against my father for tax."[53] This involved the refusal of Daniel Mifflin to pay taxes supporting the war in late 1779. Accomack County responded with a sheriff's seizure of one of the youths Daniel Mifflin had manumitted in 1775 but who was still serving his time as a minor at Pharsalia. Jailing the boy, the sheriff then sold him at auction. Appalled, Warner went to Virginia, hoping to purchase the youth and liberate him again.

This mission was what a highly principled Quaker might do in ordinary times. However, the sweep of military events in the long war for independence required someone of unusual timbre. About to push southward by horse on January 11, he doubtless heard the news that Benedict Arnold had invaded Virginia twelve days before, hurrying his twelve hundred men up the James River to Richmond, where he scattered the undermanned and terrified Patriot militia while liberating slaves plantation by plantation. Commanding the Queen's Rangers, Virginia Loyalists, Hessian Jägers, and a detachment of Bucks County Volunteers raised by Joseph Galloway, Arnold knew Virginia's capital was ripe for the plucking. When Jefferson indignantly refused Arnold's offer to spare the capital if he was allowed to seize unmolested the tobacco warehouses, Arnold pillaged the city and sent the state's revolutionary government packing.[54]

This was the situation facing Mifflin as he headed down the Eastern Shore to rescue the boy liberated by his father six years before. To be sure, the Eastern Shore lay across Chesapeake Bay from the gloomy site of Jefferson's beleaguered governorship, but nonetheless he was entering a theater of war where the British were desolating the South. Accompanied by Jacob Lindley, a widely respected Chester County elder, Mifflin located the Accomack County man and his wife who had purchased the boy. The man was Colonel John Cropper, one of the Virginia officers at the Battle of Germantown. Mifflin and Lindley pressed their case, "not only with respect to the cruelty of that particular instance but slaveholding in general."[55] Though Cropper would not yield, Mifflin deemed the case not hopeless. Eleven months later, after Cropper had been badly wounded in the final naval action of the war, Mifflin thought "it may be near time to see him again after this, whether Pharaoh is any more humbled."[56]

The Duck Creek Monthly Meeting records yield no further details on the disposition of the case. But nearly sixty years later an unnamed Delaware Quaker recounted the outcome in the widely read *United States Gazette* and then reprinted in the *Delaware Register and Farmers Magazine*.[57] The account reported that the man who bought "Thomas," Daniel Mifflin's manumitted fourteen-year-old, was "Colonel C.," an officer of "the Virginia Militia" to whom Mifflin and his brother had brought blankets and clothes when there were freezing prisoners in British-occupied Philadelphia. Each year while visiting his father, the account continued, Warner stopped by the plantation of the colonel to chide him gently. "In close, loving earnestness," the narrative ran, Warner pleaded "that it was my father's religious concern [that] he should be free" and asked "has he not amply paid thee all the purchase money—and if so, why not let him fare as his brethren?" Refused by "Colonel C.," Mifflin agreed not to bother him further but asked to say a word with Tom privately. Listening from the next room, the colonel was surprised to hear Mifflin advise the youth to serve his master well, hope for his heart to soften, and know "that thou must die, and if thou art good while here, thou will be as happy hereafter as thy master can be, for our Heavenly Father is no respecter of persons." Then "the rigid, unbending slave-holder, the warrior who had 'braved the tug of war,'" burst into the room exclaiming, "Tom is free, Tom is free." Surprised that Mifflin had not urged Tom to flee his master, and remembering how "you had administered to me when in prison," the slaveowner told Mifflin, "my heart said, 'Tom is free.'"

Though the story was deployed as radical abolitionism surged in the 1830s, it has the ring of truth. The talebearer wore his Quaker pacifism on his sleeve in ending the piece: "Love can, and nothing but love never did or ever will, accomplish a righteous reformation." Perhaps the final word on this was the action of black men and women themselves. They left no written testimonies, but they spoke with their feet—walking many miles in the late 1770s and into the 1780s without compulsion to greet Warner Mifflin and his committees. The word of his efforts on their behalf spread throughout the region with poignant, though sometimes heart-rending, results.

## A Tangled Family Story

Of all the cases where Mifflin plucked black people out of slavery, the most complex one involved his own collateral kin—and reached back to his grandfather's first involvement with Eastern Shore slavery. Part triumph and part tragedy, it illuminates the intricacies of manumission in revolutionary Virginia and the struggles of enslaved Virginians caught in a twilight zone, where the white family claiming ownership of their bodies was itself enmeshed in conflicting positions on the revolution.

Part of a geographically dispersed but emotionally close extended family, Warner Mifflin knew from his father about the case of Aunt Ann, Daniel Mifflin's older sister. Growing up at Pharsalia, at eighteen Ann had married the wealthy, slave-rich Neech Eyre, probably a second cousin, when Daniel was a boy of ten.[58] It was a tragically short marriage, probably ending in 1733 as she gave birth to a girl. With an infant named Ann on his hands, Neech Eyre, Daniel's brother-in-law, promptly remarried, giving little Ann Eyre a stepmother.[59]

Unlike her short-lived mother, Ann Eyre would have a long but troubled life that did not end until Jefferson's presidency. Every step of the way enslaved Africans were involved. Her father's death in 1738 left her orphaned at age five, but as Neech Eyre's only child, she inherited a great deal of land and most of her father's slaves. It was natural she would be taken north to Pharsalia, where her grandfather Edward Mifflin and grandmother Mary Eyre Mifflin became her guardians.[60]

At Pharsalia, Ann Eyre witnessed a dismaying rupture in the family after Edward Mifflin died in 1743, leaving a will with no provision for the disposition of his many slaves. Now master of Pharsalia at twenty-one, Daniel Mifflin brought suit at the Accomack County Courthouse, arguing that he solely was entitled to all the slaves left by his father. He lost the suit when the court ruled that the slaves should be equally distributed among Daniel, his young minor brothers Southey and Samuel, and his eleven-year-old niece Ann.[61]

Thus, Ann Eyre grew up at Pharsalia with her maternal grandmother, her uncle Daniel and his wife, and his two younger brothers.[62] She was there when Warner Mifflin entered the world in 1745. As a teenager, she saw how death stalked the Mifflin clan, claiming Warner's infant brother and two infant sisters, who died in rapid succession. With the closest Quaker meetinghouse graveyard far distant, the babes were buried in the family cemetery at Pharsalia.

Like so many in her family, going back several generations, Ann Eyre married young. And like so many others on the Eastern Shore, hers was a cousin marriage. But she reversed the flow of Philadelphia Mifflins migrating southward to the Eastern Shore, by going north to find a husband in Philadelphia.

How she connected with the Philadelphia Mifflins is unknown, but at age twenty, she married one of Warner's many second cousins—George Mifflin II (1725–1755), the son of George Mifflin I (1688–1758), her grandfather's brother. This put her in the company of the city's elite, for her father-in-law was a wealthy merchant, a member of the governor's council, part owner of Pennsylvania's first iron forge, and a considerable slaveowner. Though Ann was nominally still a Quaker, Ann Eyre and George Mifflin II took vows in Philadelphia's Christ Church in 1753.[63] She gave birth to a son Charles (1753–1783) later that year.

Like an evil spirit haunting her family, death carried off Ann Eyre Mifflin's husband in their second year of marriage.[64] In a twisted turn of family history, this reimmersed her in the life of a plantation mistress and slaveholder, a role she seemingly had left behind after her marriage in Philadelphia. But with an infant, fatherless son to care for, she returned to the tip of the Eastern Shore, where she had inherited Golden Quarter, the well-cultivated plantation, along with the slave force whose labor had provided the Eyres' genteel lifestyle for generations. Although documentation is lacking, it is probable that she had the slaves at Pharsalia she had inherited from her grandfather transferred southward from Accomack to Northampton County.

Ann Mifflin's sorrow at the death of her husband ushered in a new chapter in her buffeted life. Widowed at twenty-three, she left her infant Charles in Philadelphia in the care of her deceased husband's parents.[65] After the boy's grandfather died when he was five, Ann arranged for Thomas Wharton, one of the city's wealthiest merchants, to take the boy under his wing.[66] Returning to the ancestral Golden Quarter, Ann soon found a new husband across Chesapeake Bay, in Portsmouth, Virginia. Her marriage to Humphrey Roberts in January 1759 was destined nearly to ruin her life, though her connections with cousin Warner Mifflin renewed her Quaker ties, and, in the throes of the American Revolution, this converted her to the cause of antislavery.[67]

Ann Eyre Mifflin's new husband was anything but a Quaker. A man on the make, he had little religious commitment of any kind. Born in England in the early 1730s, he had immigrated to Norfolk, Virginia, at the onset of the Seven Years' War. Ambitious and smooth-talking, he quickly established himself as one of the merchant founders of Portsmouth, situated across the Elizabeth River from Norfolk, Virginia's main seaport, bustling with Scottish tobacco merchants. It must have seemed like an immigrant's dream for Roberts to find a land- and slave-rich widowed woman, only twenty-six, ready to become his wife.[68]

After leasing Golden Quarter, Ann took up life in Portsmouth, where she proved to be a fecund wife, giving birth to four children in the first six years of their marriage. Breaking the pattern of childhood mortality that had sorrowed the Mifflin family, all four survived infancy. The first was William (1760–1809), born in the first year of their marriage. It was William whose life would connect with Warner Mifflin—and then with Joseph Galloway and St. John de Crèvecoeur—in unexpected ways worthy of a John Le Carré mystery plot.

Raising her new family in Portsmouth, Ann Roberts played deftly on her Philadelphia connections to enroll her son William at the Academy of Philadelphia in 1770 when he was ten. There he studied as the American Revolution erupted.[69] And there William Roberts, barely a teenager, began to scribble notes on his Gulliver-like travels for the next forty years, often crossing paths with the extended Mifflin family.[70]

While her son Charles Mifflin apprenticed at Thomas Wharton's mighty mercantile house and William Roberts, his half-brother, plowed through Latin, mathematics, navigation, and moral philosophy, studying with James Cannon and Francis Alison at the Philadelphia Academy, the descent into violence between the American colonies and mother England tore apart the household of Ann and Humphrey Roberts. Yet this family fracturing gave Warner Mifflin his opening to provide freedom for the black labor force at Golden Quarter and thereby redeem another branch of the complex Mifflin family from the evil of slavekeeping.

Before 1775, Ann Roberts probably felt no pangs of conscience about owning fellow human beings, for her return to Northampton County reminded her that her enslaved labor force at Golden Quarter produced the annual crop of salt marsh hay, corn, wheat, and tobacco. Her marriage to Humphrey Roberts could hardly have changed her views about human bondage, because he had securely implanted himself in the Chesapeake Bay slaveowning elite. But to be a slaveholder in the Norfolk-Portsmouth area changed dramatically in late 1775.

The fall of 1775 was rife with rumors that Virginia's royal governor, Lord Dunmore, would offer liberty to slaves and indentured servants—immediate, unconditional freedom—for those "appertaining to Rebels" who could reach the British lines and promise to fight against the American Patriots. Terrified white Virginians called it "a Scheme, the most diabolical," to "offer freedom to our slaves and turn them against their masters."[71] As summer waned and

Patriots challenged the governor's authority, Dunmore retreated from his palace in Williamsburg to British ships anchored in the Norfolk harbor. Then, on November 14, he unleashed a contingent of British soldiers and escaped slaves who routed a Virginia militia unit at Kemp's Landing, about nine miles up the Elizabeth River from Portsmouth. On the same day Lord Dunmore promulgated his astounding proclamation.[72]

Living within a few miles of the Kemp's Landing action were Humphrey Roberts, his wife Ann, and all their young children except William, who was still enrolled at the Philadelphia Academy. A prospering merchant, Norfolk County justice of the peace, and town trustee, Roberts had two ships on the stocks in the Portsmouth shipyard, a handsome house with attending slaves, a riding coach, warehouses, and stores—all the trappings of a successful Chesapeake capitalist. Roberts watched, waited, and thought about what course to take. Five years before, in 1770, he had joined noted burgesses and Virginia merchants in signing up with a nonimportation association.[73] But that was then. What now?

By late November 1775, hundreds of slaves, responding to Dunmore's Proclamation, had fled their masters, and some three thousand Norfolk-area whites took oaths of allegiance to the king.[74] In December, after Virginia Patriots defeated a British unit led by Dunmore at the Great Bridge, up the Elizabeth River, Roberts played his hand. "He could not help declaring his detestation of the proceedings of the Americans," he later told the Loyalist Claims Commission, and "in consequence he was separated from his family."[75] Pledging his loyalty to George III, as did most merchants in the Norfolk-Portsmouth area, he piled his household goods, his wife Ann, and their children aboard one of his sloops to carry them across the Chesapeake to take up residence at Golden Quarter. Then he recrossed the bay to Portsmouth, "publicly professed himself a Loyalist," and clambered aboard Dunmore's flagship.[76]

For Ann Roberts and her children, the arrival at her ancestral home was utter chaos. By her husband's account, his family got ashore, but "an armed rebel party cut the sloop adrift before the household goods could be unloaded, letting his boat wash onto rocks," where it "was near beat to pieces."[77] What followed was mass confusion. Either Ann was unable to rescind the lease on Golden Quarter, or, more probably, the Patriots who scuttled the sloop repelled the family of a declared Loyalist. Whatever the case, Ann Roberts recrossed the bay "with her helpless children [who] had not a house to put their heads in but as a friend would let them."[78] There in Portsmouth she awaited her fate, hoping for word of her husband and son William.

If Ann Roberts's aborted attempt to take refuge in Northampton County was a nightmare, so was her husband's attempt to escape Virginia. Thinking his wife and children were removed from the war zone, Roberts wrestled four of his Portsmouth slaves, all entailed by his marriage, aboard Dunmore's flagship, the *William*. One of them attacked and crippled him, believing that Dunmore's Proclamation "extended to the whole race" not just the rebels' slaves, and enraged to find that having a Loyalist slave master left him no claim to freedom. All four had only months to live: Jacob, a carpenter, and Jemmy and Joseph, sailors, died of shipboard fever; Isaac, a carpenter, drowned at sea after Dunmore's ship weighed anchor. Of five others left behind at Portsmouth, Jemmy, a brewer, fell into American hands and was "sent to the mines," while three women and a girl fleeing to the British were "carried off by the British fleet."[79]

Aboard Dunmore's ship, Roberts watched the royal governor's floating village of about ninety vessels run short of fresh water and provisions, while a terrifying outbreak of smallpox began to sweep away the fugitive black Virginians who had tasted freedom only for weeks.[80] On January 1, 1776, from the deck of the *William*, Roberts watched the British bombard Norfolk, destroying a third of the city. A day later, he witnessed the flames plume skyward as American forces plundered and razed the houses and dockside warehouses of Loyalist Norfolkians, leaving the city all but destroyed. Patriots then turned their attention across the Elizabeth River to Portsmouth, where they converted Roberts's buildings into a prison, a hospital, and a barracks. When Dunmore's flotilla sailed up the Chesapeake Bay to Gwynn's Island in May 1776 seeking water and provisions, the march of death continued. Most of the 800–1,000 blacks he had formed into his "Ethiopian Regiment" ended their lives miserably there, scourged by smallpox and hurriedly buried in shallow graves.[81] Finally, in August, Dunmore's flotilla sailed from the Virginia Capes, half of the ships bound for St. Augustine, Florida, and Bermuda, the others for New York City. Leaving his family to fend for themselves, Roberts sailed on one of the St. Augustine-bound ships. A year later he reached British-occupied New York City.[82]

If it had not been for the plight of his oldest son, Humphrey Roberts, by his own account, would have returned directly from New York to England. But son William was having a travail of his own. Leaving the Academy at sixteen, just a few weeks before members of the Continental Congress signed the Declaration of Independence, he made his way southward through the Eastern Shore to reach his mother and siblings in Virginia. His travel notebook made only brief mention of this journey by land and was blank for the next eighteen months.[83] But his later testimony tells a harrowing story. Trying to join his family, he found that "his father, guided by his loyalty," had joined Lord Dunmore and consequently "his unfortunate family was bereft of all their property [and] turned out of their habitations." Torn between remaining with his mother and siblings and joining his Loyalist father, William Roberts made his choice: he was his father's son.[84]

Caught in the pincers of Virginia's desperate attempts to raise troops to meet the quotas set by the Continental Congress, Roberts "openly refused to bear arms." By his father's testimony, this earned him imprisonment in the Portsmouth area.[85] After escaping—and "under the necessity of flying to and concealing himself in different parts of the country"—he headed north in December 1777, hoping to reach British-occupied Philadelphia. First he reached his uncle Daniel Mifflin at Pharsalia and then took refuge with his cousin Warner Mifflin at Chestnut Grove. When unable to thread through American outposts south of Philadelphia, William returned to Portsmouth in March 1778, probably meeting briefly with his mother and siblings. Trying to reach his father in New York, he signed on to a British ship that first carried him to St. Eustatius, Tortola, and Antigua in the Lesser Antilles, and thence to New York, where in August 1778 he was reunited with his father after almost three years.[86]

Six months later, father and son arrived together in London. Humphrey Roberts pleaded before the Lords of the Treasury that he had stayed in New York for more than a year, "hearing that my eldest son was harassed, confined & cruelly treated by the Rebels," and "thought it was my duty to endeavour to get him out of their hands and for that purpose remained at New York til the latter end of the year 1778, when he arrived, having made his escape from imprisonment." Dunmore certified that the account was true. At that, they threw themselves on the tender mercies of the Lords of Treasury, who were hearing the plaintive cases of the "suffering Americans."[87] Whether they would ever see their family in Virginia was an open question.

To shelter the fugitive seventeen-year-old William Roberts was a perilous decision for Warner and his father. The Eastern Shore was largely spared the punishing warfare scarring much of the Atlantic seaboard; nonetheless, giving refuge to the son of an important Portsmouth Loyalist risked the wrath of Patriot Committees of Inspection. But family trumped politics. We can imagine how Daniel and Warner listened to the boy's first-hand accounts of his mother's attempts to weather the storm with his brother and sisters, along with the many enslaved people at her Northampton County and war-torn Portsmouth properties. Though the sources are almost silent about how she survived after her husband left with Lord Dunmore, the many memorials her husband laid before the Claims Commission, though perhaps embellished, tell much about the predicament of a woman with a checkered background of Quaker membership.

Foremost of Ann Roberts's problems was regaining residency at the Golden Quarter plantation. For sixteen years after her marriage to Humphrey Roberts, she had lived in Portsmouth, raising her young children and sharing the ease of his mounting affluence. Leasing out Golden Quarter with its scores of resident slaves, she enjoyed the benefit of a sizeable annual income. But finding Golden Quarter and the Portsmouth properties attainted by the Virginia Assembly in Patriot hands after Dunmore's departure, she had to sit out the war with friends.[88] Only in 1780, after an act of the Virginia Assembly returned Golden Quarter to her, could she return to her ancestral home.[89] This opened the way for Warner Mifflin to convert his cousin to the abolitionist cause.

In January 1782, about a year after Virginia's revolutionary government restored Golden Quarter to Ann Roberts, Mifflin made his way down the peninsula with a draft of a deed of manumission in hand to convince her to free her enslaved labor force. With Warner at her elbow, she signed the deed that showed how effectively Mifflin broke through her years of unapologetic slaveownership:

> being possessed of a number of negroes as slaves and through the adverse occurrences permitted by divine Providence under the present calamitous dispensation to overtake us (whereby I am separated from my husband and one child) thereby in my own experience have to witness the grievous hardship of being forcibly separated from those near connections whereunto the African Race has for a long series of time been subjected by the oppressive practice of making them slaves.

Then she expressed her newfound belief that holding humans enslaved was a breach of Quaker principles and policy: "I am fully persuaded it is inconsistent with Christianity and totally derogatory to the injunction of Jesus Christ our holy Lawgiver, which he enjoins his followers that whatsoever they would that others should do unto them, they should suffer it to be the governing rule of their conduct to do so by them." Hence, she continued, "I do fully believe to be indispensibly obligatory on me . . . to manumit and set absolutely free the negroes I am possessed of."[90]

Though these were her dowry slaves, Ann followed Warner's advice to take account of her missing husband, who had a secondary claim on her inherited property. "Although my husband Humphrey Roberts may yet be living," she wrote, "nevertheless as no human prospect appears of his return in a short space if ever [I] believe it my duty" to proceed with freeing the Golden Quarter slaves. Also, she had in hand her husband's written assurance that he had relinquished his interest in her chattel property. Finally, she specified that "my eldest son Charles Mifflin being under the former laws heir to all those Negroes after my decease [was] now willing to unite with me herein which for the more full and clear liberating them is concluded."[91]

The manumission deed then listed the slaves by name and age, while providing that her overseer at Golden Quarter would retain the labor of "several of the negroes aforementioned" for one year. As was common in manumission deeds, all the youthful slaves would serve at the plantation until they reached eighteen if female and twenty-one if male and would then be "at liberty to act for themselves as free people without the least hindrance or molestation."[92]

A close look at the names and ages of the manumitted slaves tells its own story, with one astounding anomaly. The names, with exact ages in all but one case, fall off the pages just as they did in the deeds of Warner Mifflin, his father, and other Eastern Shore Quakers: "Catherine upwards of 70, Catherine 47 and son Tom 15; Mary 34 and son Sam 14; Tabitha 31 and son Adam 14; Leah 30 and her James 4 years nine months and Eli one year three months; Rhoda 20 with son Jacob four years nine months; Adar 19 with her Abigail four years nine months and Peter one year three months"; and so forth.

A total of thirty slaves were now promised their freedom. But entirely absent from the deed are adult males. Not a single father or husband is named. Only fourteen boys, twelve women, and four girls were listed. In his memorial in 1783 asking compensation for lost property, Humphrey Roberts tallied fifty-three of his wife's slaves, forty-four of them at Golden Quarter.[93] What happened to the fourteen missing slaves, presumably adult males? Could Ann Mifflin have sold them away in one year after regaining possession of Golden

Quarter? This is highly unlikely. The most reasonable answer is that they fled to the British, claiming Dunmore's promised freedom in return for their willingness to help the British suppress the Patriot insurgency. In this scenario, they risked being identified as the slaves of a Loyalist's wife and therefore ineligible for freedom, but they could also have persuaded the British that Ann Roberts had never declared herself a Loyalist and was in fact in favor of the Patriot cause, thus allowing her enslaved people to claim freedom if they were able to reach British lines.[94]

Four times in the heat of war, Ann Roberts's enslaved men had a chance to reach the British. The first was in early 1776. Northampton County was largely a neutral ground, with those inclined to either side of the struggle willing to coexist while the war raged elsewhere. But to provision his floating town Dunmore frequently sent tenders ashore to obtain meat, flour, and other necessities, and it is possible that some of Golden Quarter males fled to the small boats until his flotilla sailed clear of the Chesapeake capes in July 1776. A second chance came in 1777, as the massive British fleet sailed northward through Chesapeake Bay to capture Philadelphia. "Many negroes" from Northampton and Accomack counties had fled at this time to the British, according to Virginia's Council.[95] Less than two years later, in May 1779, the British fleet appeared again, first attacking Portsmouth, where they burned a half-built ship of Humphrey Roberts', still on the stocks, while sending tenders ashore on the Eastern Shore, giving slaves a third chance to join them.[96] This kind of raiding continued when the British launched a major invasion of the South in early 1780, giving Northampton and Accomack County slaves still another chance to flee to the British, though in some cases the British seized slaves from Patriot plantations and sold them in the West Indies.[97] When Mifflin and John Parrish passed through Northampton County in May 1782, only a few miles from Golden Quarter, they found the Virginians "much alarmed on account of people [called] barge men who often come on shore." Seven months after Yorktown, British raiders were still active in Chesapeake Bay.[98]

In a cruelly ironic instance of the war's unpredictability, the adult males who disappeared from Golden Quarter may have risked all in fleeing to the British only to perish or be sold again into slavery, losing their chance to be emancipated by Ann Roberts and her son in January 1782. As for Golden Quarter's thirty women and children, who believed they had gained their

freedom, they were about to face life in a twilight zone through the machina-
tions of Humphrey Roberts and the complicity of his wife. The minor children
were obliged to stay at Golden Quarter until reaching maturity, and the twelve
women, mothers to the eighteen children, apparently stayed as well to parent
their offspring. In August 1782, several of Mifflin's close friends from Talbot
County, Maryland, looked in on the situation, meeting many times with Ann
Roberts.[99]

With talk of peace initiatives after Cornwallis's surrender of the British
army at Yorktown in October 1781, Ann, hoping to reunite her family, tried to
get a safe passage guarantee for her husband's return to Virginia. "Fearful of
displeasing him respecting liberating the Negroes," as Mifflin sadly divulged,
she silently made a cruel, dishonorable decision to withhold the original
manumission deed she had promised to send to Mifflin's father for recording
in the Northampton County court records, thereby establishing its definitive
legal standing. Then, moving across Chesapeake Bay to Portsmouth with
several blacks, she caved in to Portsmouth Patriot officials, who, according to
Mifflin, opposed the freedom she had given her slaves and convinced her to
set aside the manumission deed that had not yet been entered into the Virginia
records.[100]

Every manumitted slave's nightmare occurred when Humphrey Roberts
made his way back to Virginia, promptly doing his best to claim and then sell
the black women and children in Portsmouth and across the bay at Golden
Quarter. Hearing of this, Mifflin reached Portsmouth at the end of 1786 "to
give my assistance in an afflicting case of the poor blacks." In a long letter to
James Pemberton, he described how some of the black women had fled, while
others "came to me" at a tavern to ensure their freedom. Writing out certificates
vouching that each of the black women had been freed, Mifflin was able to
rescue several who had been held in jail, while enlisting the aid of friendly
lawyers to save the others.[101] Mystery surrounds the matter of how a barrage
of suits and countersuits were resolved and what became of the thirty women
and minor children. But we know that Humphrey Roberts, cognizant that
Virginia had repealed the traditional law of entail under which Ann Roberts's
manumission document attained its legitimacy, laid hands on as many of the
Golden Quarter slaves as he could locate. He deeded one, named Tom, to his
son Edward.[102] The fate of the others, in what surely was Warner Mifflin's most
painful rescue intervention, remains unknown.[103]

## Breakthrough in Virginia

From his work on stiffening the moral backbone of Quakers as far north as Nantucket Island and pushing for reparations for liberated blacks in the later stages of the Revolutionary War, Mifflin launched a new dimension of his reform agenda. Up to this point, except for the 1777 peace embassy to Generals Howe and Washington, he had devoted himself to working *within* the preparative, monthly, and quarterly meetings to end Quaker slaveowning, while ministering to the needs of freed people. Now he turned to a more difficult task: how could he reach legislators who deplored the pacifist Quaker refusal to support the war for independence—some called it cloaked Toryism—convincing them that perpetuating slavery while founding a nation on natural rights was to build a house on sand, to practice a shameful hypocrisy, to shout the doctrine of freedom across the Atlantic while denying it to one-fifth of the population?

With the war drawing to a close, Mifflin seized on the notion that something concrete could be accomplished at the state level to advance the cause of freedom for enslaved blacks. Referring to the preamble of the Declaration of Independence, with its ringing assertions of inalienable rights and self-evident truths that "all men are created equal," he wrote of how "seeing this was the very substance of the doctrine I had been concerned to promulgate for years, I became animated with a hope that if the representatives were sincere and inculcated these views among the people generally, a blessing to this nation would accompany those endeavours." Thus, he began to plan a coordinated lobbying effort with those in the growing Quaker network "in representing the case of the enslaved Africans to different legislative bodies."[104]

The first target of opportunity was Virginia. It was the state with by far the most enslaved Africans—in fact, more than in the other twelve states combined. Quakers there had tried unsuccessfully since 1769 to repeal a particularly offensive law that put a chokehold on any slaveowner wanting to free an enslaved person. Passed in 1723 and reaffirmed in 1748, the law forbade private manumission "upon any pretense whatsoever," except when the governor and council approved freedom "for some meritorious services."[105]

Swept up in the growing antislavery sentiment emanating from Philadelphia, where slaveholding had become a moral gauge of practicing the Golden Rule, Virginia Quakers began to examine their consciences and to take incremental steps to cleanse themselves of the sin of slaveholding. In 1771, seventy-five-year-old John Pleasants, brother-in-law of Philadelphia's Israel Pemberton,

shocked the slaveocracy by penning a will granting freedom to his 215 slaves ✓
when they reached the age of thirty—and if "the law of the land will admit
them to be set free without their being transported out of the country." But
that was the rub, that the law of the land forbade exactly what Pleasants was
trying to do.[106]

Some Virginia Friends, now convinced that slaveholding was poisonous
to themselves and the nation, skirted the law by freeing slaves in deeds and
wills without legal sanction, hoping that sheriffs or other authorities would
not bring them to court. Daniel Mifflin, inspired by his eldest son, had done
just that in April 1775, granting the slaves at Pharsalia "their natural, just and
inherent right and privilege, the liberty of their persons (which they are entitled
to by nature)." Other Virginia Quakers followed Mifflin's lead. Similarly ignoring the law, John Pleasants's son Robert gave eighty slaves quasi-freedom in
1777, setting them up on his land as tenants and hoping that the wartime crisis
would divert the attention of the authorities.

Over the next few years, Virginia Quakers, speaking through the Virginia
Yearly Meeting, kept up a drumbeat of petitions to the legislature urging a law
allowing manumissions. In 1779, one bill gained legislative traction for validat-
ing, ex post facto, the freedom of men and women already manumitted, but in
the end it failed. The next year brought another Quaker petition. It too failed.
Not easily discouraged, the Quakers pledged to try again.[107]

At this point Warner Mifflin entered the fray. Six months after the British
debacle at Yorktown, he agreed with his kinsman John Parrish (1729–1810), a
Quaker bricklayer from Philadelphia who was an increasingly vocal antislavery
spokesman in the Philadelphia Yearly Meeting, to take their horses down the
Eastern Shore and across the Chesapeake Bay to Virginia. It was planned as a
double-edged mission. First, they would visit monthly meetings and the homes
of slaveowning Quaker families to spread the antislavery doctrine, and then
attend the Virginia Yearly Meeting in Black Water in late May 1782. From there
they would alight at Richmond to bear testimony on behalf of enslaved Africans
and try to push a manumission bill through the General Assembly.

For Parrish and Mifflin the trip sealed the melding of heart and soul, what
the former jotted in his notebook as something akin to the Old Testament
"knitting of love between Jonathan and David" (1 Samuel 18:1). "How necessary
it is to be thus united in traveling," he mused.[108] Stopping at Pharsalia, they
conducted family worship with Warner's father before reaching the Accomack
County Courthouse, where they pleaded the case "of the oppressed Africans"

before the presiding judge. Riding farther south, they left their horses to boat across the Chesapeake to mainland Virginia, where they lectured slaveholders on "the absurdity of contending for liberty while they themselves were keeping others in a state of slavery." At some home visits they succeeded. Thomas Seats in Isle of Wight County, for example, rose from a dinner discussion about the iniquity of slavery to scratch out a manumission document freeing his ten slaves. In other cases, they met only with rejection. At homes where this occurred, Mifflin followed the example set by John Woolman years before by refusing to take dinner, at one point eating food only once in forty-eight hours rather than break bread with Quaker families who would not agree to relinquish their enslaved fellow humans.

From there, with new horses, they went on for several days to attend the Virginia Yearly Meeting. There too they carried the torch of antislavery to timid Friends. Continuing to Petersburg, Mifflin and Parrish were joined by Edward Stabler, a staunch abolitionist Quaker with ties to many of the state's legislators. Plotting their lobbying strategy and composing a remonstrance on "the oppressive laws that prohibit the holders of the blacks setting them at liberty," the trio made their way to the new Virginia capital in Richmond. There they spent the next nineteen days in the most extensive lobbying effort ever launched by the Society of Friends.[109]

The address they prepared played to the top of their agenda in words more sharp-edged than Friends had dared to express in the long years of war: that "professors of Christianity . . . [knowing] that freedom is the natural right of all mankind, could not continue their fellow men in slavery and transmit them from one generation to another as brute beasts, thereby subjecting them to the arbitrary treatment of others and a separation from the[ir] tenderest connections." Unless inconsistency was a virtue, Virginians could not trample on the principles "set forth in [Virginia's] Declaration of Rights." The remonstrance went on to indict the "most flagrant violation of justice and the rights of mankind" that occurred when sheriffs seized blacks who had been emancipated by Quakers, then selling them at auction as slaves to satisfy fines imposed on Friends who could not support the war. Left aside for the moment was the real prize sought after—a law permitting private acts of manumission.[110]

Allowed to present their memorial—only after the doorkeeper removed their broad-brimmed black hats—Mifflin, Parrish, and Stabler sat in the gallery watching the debate as their memorial and a manumission bill were committed to committee. This led to earnest evening discussions with committee members.

Day after day, the General Assembly debate plodded along in the early summer heat. On one day, the prospects of passage seemed bright; on others, avid defenders of slavery almost scuttled the bill. Finally, on June 10, 1782, the manumission bill passed, allowing the traveling Friends to repair to Curles, the plantation of Robert Pleasants, before starting the long journey home.

It was a triumph for lobbying and one that modeled future lobbying efforts. The perseverance of a few Quaker men importuning the legislators in their lodgings, in the streets, and outside the legislative chambers made the crucial difference. Edward Stabler, the one Virginian in the lobbying cadre, drew on his network of connections as a tobacco merchant to gain access to the Virginia legislators. Sweet-tempered John Parrish, a Marylander by birth, proved an adept tactician in lobbying. But it was Mifflin, imposing in stature and deploying a disarming, warm-hearted, hand-on-the-sleeve approach, who was perhaps the most persuasive in dislodging legislators from previously held positions. In their minds, the Quaker delegation believed "our being present to espouse the cause of these poor oppressed people . . . was of singular use in preventing the matter being thrown out of the house."[111]

The 1782 manumission bill, much less restrictive than those the Virginia legislators had battered down in previous years, was remarkable in several respects. Foremost, it removed the roadblock that had stood in the way of voluntary manumissions for more than half a century. In a critically important clause, it allowed freed men and women to remain in Virginia, preserving their kin ties and, in spite of their enslavement, their love of the land where they had toiled. The law also required protection of those who were not in a position to maintain themselves. For any black not of "sound mind and body," for any over forty-five years of age, and for all males under twenty-one and females under eighteen, the manumitting slaveowner, or, if the slave was liberated by will, the estate of the deceased, was held responsible for support and maintenance. Equally important, every liberated man and woman was to receive a copy of the "instrument of emancipation"—the freedom papers that would serve him or her if seized as a runaway slave. This benefited slaveowners as well, by making it easier to reclaim runaway slaves who could not produce freedom papers. Finally, giving white Virginians some comfort, the law provided that the county sheriff could hire out any freed person who failed to pay the taxes imposed on all adult inhabitants of the county. Though a compromise piece of legislation, it was nonetheless a revolutionary era high water mark south of the Mason-Dixon line.[112]

Virginia's first step toward reconciling revolutionary principles with the entrenchment of slavery raised the hopes of Quakers on both sides of the Atlantic. Upon hearing the word, Philadelphia's Meeting for Sufferings exulted. "The Light of Truth," its clerk recorded, had finally reached Virginia, where "temporal considerations and long accustomed prejudices have held [slaveowners] in obdurate blindness."[113] Mifflin remembered it well in his later reflections. "From these encouraging circumstances I was induced to hope that Divine favour might yet be continued to this land."[114] In Virginia, it opened the door for Quakers to implement the Philadelphia Yearly Meeting dictate, making the failure to free enslaved humans a disownable offense. Within six years, most Virginia Quakers had complied. This, in turn, encouraged other Virginians, including some of Jefferson's neighbors, to free their slaves, particularly on Virginia's Eastern Shore, where the antislavery movement sank deep roots.[115] Promoting a gradual abolition plan in 1796, Virginia's St. George Tucker credited the 1782 manumission law with freeing "upwards of ten thousand" slaves.[116]

Success in Richmond confirmed Mifflin's belief that he was doing the work God intended for him and that which he believed the Scriptures required. It convinced him that other states—Delaware, Maryland, North Carolina, and New Jersey—could also be moved to purge the noxious institution that ran athwart the revolutionary principles for which the Patriots had shed their blood. From this point forward, at thirty-seven, Mifflin made the campaign against slavery and the protection of free blacks his life's work.

Crossing the Chesapeake a few days after the signal victory in Richmond, Mifflin and his bosom friend Parrish reclaimed the horses they had left on the Eastern Shore. With refreshed steeds, they jogged twelve miles to confer with Ann Roberts at Golden Quarter about the confused state of her manumission deed. Three days later, Mifflin reached Chestnut Grove after an absence of more than eight weeks. Their mission accomplished, Parrish scribbled in his notebook that they were encouraged "to put our trust and confidence in the never failing helper and shepherd of his sheep, who watches over his flocks by day and night so that not a hair of our heads shall fall without his permission."[117] Such was their providential understanding of human affairs.

Back home at Chestnut Grove, Mifflin reprised the Virginia lobbying mission. Might he and Parrish have done more to convince slaveholding families to release their chattel property? Could they have lobbied more strenuously when the legislature considered a gradual abolition plan?[118] Brooding about this, he penned an essay urging further action among Virginia's owners of some

200,000 slaves. In a passionate, Bible-studded disquisition of several thousand words, he insisted he was "a countryman," a "lover of mankind," a man "feeling my mind influenced with love toward the people in general." He larded his remarks with references to how the British sword in the past year had terrified Virginia and how God "is justly offended with us for our multiplied transgressions against his holy laws" by oppressing fellow humans. Was not the black woman he saw auctioned off in Richmond one "of the number of those for whom Christ died?" Was she not among those "to whom [Christ] enjoins his followers to do as they would be willing to be done unto?" Was she kept "toiling and drudging and faring as poor Lazarus in order to [provide] our sumptuous fare" because her skin is black?[119]

Hoping to reach a national audience by publishing his appeal to Virginia slaveowners, Mifflin reached out to Anthony Benezet. He hoped the nation's consummate abolitionist would guide "Some Remarks" through the Philadelphia Yearly Meeting's Overseers of the Press. It failed. Indeed, Benezet himself was encountering resistance in publishing an essay calling for immediate, universal emancipation. "I generally met with difficulty," Benezet wrote a friend, "[and] . . . perhaps it's best to check my natural activity & vehemence." The Meeting for Sufferings had sat on his essay for more than six months, though John Parrish, Nicholas Waln, and Warner Mifflin were among those who strongly favored putting the essay "in the hands of all the men [in] power on the continent particularly to the southward."[120] Mifflin's essay suffered the same treatment as Benezet's. He realized, he wrote Parrish, that his essay was "doomed," that "my trials on the account of them [blacks in Virginia] . . . are great and appear to increase of late; sometimes I am ready to conclude it may be I am too fast and that it may be best to set down quietly and endeavour to keep under a silent exercise submitting all to the working of the invisible arm who can without any aid of poor worms perform according to his unbounded pleasure."[121]

This was Mifflin's dilemma—before, now, and in the future: should he continue his efforts in the face of opposition from the Philadelphia-centered moderates, or should he shrink into the shadows? The answer was always the same: push ahead, pull back, and push ahead again. He was resigned, he wrote, to "leave to the better judgment of my Friends" the publication of his "Remarks for the Consideration of the People of Virginia," though he was "willing to defray the expence. . . . Yet at times I think I see and feel so much that I durst not hold my peace."[122]

As happened so many times in his life, tragedy again struck Mifflin's family after his return from Virginia. Mary, his firstborn child, died of unknown causes two months before her fifteenth birthday, on February 23, 1783. Mifflin had earlier lost two daughters in their first few weeks of life, but this time the pain cut deeper to the bone. Gathering himself, he sought comfort in reading from Job: "The Lord gave, and the Lord hath taken away, Blessed be the name of the Lord." Then he reminded himself that when smitten by the rod and staff, it was his role "to be enabled to bless and praise His ever adorable name." Duty still awaited him. Not to respond would mean he would be "shut out from His life-giving presence, in which alone is the true comfort."[123]

## Challenging Congress

Though it was a poor remedy for his loss, Mifflin wrenched himself away from Kent County to redouble his antislavery efforts. This time he became a key figure in a carefully coordinated effort linking Quakers on both sides of the Atlantic to bring pressure on the heads of government to live up to the principles of the American Revolution.

Seven months after the death of his beloved daughter, Mifflin made his first appearance before the national Congress, as part of a Quaker effort to stop the resumption of the slave trade that had been halted during the revolution. This began with the decision of the Philadelphia Yearly Meeting at its fall meeting in 1783 to memorialize the nation's legislators on the slave trade.[124] It is not clear who fashioned the carefully written petition, endorsed by the yearly meeting on October 4, 1783, but it bears the marks of Anthony Benezet. Among the concourse of more than a thousand Quakers attending the yearly meeting, convening for the first time in peace in almost a decade, 535 Quakers from five states signed the petition, including nearly every notable figure of Philadelphia-centered Quakerdom. One of the first signers was Warner Mifflin, followed by his father, by now an abolitionist activist.

The choice of Mifflin as one of those appointed to carry the petition to the Continental Congress marked his emergence as a major figure within the Quaker antislavery patriciate. In ordinary times, he and his fellow delegates would have walked only a few blocks from the Great Meetinghouse to present the petition at the Pennsylvania Statehouse on Market Street, where the Continental Congress had conducted the war for eight years. But in fact, Congress

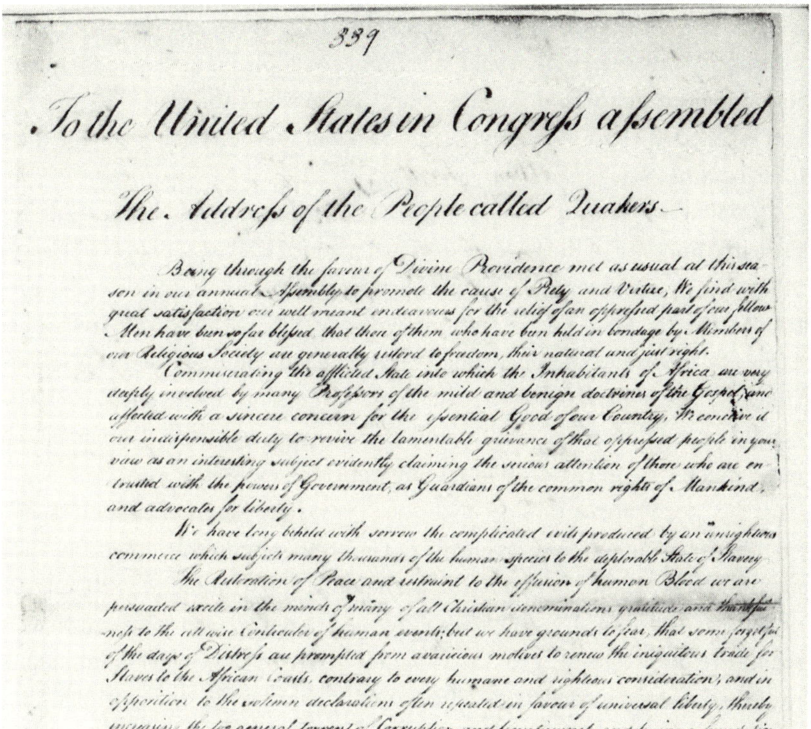

339

To the United States in Congress assembled

The Address of the People called Quakers

Being through the favour of Divine Providence met as usual at this season in our annual Assembly to promote the cause of Piety and Virtue, We find with great satisfaction our well meant endeavours for the relief of an oppressed part of our fellow Men have been so far blessed, that those of them who have been held in bondage by Members of our Religious Society are generally restored to freedom, their natural and just right.

Commiserating the afflicted State into which the Inhabitants of Africa are very deeply involved by many Professors of the mild and benign doctrines of the Gospel, and affected with a sincere concern for the essential Good of our Country, We conceive it our indispensible duty to revive the lamentable grievance of that oppressed people in your view as an interesting subject evidently claiming the serious attention of those who are entrusted with the powers of Government, as Guardians of the common rights of Mankind, and advocates for liberty.

We have long beheld with sorrow the complicated evils produced by an unrighteous commerce which subjects many thousands of the human species to the deplorable State of Slavery.

The Restoration of Peace and restraint to the effusion of human Blood we are persuaded excite in the minds of many of all Christian denominations gratitude and thankfulness to the all wise Controuler of human events; but we have grounds to fear, that some forgetful of the days of Distress are prompted from avaricious motives to renew the iniquitous trade for Slaves to the African Coasts, contrary to every humane and righteous consideration, and in opposition to the solemn declarations often repeated in favour of universal liberty, thereby increasing the too general torrent of Corruption and licentiousness, and laying a foundation for future Calamities.

We therefore earnestly sollicit your Christian interposition to discourage and prevent so obvious an Evil, in such manner as under the influence of Divine Wisdom you shall see meet.

Signed in and on behalf of our Yearly Meeting held in Philadelphia for Pennsylvania, New Jersey, and Delaware, and the western parts of Maryland and Virginia dated the fourth day of the tenth Month 1783.

Isaac Lane; John Reynell; Thos. Ross; John Price Jun.; Hugh Roberts; Joseph Moore; Isaac Pickering; William Harvey; Joshua Morris; Jacob Haviland

Joshua Brown; George Evans; Thomas Ruston; Anthony Benezet; James Thornton; Warner Mifflin; Saml. Emlen jun.; Daniel Byrnes; Geo. Dillwyn

Saml. Pemberton; Jacob Lindley; Thomas Lightfoot; Mark Reeve; William Savery Jun.; John Hoskins; George Churchman; Thomas Milhous

Wm. Hersey; David Cooper; Benj. Swett; Owen Jones; Eli Yarnall; David Evans; Silas Downing; Aaron Lancaster

*Figure 11.* Signers of this petition in 1783 to the Continental Congress calling for ending the slave trade and reminding Congress of the "solemn declarations often repeated in favor of universal liberty" nearly doubled the number in London who had signed a similar petition to Parliament four months before. Mifflin's name is in the second column, six from the top. National Archives.

was ensconced fifty miles to the north because, three months before, the mutinous Pennsylvania Line of Washington's Continental Army had surrounded the statehouse, enraged at empty promises of back pay. Congress fled and for the fetid summer of 1783 camped out at the slumbering college town of Princeton, New Jersey.

On October 8, Mifflin and his fellow delegates entered Nassau Hall, the principal building of the College of New Jersey, to wait on Congress. Dressed in Quaker gray and their black broad-brimmed beaver hats, the Friends negotiated with President Elias Boudinot, who told them it was not customary to allow petitioners an audience. But relenting, he introduced them to a solemn Congress. After distributing to Parliament the London Yearly Meeting address deploring the slave trade, the Friends stood gravely as James Pemberton, his head covered, read the yearly meeting petition aloud. The memorial began with the "great satisfaction" that "those . . . who have been held in bondage by members of our religious society are generally restored to freedom, their natural and just right." But now, with the bloodletting at an end, would Congress not step forward to stop those who "are prompted by avaricious motives to renew the trade for slaves to the African Coast, contrary to every humane & righteous consideration & in opposition to the solemn declarations often repeated, in favor of universal liberty"? The sordid contradiction that a nation birthed in liberty was resuming the inhuman slave trade would be an offense to the Creator and mock the nation's founding principles.[125]

The Quaker delegation reported that they were "respectfully received," and some Congressmen dined with Quaker lobbyists to hear their arguments.[126] More than that, Congress did nothing. However, in November President Boudinot carried the petition to Annapolis, where it was referred to a committee of Thomas Jefferson; David Howell of Rhode Island, a lawyer and future president of Brown University; and Maryland's Jeremiah T. Chase, an Annapolis lawyer with liberal leanings. Referral to a committee provided some cause for optimism, but the committee recommended only that individual states enact laws consonant with the Non-Importation agreement of the First Continental Congress that pledged (but could not enforce) the banning of the slave trade after December 1775. The full Congress in early 1784 voted down the committee report, dashing the Quakers' hopes for a national commitment to prohibit human trafficking.[127]

Yet the petition may have influenced the debate already in motion to settle a plan of government for the western territories that the states were relinquishing to the national government. In the "Plan of Temporary Government of the Western Territory," a clause specified that "after the year 1800 there shall be neither slavery nor involuntary servitude in any of the said [Western Territory]." Congress voted down this clause on March 1, 1784, by a single vote, with the fate of countless enslaved people hanging in the balance.

While in Princeton, Mifflin also met with Nathanael Greene, Washington's ranking general at the end of the Revolutionary War. Greene's abandonment of Quaker pacifism lay heavy on Mifflin's mind; but finding Greene fully engaged with members of Congress, he waited until returning home to unburden himself. So far as the surviving sources disclose, Mifflin never upbraided Thomas Mifflin, his second cousin, for becoming a fighting Quaker. But with Greene, he poured out his disappointment. Spilled over several pages, his words offered his belief that "forbearance of the Merciful Creator of man" might still have "the door of mercy open to rebellious and backsliding creatures who have so deeply revolted from his Divine Laws." What good would all of Greene's generalship do "to procure any treasure in Heaven . . . or whether it is not more likely that all thy great exploits will . . . terminate in anguish of soul, disappointment, and perplexity?"[128]

Having said his piece on a Quaker raising the sword, Mifflin, knowing that Greene had accepted a large plantation replete with a slave labor force from a grateful South Carolina legislature, implored the lapsed Quaker to set a precedent. To "publicly . . . protest against having the labour of slaves" at the plantation, would provide "a degree of consistency . . . in thy contending for others to enjoy what thou holds so dear to thyself, that is liberty [and] the odiousness of slavery." For a war hero not to forswear the use of enslaved fellow creatures would "tend to encourage the petty tyrants of America to hold on [to] their oppression, also to strengthen the infamous trade to Africa, and so draw down renewed displeasure from Heaven."

Greene responded temperately to the scolding but defended his decision to abandon pacifism with an argument about the universal condition of man. "Nature has linked us together," he wrote, "into different societies, from a social principle; and where the happiness of one is disturbed by the inroads of another, opposition becomes both just and necessary." He was as prone as anyone to deplore the "calamities" of war; but "Nature has armed all creation, more or less, with weapons of defence; and when the temper and means are so admirably suited to this end as in man, it is difficult to suppose it was not in the original order of creation."

As for accepting enslaved Africans on his South Carolina plantation, Greene agreed that "nothing can be said in its defence," but reminded Mifflin that he had implored the Continental Congress to allow him to enlist manumitted slaves for service in Washington's much depleted Continental Army. In keeping slaves in South Carolina, he pleaded only that he would better their condition and believed "they are, generally, as much attached to a plantation as a man is to his family, and to remove them from one to another is their great punishment."[129]

Six months later, on May 3, 1784, seventy-one-year-old Anthony Benezet died in Philadelphia. The funeral procession was the largest ever seen in the city. About a third of the mourners following the coffin were black, bidding farewell to their greatest white ally.[130] After Benezet's death, Mifflin tried to fill his shoes, not mainly as the publicist of antislavery sentiments but rather as the Quaker of high principles fashioning published antislavery appeals into antislavery action to be played out in the centers of state and federal political power. He took the self-abnegating schoolmaster's last words as his rule: "I am dying, and feel ashamed to meet the face of my Maker, I have done so little in his cause."[131] In this vein, Mifflin intensified his commitment to self-denial and service to the antislavery cause.

# Chapter 4

## Widening the Circle

*"Some things I have to meet with,"* Mifflin wrote in 1782, "that I have thought might be compared to the thorn in the flesh—a messenger of Satan by which I am buffeted." As usual, he "felt my mind engaged under a state of resignation to beg that nothing might be spared me that was offensive but that judgment might be laid to the line and righteousness to the plumb line."[1] It was a refrain his friends and family would hear frequently in the years ahead.

By the time Warner Mifflin returned from lobbying the Continental Congress regarding the slave trade in late 1783, he was committed to moving outward from Kent County to play a role on the larger stage of the abolitionist trans-Atlantic crusade. If his efforts at the Continental Congress were largely fruitless, there was much to do at the state level. Success in Virginia in 1782 gave some hope that a campaign to remove roadblocks to emancipating enslaved people in Delaware, Maryland, and North Carolina might bear fruit. For the next five years, while battling self-doubt and coping with family tragedies, Mifflin "bowed to the cross of our Lord Jesus Christ," as it was later said of him, and "did for the slave in obedience to what he believed his Master required at [his] hands."[2] Thus began his campaign to convince the state legislatures of their Christian duty to lighten the suffering of enslaved Africans and protect the fragile security of blacks just beginning to taste freedom. In the process, he acquired as his second wife and stepmother to his children a remarkable Quaker woman, whose Philadelphia family had risen to the upper echelon of the mercantile and entrepreneurial elite.

Then, as the first federal Congress under the newly ratified constitution met in New York, Mifflin's developing skills as an unswervable, innovative lobbyist brought him to the nation's attention. Admired by a chorus of anti-slavery publicists, he pushed the Quaker grandees to raise their banner as the keepers of the nation's conscience, forced Congress to debate the issue of

slavery that most delegates had tried to bury, put proslavery Southerners on
the defensive to the point of painting slavery as a positive good, and placed a
target on his back as a dangerous—some said fanatical—disturber of the peace.
In so doing, he cut across the grain, as one recent historian has put it, of "a
historiography invested in the seemingly inevitable failure of eighteenth-
century American antislavery."[3]


## State Initiatives

Starting in Delaware, Mifflin resembled a one-man abolitionist society on the
Eastern Shore, for there was no equivalent on the peninsula of the Pennsylvania Abolition Society. Nor was there in Delaware a coterie of dedicated abolitionist figures such as Philadelphia's Anthony Benezet, Thomas and Sarah
Harrison, John Parrish, and the Pemberton brothers (working with Samuel
Allinson, David Cooper, John Hunt, and George Dillwyn from across the
Delaware River in New Jersey). Though operating largely on his own, Mifflin
was far from autonomous. Given the layered structure of the Society of Friends
and the procedures its leaders had followed for generations, it was all but
obligatory that Mifflin conduct his efforts under the auspices of the Philadelphia Yearly Meeting and its Meeting for Sufferings. Of course, this was
also a way to give weight to his efforts. His main conduit to the yearly meeting was James Pemberton (1723–1809), a former Pennsylvania assemblyman,
Winchester exile, and clerk of the yearly meeting in most years since 1761.[4]
It is no wonder Mifflin cleaved to Pemberton, his elder by twenty-two years.
Though one of Philadelphia's wealthiest men, Pemberton had been drawn
into the Quaker reform movement in the 1760s, stricken with the devotion
and asceticism of John Woolman and Anthony Benezet. In his short sojourn
in Philadelphia, Jacques-Pierre Brissot de Warville lauded Pemberton as "a
man whose virtues place him among the most respected of their [Quaker]
leaders. His coat was threadbare but spotless; he prefers to clothe the poor
and spend his money in defense of the Negroes rather than have a large
wardrobe."[5]

Within months of returning from Princeton, Mifflin began laying the
ground for lobbying the Delaware legislature on slavery. The first part of what
quickly blossomed into a frontal attack on bondage was an effort to repeal laws
requiring masters, when freeing an enslaved person, to provide indemnity

bonds that would relieve county governments from providing support for indigent freed people.

Posting security bonds for freed slaves had a long history in the American colonies, always clogging the road to freedom for Africans. In Delaware since 1731, masters had been required to compensate counties for supporting indigent freed men and women. Nine years later a bond of thirty pounds was required for any liberated person in poor health or over thirty years in age. Then in 1767, when slavery in Delaware was peaking and Quakers were beginning to free their slaves, the legislature upped the ante, now doubling the indemnity bond to sixty pounds for any slave, regardless of age or condition, released from bondage. Controlling the legislature, the slave interest hoped to frighten off slaveowners with some inclination to free their chattels. Even Friends, soon under compulsion to liberate bond people, cited the law as a reason to resist manumission.[6]

Spurring Mifflin into action on this roadblock to manumission was the heart-wrenching case of an unscrupulous master who had freed his female slave and neglected—or purposely failed—to post the security bond. Then, after she believed she was a free woman, he cited the law's provision that the freedom was not legal until the bond was posted and used this loophole to seize the woman and her children with the intention of selling them. Already the go-to reformer in Kent County, Mifflin found himself solicited "by many to promote a petition to the Assembly for a repeal of the law," and by his account three of the judges promised to sign the petition.[7] Meanwhile, the case entered Kent County's court of common pleas.

Mifflin proceeded cautiously after the frightened woman reached him in 1783 with her story. He urged the Meeting for Sufferings in Philadelphia to find a way to support the woman in court after her former master had retained Edward Tilghman, one of the state's most prominent lawyers. "I am doubtful sometimes whether I do right to move in this way," Mifflin wrote James Pemberton, though he believed Friends should not "be silent spectators of such flagrant violations of the Rights of Mankind."[8] Not a lawyer, and unsure of himself, Mifflin appealed to Pemberton for guidance, while the case moved toward the Delaware Supreme Court. Meanwhile, he worked to repeal the personal security law altogether. It would take four years.

Before he could get much farther with his campaign in Delaware, Mifflin was struck at age thirty-nine with the second medical crisis of his life. In order to coordinate his efforts with Philadelphia's Quaker antislavery leaders, he had attended the Philadelphia Yearly Meeting in the fall of 1784, working for several days with the Meeting for Sufferings.[9] On the way home in early October, he was stricken with the autumn fever that had scourged parts of the Eastern Shore for years. This time it struck with a vengeance. Unable to go beyond Wilmington, thirty miles south of Philadelphia, he lay at a friend's house for six days. Only after his wife and his brother Walker arrived with a wagon could he move southward toward home. Back at Chestnut Grove, he was afflicted for weeks by violent headaches, which he feared would rob of him of "the use of my reason." By November, he was recovering. Far from discouraged, he took the disabling bout with the fever "as a fresh reminder of what must surely come to pass some day that is not at a great distance forward." He must prepare, he wrote James Pemberton, his constant Philadelphia correspondent, "for that awful moment" by taking up his abolitionist work.[10]

With renewed energy, Mifflin tackled a second reform—to stop the internal domestic slave trade that was increasing at the end of the long war. With grain the principal and less labor-intensive crop, many slaveowners were eager to sell surplus slaves out of the state to where they were still in demand, especially in the Deep South. For abolitionists such as Mifflin this directly threatened attempts to spur manumission. For the enslaved, it was pure terror—the prospect of sundering family ties while consigned to a harsh slave regimen in rice and cotton fields far from home.[11]

In mounting his campaign, Mifflin moved artfully to line up support from outside the Society of Friends, knowing that Quakers were hardly in good repute at the end of the war and, moreover, represented only a small minority of Delawareans. His best prospective allies were the Methodists, the fastest growing denomination in the new nation. Led in the 1780s by Richard Bassett, a well respected Dover lawyer, and Allen McLane, a Revolutionary War hero who had been with Washington at Valley Forge and was a veteran of battles at Long Island, White Plains, Trenton, Princeton, and the siege of Yorktown, both Methodists were well known to Mifflin as men with strong antislavery views.[12] In October 1785, McLane introduced the bill prohibiting the exportation and importation of slaves, probably armed with a copy of just such a law passed in Maryland in April 1783 that Mifflin had obtained.[13] To Mifflin's disappointment, the matter was deferred until the next year.

But even more important, Mifflin hoped that Delaware might follow Pennsylvania by putting slavery on the road to extinction with a gradual abolition act. To soften up the legislature, he drew on the lobbying tactics used in Virginia in 1782, putting in the hands of legislators copies of abolitionist pamphlets such as David Cooper's *A Serious Address to the Rulers of America on the Inconstancy of their Conduct respecting Slavery, Forming a Contrast Between the Encroachments of England on American Liberty, and American Injustice in Tolerating Slavery* (1783) and Benezet's *Short Observations on Slavery* (1783).[14]

Mifflin understood that the best chance for success in obtaining a gradual abolition act was to work behind the scenes while a man of great repute took the lead. If there was a single high-profile person capable of reaching non-Quakers in the effort to end slavery altogether in Delaware, that man was John Dickinson. Long an acquaintance, if not a close friend, Dickinson, both as president of Delaware during several war years and as a member of Pennsylvania's Supreme Executive Council, had the gravitas to sway the Assembly, all the more since he had freed most of his own slaves. Indeed, as Delaware's president in 1781–1782, he had urged the Assembly to pass laws "for alleviating the afflictions of this helpless, and too often abused part of their fellow creatures," including a clause so that black families would not be "cruelly separated from one another, and the remainder of their lives [be] extremely embittered."[15]

For Mifflin, it was a godsend that Dickinson was moved to draft a gradual abolition act in 1785.[16] Not only was Dickinson a skilled lawyer and legislative veteran, but he commanded national attention as one of the ablest constitutionalists of his generation. Working from Pennsylvania's 1780 landmark gradual abolition law, Dickinson's draft went beyond it in several respects. First, his proposal provided for freedom at age eighteen for females and twenty-one for males born into slavery, as opposed to the Pennsylvania law where freedom was gained only at twenty-eight. Another clause banned building or outfitting of any vessel engaging in the slave trade, with an unusually severe penalty of one thousand pounds, and another criminalized the breakup of slave families through sale.

With McLane introducing Dickinson's abolition bill, Mifflin swung into action. Drafting a "memorial" in late 1785, he garnered signatures from 106 Friends from the Duck Creek and Wilmington Monthly Meetings, submitted it for approval to the Philadelphia Meeting for Sufferings, and then, with 204 signatures, had it ready for the January 1786 session of the Delaware legislature.[17] Accompanied by six other Friends, Mifflin presented the "afflicted case of the oppressed Negroes in this state," pleading for "such relief as justice, humanity, the common natural rights of mankind, and, above all, the precepts and injunctions of the Christian Religion require." Decrying "the oppression exercised over the Black People" and the "withholding from them their just and natural right of personal freedom," the petition urged the repeal of the indemnification law, insisted that those freed should be given full legal rights, and supported Dickinson's gradual abolition act.

Hope took hold when the assembly appointed a committee to consider the gradual abolition bill and then agreed to debate its positive recommendation. It was not to be. After two weeks of negotiations, proslavery legislators submitted a substitute bill "for the better regulation of servants and slaves"—a parliamentary maneuver to pull the floor from beneath the abolition act while testing the waters for a bill aimed at curbing the growth of free blacks by prohibiting bondsmen and women freed outside Delaware from entering the state. Though the abolition bill was reintroduced and read a second time, the assembly adjourned in February 1786 without bringing either bill to a vote. An antislavery attempt to break the stalemate four months later provoked another reading of the bill and another debate—all to no avail.[18] Years later, Dickinson wrote that he had tried to "bring the affair forward," but after being advised by one legislator that "the legislature were in such a temper that it would be in vain . . . to renew the attempt," he backed off, hoping for a better day.[19] Nor did the other bills pass.

On June 3, 1786, five days before the legislature deferred Dickinson's abolition bill "for further consideration," effectively dealing it a death blow, Mifflin lost his wife Elizabeth, the mother of his five surviving children, aged fifteen, twelve, nine, seven, and two. For four months she had been in great pain—"her agony was great," Warner recounted, suggesting advanced cancer. In the last few weeks of her life several of their children also hovered on the edge of the grave, perhaps seized by the unwelcome seasonal visitor that carried Kent County young away in raging fevers. "Several of the children [were] so ill that we did not know which would go first," Mifflin wrote his father. He recounted further how in the latter stages of her disease Elizabeth wondered "why she should be so afflicted more than others that she had been concerned to inspect into the cause." Yet "if it was her master's will . . . for the promotion of his glory, she was resigned to his will." Sitting at her bedside just before she died, Warner heard her say in prayer: "Gracious Lord, if it be thy will, receive my soul; thou knows I have had no desire to be continued but to serve thee." Now, she murmured, she "was entirely willing to leave us."[20]

Mifflin was unstrung by grief. At the death of his wife, not yet forty, he wrestled with what had befallen him. "I did think if a sacrifice of all things I had in the world besides, [it] would [have] been acceptable and I had to labour with my hands for our support if she might [have] been allowed to remain with me while I remained, it would have been my choice." But true to the Quaker code of resignation and remorse, he wrote his father that "it is my duty to submit, which would not be so hard to do if some fears did not get up at times that she might have been continued with me had I been more what I ought." For more than a year, his letters spoke of writing from his fireside with his "motherless babes around me."[21]

Though anguished by the loss of his wife, Mifflin did not diminish his efforts on behalf of African Americans. Indeed, his peripatetic behavior over the next few years tempts one to think that life on his horse was his way of filling the emotional hole left by Elizabeth's death.

Three months after burying Elizabeth in the Murderkill meetinghouse yard, Mifflin left his five children at Chestnut Grove in the hands of his black and white housekeepers to attend the Philadelphia Yearly Meeting in September. He was back a month later for a meeting of the Meeting for Sufferings. There it was decided to memorialize the Continental Congress, now in the last year of its checkered career, to reconsider the Quaker address of 1783 that had pleaded the case of "the greatly injured and oppressed part of our fellow men, the enslaved Africans," and warned of the "additional national guilt [that] is daily accumulating."[22]

Mifflin joined eight other Quaker activists in traveling to New York City in November to inveigh against slavery and the resumption of the slave trade.[23] Pledging their commitment to "universal liberty and the common rights of man," they asked Congress to urge states to halt the "national iniquity" of the continuing slave trade. Finding that Congress lacked a quorum, they used the tactic that Mifflin had found productive in Virginia to push through the manumission act four years before—visiting members of the Congress at their lodgings to speak with them individually. With New York Friends and the mayor of the city aiding them, they visited sympathetic northern representatives but also, as unlikely as it might have seemed, those from Georgia, the Carolinas, and Maryland. Though they returned empty-handed, they had reminded the nation's leaders that Friends were not surrendering their role as the nation's conscience, and they had laid the groundwork for appeals to a stronger federal Congress, as the weakness of the Continental Congress fueled the move toward a constitutional convention. As well, the Quaker visitations may have had some influence on Congress's famous Northwest Territory ordinance, passed the next summer, which prohibited the carrying of an enslaved person north of the Ohio River—the most important piece of antislavery legislation done during the thirteen-year life of the Continental Congress.[24]

Mifflin's return to his family left him little time before the meeting of the Delaware legislature in January 1787.[25] Though he had intended to visit Pharsalia, where his father had just lost his wife of thirty years, Warner was beset by another "afflicting piece of business" in Murderkill Hundred that impelled him to stay in Delaware to help push through antislavery reforms. When a slaveowning planter moved close to Mifflin from Snow Hill, Maryland, just below the Delaware boundary on the Eastern Shore, he commissioned a ship captain to carry "a cargo" of his slaves to South Carolina, along with eighteen others he purchased locally. "This affected me much," Mifflin wrote John Parrish in Philadelphia. He visited the "much hardened man," who told Mifflin he was too late to do anything about it. But just as he had put everything aside to travel to Richmond five years before to lobby the Virginia legislature, Mifflin now "laid aside the pretentions to other business" to spend the next four weeks lobbying in Dover.[26]

In Dover, Mifflin found that few Friends had the stamina to sit through days of legislative maneuvering. Most of the Wilmington and Duck Creek Monthly Meeting Quakers who turned out for the first legislative session, including his brother Daniel, stayed only briefly, leaving Mifflin to carry the load. When a motion to allow him to speak failed, Mifflin did the next best thing—sitting "for hours on the stair steps" to buttonhole representatives or visit them "out doors as we did in Virginia."[27]

Even though by this time he was a toughened lobbyist, Mifflin doubted himself. "I hope the cause and testimony is not hurt," he worried, "though ... fearing I was about what perhaps might as well be let alone." Yet he believed "that everyone had not the same influence with men of this [proslavery] cast as myself, and if I might . . . sufficiently to keep under the last Regulator it might be well employed." Mifflin was aware that many Quaker leaders regarded him as passionate to a fault; but in the heat of a legislative battle he was incapable of standing down. "Thou knows that with my disposition there is great danger," he wrote; but while "I had ups and downs" and the "need of care on my part," he felt empowered by his conviction that "neither riches, honor of men, nor long life were the inducements to my [efforts] . . . but to endeavor to fill up my allotment and for the good and welfare of my fellow mortals."

By late February 1787, the prolonged efforts of several years in Delaware produced results. Spurred by Methodist Richard Bassett, Kent County's leading legislator and future governor of the state, the legislature passed a law bundling several previous propositions. It was hardly the breaking of dawn that Mifflin hoped for; yet it was a significant step forward. The personal security bond, always an impediment to private manumissions, was eliminated for healthy slaves liberated between eighteen and thirty-five. The law also tried to bottle up the domestic slave trade that was bringing slaves into Delaware for sale and funneling a much larger flow outward for sale as disposable workers. Thus, the law criminalized the sale of enslaved and indentured blacks out of state to the Carolinas, Georgia, and the West Indies—almost a guarantee of a much shortened life in the life-sapping sugar, rice, and indigo fields—except by approval of three justices of the peace. Any enslaved person brought into the state would be granted freedom. The effect was limited, however, for the law was nearly toothless, with enforcement mechanisms all but nil. The law also aimed at stopping the practice of kidnapping free black Delawareans and shipping them southward, sanctioning a hefty fine of one hundred pounds. Again, the effect was limited, for many men in the dirty business simply factored this into the price at which they offered their victims to the slave traders. Moreover, it was nearly impossible to pursue a body snatcher and rescue the manhandled freed person once the state line had been crossed. The law also denied to free blacks the franchise enjoyed in most northern states, the right to hold office, and the right to testify against a white person. This emphatically defined the meaning of black citizenship—that free blacks did not have "any other rights of a freeman, other than to hold property, and to obtain redress in law and equity for any injury to ... person or property."[28]

While ignoring the gradual abolition initiative, the legislators of the 1787 code hedged in the maneuvering room of slaveowners and slave traffickers. It also wounded the proslavery cause, as one historian has written, by providing "a legitimate avenue for slaves seeking freedom." Armed with the right to sue, many slaves sought out Mifflin as an advisor and "next friend" when they believed their master had flouted the law or tried to squeeze through supposed loopholes.[29] How many slaves got their freedom, or regained freedom after being reenslaved, is difficult to measure. But the limited gains of Mifflin and his supporters were enough to worry slaveowners and traffickers. On the other side of the color line, the word was out, impelling black Delawareans to beat a path to Mifflin's Kent County home in search of his help.

At moments like this, Mifflin's unconscious night life gave him a new feeling of assurance. After his weeks of lobbying in Dover, he dreamed he was perilously embarked "on a boisterous water" in a small bark; but gratefully he washed ashore safely on Chincoteague Island, his boyhood playground at his father's land. There he landed his cargo of five fat bullocks and put them out to pasture. "This dream had such an effect on my mind," he wrote John Parrish, that he was stirred to think deeply on "the matter that I was then engaged in." The dream told him that "something satisfactory would be the result" of his antislavery efforts, "for I thought if nothing but common natural justice" was operating in the world, his ship would not be sunk except by an extraordinary storm. Here self-doubt inflected with optimism revealed itself in his nocturnal subconscious.[30]

Partial success in Delaware was enough for Mifflin to launch new sojourns down the Eastern Shore and across the Chesapeake Bay. While the nation's attention was riveted on the drama unfolding in the suffocating summer of 1787 in Philadelphia, where fifty-five delegates converged to abandon the Articles of Confederation and write a constitution, Mifflin left Chestnut Grove for two long trips southward. The first spanned about five weeks in May and June, the other more than eight weeks in November and December. Both trips required him to measure parental responsibilities against what he saw as his duty to testify against the evils of slavery. As so often in the past, the latter was the winner.

Stopping to visit his father, Mifflin met with Quakers on both sides of the Chesapeake in Maryland and Virginia in mid-May 1787, attending several monthly meetings and the Virginia Yearly Meeting. Traveling with his friend and kinsman John Parrish, he wrote of how "I feel my tryall great to leave my dear and tender babes, but through mercy I have experienced hard things made easy."[31] Such guarded optimism was almost immediately confirmed when Mifflin intervened in a case of an enslaved woman and her children in Worcester County, Maryland. Hearing that the woman had been transported from Virginia to Maryland, contrary to state law, Mifflin, "in company with his father," petitioned the county court with "proper evidences to prove the fact." Though some of the slaveholding justices "would fain have waived the subject," Mifflin pressed the case—and won freedom for the woman and her children. The first of its kind in Eastern Shore Maryland, it was a "matter of importance," wrote John Parrish, who witnessed the court proceedings, for it gave promise of "put[ting] a stop to this cruel traffic, such as transporting [slaves] from one government another."[32]

From this precedent-setting victory, Mifflin proceeded to Annapolis, where a bold bill "for the total abolition of slavery" was under discussion at the Maryland legislative meetings. Mifflin had already taken the issue to Maryland's governor, William Smallwood (1732–1792). In a long, passionate letter to the Revolutionary War veteran, after preaching the antiwar doctrine and invoking scripture about "the Almighty creating of one blood all nations of men however diversified as to colour or language," Mifflin implored the "helmsman of the government . . . of Maryland" to raise his voice against the "cursed practice" of slaveholding and the domestic slave trade that was tearing black slave families apart. Though doubtless aware that Smallwood was a major slaveowner, Mifflin pressed on him the recent account of how several ship masters employed in the shipment of Maryland slaves to South Carolina witnessed heartsick slaves, wrenched from their kin and never expecting to see them again, casting themselves "into the great deep whereby to end their sorrow." "Oh poor America," Mifflin pleaded, "what will be thy fate" as God judged "the sins of the people."[33]

Taking lodgings in Annapolis, Mifflin found "some very warm advocates" speaking on the necessity of excising the cancer of slavery. Among them was Samuel Chase, a zealous Patriot during the war and a tribune of the common man. In a spirited debate of several days the Assembly considered what no state legislature in the South had broached.[34] Though the abolition bill was stalled at the hands of a proslavery majority, Maryland Friends did not give up, soon submitting another emancipationist petition, supported by Chase, from the Baltimore Yearly Meeting. Mifflin witnessed this when he returned at the end of the year, again disappointed that the legislature refused to discuss the abolition bill, though only by a vote of thirty to seventeen.[35]

Failure at the state level in Maryland did not deter Mifflin from doing what he could at the local level, where he often saw displays of human behavior at its worst. Lacking the support of any equivalent of the Pennsylvania Abolition Society, whose lawyers took on individual cases when presented with presumed illegal activity by slaveholders, Mifflin tried his best to provide a beacon to distressed blacks. When a Sussex County, Delaware, slaveowner prepared to take a slave across the state line to Maryland to his other plantation, Mifflin tried to intervene. He hoped that Delaware's laws, more favorable to slaves "in protecting them from outrage of despotic men," should make it impermissible "to suffer them to be brought from a better to a worse state." But human kindness, not much the habit of slaveowners, was not legally negotiable. In this case, the matter fell into the hands of the Maryland courts, which were beyond Mifflin's reach.[36]

His second extended trip took Mifflin southward in late 1787, this time through Virginia to North Carolina. Mifflin wrestled with the familiar dilemma of reconciling fatherly care of his children with his duty-bound complex—the fear of disappointing his Maker. This time, he almost wished for a disabling sickness that would excuse him from an arduous absence from home. "My strait has been great in leaving home on many accounts," he wrote his Philadelphia confidant, "insomuch that I thought it was a bitter cup that I should have been glad to have been excused from. I thought if a small spell of sickness had prevented my going, it would have been more pleasant; but I was left without sufficient excuse of this kind, though I have a cold and have had on my journey severe pain in my breast." For a man intensely committed to serving God, even severe chest pain was no excuse to remain with his children. "My journey has been undertaken . . . to follow Him. . . . It has fixed in my mind, that if He require me to go . . . it will not be without its reward."[37]

The first leg of the trip took Mifflin to preparative, monthly, and quarterly meetings to reinforce the decades-long attempt of reformist Quakers to persuade Friends to cleanse their hands of slaveholding. Six years before, the North Carolina Yearly Meeting had followed the Philadelphia Yearly Meeting when it agreed to disown masters who did not free their slaves.[38] That they would take such a step was in itself extraordinary, because North Carolina legislators had made manumission nearly impossible.

Mifflin knew all too well the peculiar situation of North Carolina Quakers. Those willing to comply with the strictures of the Society of Friends had to do so in virtual defiance of state law. Since 1741, the law allowed private manumissions only for "meritorious service" as approved by a county court, and further provided that any white freeholder could detain a slave liberated in defiance of the law for delivery to the sheriff, who, unless the freed person had left the state within six months, would then sell the person at auction back into slavery. The only state with such a prohibition, the law operated as a formidable barrier to numerous Quakers eager to clear their conscience. Strengthened in 1779 after a series of court cases, the law made Quaker manumissions all the more difficult.[39]

Yet many North Carolina Quakers—some were conscience-stricken, others yielded to continued efforts of monthly and quarterly meetings to purge Friends of a deep-dyed sin—were willing to evade the law. Some county courts,

sympathetic to slaveowner rights to manumit their slaves, expanded or ignored
the common understanding of "meritorious service," particularly in the coastal
counties of Pasquotank and Perquimans, where Quakers were concentrated
and served as justices of the peace. In 1777, for example, eleven Quakers had
freed forty slaves, not for "meritorious service" but from the conviction that
human bondage was an evil no longer to be tolerated.[40] The legislature tried
to retaliate with stricter definitions of the law, and for several years the matter
was fought out in the courts.

Threading his way through this disputed legal and legislative terrain, Mifflin traveled with his friend Sarah Harrison, the wife of Philadelphia's Thomas
Harrison, a workhorse of the Pennsylvania Abolition Society. Visiting slaveowning families, they urged them to free their fellow human beings, while
Mifflin wrote deeds of manumission for them to use. At the same time, they
visited monthly meetings, gently twisting arms to have those who "disregard[ed]
the wholesome advice of the body" disunited.[41] It was heartening to see how
many Friends were willing to evade the law and how these unauthorized
manumissions swelled the free black population.[42] But he also heard about
some sixty heartbroken men and women who had been manumitted, only to
be seized by sheriffs and sold back into slavery.[43]

With news that the Constitutional Convention in Philadelphia had completed its work and newspapers bristling with arguments for and against ratification, Mifflin rode deep into the interior to attend the North Carolina Yearly
Meeting and help write a petition calling for the repeal of the law that forbade
private manumissions.[44] Then, after reaching Tarborough, about fifty miles
east of Raleigh, he presented the Friends' petition to the North Carolina legislature. "My coming was much talked of among the members," he confided
with a touch of embarrassment to James Pemberton, and "some said they
understood I was one of the greatest men in America, which thou may well
think cowed me not a little." That said, Mifflin related his cautious approach
to lobbying. At first, he kept quiet and "pretty close at my lodgings," where he
gladly received the former governor, Josiah Martin. Then he called on Governor Richard Caswell and "ventured a little among them [the legislators]" for
several days.[45] Using a now established lobbying technique, he visited legislators individually for more than a week. Gratified that he was asked to speak to
the lower house, he found "there was a majority of the members in both houses
who would have been willing that liberty should have been given to emanci-
pate," except for "the artifice of one violently opposed" member who blocked

the measure. In fact, the bill passed both houses on its first reading, fell one vote short of a majority in the Senate on the second reading, and was buried when the speaker cast the deciding vote.[46]

Mifflin remained optimistic that the North Carolina legislature would soon repeal the law severely limiting manumissions. However, his optimism was misplaced. He did his cause no favors by objecting that five Quakers elected to the lower house had agreed to fill civil positions. Even the Friends who helped elect them aroused Mifflin's censure. This purist position on Quaker participation in public policy led him even to oppose Friends serving as justices of the peace, though this had enabled several courts to shield manumitted slaves from reenslavement. Never lacking scriptural backup, Mifflin quoted Jeremiah 2:13: "My people have . . . forsaken me [and] the fountain of living water and hewn to themselves cisterns that will hold no water."[47] To be sure, this followed Quaker policy to withdraw from government during the Revolution, but that was based on upholding their peace testimony. In matters of abolitionism, withdrawing from government in North Carolina lessened the chance for removing the barrier to manumissions. Despite a new remonstrance in 1788 from the North Carolina Yearly Meeting to repeal the anti-manumission law, the legislature instead, claiming that free blacks were "going at large to the terror the people of this State," strengthened the law by authorizing any white adult to identify illegally liberated slaves and thereby facilitate their seizure and reenslavement. For Mifflin, it was a nearly fruitless trip.[48]

Returning home on December 19, 1787, as the ratification debates on the Federal Constitution absorbed the nation, Mifflin found "my little flock [surviving] bravely" in the hands of hired housekeepers. Even if the North Carolina effort had produced no results, there was still work to do in Pennsylvania, Maryland, and Delaware. In March 1788, following the old King's Highway north to Philadelphia, as so many times before, he joined leaders of the Pennsylvania Abolition Society and the Philadelphia Yearly Meeting to attend sessions of the Pennsylvania legislature and present a memorial for an extensive revision of the 1780 gradual abolition act. This time the Friends' efforts succeeded. The 1788 law outlawed the outfitting of vessels for the slave trade, forbade slave masters from transporting pregnant slaves out of state so that their children would enter the world as slaves, prohibited the separation of slave families, and imposed condign punishment for kidnappers of free blacks who were hustling their victims southward to be sold as slaves.[49] While in Philadelphia, Mifflin visited General Thomas Mifflin—a rare visit suggesting rekindling of a familial relationship fractured by his cousin's abandonment of Friends' peace testimony.[50]

After planting season, in late April 1788, Mifflin returned to Annapolis with John Parrish for another bout of legislative lobbying. This time he faced charges that would soon become familiar. Some told him they had wisdom enough to make their own laws without the advice of ideologues from another state. Another legislator charged that "I sold all my Negroes before I entered on the promoting [of] emancipation and that I gave runway Negroes passes." When Mifflin asked the man to meet to discuss this, the legislator refused. Mifflin mused that such affronts were "not equal to that [which] the poor blacks meet with." But he was wounded. "At Annapolis after I had been there a day or two," he wrote, "I never could enter on such business again, if I might be exempt from it—it felt so exceeding disagreeable to me."[51]

But he set aside the hostility of some lawmakers, accepting an invitation to read before the lower house the memorial he and Parrish had prepared. Arguing that the enslavement of fellow humans was a monstrous trespass against the simplest of all Christian doctrines—the Golden Rule—and the natural rights doctrine expressed in the nation's founding documents, they called for a gradual abolition law and laws easing the manumission process. Reporting his efforts to James Pemberton, Mifflin thought he was regarded as "a devilish clever fellow," but "he read the memorial well." At least Mifflin and Parrish had the encouragement of Thomas Cockey Deye, Speaker of the House, who "was disposed to do what he could for our Society." That turned out to be an empty promise, as the House referred the matter to the next session. The stress was enough to send Mifflin home to his bed for almost five days with a severe case of piles.[52]

Returning to Delaware, Mifflin coordinated a new campaign to move the state's legislature to further antislavery action. With ratification of the Constitution, the topic of the day, Mifflin kept his eye on something else happening in Philadelphia—the reorganization of the Pennsylvania Abolition Society, with outreach from its earlier Quaker base to a more religiously diverse organization. Delaware was late in the game but got started in 1788, when Mifflin and Bassett founded in Dover the Delaware Society for Promoting the Abolition of Slavery. Like the Pennsylvania Abolition Society, the Delaware society staked its future on reaching across denominational lines. Recruiting the state's governor, Thomas Collins, as president, it enlisted Revolutionary War heroes such as Allen McLane, James Tilton, and John Vining to fill leading offices.

Quakers such as Mifflin and his brother-in-law Charles Hilliard quietly operated in the shadows as a working committee to deal with individual cases of
white malfeasance.[53]

A parallel society got under way in Wilmington—the Delaware Society
for the Gradual Abolition of Slavery, with Quakers more conspicuous in leadership roles. Though never able to match the effectiveness of the Pennsylvania
Abolition Society, both Delaware societies backed legislative initiatives, put
antislavery petitions before Delaware's lawmakers, participated in freedom
suits, and appointed delegates to the American Convention of Abolition Societies when it formed six years later.[54]

Sparking the founding of these two societies was an alarming attempt to
outfit a British slave ship in Wilmington. The year before, in 1787, after unloading its cargo of enslaved Africans in the West Indies, the ship had refitted in
Philadelphia, but now, after completing another trans-Atlantic voyage, it was
blocked by a new Pennsylvania law that prohibited servicing the carrying trade.
Thus it coasted down the Delaware River to refit in Wilmington.[55] Philadelphia
Yearly Meeting's Meeting for Sufferings sprang into action, joining the two
new Delaware abolition societies and two other groups of citizens to petition
the legislature for prompt action. The Delaware Abolition Society petition
bore fifty-seven signatures, including those of Warner Mifflin and his brothers
Daniel and Walker. Important legislators such as Allen McLane and John
McKinly signed as well.[56]

The society's petition, probably written by Mifflin and Bassett, prefaced
their specific requests with the assertion that "the principles of impartial justice
... equally entitled [enslaved Africans] to their just and natural right of personal
freedom." It asked for laws to remove Delaware from the states allowing,
covertly or not, the outfitting of ships for the slave trade; to "restrain the punishment of slaves at the mere will and pleasure of their masters, which is often
very tyrannically and cruelly exercised"; and to add teeth to the 1787 law
restricting the transportation of slaves out of the state. Though a legislature
committee prepared such a bill, action awaited the next legislative session in
January 1789. As usual, Mifflin attended many days of the legislative sessions,
muttering in his usual way that he was "in much fear that I might be a busy
body and meddling where I had no proper business."[57] But this time he mainly
succeeded. The legislature strengthened the bill prohibiting the sale of slaves
out of state except with the approval of five justices of the peace and—most

important—closing off Virginia and Maryland to internal trafficking. In addition, the fine for convicted offenders was augmented.[58]

## An Aborted Mission Abroad

Mifflin's lobbying efforts in Delaware, Maryland, and North Carolina brought only piecemeal reforms—in the main disappointing. To a man absorbed in natural rights doctrine and his Bible, his countrymen were betraying their birthright principles and offending God in the process. With perseverance as his strong suit, he was by no means ready to abandon his antislavery efforts. And whatever doubts he had about his "meddling," they were swallowed up by the intensity of his religious convictions. Also sustaining him was his growing connection to the trans-Atlantic antislavery crusade that had been gaining momentum in the decade following the achievement of American independence.

Mifflin had first felt "urgings" to spread his wings abroad in 1785. Believing he was called to cross the Atlantic to confer with the "meetings for discipline" of fellow Quakers in England so as "to build up Israel," he sought a traveling certificate from the Philadelphia Meeting of Ministers and Elders in the spring of 1786. Though he had the endorsement of the Duck Creek Monthly and Western Quarterly meetings, Philadelphia Yearly Meeting's Ministers and Elders would not endorse the trip, though they had no "doubt of the rectitude of his concern." Possibly, the Quaker leadership saw Mifflin's intended embassy as an intrusion on their growing connections with the London Yearly Meeting, or they feared that his impassioned demeanor would offend some of the diffident English Quakers. Mifflin "was very submissive," according to Job Scott, one of the elders present at the meeting. But this was not his last attempt to follow many Philadelphia-area elders and ministers drawn after the war to England, Ireland, and continental Europe.[59]

If he could not cross the Atlantic to visit English Quaker meetings, Mifflin implanted himself in the efforts of the Philadelphia Yearly Meeting to strengthen bonds with their English counterparts, and especially to urge the London Yearly Meeting to participate more vigorously in the growing trans-Atlantic antislavery crusade.[60] His frequent trips to Philadelphia kept him informed of these efforts at coordination, because the drafting committee of the Philadelphia

Yearly Meeting's lengthy epistle to its London counterpart in May 1786 included his close friends in Philadelphia—Henry Drinker, James Pemberton, and John Parrish.[61] Then he took a singular action to make himself heard across the Atlantic.

First, he started with no less a figure than John Moore, Archbishop of Canterbury, head of England's Anglican Church. Knowing of the London Yearly Meeting's petition to Parliament "to stop the abominable slave trade," he implored the archbishop to exert his influence as the "father in the national church" in support of the petition.[62] Striking a pose of a sinner in the hands of an angry God, Mifflin launched into the story of how he was converted from slaveholder to slave liberator, how he participated in the peace mission to the warring armies in 1777, and finally how he lobbied the legislatures in Virginia, Delaware, Maryland, and North Carolina to speed the manumission of the enslaved and work toward universal freedom. Surely, he maintained, a vengeful God who made all people of one blood would punish nations that continued the enslavement of fellow humans. To seal his case, he relayed the frightful account he had received from a schoolmaster who had lived in South Carolina for many years. The teacher told of how a slave master of his acquaintance urged one of his male slaves "to copulate with his [enslaved] women, not regarding whether they had husbands or not and, if they had, . . . the woman must comply with their tyrant's will," he reasoning that this was no different from breeding cattle. "How shameful is chastity thus prostituted," Mifflin sputtered, "and the divine law trampled upon."[63]

On the heels of this letter, Mifflin made a second attempt in late 1787 to cross the Atlantic to participate in the London Yearly Meeting scheduled for June 1788. In spite of his years of service and leadership at the Duck Creek Monthly Meeting, he encountered reservations from his local approving body. Perhaps it was because the Philadelphia Meeting of Elders and Ministers had rebuffed the earlier attempt. But the hesitancy of a committee of seven appointed to consider the application suggests something else. Was Mifflin going too far in his incessant, almost obsessive, ministries away from Chestnut Grove, while leaving his young children behind? Meeting six times between December 1787 and July 1788 to consider Mifflin's request, the committee—it included the brother-in-law of his deceased wife and close friends such as Ezekiel and John Cowgill—could not bring themselves to approve the request. Buried in the monthly meeting minutes are tell-tale warnings to the passionate reformer that he needed to rein in his impulses, even if he believed God was speaking to him, in order to parent his "motherless babes." One minute read: "the concern of our Friend Warner Mifflin being revived and weightily considered by this meeting, it appears to be the prevailing sense of friends that the subject be yet left for further deliberation." Another read: "it appears most easy to the minds of friends that it be yet continued for further consideration recommending a serious and weighty attention to the pointing of truth in his [Mifflin's] mind in the ripening up or the further procedure of his concern." After meeting twice with Mifflin, where he pleaded his case, the committee was still concerned: "six of them have had an opportunity with him since our last [report] but are not yet prepared to make a final report or produce a certificate, they are therefore continued to pay the further needful attention thereto." Even after the committee reluctantly recommended a travel certificate, the matter lingered on through the summer and fall of 1788, while the Western Quarterly Meeting considered the case.[64]

But if Mifflin could not go Europe, Europeans came to him. Especially they came from France. One who would arrive a few years later, entirely unknown to Mifflin, had sent ahead a moving letter confessing that "thou whose virtues have penetrated me . . . with gratitude to the Supreme Being, who amidst a race of carnal, perfidious men, has sent into the world such a person as thou art for the consolation and honor of human nature." Authoring this letter was Louis Philippe Gallot de Lormerie, a wealthy aristocrat who frequented Enlightenment salons in Paris, where Lafayette had introduced him to Jefferson in 1786. A member of the Philanthropic Society of Paris and the London Society of Arts, de Lormerie pledged that after his retirement he would "consecrate to thee a monument in the midst of my groves," inscribed with "a recital of the benefits thou has bestowed on mankind . . . to my children and to our remote posterity."[65]

Perhaps carrying de Lormerie's letter, Jacques-Pierre Brissot de Warville had much more to say about Mifflin, and he wanted the world to know it. One of the remarkable Frenchmen coming to Philadelphia in the post-revolutionary period, he arrived in August 1788, and Mifflin was on his must-see list. Nine years Mifflin's junior, Brissot officially came to represent a French consortium eager to speculate in the American revolutionary debt and western lands. But unofficially he came to nourish his antislavery commitment by making connections with Philadelphia-area Friends. A few years before, his abolitionism had been inspired by the American Quakers, whom he regarded as models of Enlightenment humanitarianism. In France, he had already forged a friendship with Crèvecoeur, whose Paris edition of *Letters from an American Farmer* in 1784 had converted Brissot to universal freedom and brought Mifflin to his attention. Then, in February 1788, only three months before his departure for North America, he co-founded the Société des Amis des Noirs (Society of Friends of the Blacks).[66] "One of the purposes of the journey I made to America," Brissot wrote in his memoirs, "was to serve the cause of the blacks and to spread the branches of the Society I had just instituted in Paris."[67]

When Brissot reached stifling Philadelphia on August 26, 1788, Mifflin was among the first antislavery stalwarts he met. Confined to his lodging by a violent intestinal disturbance, Brissot was glad to find Mifflin at his door four days later. Mifflin did not disappoint. Recording some of their conversation in the notes he gathered for a book relating his brief sojourn in the United States, Brissot gushed about "this angel of peace and charity . . . What humanity! What charity! It seems that his only pleasure, his very existence, is to love and serve mankind. He devotes himself entirely to the task of gathering all men into one family, and he does not despair of being able to do so." Taken by "this good Quaker's heart," Brissot confessed, "How small I felt as I gazed on him!" But "the loyalty of an angel such as Warner Mifflin . . . is the best possible defense for that society." When Brissot mentioned the mountain of obstacles that Mifflin and his abolitionist friends faced, Mifflin responded, "But my friend, is not the arm of the Almighty stronger than the arm of man? What were we when the Society was born in England? What was America thirteen years ago when Benezet rose in protest against Negro slavery? Let us do good, let us not fear obstacles, and the good will come to pass." Brissot also injected sorrowful comments on how Mifflin's integrity and ardency in fighting for the abolition of slavery "has been repaid with the most atrocious calumny." Yet Mifflin responded only with "patience, kindness, forgiveness, and logic."[68] It was this outward calm and forbearing disposition that Mifflin was soon to display on the national stage.

Returning to France in late 1788, where he became deeply involved in the Paris Commune as the French Revolution erupted, Brissot published *Nouveau voyage dans les États-Unis de l'Amérique* in 1791. Joel Barlow, the American poet living in France, quickly translated and published it as *New Travels in the United States*. Published in London, Dublin, New York, and later Boston, it devoted three chapters to the Quakers, including one on "The Good Warner Mifflin." Brissot gave authenticity to Crèvecoeur's account of Mifflin and added reason to celebrate the fearless Quaker. Stripped of dialogue and lavish detail, Brissot repeated the story of how Mifflin, "without a passport," reached Howe's headquarters and spoke to him "firmly and with so much dignity" about turning swords into plowshares; then, again without passport, risked "being taken a spy" to reach Washington's headquarters to preach the peace testimony.[69] If Crèvecoeur's celebration of Mifflin had not yet made his name a byword in Europe, Brissot's fulsome praise completed the task. Within a few years, townspeople in Amsterdam, Stockholm, and Berlin, Leipzig, and other German cities were reading about "the serenity of [Mifflin's] countenance and . . . pleasing gestures," about "a life committed to the good of humanity," and about the shallow, toxic attacks on the Quakers "as a hotbed of hypocrisy and duplicity."[70]

## The Vital Marriage

Before Mifflin left Brissot's lodgings on August 30, 1788, he asked the Frenchman to visit a woman whom he had been courting for many months. Like his attempt to travel to London, the courtship had not gone smoothly. He told Brissot that the marriage was to happen "in a few days," but in fact it was delayed, as we will see, for six weeks. Nonetheless, Brissot obligingly made his way to the home of Ann Emlen ("Miss Ameland" in Brissot's *New Travels*). Brissot was charmed. Once a frivolous, beautiful young Quaker girl who "loved the world, wrote poems, composed music, and danced," she had turned her life inside out despite jesting from her friends. She "renounced all these amusements to embrace the life of an anchorite in the very midst of society. . . . What sweetness! What modesty! And at the same time, what a pleasant conversationalist."[71]

In Mifflin's mind, what Brissot found attractive about Ann Emlen was rewarding but hardly sufficient. It did not hurt that she was a woman of calm and beautiful countenance—and a woman of considerable wealth. But what he needed most of all was a consort to co-parent his five children while he was at home, to run the household while he was away on his incessant missions, and to stand with him as a deeply spiritual person committed to benevolent reform both inside and outside the Society of Friends.[72] As to that latter quality, he had no doubts, for Ann had spent most of her twenties seeking spiritual authorization to map out ways to purify herself and the Philadelphia Quaker community. As a young single woman, she could not hope to intrude on the management of the Philadelphia women's meetings controlled by older married women. Nonetheless, she had attracted attention for the depth of her spirituality and simplicity, along with signs of that special gift from God that was preparing her for the role of public minister.[73]

Ten years younger than Warner, born in 1755 in a family of great wealth, Ann Emlen was the youngest daughter and sixth of eight children of Ann Reckless Emlen and George Emlen, a Quaker merchant whose country home in Whitemarsh, willed to her brother, had served briefly as Washington's headquarters after the British occupation of the city in 1777. While many comely young Quaker women were entertaining British occupying officers, she would don only drab dresses and shun all "gay society." Her conversion to extreme plainness, her devoutness, and her descent into private, often gloomy meditations worried her family and friends.

After her father died in January 1776, the month Thomas Paine's *Common Sense* appeared on Philadelphia's streets, she fell deeper and deeper into religious ruminations, mostly keeping to herself, as she pondered the bloody war swarming around her. At twenty, she wondered, was she an empty vessel that God would fill?[74] Becoming utterly disdainful about the social life of her age group, she filled copybook after copybook: extensive "Notes on the Bible"; 120 pages of details from Samuel Bownas's *Account of the Life, Travel, and Christian Experience* (London, 1756); a moody "Account of My Religious Progress"; an indignant thirty-five-page "Address to Methodist John Wesley on his derogatory *History of the Quakers*," where she countered, point by point his "unfair account of us"; an oversized commonplace book titled "Notes on Quaker Doctrine," and abstracts of minutes and advices from the London Yearly Meeting organized by topics—among them Education, Mourning Habits, the Poor, Slaves, Sufferings, Plainness, and Youth. In another twelve-page expostulation, "Notes on the Payment of Taxes Appropriated for Military Purposes," she ransacked world history to detail bloody wars waged over the centuries to subjugate innocent peoples. How the British in Africa used their military power "to enable the heathen in conjunction with professed Christians to make war with and make merchandize of their brethren" especially excited her indignation. So did the long history of European-Indian violence in America, where "the Indians [have] been instigated to acts of evil and murder [of] Christians" and how "Christians scalping Indians have stained the earth with human blood for a miserable share in the spoil of a plundered world."[75]

All the while, she sponged up the tense debates about the crisis with the mother country and how Friends could weather the storm besetting them. With the Continental Congress meeting in the city and delegates lodging around the Emlen house at Sixth and Chestnut Streets, she was accustomed to seeing men in powdered wigs from all the colonies. She was not the least intimidated by any of them. Though brought up, like all young women, to regard public affairs as best left to the men, she could not remain aloof. "How shall I impose a silence upon myself," she scribbled in a commonplace book, "when the subject is so very interesting . . . and what every member of the community is more or less concerned in?"[76] In 1779, at twenty-four, she blistered a member of the Congress with an eight-page letter, expressing "in no small degree" her shock at his assertion that importing "luxuries are necessary to employ the . . . labouring poor." Was he "too much blinded by a false reasoning or biased by the politicians"? "So mistaken a sentiment," she railed, was "a pursuit of needless wealth."[77] To the famous John Dickinson, also a Congressman, and variously president of both Delaware and Pennsylvania, she wrote with words that most would have regarded as the height of impudence, advising him that if he acted more in compliance with Quaker principles, it might "induce us to address thee in the character of John Dickinson the Worthy, not J. D. Esq., or [J. D.] the Great." She signed off with "Thou wilt say I suppose I am a strange girl to write as I do. Farewell however, Thy Friend, A. Emlen, Jr."[78]

Living through the British occupation of Philadelphia in 1777–1778, Ann was close at hand to witness the Galloway family trauma. While most Friends trimmed their sails by keeping their distance from Grace Galloway, Joseph Galloway's wife, Ann visited her on many occasions for the next few years, after her husband and daughter left with the British in June 1778. All the while, she absorbed herself in deep religious meditation. "It is not marriage or celibacy," she confided to herself, "[that] gives merit or demerit to a person, but a life ordered in the fear of The Lord."[79] Her mother, worried about her daughter's gloomy search for identity, advised that spinsterhood was the best choice for her.[80]

Even the uppermost Quaker leaders, men she encountered nearly on a daily basis, could not escape Ann's finger-wagging. Though she prayed to God for "prudence, divine prudence, which may prove a stay to my mind and a bridle to my tongue," she never could adopt the passive stance of most women, who were inured to a subservient role or, in the case of elder Quaker women, poured their energy into monitoring the Friends marriage process and overseeing the care of the poor. This was on full display when she staked out a position on the use of Continental currency, an issue that cleaved mid-Atlantic Friends and made enemies of friends.

Ann had brooded about the issue for several years after her father's death. Then in November 1779 one of her friends had a dream so unnerving that she knew that the bedrock Quaker principle of pacifism required her to take the unpopular political stance of forswearing any form of involvement in the war, including the use of Continental currency. Her friend, she wrote in her commonplace book,

> had a vision of children wading through a sea of blood, crying for bread, when a table was spread of it, unbaked and mixed with blood of which they could not partake and went away weeping. Some of small growth, children in religion, have been led off the use of this money . . . and we know not how deep our wadings may further be in rejecting this mark of the beast and spirit of war as in the right hand or otherwise by the mark on the forehead.[81]

Eerily, Ann had visited the chapter in Revelation that Warner Mifflin, eighty miles to the south, had consulted two months before when he had stumbled from the forest at midnight, tortured by the issue of dealing in Continental currency. Ann reached the same conclusion that "the hand of the most High is upon me . . . sent I believe in love, that it may tend to spiritual refinement and greater subjection of will." The dream had confirmed her view that the true Quaker would not partake of any sustenance mixed with war-induced blood. Showing her distaste for Pennsylvania's revolutionary government, which she described as pursuing "a restless search after a licentious liberty," she shook off a prolonged illness and decided she must "leav[e] my dear mother's house until she can see her way to forsake the use of Congress currency and the support thereof in the payment of taxes." While a "bodily indisposition shook over me," she wrote, she pledged "to guard with increasing care through thine holy aid against indulging in what may come through the channel of a polluted currency."[82]

A year later, with the currency issue still hotly debated by Friends, Ann left Philadelphia to stay with friends in Chester County. Several of her female friends found this "extraordinary" and believed "she carries the matter too far."[83] John Pemberton, eighteen years Ann's senior and a revered elder and traveling minister, tried his best to dissuade her, urging her "to return to thy mother's home to avoid any censure which an uncharitable world may cast out." Sounding like a stern uncle, he told her "calmly resign to the voice of pure wisdom."[84]

But Ann held her ground. In fact, she hurled back at the gentle Pemberton her indignant refusal to return to her mother's home. If he was trying "to preserve me from the shafts of calumny," he was wasting his time; instead, she was fully prepared to bear "a winter season of reproach." "It is not in mine own will," she insisted, "but in the Cross thereto that I have submitted to become as a mark to shoot." As if this wasn't clear, she concluded by telling him, "I must endeavour to stand my ground, knowing in the depth of some painful experience on what ground and foundation I do stand on."[85] Never in Philadelphia Quakerdom had such a woman, in such a season of stress, drawn such a line in the sand.

By the summer of 1781, fighting one of her periodic depressions, this time most likely the result of a broken love affair, Emlen felt her way toward becoming a female "messenger of the truth," a well-trodden path followed by many English and American Quaker women.[86] For weeks, she worked through a spiritual crisis over whether she was fit to speak before men, though Quaker women had been doing that on both sides of the Atlantic for more than a century. Attending a Methodist service, she bristled at the refusal of a request from a young woman to speak. "Male and female are declared to be one in Christ," she wrote in her diary, and soon, deeply troubled, she decided again to leave Philadelphia. "I see no other way for true peace," she confided to her commonplace book of religious notes. "What is before me I know not but must rely solely on thy divine sufficiency, Gracious Creator, who hath hitherto sustained me and knoweth how to deliver [me] safely . . . into Jordan."[87]

After peace returned, Emlen returned to Philadelphia. Ann Warder, the English Quaker visiting the city after the war, found Ann unmoored from worldly concerns—a person whose "mind appears to be a perfect symmetry of heavenly love." But her dress—a brown dress and a cap of "coarse muslin without either border or strings"—was decidedly unattractive. Meeting for tea or supper, Warder hardly knew what to make of this woman, now turning thirty. Amid the scene of postwar young Quaker women addicted to gaiety, she found Ann Emlen alarmingly other-worldly, as if she floated above the city, wearing altogether dowdy clothes.[88] That mattered little to Ann Emlen, for she had found her way home, literally and vocationally. In a long letter to John Pemberton, Ann poured out her desire "to preserve my integrity (if favoured to have any) Godward, that no erroneous influence whatever may ever cause my feet to slide from the beaten path of Christ's Companions." Her life, she vowed, would be "a way of self-denial or abasement of self." Breathing the language of the Lamb's War of early English Quakers, she hoped "to join the already enlisted Troops, the Captains, Generals, and Commanders in chief of the heavenly Militia, whose king and awful rule and commissioner is the Majesty on high."[89]

This was the woman Mifflin assiduously sought out as his hopes to go abroad fell to pieces.

The courtship was far from easy, because Ann Emlen was all but determined to forgo marriage. How many days Warner spent in Philadelphia courting her is uncertain, but Ann's "Notes on Religion" traced the course of her resistance—and his persistence. "How far this may be founded on the Rock, I know not," she wrote about his first professions of love. "But if it be a seed of faith sown by the everlasting Shepherd, . . . I wish it to flourish. . . .; if not that it may be rooted up." For Warner, it was an uphill struggle. He pleaded that "he believed it was under divine sanction," but admitted, "there would be likely much outward opposition." She battled with her "inward doubtings." Later, worried that he lived "in a distant city," she prayed that "the merciful God of my salvation be pleased to teach me how to walk herein and lead me safely . . . that I may not stumble through the dark mountains." Mifflin implored that his marriage to her would be "interwoven with his religious faith . . . as to be inseparable." When Ann warned him that she "desired the matter wholly to drop," Warner's friends suggested other possible wives.

This would not do. Eager to continue his efforts to gain sanction for his ministry to England, he desperately needed what his friend Henry Drinker unromantically termed "a housekeeper to superintend his family concerns and discharge a parental duty to his children during his absence from them."[90] Facing the prospect of losing the prize he coveted, Warner pulled out all stops. Skirting the edge of acceptable behavior, he had "papers prepared," in the Quaker tradition, with names and dates of the marriage filled in for the first announcement of an intention to marry, to be submitted to the women's monthly meeting. "It was withheld from him for a season which was a state of painful suspension," Ann recorded. Then, still haunted that she was making an unwise step, she acceded. "This day, 10 mo. 1788," she wrote morosely, "is the expected time of my second espousal, not unto God as formerly but unto one of his devoted servants. May the connection be a happy one, but if the gloom that has overspread my mind at this season with plenteous tears flowing from mine eyes, may I be able to endure to the end in the fire and in the furnace, Jesus Lord be with me. Amen."[91]

And so they were married on October 9, 1788. The always gossipy Ann Warder clucked that "the marriage of Nancy Emlen is to be accomplished to Warner Mifflin, an eminent Friend but yet apparently an unsuitable husband for her, having five children, the oldest eighteen, and living eighty miles from here in an unhealthy part of the country."[92] What Ann Warder regarded as unsuitable was exactly what mattered to Warner with his brood of children, the youngest not yet four years old.

Consistent with their pledge of simple living and Warner's commitment to blacks, the couple shunned the handsome meetinghouse at Second and High Streets, where Ann's family had worshiped for generations, in favor of the seldom used, much smaller Bank Meetinghouse on Front Street north of Arch. Built in 1685 and used for two decades thereafter by the Pennsylvania legislature, since 1756 it had been the meetinghouse for black Philadelphians drawn to Friends' quiet worship. Few of the Quaker patriciate attended. Witnessing the brief ceremony, Rebecca Jones, Philadelphia's greatly admired traveling minister, noted that in contrast to other Quaker weddings it was "more in simplicity and with less parade than I have ever seen on the like occasion." "I fear," she wrote, "they will not have many followers in this city," in itself a reflection on Ann Emlen's singularity.[93]

The ceremony was indeed simple. In a stripped-down version of the usual vows, Warner stood with hat covering his head and, as custom required, spoke first:

It is I trust in a measure of the reverent sensibility of the presidency of the holy fear of God Almighty that we now appear in order to enter into the solemn covenant of Marriage which I now on my part do, by proceeding to say: that I take this my Friend Ann Emlen to be my Wife, promising through the Lord's Assistance to be unto her a Loveing &

**Figure 12.** The meetings for black Philadelphians had been held at Bank Meetinghouse since 1756, giving poignancy to the marriage there of Warner Mifflin and Ann Emlen. Haverford College Library.

Faithful Husband until we shall be by Death separated or until Death shall separate us.

Ann's response was even simpler:

Under a sense of the fear of God & in the presence of this assembly, I take this my Friend Warner Mifflin to be my Husband promising through the assistance of God to be unto him a loveing & faithful Wife until Death shall separate us.

If the vows were lean, their dress was equally simple. Witnessing the ceremony, one of the attending Friends described Warner as dressed in a suit of "plain clothes, far from being new, but the majesty of his presence caused all trivial circumstances to be overlooked." Ann said her vows clad as plainly and colorlessly as possible: the dress, bonnet, shawl, and cloak were all of "brown Holland linen." Only her cap was white, "made of fine linen perfectly plain and tied with white linen tape under the chin." For this observer, Ann's glowing countenance still shone through: "Under this peculiar garb," wrote Elizabeth Brookes, daughter of one of the founders of the Quaker Sandy Spring meeting north of present-day Washington, D.C., "the beauty for which she had been conspicuous was not impaired." Staying after the bridal pair left the meeting-house, "her fashionable friends" were united in thinking that "she had done all in her power to disfigure her beautiful face and person, but to no purpose."[94]

Warner was now yoked with a woman of fierce religiosity who was to become one of the mid-Atlantic's most notable female Quaker ministers. He could only hope that she would be a pillar of support for his efforts on behalf of enslaved and freed Africans. Five weeks into the marriage he wrote his kinsman John Parrish: "I think I have got a companion that is likely to exceed my expectation for a country wife, and the harmony among the children is yet comfortable and I have no doubt of its continuance."[95]

Once settled at Chestnut Grove, Ann adjusted to life with a spouse she had never imagined she wanted. While becoming stepmother to five and household manager supervising free blacks and their children awaiting freedom, she threw herself into the work of the Murderkill Monthly Meeting. Within a few months she was appointed to committees of the women's meeting, and in less than a year as a representative to the Southern Quarterly Meeting that met across the peninsula at Third Haven, Maryland.[96]

Several weeks after their marriage, with the opportunity to resume his political lobbying but stymied by his desire to carry his mission to England, Mifflin saddled up, this time bound for Annapolis to deliver a petition to the General Assembly for repealing a law blocking the manumission of slaves and another "respecting the Mulatto children." Mifflin thought the friends of Africans in Maryland were gaining ground among younger members of the legislature's lower house, some of whom "expressed some noble sentiments" after the Quaker petition was considered paragraph by paragraph. Older hands in the upper house squelched the efforts, though the legislature would shortly repeal the 1752 law barring testamentary manumission.[97]

Rebuffed once more in Maryland, Mifflin turned again in late 1788 to his fixation with visiting the London Yearly Meeting and other English meetings of discipline, convinced he could bring lost sheep back to the fold and eager to spread his antislavery doctrine. Again the Philadelphia Ministers and Elders would not approve. Undisclosed in their minute books are explicit reasons to deny a traveling certificate, but it can be deduced from the sources that the ministers and elders worried about Mifflin's inability to rein in his passionate commitment to what many Friends saw as a hopeless cause. Rebecca Jones, his Philadelphia friend and a veteran minister who had logged thousands of miles traveling through England, Scotland, Ireland, and most of the Atlantic coast as a "publisher of the truth," counseled him to "to let patience have its perfect work."[98] The Quaker leadership—some of them were his closest confidants in the city—struggled for a full year to find a way to keep him homebound. The matter became a major topic of discussion without resolution until one member—in Quaker fashion the name was carefully left unmentioned in the minutes—raised a procedural question about the "propriety and authority" of the Duck Creek Monthly Meeting granting a certificate "for a member in his station." Thus, because he was not a minister (though an elder), Mifflin's application was denied. He acceded quietly. "My mind feels quite calm and composed respecting England," he wrote Henry Drinker, his constant correspondent. Though he thought he had "been right in opening the matter before my friends," he believed "it is my duty patiently to abide their determination . . . and I love the brethren." Perhaps part of the sting was removed when Mifflin was elected to the Pennsylvania Abolition Society.[99] That Ann was now three months pregnant may also have settled his mind on the matter.

## In the Nation's Capital

In her eighth month of pregnancy, Ann Mifflin bade her husband farewell in February 1790 as Warner left Chestnut Grove to join ten Quaker leaders, mostly from Philadelphia, in a campaign to persuade the first Federal Congress to consider ways to end the slave trade, to consider gradual abolition plans, and to ameliorate the conditions under which some 700,000 enslaved blacks suffered. Quakers were well aware that the southern states were determined to put slavery beyond the reach of federal authority and that the slave trade, already banned in ten states but given a twenty-year lease in the Constitution, was regarded only as a state matter. South Carolina had used that option by reopening the slave trade in 1783 after a ten-year hiatus. As for a plan to end slavery, the odds seemed insurmountable. And asking for legislative remedies for slave masters to treat their bound laborers as human beings rather than "brute beasts" required convincing the new national Congress to privilege human rights over property rights.

Yet Friends knew that a pool of antislavery support lay outside the Society of Friends and that the immunity of slavery and the slave trade from federal regulation had not yet been definitively determined. They also knew that rancor still existed over the Constitutional Convention's extension of the slave trade for twenty years.[100] Indeed, the Lower South—South Carolina and Georgia—were the only fierce backers of a continued slave trade.

Meanwhile, the gradual abolition of slavery in the Upper South had the support, at least in the abstract, of such luminaries as Luther Martin, William Pinkney, and Gustavus Scott of Maryland; and George Washington, Edmund Pendleton, Patrick Henry, Thomas Jefferson, George Wythe, and St. George Tucker of Virginia. Just five years before, a Methodist petition to the House of Delegates in Virginia to enact a gradual general emancipation of slaves, though dismissed, was not, according to James Madison, "without an avowed patronage of its principle by sundry respectable members."[101] From Paris, Jefferson in 1787 wrote that "from the mouth to the head of the Chesapeake, the bulk of the people will approve it [the extirpation of slavery] in theory, and it will find a respectable minority ready to adopt it in practice, a minority which for weight and worth of character preponderates against the greater number, who have not the courage to divest their families of a property which however keeps their consciences unquiet." When Brissot de Warville visited Washington in 1788, he found the president-to-be in favor of gradual abolition, though convinced that most Virginians were not ready for it.[102]

Whether or not the time was ripe, a broader matter that had surfaced during the ratification debates could not be driven underground. "A renewed sense among some politically aware Americans" existed, writes David Waldstreicher, "that morality, and ideas, could not be compromised without great risk." This is exactly what the Quakers had in mind, tapping into the refusal of many Americans, even though the constitution had been ratified, "to believe that the Constitution, or even America, was the ultimate source of their cherished ideals," and that "some standard outside the nation, one that did not require the benediction from the founding fathers, ought to be the source of legitimacy, a polestar in making political judgments."[103]

Far from being the hopelessly naïve, delusional idealists that many historians have depicted, Warner Mifflin and his fellow Quakers were experienced lobbyists and men fiercely intent on trying to save the nation from the seeds of self-destruction that continued to germinate with slave dealing and slaveholding.[104] Attuned to the widespread hatred of the slave trade and the considerable sentiment for a gradual abolition of slavery, they were especially encouraged by the glare of publicity on both sides of the Atlantic occasioned by a bone-chilling depiction of "tight packing" on the English slave ship *Brooks* that proved "to be among the most effective propaganda any social movement has ever created." First published in Great Britain in November 1788, it made its American appearance six months later when the Pennsylvania Abolition Society, working closely with the Philadelphia Meeting for Sufferings, arranged for Mathew Carey to print it in his *American Museum*, the nation's most widely read magazine. At the same time, Carey cast it off as a broadside, with 2,500 copies to be sent to antislavery supporters as far south as Charleston, South Carolina. The Pennsylvania Abolition Society rewrote the text written in London beneath the image, deleting the assurance that stopping the slave trade in no way implied the emancipation of slaves. "We have had an engraving of the print done here," wrote James Pemberton for the society to Friends in London, "in order to introduce it into one of our monthly publications, the American Museum, which hath a very extensive circulation, but we shall be obliged to accompany it with some additional remarks, suited to our more advanced stage of the business; because we observe that [your] publication cautiously avoids the Idea of Emancipation, & is confined solely to the abolition of the slave trade."[105]

Thus, the Quakers saw an opening. Mifflin and his friends knew that the effort before them faced mountainous obstacles, warranting a guarded optimism at best. But "we are not without hopes," wrote Pennsylvania Abolition Society vice-president James Pemberton, "that we shall acquire some strength from the proceedings of the Parliament of Great Britain," referring to the first time Parliament had debated the slave trade. And they could do no less. If God was on their side, this was no time for slackers. Appointed to the delegation to visit Congress, Mifflin would play the leading role in a carefully calculated lobbying effort, which set a precedent for modern pressure group American politics.[106] As for leaving Kent County in the middle of winter and placing his family responsibilities in the hands of his wife, it was not in his imagined range of possibilities to spurn the opportunity of influencing the national government.

Intending to travel by horse the 180 miles from Kent County to New York City, Mifflin was obliged by dirty weather and violent headaches to join other Philadelphia delegates on the stagecoach to Manhattan on February 5.[107] Whether Mifflin was suffering from migraine headaches is unclear, but this was the beginning of a recurrent problem that would plague him for the next

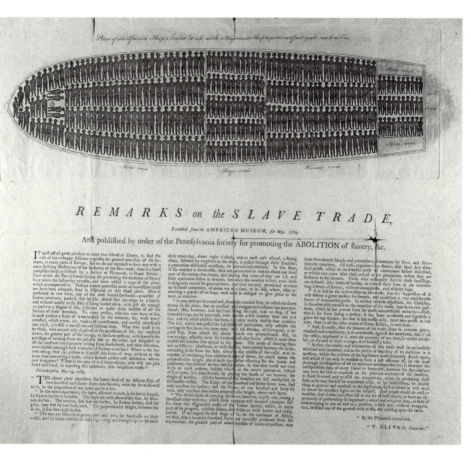

**Figure 13.** Cross-section of slave ship *Brooks*, Pennsylvania Abolition Society broadside (1789). Its depiction of the lower deck's "tight-packing," with labels for men's, women's, girls', and boys' sections, "presented to our view, one of the most horrid spectacles—a number of human creatures, packed side by side, almost like herrings in a barrel, and reduced nearly to the state of being buried alive, with just air enough to preserve a degree of life sufficient to make them sensible of all the horrors of their situation." Courtesy Historical Society of Pennsylvania.

eight years. The eleven-member Quaker delegation that reached New York City to launch the antislavery offensive (in the first sustained lobbying effort in American history) was an impressive lot. Bundled up in the stagecoach were two of the Winchester exiles—John Pemberton and Henry Drinker—and others with whom Mifflin had communed for years, including John Parrish, Jacob Lindley, his wife's uncle Samuel Emlen, Sr., Abraham Gibbons, and

Nicholas Waln. Staying in the city with the Quaker ironmonger William Shotwell, Mifflin soon emerged as the delegation's leader, though at age 46, he was much junior to such Quaker worthies as John Parrish (1730–1809), Henry Drinker (1734–1809), and John Pemberton (1727–1795) and much less eminent than others in the Society of Friends' legal and commercial transactions. But none matched him in depth of emotional attachment to suffering blacks, persistence in face-to-face contacts, and disarming forbearance even when viciously attacked.[108]

Clad in drab suits and broad-brimmed hats, Mifflin and his fellow lobbyists took their seats in the gallery of Federal Hall on February 11, observing the opening volleys on the issue widely regarded as the Congress's consummate concern—the adoption of Alexander Hamilton's "Report on Public Credit" that was meant to stabilize the nation's chaotic fiscal affairs (but made a mockery of the pay certificates issued to ordinary soldiers who, out of necessity, sold them to speculators at a fraction of their face value). Then, the dramatic moment struck. Roman Catholic Thomas Fitzsimmons of Pennsylvania brought forward the Philadelphia Quakers' memorial.

The Quaker petition, bearing Mifflin's name along with those of eighteen other Quaker leaders, appealed to Congress's authority as "guardians of the common rights of humanity . . . and the general well-being of the people over whom they preside." Citing the "public detestation" of the "wickedness of the African trade for slaves and the inhuman tyranny and blood guiltiness inseparable from it," as evidenced in the prohibition of the slave trade by ten states, the Quaker petition urged Congress to use "the full extent of your power" to "produce the abortion of the slave trade."[109]

With delegates from the Deep South already in a froth, John Laurance of New York presented a second petition from the New York Yearly Meeting, imploring Congress to plug a legal loophole used by Massachusetts and Rhode Island slave traders, who were banned from outfitting slave ships in their states, by contracting with New York shipbuilders to do the bloody job for them. In this way, American merchants and seamen, almost entirely northerners, carried many thousand slaves from Africa to the West Indies.[110]

Though the Quaker petitions were couched in circumspect language— neither mentioned the abolition of slavery—they set Congress aflame as if a lightning bolt had struck Federal Hall. South Carolina's Aedanus Burke, pointing to the Friends in the gallery, charged they "had come here to meddle in a business with which they have nothing to do." Georgia's William Jackson, "very violent and abusive," snarled that if the Quakers were "so desirous of freeing the negroes," they should provide "funds sufficient to pay for them." Moreover, they had not supported the war for independence or formed the Constitution. "Do they understand the rights of mankind, and the disposition of Providence, better than others?" he asked.[111] Thus began the new republic's first national debate on slavery.[112]

The next day, with the temperature just above zero, Federal Hall heated up quickly with the introduction of a third petition, this one from the Pennsylvania Abolition Society. In his near-death expiation of his previous slaveholding, ninety-year-old Benjamin Franklin had lent his vast prestige as president of the expanded, religiously diverse society membership and set his hand to a petition more radical than those of the previous day. It urged Congress to go "to the very verge of the power vested in you for discouraging every species of traffic in the persons of our fellow men" and to consider "all justifiable endeavors to loosen the bands of slavery" and "countenance the restoration of liberty to those unhappy men, who alone, in this land of freedom are degraded into perpetual bondage."[113] Whereas the Quaker memorials were limited to the traffic in slaves, the Pennsylvania Abolition Society memorial struck at slavery itself. As would soon become apparent, this was akin to pouring fuel on smoldering tinder.

Watching from the gallery, Mifflin had more than a hint of the work before him. "Do [these men] expect a general emancipation of slaves?" thundered South Carolina's Thomas Tucker. "This would never be submitted to by the Southern states without a civil war." Jackson of Georgia, a leading flame thrower, warned that even taking up the three memorials would bring "revolt, insurrection, and devastation." In retort, Pennsylvania's Thomas Scott declared if he were appointed a federal judge, he might rule in favor of any slave making a claim of freedom, to which Jackson replied that such a judge would shorten his life immediately. Infuriated, Aedanus Burke growled that "too much attention has been paid" to Mifflin and his friends and even made a motion for clearing the gallery.[114] At stake, it now became clear, was not only Congressional action on slavery and the slave trade but the right in a democracy to petition elected representatives.

Trying to extinguish the flames and get back to the funding and assumption issue, Speaker of the House James Madison urged referral of the petitions to a committee charged with probing the boundaries of Congress's power over slavery and the slave trade. After two days of sulfurous debate, featuring attacks on the Quakers as unfaithful Americans who had sat out the Revolution, the House voted 43–11 on February 12 for referral to a special committee chaired by Abiel Foster, the stern Congregational minister from New Hampshire.[115] The right of petition was thus affirmed. Mifflin must have been encouraged that most Congressmen representing states that had already banned slave importations, including eleven of the fourteen delegates from Virginia and Maryland, agreed that the implied powers clause of the Constitution had left uncertain the extent of federal authority to deal with slave traffic and slavery itself.[116]

With an initial victory in getting full consideration of the antislavery memorials in the House, Mifflin and his friends pushed to get the petitions introduced in the Senate as well. Presiding over the upper house, Vice President John Adams, never interested in the antislavery issue, first delayed consideration of the memorials and then, "rather with a sneer," introduced "the silly petition of Franklin and his Quakers" on February 15. After brushing off a visit from one or more of the Quakers—Mifflin was almost certainly one of them—he said, sarcastically, that "he had been honored with a visit from a Society, a self constituted one he supposed." Adams engineered a "lie-on-the-table" response to the memorials.[117]

Once the Quaker and Pennsylvania Abolition Society memorials had been referred to a special committee, seven of the Quaker lobbyists headed home on February 16, concerned that their entreaties would amount to nothing. They reached Philadelphia after a bone-rattling overturn of the New York-Philadelphia carriage while crossing a stream. Only John Pemberton, Warner Mifflin, John Parrish, and Samuel Emlen remained, though now joined by the talented Quaker lawyer Miers Fisher, a Quaker exiled to Virginia during the revolution.[118]

Mifflin now moved into high gear. At the Foster committee's request for grist, Mifflin and his friends gathered a collection of antislavery materials, including Thomas Clarkson's by now widely known *Essay on the Slavery and Commerce of the Human Species, particularly the African* (1786) and *Essay on the Impolicy of the African Slave Trade* (1788). Meanwhile, Mifflin wrote out testimony for the committee's first meeting to guide their deliberations. This was encouraging—that the committee would look to a maligned Quaker for worthy arguments.[119]

Though suffering from a respiratory infection, Mifflin conferred with members of the Foster committee, giving them talking points to consider. On

about February 15, he appeared to provide the first recorded oral testimony
before a Congressional committee. How, constitutionally, could Congress
stop New York City entrepreneurs from fitting out ships for the slave trade?
Could Congress frame "regulations respecting the conditions of the oppressed
Africans now held in Bondage"? How might Congress stop the reenslavement
of manumitted blacks in North Carolina and Virginia? And would Congress
recommend to Georgia and South Carolina, the only states still allowing slave
importation, that they halt the nefarious trade?[120]

Then came a moment that surely buoyed Mifflin's spirits while solidifying
his connections with the Atlantic-wide antislavery network. St. John de Crèvecoeur, who through his 1784 French edition of *Letters from an American Farmer*
had nearly enshrined Mifflin in French Enlightenment circles and made him
a byword for such French antislavery advocates as Brissot, had taken up the
position of French consul to New York in 1787. A dinner was arranged on
February 22, when Mifflin and Miers Fisher, a close friend of Crèvecoeur and
Brissot, "spent several hours there much to their satisfaction."[121] Doubtless,
the three men talked about the antislavery petitions in the hands of every
Congressman.

While the Foster committee deliberated, Mifflin continued his multi-
pronged lobbying campaign through what had become face-to-face tactics.
He did not spare button-holing Congressmen. "Members were way-laid in the
lobby of Congress [in Federal Hall] [and] were assailed in their own houses,"
grumped William Loughton Smith of South Carolina, pointing his finger at
Mifflin, who had appeared without warning at their lodgings to press the
Quakers' cause. Even the most fire-eating proslavery southerner, Mifflin told
himself, was not beyond his ability to reach. Putting aside the invective William
Smith had heaped on the Quaker lobbyists, Mifflin arrived at the South Carolinian's lodging on February 28. "Mifflin, a great fellow near seven foot high,"
Smith sputtered, "stalked into my parlour and sat two hours" whereupon "we
endeavoured to convert each other in vain." From there, Mifflin went on to
the lodging of South Carolina's Ralph Izard, where Smith found them an hour
later "attacking each other with texts of Scripture." With his usual equanimity,
Mifflin asked Smith and other southern Congressmen to dine with the Quaker
delegation to continue the discussion.[122]

After the Foster committee resumed its work, Miers Fisher obtained a draft
copy of a rough outline, springing Mifflin into action with "Queries to the
Committee" that asked "whether Congress have not full and clear power to

prevent any citizen . . . from being concerned in the African slave trade to foreign parts" and "whether their power do not extend to prevent foreigners fitting out vessels in any of the ports of the United States, for the slave trade, under heavy penalties." This was a fallback position, zeroing in on Manhattan's ship fitters intent on capturing profits by way of an end run around New York's ban on the slave trade.[123] Meeting with the committee, Mifflin followed up by insisting in writing to the committee chair that, notwithstanding the claims of southern Congressmen that Quakers had no standing on matters of slavery since they were not themselves slaveowners, "we have a right to propagate from one end of the earth to the other [their Golden Rule maxim] even if some might be touched in a tender spot thereby, to the raising a tumult against us, as the shrine-makers to Diana of Ephesus did against Paul." Noting that "we are from our homes, on no other business," Mifflin pressed for expediency in delivering the committee report.[124] That the committee would entertain Mifflin enraged Deep South Congressmen. Smith of South Carolina deplored how the Quakers "obtruded themselves into the committee with a ready made report in their hands, calculated to violate the constitution and overturn the government."[125]

Mifflin must have had mixed feelings when he saw the committee report released on March 5. Though "the general spirit of the report was antislavery" in the view of one historian, in most of its particulars it provided little comfort. Sections 1 and 2 reported that the committee could find constitutional grounds neither for interfering with the slave trade until 1808 nor "interfering in the emancipation of slaves." Yet Section 3 presented the hope that states would "revise their laws from time to time . . . and promote the objects mentioned in the [antislavery] memorials"—"instruction of slaves in the principles of morality and religion," "comfortable clothing, accommodation and subsistence," "the regulation of their marriages and the prevention of the violation of the rights thereof," an avoidance of "the separation of children from their parents," maintenance of those sick, aged, or infirm, and ways to prevent "the seizure, transportation, or sale of free negroes." This did nothing to curb the master's total control of his human property, but only appealed to "the wisdom and humanity of the legislatures of the several states." Additional sections asserted Congress's authority to lay a tax up to ten dollars for each imported slave and to prohibit fitting out of ships in any American port "for transporting persons from Africa to any foreign port."[126] The latter was a signal victory for the antislavery activists.

Mifflin and his Quaker compatriots eagerly awaited the debate over the committee report, sitting day after day while the House debated Hamilton's funding and assumption bill. "We attend generally at the [Federal] Hall to shew ourselves," wrote John Pemberton, "& to remind them we are waiting upon them"—that is, sitting in the gallery, eagle-eyed, to let them know that as representatives of the people, they were being held to account.[127]

Hard-shell southern delegates, led by Smith of South Carolina, maneuvered to postpone debate on the Foster report for as long as possible, hoping to exhaust Mifflin and his friends, already a month away from their homes.[128] This did not take measure of Mifflin and his cohort's tenacity. Still hoping to soften the Carolinian's hostility, Mifflin composed a long letter delivered to Smith while he was seated in Federal Hall. "I love thee—I wish thee well—and would not injure thee knowingly more than I would myself; then why is it not proper to stile thee my friend?" wrote Mifflin. "I never have been offended with thee—not even . . . when in thy company what thou hadst said about Quakers." That said, Mifflin assured Smith that he was not in favor of an immediate emancipation of slaves, but only one "by gradation." He tried to scotch the notion peddled by the southern delegates that he abetted runaway slaves. He did insist, however, that holding slaves violated scripture in Mark 12: 30–31, that "Thou shalt love the Lord thy God, with all thy heart, soul, and strength, and thy neighbour as thyself"—a command understood "to include all the sons and daughters of men, of all nations, colours, and languages." In the meantime, he pleaded for action on ending the slave trade. "My concern is great, to stop . . . the wicked, barbarous, inhuman, and devilish trade to Africa for slaves. . . . Did the people of Africa injure us in any sense?" he asked. "Then why should we desire to so grievously afflict them?"[129]

Finally, after a series of delays, the Foster report was scheduled for discussion by a Committee of the Whole on March 16. Quick off the mark, Mifflin penned a last appeal to members of the House, engaging young men to make fourteen copies to be distributed by the doorkeeper. Imagine your mother, father, brother, sister, or wife, Mifflin asked the representatives, "torn from all, which men call dear, and put on board a vessel owned by a citizen of America, and to be fitted out of one of the ports of the United States . . . or by a foreigner coming . . . to procure a cargo, for such a voyage, among which cargo were hogsheads of iron handcuffs made by an American in this land of freedom." Writing when his wife was in the ninth month of her pregnancy, he concluded by insisting he was "as tenacious of supporting the union as any of the southern delegates" and "a well-wisher to the true interests and welfare of America." But in the face of "this ugly monster" of slavery, "I should rather my children had a period put to their existence, than to be" subjected to a slavery "worse than death."[130]

On the same morning, Mifflin stopped by President Washington's house on Broadway, hoping that an appeal made in person would move the man he had last seen thirteen years before to intercede or at least lend moral support.[131] Mifflin knew that, just months before, his Philadelphia Quaker friends had sent a delegation to salute Washington's ascent to the presidency and had presented him with Robert Barclay's *Apology for the True Christian Divinity* (1676)—a pillar of Quaker beliefs. Washington publicly replied that "(except their declining to share with others the burthen of the common defense) there is no denomination among us, who are more exemplary and useful citizens."[132] To Mifflin's delight, the president gave him ample time to present his arguments, all too familiar to the president, concerning the "immorality, injustice and impolicy" of maintaining slavery. Mifflin assured Washington, as the president noted in his diary, that the Friends "did not wish for more than a gradual abolition or to see any infraction of the Constitution to effect it." Washington carefully parried Mifflin's arguments—"I was not inclined to express any sentiments on the merits of the question"—but at least Mifflin had reestablished his credentials with the nation's president.[133]

It became clear later on the snowy morning of March 16, the first day of debating the Foster committee report, that Mifflin's entreaties had no effect on the Deep South Congressmen. Taking his accustomed seat in the gallery, where raffish, often jeering, and generally indecorous spectators shared space with the staid Friends, Mifflin quickly found that representatives from the Deep South had concocted "a carefully conceived strategy of character defamation."[134] Even a modicum of dignity was in short supply when proslavery representatives took the floor, first trying to block consideration of the Foster report, then filibustering to wear down the opposition, and finally attacking it with a vitriol that shocked even some of their northern supporters, as well as James Madison. The verbal assaults on Quakers went on for days, closely noted in the New York newspapers. In a double-barreled strategy, Georgia and South Carolina delegates defended slavery by picturing Africa as a misery for its inhabitants, the slave trade as a humanitarian rescue operation, and lifelong and heritable enslavement as a benevolent and gentle system of labor, where slaves were well housed, clothed, fed, and doctored, and in old age lived "at ease and in great plenty." Coupled with this were attacks on the Quaker "fanatics," the "rascally society of people called Quakers." "The northern States adopted us with our slaves," expostulated William Loughton Smith, "and we adopted them with their Quakers." Pointing to them in the gallery, Smith brayed that they sat in their broad-brimmed hats "like evil spirits hovering over our heads in the gallery."[135]

Laced through the attacks on the abolitionist petitions was the white southern specter of racial intermixing. Six years before, in his famous *Notes on Virginia*, Jefferson, despite his liaison with his slave Sally Hemings, had frankly stated his aversion to racial intermingling, insisting that once freed, the black male had "to be removed beyond the reach of mixture" lest the nation be stained. Reflecting Jefferson's dark fear of interracial sex, Deep South delegates riddled the debate with portrayals of a "mongrel" nation that the likes of Warner Mifflin, in their reading, would produce. Reading aloud the telling excerpts from *Notes on Virginia* where Jefferson labeled Africans "by nature an inferior race of beings" and called the mixing of races a crime against nature, Smith sputtered that interracial sex would be the inevitable result of emancipation, that if such a mixture of blood should take place, "then the white race would be extinct and the American people would be all of the mulatto breed."[136]

Mifflin was an unlikely target on the face of it in the fear-mongering about miscegenation, for he had never spoken a word on the subject and was a stalwart member of the Society of Friends, who had not, to this point, made more than occasional moves toward welcoming blacks into their worship. But knowing that most white northerners shared the southern white distaste for interracial intercourse, the southern firebrands jumped on the issue as a rhetorical bludgeon to bring Northerners to their side. Seeing Mifflin and his friends in the gallery, Jackson of Georgia leered "however fond the Quakers may be of this mixture and of giving their daughters to negroes' sons, and receiving the negro daughters for their sons, there will be those who will not approve of the breed, and a motley breed it will be." Let the Quakers go to Africa to practice their "humane speculations," he dilated; "There they may marry and be given in marriage, and have a motley race of their own."[137]

Heralded by Crèvecoeur and Brissot as the epitome of Quaker humanitarianism, Mifflin now became for Lower South representatives the embodiment of hypocrisy, smug moralism, and officiousness. Singled out for particular venom, he was the only Quaker named in six days of verbal abuse. Ridiculing "the foolish petitions from the people called Quakers," Jackson ranted about Mifflin's role in leading the Quaker delegation. Should the Congress tamper with slavery and the slave trade "for the gratification of a volunteering society of Quakers?" he spouted, "for the gratification of a *Warner Mifflin*?" Mifflin emancipated his slaves, Jackson thundered, not as an "act of humanity"; rather, it was a feeble attempt of a man "trembling under the lash of an evil conscience and fearing the just punishment of an avenging rod in a thunder storm to atone for his numerous hoard of former sins."[138] Calling Mifflin "this leader of sedition," Jackson's attack left Madison shaking his head that "the Gentlemen from S. Carolina & Georgia are intemperate beyond all example and even all decorum. They are not content palliating slavery as a deep-rooted abuse, but plead for the lawfulness of the African trade itself" and "lavish the most virulent language on the authors of [the Quaker memorials]."[139]

As the slavery debate reached a climax, one of the Lower South delegates published the most lacerating and scurrilous attack on Quakers that had reached public prints in a century. Readers of the *New York Journal*, treated to a new high in journalistic billingsgate, learned that only "avarice, interest, passion, or fanaticism" motivated Quakers. Their "illiberal, violent, and abusive petitions," aiming at a general emancipation, "may loosen the fidelity of the slave to his master; the bloody standard of rebellion may be raised, reciprocal massacre and carnage may ensue." The slave, "who was contented with slavery, who whistled and sung in the field of his master," would curse the "cruel mercies of the Quakers," and if "friend M-ff-n [Mifflin] was on the slave coast [of Africa], they [the Africans] would hang him for his doctrines" because enslavement in America was for them a supreme blessing. Once emancipated, the black male would head north "to marry Quakers' daughters, and to drink cider with eastern representatives."[140]

The attacks on the Quakers and the defense of slavery as a benevolent institution continued through lengthy speeches on March 19, 22, and 23. Still hoping for a last-minute change in the positions of representatives, Mifflin invited a number of them to dinner on March 23. However, the cause was already lost, when the House that day tabled the Foster committee report, agreeing to Madison's compromise to end debate while allowing both the committee report and an amended report of the Committee of the Whole House to be recorded in the House journals. Madison's compromise brought the five-week matter to a close. The closest analyst of the First Congress's pyrotechnic debates on the slavery question calls this the "burial" of the two reports "in an unmarked grave."[141]

The satisfaction that Mifflin could take from his six weeks in New York owed little to the final result, since the Congress asserted no authority to regulate the conditions of slavery or stop the slave trade. The Quaker delegation knew the chances were all but nil and noted this to their London friends.[142] But for Mifflin, beyond becoming a practiced lobbyist, there were two small victories. First, the Quakers' long vigil in New York protected the right to petition Congress, defeating southern attempts to implant a gag rule to foreclose any discussion of Congress's authority to deal in any way with slavery or the slave trade.[143]

Second, the Friends succeeded in capturing national attention.[144] The diatribes of Jackson, Burke, Smith, and Baldwin roused Benjamin Franklin, revered on both sides of the Atlantic, to strike his last blow against slaveholding. Nearly on his deathbed, Franklin sent his last prose piece to the *Federal Gazette*, satirizing the Deep South attacks on the Quaker petitions and casting Mifflin as the central figure in the affair. Substituting Algerian Muslims who kidnapped Christians and held them in slavery for Lower South slaveholders and billing Warner Mifflin as a member "of the sect called Erika or Purists," Franklin had Sidi Mehemet Ibrahim, the Divan of Algiers, proclaim, "If some of the religious mad bigots who now teaze us with their silly petitions have in a fit of blind zeal freed their slaves, it was not generosity, it was not humanity that moved them to the action; it was from the conscious burthen of a load of sins, and hope from the supposed merits of so good a work to be excused from damnation. How grossly are they mistaken in imagining slavery to be disallowed by the Alcoran." Nobody conversant with the extended debate at Federal Hall could mistake Sidi Mehemet Ibrahim from Jackson of Georgia or the Erika-Purist from Warner Mifflin. Closely dovetailing Jackson's and Smith's intemperate speech with Ibrahim's arguments, Franklin had the Muslim repeat all the threadbare Deep South arguments: that Algerians rescued Christians from a sunless and sordid existence; that when they were enslaved they were treated with kindness; if they were freed Algiers would become an economic sink. If the Christians were emancipated they would not adopt Islam but would have to be supported as beggars, because "men accustomed to slavery will not work for a livelihood when not compelled," and would curse their liberators, since "our people will not pollute themselves by intermarrying with them."[145] Reprinted in Boston, Newport, Providence, New York City, and Baltimore, Franklin's mordant satire put him on the side of the Quaker emancipationists. Less than a month later, he died on April 17, 1790, heralded for a long life as the globe's most accomplished American.[146]

A weary Mifflin, plagued by headaches and winter colds, left New York on March 25, arriving at Chestnut Grove only twelve days before Ann Mifflin delivered their first child. By this time, he was marked by Deep South slaveowners as the most dangerous man in America. When Ann delivered a boy on April 6, 1790, she and Warner named the infant Samuel Emlen Mifflin after Ann's brother and uncle, the latter Warner's fellow delegate in New York. A few days later, Ann wrote in her commonplace book prayer-like verses to express her religious devotion and her awareness of the precariousness of life among the newborn:

> Thanks to thee my sovereign Lord
> For mercies thou has sent
> Who with the blessings thou affords
> Adds that of sweet content
>
> Preserve him 'midst each dangerous ill
> That oft encounter youth
> As though thy grace his bosom fill
> With righteousness and truth
> . . .
> And in like faith which they professt
> As ancient records tell
> A name is given in which I rest
> And name him Samuel.[147]

Warner's emotions at his wife's safe delivery are not revealed in his correspondence or autobiographical writings. But it is clear, as we will see in the next chapter, that the advent of his second set of children did nothing to diminish his antislavery fervor and his determination to purge the nation of its indelible sin of oppressing African people.

# Chapter 5

## Finish Line

*"I think it my duty* to tell you plainly that I believe the blood of the slain, and the oppression exercised in Africa promoted by Americans and in this country also, will stick to the skirts of every individual of your [legislative] body, who exercise the powers of legislation and do not exert their talents to clear themselves of this abomination, when they shall be arraigned before the tremendous bar of the judgment-seat of him who will not fail to do right in rendering unto every man his due."[1] Such were the words of Warner Mifflin in 1793 when again, after facing off against the nation's Congress in his emancipationist crusade, he took to the public prints to mobilize public opinion. As for almost two decades, this mission of mercy on behalf of black Americans had been his consuming passion.

This chapter chronicles the final eight-year chapter of Mifflin's travail, much of it as his struggle for life with a failing body was compounded by family tragedy and setbacks in managing his properties in mid-Delaware. Always fighting against an incoming tide of southern determination to protect slavery in Congress and to extend it to the vast Mississippi Territory opening up to cotton production, he had at his back a countervailing wave of antislavery sentiment sparked by the mass rebellion of slaves in French St. Domingue. Mifflin's antislavery work in the early 1790s had particular resonance as the volcanic eruption of slave rebellion in the Caribbean triggered intense discussion in the seaboard cities, particularly in Philadelphia, about whether the universalistic principles of the American Revolution were not at work in the overthrow of the Caribbean's most horrendous slave regime—and how that might awaken Americans to the danger of turning a deaf ear to calls for a gradual abolition of slavery.[2]

But Mifflin would have to convince an unstable court of public opinion, torn between celebrating and deploring the tumultuous French Revolution,

trammeled by the rise of a Jeffersonian party that contested Federalist domi-
nance, and caught up in the Whiskey Insurrection and war against native
peoples west of the Allegheny Mountains. Quaker abolitionists such as Mifflin
had always been a sliver of the populace, regarded by many as naïve, misguided,
and piously judgmental, and by the mid-1790s the tide of antislavery opinion
had crested. Yet Mifflin pushed on, plodding by horse to state legislatures, one
after another, where incremental advances might be gained as the omnipresent
God, as he understood it, watched from above and allowed him another lease
on life. The lease, fate decreed, would come to an abrupt end.

## Playing to the Public

Though historians have almost uniformly regarded the Quaker efforts at the
first Federal Congress as a failure, mid-Atlantic Quaker leaders were far from
discouraged. Indeed, their admiration for Mifflin's unceasing efforts grew.
"Warner Mifflin has been abusively treated," wrote James Bringhurst, a Philadelphia merchant and Quaker activist, "for his valiantly standing forth and
doing all he well could in that cause in favor of those injured and oppressed
Africans, a cause wherein he has long labored and I believe to some good
purpose." "He and other friends," Bringhurst continued, "seem well satisfied
with having been industriously engaged in the service; although that success
has not immediately attended their labours that was desirable, yet have a hope
real benefit will be the result from it in time."[3]

Was this whistling in the wind? Mifflin thought not, and he had the encouragement of men such as George Thatcher of Massachusetts, who was sure "that
righteousness will finally prevail" and that nothing was "more delicious than
those of beholding the happiness of others springing from our labour and toil."[4]
Further encouragement came from James Madison. Opposed to slavery in
theory and sympathetic to Quaker efforts to ameliorate the condition of the
enslaved, the speaker of the House of Representatives had advised John Parrish
that, while it was hopeless to raise the issues tabled in March 1790, he encouraged Friends to bring forward any information on the fitting out of foreign
slave ships in American ports or instances of "American bottoms to supply
foreigners with slaves," for the House had voted that it was within its power to
prevent this without "infringing on the Constitution." Parrish did just that.
Enclosing a list of ten Rhode Island ships clearing port for the slave trade and

reporting that fourteen others had been fitted out in New York, he pleaded that "may it never be said that the Americans have so little sense of true liberty . . . that after having establishing their own liberty they continue to make depredations upon others."[5]

And so Mifflin moved forward. In May 1790, intent on keeping the slave trade and slavery issue before the public, he sent the House of Representatives, just before the first session of the first federal Congress adjourned, a long defense of the Quakers' petitions and their lobbying efforts as a conscience-driven effort to remedy what much of the nation admitted was a shameful contradiction of its founding principles—the continuing slave trade and the incessant trampling on the natural rights of hundreds of thousands of black Americans.[6]

Testifying on behalf of "that cruelly oppressed part of our fellow men, the people of Africa," Mifflin proffered that his was a duty owed to "my country and countrymen." Carefully thanking "the kind reception" offered to the Quaker delegation by many members of the House, he asked readers to consider the charges that Quakers were "useless to civil community" and think "whether such scoffers and revilers do not, either blindly or willfully, reproach the Christian religion," with its Golden Rule a fixed principle. Then he slipped in a pacifist dig against those "who found their boast of usefulness in the world on their attachment to the exercise of arms, or what in their creed is styled military virtue." But his central argument was that the new nation dared not turn away from spurning "the common rights of men" and "the violated rights of humanity." It was "clearly in the power of the Legislature of the United States, greatly to obstruct . . . the pursuit of this iniquitous traffic, if not to put an effectual stop thereto, without infringing the constitutional right of any branch of the confederation." Only in this way could the nation's elected representatives "remove the foul guilt and reproach from our land" flowing from the "sordid and dishonest practice of trading in the life and liberty of our fellow men." The "well being of either our Christian community in particular, or that of civil society in general," hung in the balance.[7]

Whatever the House of Representatives thought of Mifflin's piece, the real point was to put it before the public.[8] In his first effort to thrust himself into the public prints—newspapers and magazines filled with political opinion were proliferating in the early 1790s—Mifflin found a willing ally in Benjamin Rush, a warm-hearted friend of the emerging free black community in Philadelphia. Already, Rush had prevailed on Mathew Carey to publish Mifflin's

March address to the House of Representatives, his long letter to William Loughton Smith of South Carolina, the "Queries" presented to the Foster committee, and a letter to its chairman, Abiel Foster, in the August 1790 issue of the widely subscribed *American Museum*.[9] In October, Carey followed up with Mifflin's Address to the House of Representatives, and in December he published the plan for gradual emancipation in Virginia by Ferdinando Fairfax, a protégé of Washington and a man deeply embedded in the Virginia planter aristocracy.[10]

Of course not everyone was convinced by Mifflin's efforts, but such closely constructed appeals to universal liberty and the brotherhood of all mankind gave the reading public the chance to measure who was fanatical and who was humane and truly Christian. Through it all, Mifflin showed his forbearance. Noting that while he was lobbying in New York, Deep South firebrands "personally held [me] up as a ringleader of sedition"; he assured Rush that "Tho the flames from the South should yet raise, I see nothing terrible in them, they are but men whose breath as well as mine is in their nostrils."[11]

Another entirely unexpected event, one of volcanic proportions, gave resonance to Mifflin's published pieces from the Congressional antislavery debate. The black rebellion in French St. Domingue, erupting in early 1791, was by far the greatest uprising of enslaved Africans in the Americas, and it promised to overthrow the most extensive exploitation of humans in the hemisphere. While the cauldron of bloodshed only a few hundred miles offshore shook southern slaveholders to their boots, leading them to stiffen discipline in the slave quarters, the reaction in the northern cities encouraged emancipationists to believe that the masters of the American slave regime had fair warning that it was time, with God watching, to deliver on the revolutionary promises that the adolescent republic was the beacon of universal freedom. Among those whose support of the insurrection in St. Domingue was published in Philadelphia was Connecticut's Abraham Bishop, a young egalitarian teacher, public orator, and lawyer (and previously an opponent of ratifying the Constitution). Ringing out from the pages of the city's *Federal Gazette* and *American Museum*, his words could not help but fortify the resolve of Mifflin, Pennsylvania Abolition Society stalwarts, and leaders of the Philadelphia Meeting for Sufferings: "Let us be consistent Americans; if we justify our own conduct in the late glorious Revolution, let us justify those who, in a cause like ours, fight with equal bravery." In words that Mifflin would have found familiar, Bishop proclaimed that the "Universal Father," looking down on the cataclysmic events playing out in St. Domingue, was finding further confirmation that "of one blood, he has created all nations of men that dwell on the face of the earth" (Acts 17:26).[12]

Others joined the chorus.[13] A stirring speech put before a Kentucky constitutional convention by Princeton-educated Presbyterian David Rice of Kentucky, titled "Slavery Inconsistent with Justice and Good Policy," came off the press in Philadelphia a few months later. Rice's claim that slaves in St. Domingue were pursuing "the natural rights of all rational beings" echoed Mifflin, reminding readers of Philadelphia's many newspapers and magazines that "universal freedom was part of a Providential plan."[14] As a pacifist, Mifflin no doubt regretted the death-dealing violence that consumed the French island; yet how could he not applaud how the standard of racial equality and universal human rights had been raised? Bishop and Rice's pronouncements, obliterating the color line, were only the prelude of a torrent of antislavery missives that populated the columns of the seaboard newspapers in the early 1790s. From across the Atlantic in 1791 came copies of William Fox's *Address to the People of Great Britain on the Propriety of Abstaining from West India Sugar and Rum*—a runaway bestseller that easily eclipsed Thomas Paine's *Common Sense* as "the most widely distributed pamphlet of the eighteenth century."[15] Quickly reprinted in Philadelphia, Lancaster, New York, and Boston, Fox's chilling cries that every pound of West Indies sugar cost two ounces of African flesh and that every consumer became an accessory to murder pumped new life into Mifflin's continued antislavery lobbying.[16]

## Another Season of Lobbying

It did not take long for Mifflin to regroup after returning home. For the next three years he would shuttle between the nation's capital, resituated from New York to Philadelphia in December 1790, and the state capitals of Delaware and Maryland. He did so with his usual trepidation. "Fears and doubts assail [me] often," he wrote John Parrish, hoping he "had not overlaid the time" in New York. It was no mystery to him that some Friends thought his passion exceeded acceptable bounds, and he knew that he should not "be too confident in any of my steppings but to pursue the right direction through good report and bad report, craving that neither in heights nor depths, neither by smiles nor frowns," so that he should be able to please "his Holy will."[17]

Leaving the parenting of his older children and infant son to his wife and household servants and cutting himself adrift from his limping plantation economy, Mifflin resumed what he regarded as God's plan for him, when Delaware's legislature in early 1791 called a constitutional convention to revise the state's organic law. Mifflin immediately jumped into the fray. His five-page, closely written jeremiad, studded with biblical references, went to the state legislature even before the convention met. Could those elected to serve all the state's people sit by idly while existing laws are "trampled upon and evaded," whereby "not only have slaves been sold and carry'd off [out of Delaware]," while other black Delawareans who were freeborn or given freedom were cast into slavery? Could they tolerate bearing witness to Delaware slaveowners selling their fellow humans to a slave dealer who clapped them into irons at the county jails "for no crime whatever but for fear they might fly from the monster who had purchased them to carry [them] to the Carolinas or Georgia"? How could legislators charged "as guardians of the welfare of the people of this state" square this with the nation's founding declarations of human rights and universal freedom? "Divine indignation," he lectured, is on "the eve of being poured down upon the tyrannizing over fellow men." "I am both sorry and ashamed for my country," he confessed.[18]

While waiting for the Delaware constitutional convention to meet, Mifflin turned his attention to Maryland. As he had done so many times before, he crossed the peninsula as a delegate from Murderkill Monthly Meeting to the Southern Quarterly Meeting in Easton on the bayside. After stopping at the Third Haven Monthly Meeting to gather evidence of the "striking instances of cruelty" by which black families were sundered after one parent, or both, was sent in chains to the Carolinas or Georgia, he arrived in Annapolis in July. There, he provided details on how slave masters with surplus workers on their hands found a loophole to evade the Maryland law proscribing the sale of slaves out of state. It was all too easy: construct a deed of manumission with freedom to take place at age thirty-one, then offload the person to North Carolina to be sold for the years remaining until he or she reached thirty-one. The seller "incurs no penalty" and the purchaser "may hold the Negro a slave for life," since North Carolina law "prohibits liberation entirely." Though it was too late to present petitions to the Maryland legislature, Quaker lobbying eventually convinced the Maryland Assembly to pass a law levying fines for kidnapping and trafficking free blacks out of state, though the fines were so light they could easily be factored into the terms of the trading in human flesh.[19]

Disappointing results in Maryland did not deter Mifflin. When delegates elected by the Delaware legislature gathered to revise their constitution, Mifflin and his friends pressed the case for excising the cancer of slavery. His long letter to "the citizens of the Delaware State, and more particularly to the members of the convention now sitting at Dover," predicted that "the just judgments of GOD Almighty will be yet conspicuous in this land," in view of the "havoc there is made of the human species, as tho' they were the brute creation." Would the constitution writers allow the "seeds of slavery" to "vegetate," denying that "every human being in this state" should be "born free"? To do less, "our new Constitution, I believe will be a disgrace to the state in the eyes of the nations of the earth; and that it will be a Rottenness...that will sap the foundation, and I believe the just indignation of Heaven against it."[20] Submitted to the first session of the convention, it was read aloud but set aside as the delegates drafted a new constitution, printed it for consideration of the citizenry, and adjourned to meet in May 1792.[21]

Though the convention delegates included emancipationists such as Methodists Richard Bassett and Allen McLane and Presbyterians such as James Tilton and John McKinly, the hope for a gradual abolition clause faltered when the convention reconvened. It was not for lack of effort on the part of the Friends. Jumping into the deliberations, the Philadelphia Meeting for Sufferings drew up a strongly worded memorial that Mifflin presented to the convention in June 1792. Warning that "the eyes of distant nations are turned to view the conduct of the people of the American States," the petitioners exhorted the convention to live up to the inalienable rights clause of the Declaration of Independence by bringing slavery and the slave trade to an end. The Pennsylvania Abolition Society also weighed in with James Pemberton, its president, urging Dickinson, his kinsman, to "propose some means to alleviate the afflictions of the slaves and prevent the oppression and miseries to which they are subjected...by the separation of the nearest connections which...sorrowfully prevails in defiance of every obligation of humanity."[22]

President of the convention Dickinson reported that the memorial was "repeatedly and respectfully taken into consideration," and Mifflin was granted permission to address the convention.[23] But Dickinson did little to help. Though by this time more than half of all black Delawareans were free, and though he claimed that "It is and has been for some time past my earnest concern that slavery may be gradually and totally abolished," Dickinson waffled in the convention's final session. To be sure, the proslavery sentiment still ran strong, especially among Sussex County delegates. Dickinson was probably right that the efforts of reformers to get constitutional remedies for shipping slaves out of state and kidnapping free blacks for sale as slaves across Delaware's borders were asking for what should be legislative prerogatives. Nonetheless, he sounded much like the Lower South representatives from the first federal Congress. Measures that "irritated" slaveowners, he warned, "would really add to the distresses of those whom the humane desire to relieve." As well, "any pruning of this tree of bitter fruits would only strengthen it and make it last longer." In an astounding assertion unbecoming an astute lawyer and constitution writer, Dickinson further argued that any "alleviations of slavery by the convention would have been constitutional sanctions of it," as if slavery did not already have legal standing in Delaware.[24] Dickinson reminded Pemberton that he had drafted a gradual abolition law several years before but had withdrawn it when he saw no hope for its passage, and was still waiting for "a better prospect of success."[25] Living until 1808, Dickinson never found that "better prospect," though by the time of his death the percentage of blacks in Delaware who were enslaved had shrunk to less than 30 percent. Attending the meetings of the convention for all but one day from May 29 through June 12 to lobby the delegates, Mifflin had no success in getting his state to set slavery on the road to extinction. Pemberton made a last-ditch effort to get Dickinson to introduce a gradual abolition act in October 1792, to no avail.[26]

Where Mifflin did succeed was in beating back Dickinson's proposition to overturn the 1787 law that allowed free blacks to purchase and inherit land. No biographer or student of Dickinson's political writings has explained why this thoughtful man, supposedly sympathetic to the plight of black Delawareans, wanted to deny them one of the few liberties they held and one that formed the cornerstone of self-reliance. Nowhere in the northern states except New Jersey had such a cruel measure been contemplated. If passed—Dickinson's draft bill provided that "none but white persons shall hereafter be capable of becoming freeholders within this state"—it would have severely compromised the promise of free black life. Outraged, Mifflin wrote Dickinson that "he was as great an enemy to the cause of righteousness as [there] was" in the convention.[27]

Approved on June 12, 1792, the new constitution mainly advantaged ordinary white Delawareans. Following Pennsylvania's example, it extended the franchise to all free adult white men who paid even the slightest tax, while shifting the election of the governor, previously called the president, from the legislature to the people at large. At the same time it strengthened the governor's executive powers by giving him veto power over legislative bills. Lost in the process were some thirteen thousand blacks, nearly 70 percent of them still enslaved.

Even before Delaware's constitutional convention completed its work, Mifflin had resumed his attempts to sway the national government. He started with the president. To Washington, now installed in Robert Morris's house in Philadelphia, Mifflin composed a long, emotional letter in February 1791 about how the patriarch of Mount Vernon entered his mind, ghost-like, as he sat in silence at a Friends meeting. Describing how the president invaded his dream life as well, Mifflin offered this as a sign that the ever-watchful God "might design thee as an instrument" of his intentions for humankind. Generating these visions was the outbreak of war against Native Americans of the Ohio River valley, where Washington had ordered the Federal army, largely composed of Revolutionary War veterans, to proceed west under General Arthur St. Clair. Mifflin did not doubt that the new nation could overmatch the Indian nations, but he was also sure that "almost as barbarous treatment is exercised by whites on Indians and Negroes as any I have yet heard of by Indians toward whites." Surely drenching the earth with blood would bring chastisement from God.[28] By the end of the year, the Meeting for Sufferings memorialized President Washington and Congress with a similar peace testimony, urging a policy of "peace and friendship with the original owners of this land."[29] Received and read in the House of Representatives, it was promptly tabled.

A year later, Mifflin and the Philadelphia Yearly Meeting relaunched their campaign. In Mifflin's handwriting and signed by fifty-two others, their petition in November 1792 repeated the call for stanching the "effusion of blood" in the Ohio Valley and treating with native peoples in a just way. Though expressing their sympathies for "the distressed situation of the frontier [white] inhabitants," they urged that whites should not be permitted to settle on lands "which have not been purchased of the original owners." The petition was almost guaranteed a quick defeat when the House referred it to a committee of five that included two of Mifflin's chief tormentors from the First Congress—Baldwin of Georgia and Smith of South Carolina. Two weeks later, the House ordered the petition "to lie on the table," thus burying it. Yet the House upheld the right of petition.[30]

A few days later Mifflin shifted his attention back to what he regarded as the obligation of the American government, under the Constitution's general welfare clause, to address the festering cancer of slavery. While the leaders of the yearly meeting were unwilling to remount their 1790 campaign at the first Congress, they were content to see Mifflin strike out on his own.[31] In a memorial to President Washington and the Congress in November, Mifflin quoted the Declaration of Independence on self-evident truths and asked, "How then have those rights become alienated, that Americans shall be permitted to continue to ravage the coast of Africa, thereby promoting murder, pillaging, plundering and burning its towns and inslaving [sic] its inhabitants?" If the enslaved included "one of your beloved, delicate wives, your tender babes, or near relatives, how then would you feel?" As if sensing the biological holocaust that would strike Philadelphia nine months later, he predicted that "If measures are not taken to redress the wrongs, and alleviate the sufferings and oppression of the African race in these states, the Almighty will manifest his displeasure in a more conspicuous manner than has yet appeared."[32]

Mifflin surely knew that many in Congress were deists rather than providential Christians, but he played, as always, to God-fearing Protestants. "Do not you with me believe that there is a God of Justice?" he asked. Or, as children of the Enlightenment, how could signers of the Declaration of Independence avert their eyes when "avaricious men shall be permitted to pass through the country, steal, buy, traffick, barter and exchange the blacks, as though they were indeed brute beasts, separating husband from wife, parents from children, even mothers from infant babes?" Could the president and Congress put themselves in the place of their "suffering African brethren, who in this country may be loaded with irons, under all the pangs of sorrow the human heart can be capable of enduring, for no crime whatever but because it pleased God to suffer them to come into the world with a black skin?" Mifflin called for no specific legislative measures but, referring to foundational documents, simply called for American compliance "with their covenants and engagements."[33]

When this was introduced as a petition by Fisher Ames of Massachusetts on November 26, the resulting fireworks were entirely predictable given the sensitivity of southern representatives to the massive slave revolt in St. Domingue the previous year. John Steele of North Carolina unleashed the first salvo, surprised that the long debates in March 1790 had not convinced Mifflin, "a fanatic," to keep his silence. He was "not content with keeping his own conscience" but "to become the keeper of the consciences of other men." When Ames reminded the House that the first Congress had agreed to protect the right of petition, Smith of South Carolina fumed that the right to petition did not cover the "mere rant and rhapsody of a meddling fanatic, interlarded with texts of scripture and concluded with no specific prayer." Smith warned that even reading the petition or entering it into the House journals risked spreading word of antislavery advocacy southward. Should slaves hear of it, their presumed affection for their masters might lead to restlessness, thereby making "greater severity towards them necessary." The House summarily tabled the petition and returned it to Mifflin, "setting the stage for the infamous gag rule that [decades] later would distinguish the antislavery petition campaigns of the early nineteenth century."[34] The only morsel of satisfaction Mifflin could get was the House decision to allow his petition to remain in the House journals, thus preserving the right of petition.

Before leaving the city, Mifflin visited Washington once more to plead his cause. Then he took his case to the public. Even if Congress could bury his memorial on the abolition of slavery and the slave trade, he could still reach the citizenry with his argument that the nation's integrity and global reputation hung in the balance. And he meant to show he could not be silenced. Within a week the *Baltimore Evening Post* published his memorial; then, probably through the intervention of John or James Pemberton in Philadelphia and Moses Brown in Providence, the editor of the *Providence Gazette* published it a month later, with his comment that Mifflin "has been well known to many, in almost every state in the union, to be a man of good sense and solid discernment, of a plentiful estate and unsullied character, a citizen of one of the southern states, and a firm friend to the universal liberty of mankind, both in principle and practice."[35]

Returning to his Kent County home, still undaunted, Mifflin wrote Washington that he was not leaving the arena of contest. Assuring the president of his deep respect, he expressed his "wish with all my heart that thou were not a slaveholder." As for his Deep South detractors who had pilloried him on the floor of the House of Representatives, Mifflin wrote that "I have no doubt this country will find some day we are right, let southern blasts storm as they may and insinuate what they will respecting the Africans." Meanwhile, he asked the president, in any case where the Society of Friends or individual Quakers "give thee uneasiness," to communicate directly with them, understanding that most Quakers "are favourable toward thee."[36]

Even before reaching Chestnut Grove, Mifflin had begun drafting a long retort to the charges hurled at him in Congress Hall. Now, in January 1793, planning to reach a national audience, he hastened to submit it to the Philadelphia Yearly Meeting for approval.[37] Sixteen pages in print, he titled it *A Serious*

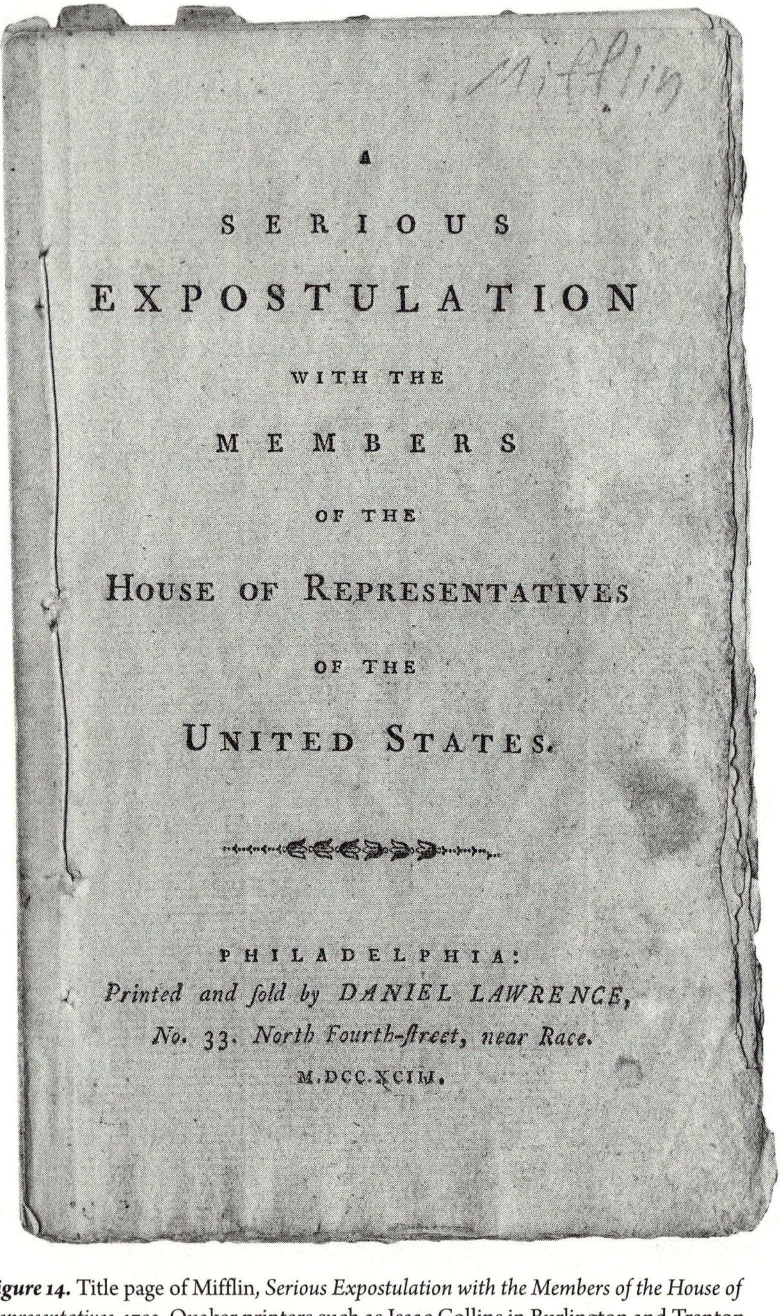

Mifflin

A

SERIOUS

EXPOSTULATION

WITH THE

MEMBERS

OF THE

HOUSE OF REPRESENTATIVES

OF THE

UNITED STATES.

PHILADELPHIA:

*Printed and ſold by DANIEL LAWRENCE,*

*No. 33. North Fourth-ſtreet, near Race.*

M.DCC.XCIII.

***Figure 14.*** Title page of Mifflin, *Serious Expostulation with the Members of the House of Representatives*, 1793. Quaker printers such as Isaac Collins in Burlington and Trenton and Joseph Crukshank and Daniel Lawrence in Philadelphia were vitally important in publishing Quaker antislavery essays, memorials, and addresses to the public. Courtesy Library Company of Philadelphia.

*Expostulation with the Members of the House of Representatives of the United States*. Published in Philadelphia, and shortly thereafter in Poughkeepsie, New York, and New Bedford, Massachusetts, it reintroduced the Delaware reformer to the wider public with his abolitionist arguments.[38]

Mifflin began by reminding his hoped-for readership that the "harmony of the union" that his antagonists claimed he was disturbing was far from harmonious and could never be so while the stain of slavery disfigured the newborn republic. From there, he put on display excerpts from the Continental Congress's 1774 promise to halt the slave trade; the "Causes and Necessity of Taking Up Arms" of July 1775, where Congress proclaimed that "the Divine Author of our existence" never "intended a part of the human race to hold an absolute property in, and unbounded power over others"; the Declaration of Independence with its ringing clauses about inalienable rights; and other Congressional statements that pronounced "the great principle (of government) is and ever will remain in force, that men are by nature free." As for his public pronouncements, they were no more fanatical than the Continental Congress's defense of American liberties: "If this is fanaticism, enthusiasm, &c., may the Almighty grant a double portion to what I ever experienced, if it be his holy will."[39]

Calling slavery a "national iniquity" and "a national guilt," Mifflin reminded the House that "[I] plead the cause of injured innocence" and "open my mouth for my oppressed brethren, who cannot open theirs for themselves." Hardly a day passed when he did not encounter accounts "of the inhumanity perpetrated in these states on this race of men." How could he not speak out, as "the Prophet did when he was ordered to cry aloud, spare not, lift up thy voice like a trumpet, and shew my people their transgressions, and the house of Jacob their sins?" They would be arraigned at the judgment seat, he assured them, for God would not forgive "such degradation" visited on those with nothing more offensive than "the natural black skin of the body."

Mifflin had little reason to believe that his *Expostulation* would move Congress or the president toward substantive action. Rather, his quarry was the public at large. In this strategy to reach a national audience, where a militant moral confrontation was at the heart of the matter, he knew he was in this endeavor for the long run. That thought must have been in his mind just three weeks after the publication of *Expostulation*, when Congress passed the Fugitive Slave Act of 1793, a crushing defeat for Quaker abolitionists. Strengthening the hand of bounty hunters roaming the North to capture and reenslave escaped Africans—and seizing free blacks in the process—the act ramped up the slave-catching industry and discouraged those intending to make their break for freedom. For Mifflin, the only solace was the belief that the law would not go unnoticed from above, where a watchful God would smite the Americans for defiling their founding principles.[40]

Still, cascading news from France and St. Domingue gave resonance to Mifflin's *Expostulation*. The arrival of Edmond Charles Genet, the French minister, in April 1793; the razing of Le Cap Français by black insurrectionists in June; and the proclamation from the French revolutionary government abolishing slavery in St. Domingue made universal freedom a topic of intense public scrutiny and argument up and down the seaboard, and particularly in Philadelphia.[41]

While the nation's capital churned with news of violent black self-emancipation, God's vengeance that Mifflin had prophetically warned about struck horrifically at the center of Quaker abolitionism. Signs of the dreaded yellow fever appeared in July 1793. By early September, with the Philadelphia Yearly Meeting sessions impending, yellow fever had swept through the city like an avenging angel. Before it ran its course, some seventeen thousand Philadelphians had fled the nation's capital, and nearly five thousand lay in their graves. Attending the yearly meeting—only sixty of the 140 delegates appointed by their local or regional meetings dared come—Mifflin grimly watched the death carts, driven by leaders of the free black community, carrying the dead to the cemeteries.[42] Mifflin witnessed the deaths of many Friends, including his wife's sister-in-law, married to her brother George Emlen of Chester County. Like many other Friends, she believed that the perilous epidemic in Philadelphia did not entitle true Quakers to shirk their duty if their monthly or quarterly meeting had appointed them representatives to the yearly meeting.[43]

Mifflin survived the ordeal and returned home to Chestnut Grove. By January the next year he was back in the broken city. Hearing that Richard Allen and Absalom Jones had just published their *Narrative of the Proceedings of the Black People, During the Late Awful Calamity in Philadelphia*, an indignant response to Mathew Carey's *Short Account of the Malignant Fever*, where the Irish immigrant publisher unfairly accused black Philadelphians of profiting from the misery of white citizens, Mifflin promised to sell "a great number" of them and supported the proposal that Allen and Jones procure a copyright for their pamphlet.[44] It was a small contribution to an interracial, intersectional alliance and not unnoticed by Allen.

If 1793 was a year of setbacks and sorrow, 1794 yielded better results. On January 1, in an effort to coordinate the work of the abolition societies dotting the Eastern Seaboard and create a national lobby, the American Convention for Promoting the Abolition of Slavery and Improving the Condition of the African Race met in Philadelphia. Appointed to the steering committee, Mifflin joined such Philadelphia notables as Benjamin Rush and William Rawle to seize on Congress's 1790 concession that it had the authority to prohibit American ships from carrying slaves to foreign ports—termed the carrying trade.[45] Hoping for a small victory, Mifflin stayed in the city to lobby Congressmen on possible further steps. He decamped, however, before the legislative debates ran their course, ruffled that some Quaker leaders in the city felt he was pushing too hard. "It was not fear of Congressmen or Presidents that drove me [out]," he wrote Moses Brown, who had come from Rhode Island to join the Quaker delegation, "for I feel an open door toward them and I am fully of the faith it would have been more so if I had stayed a little while to have been more among them."[46]

The American Convention petition convinced Congress to pass the 1794 Foreign Slave Trade Act, the first federal legislation curbing the slave trade. The law prohibited American ship captains (almost always backed by eastern seaport merchants) from carrying captured Africans to foreign ports, usually the West Indies, or fitting out slave ships in American seaports for use by slavers from other countries. Rhode Island and Pennsylvania had passed such a law seven years before, and several other states soon followed. Though a small step, the law put off-limits the foul but profitable business that was enriching scores of investors. It culminated Quaker efforts since 1783 to hobble the slave trade, while upholding the Quakers' position that the federal government had the authority to hem in its boundaries.[47]

## At Chestnut Grove

The prophetic impulses that kept Mifflin traveling, lobbying, and writing like a man possessed in the name of Jesus left little time in the early 1790s for parenting his growing brood of children or managing his Chestnut Grove plantation.

Without his finding Ann Emlen as a second wife, this could not have happened. A touching letter she sent Warner's nine-year-old daughter a few months before the marriage reflected how important she would be as a stepmother. Susanna, perhaps with gentle prodding from her father, had written her stepmother-to-be that she intended to act in every way possible to please her. "My dear Susannah," Ann replied, "seek to please thy heavenly Father and in that thee will please me." Trying to clear Susanna's mind of any thoughts of the age-old trope of the cruel stepmother, Ann promised, "I shall rejoice to see you do well as much as though you were my own dear child, for I shall consider you as such and I hope you will allow me to treat you as such." At the same time, Ann was candid that an affectionate parent did not stint in providing "advice, admonition, counsel, or even reproof." Along with the letter she sent a bag of shells "to view in the variety and beauty thereof, the wonderful works of Providence," along with a parcel of raisins and an advice book and a parcel for her brother Warner.[48]

Despite this promising start, the years ahead were full of stressful moments and hard decisions at Chestnut Grove. The challenges were multiple: first, life at his Kent County plantation churned with marriage, death, emotional crises, and his frayed and weakening body. Also, the management of Chestnut Grove ran afoul of difficult circumstances, some of Mifflin's own making. Finally, he was overwhelmed by how his efforts on behalf of Eastern Shore blacks turned Mifflin's Crossroads into a precursor of the nineteenth-century Underground Railroad.

At Chestnut Grove, Warner's "bodily indispositions"—Friends used this term to cover a multitude of ailments and diseases—kept him off balance, feeling every year of his age and aware that his health was ebbing. In October 1791, he reported a return of "my disorder" and how "[my] very weak situation" produced thoughts "that my days may not be many more."[49] Meanwhile, he feared his wife Ann would miscarry in her second pregnancy in the winter of 1791–1792, while their son Samuel, not yet two, suffered from ague and periodic fits that signaled epilepsy. To their joy, in late March 1792, Ann safely delivered a son. Ever meditative, she scratched out verses while nursing him:

> The perils of a Lying in
> > Are many, great, and sore,
> > Thou hast preserv'd from such therein
> > And I'll thy name adore.

Thy word was giv'n, a son was sent
    Preserve him if thy will
    With thy pure mind to be content
    Thy precepts to fulfill . . .
As names significant were giv'n
    By ancient Israel
    Not without cause I'll do so ev'n
    And name him Lemuel.[50]

In an ever-changing household, marriage and death, joy and grief commingled. The wedding of Warner's oldest child, daughter Elizabeth, at Murderkill meetinghouse in July 1792 was cause for satisfaction because the groom, Clayton Cowgill, was the upstanding eldest son of Mifflin's friend, John Cowgill, who had been mobbed during the revolution for refusing to deal in Continental currency. Yet even the good reminded Warner of the bad. "Tho [the marriage was] agreeable to me, yet I found it a great thing to give up to the parting with a child—what would I do then if I was a Negro and had a daughter carried from me to Carolina?"[51] Adding to that departure from the household was the decision in 1794 that fifteen-year-old Susanna, to whom her stepmother had written so affectionately six years before, should be apprenticed to housekeeping in the family of Quaker Josiah Bunting in Chester County.[52]

Only a few months after this, Ann Mifflin gave birth to a third child, only to see the babe take sick and die after five months. It was the only daughter she would ever have. Four months later, on the last day of 1795, Warner's seventy-three-year-old father died at the old family homestead in Accomack County. Warner and Ann made their way down the Eastern Shore for the burial in the family plot at Pharsalia. In his complicated will, scratched out just nine days before dying—very probably it had Warner's input—Daniel Mifflin gifted his many children and grandchildren. True to the reparationist doctrine Warner had tried to spread, Daniel enjoined his children and grandchildren "to take care of and administer to the necessities and relief of such Black people as myself and former wife Anne manumitted and are or may be in circumstances any ways not able to help themselves."[53]

While Mifflin framed his life around political and religious affairs in the 1790s, he had the inconvenient matter of maintaining his household and financing his extensive travels. His wife Ann shouldered more than her share of the load. With four stepchildren to mother, two babes from her own body to suckle, and recurrent illnesses stalking her husband, it was indispensable to have household servants and plantation hands.[54] Oversight of such a workforce, even if small, brought troublesome situations and often grief. On one occasion, Warner recorded his sadness at the death of a twin black boy living at Chestnut Grove. "I lost a Negro boy yesterday with a lock'd jaw by a small hurt in his heel," he wrote in sorrow; "It was a trial to me . . . from the pinching trial in the separation of two brothers [and] the one that survives; I never in any colour saw more affection from one brother to another . . . than was manifested through his illness [of] about 4 days. I was almost ashamed of myself on reflection; I thought the tender care of a mother to her darling child was never more conspicuous."[55]

Another case involved finding a woman "to keep house" for the "clever, sober young man" and his family who managed the Mifflins' subsidiary plantation at their marshland, where they pastured their stock. The candidate was Rachel Love Freedom, a free black woman with a load of troubles. She and her husband had tended the oceanside Chincoteague property of Mifflin's father, but when her husband had been kidnapped and sold into slavery for shipment south to the cotton frontier, the distraught Rachel had fled with her three young children to Pharsalia. Finding Rachel "so full of Methodizing" that Daniel Mifflin found her unmanageable, he hoped Warner and Ann would take her on a trial basis. And so it was arranged to bring Rachel and her three children by shallop to Chestnut Grove, where she was promised an increase in wages. In this fluid, danger-filled world for blacks on the Eastern Shore, Warner and Ann did what they could to help Rachel while getting "help" themselves for managing their properties.[56]

Property management itself had become precarious by the 1790s. In freeing his slaves—by his account this halved his worldly assets—Mifflin had sharply curbed the income he could derive from his extensive properties.[57] Replacing a plantation workforce was the problem confronting all Delawareans who had liberated their enslaved people. This meant hiring agricultural workers on share cropping or wage labor terms, neither of which produced more than marginal profits. Never an astute plantation owner with much interest or aptitude for new agricultural practices, and almost determined to eschew making money, he extracted only a modest surplus from his plantations. Like all his neighbors, he was also affected by the commercial downturn of the late 1780s that dampened profits for Delaware grain producers. But this cast only a pale shadow on agricultural production, compared to the devastation wreaked by the Hessian fly infestation. By the early 1790s, swarms of the deadly insect nearly invisible to the human eye had sapped the livelihoods of most Delaware wheat farmers.[58]

In such unfavorable circumstances, Mifflin's fallback strategy was to draw down his extensive property holdings, most of which had come to him through his two marriages. In 1786, even before his first wife died, he and Elizabeth cashed in part of her dowry land, selling a 1,214-acre plantation to the south of Chestnut Grove. Shortly after her death, he sold another part of her inheritance—a 74-acre farm close to his home plantation. The next year, he disposed of three small tracts along the Dover River (now named St. Jones River) that he had purchased sixteen years before.[59] In 1789, a year after his second marriage, Mifflin and his wife, in conjunction with his father, sold 500 acres of the dowry land with grist and saw mills that Daniel Mifflin's first wife had inherited from her father in Kent County, Maryland, a half-century before. Ann Emlen's dowry land, part of a portfolio of properties she had inherited from her wealthy father, also became part of their support system. In 1791, with Chestnut Grove barely subsisting, she and Warner agreed to new leases on land in Philadelphia and Darby (Delaware County) that Ann brought to the marriage.[60]

In his now numbered years, Mifflin threw the dice in an un-Quakerly fashion to prop up his precarious finances. His wife and Henry Drinker, his lifelong Philadelphia mentor, had warned Warner not to invest in a risky enterprise hatched by Samuel Hopkins, an entrepreneurial Quaker well known in Philadelphia. Hopkins had fixed on a new method to process potash and pearl ash, an essential ingredient in producing soap, glass, dyes, and saltpeter. Obtaining the first patent in American history in 1790, he set about attracting investors. By the time he reached out to Mifflin in 1797, he was infamous for shady accounting and deceptive enticements to prospective investors.[61] Nonetheless, Mifflin entered an agreement to strip seventeen and a half acres of woodland, using one of his black wage workers, to convert the forest into cordwood. Shipped to Rahway, New Jersey, where Hopkins had set up his latest ashery, the wood would secure a share in the potash production profits for Mifflin.

It was a deal gone bad. With no return on his investment—the potash operation never flourished—angry letters from Mifflin brought silence from Hopkins and finally a long letter charging Mifflin with unkind words and ill feelings, along with vague promises to settle the accounts. "He meant only to gull my husband," lamented Mifflin's distraught wife. With his body failing, it put a punctuation point, like a foreclosed mortgage, on Mifflin's financial decay.[62]

Added to his personal and business concerns was the reality that Mifflin had become the living magnet on the Eastern Shore for frightened slaves in danger of being sold south to South Carolina and Georgia. Indeed, the stress attending this likely contributed to shortening his life. Once Chestnut Grove became known as the place of counsel, succor, and encouragement for those making their break for freedom, slaves found their way, sometimes from more than one hundred miles, to Mifflin's home. This made him a marked man, often having to defend himself from encouraging the flight of the enslaved and forging passports for those seeking refuge to the north. "It has been reported," he wrote, "that I have persuaded the blacks to run from their masters, and that I give them passes whenever they apply." But Mifflin denied this. "I believe a cause that is sanctioned by omnipotent Goodness, needs no such efforts to make it successful; . . . I am troubled at seeing any run from their masters, and generally counsel such, that it is my judgment they had better remain at home, in quiet resignation, as much as possible, to their allotment." Mifflin admitted that some, having made it this far northward, continued their flight, but others returned to their masters. On another instance, in a letter to a South Carolina political leader who had lashed out at him and the Quakers, Mifflin turned his cheek: "I wish thee happiness, I wish thee no more ill than I wish for myself," and then reminded his tormenter that while he knew most slaves "know full well that their slavery is against all principle," he urged them "to be resigned, to expect all things from God and their liberty from the law." Very probably Mifflin did not deny them hints on the best routes northward toward Philadelphia, and he certainly fed the sometimes half-starved refugees; but he also sometimes gave them money to return to their masters with a "letter requesting that they not be punished."[63]

As word spread along the African American grapevine that Warner Mifflin was the best white friend they could find in making their way north, road-weary blacks beat a path to his door, taxing Mifflin almost beyond his limits. As early as 1790, he wrote that "I am so beset with the complaints of the poor blacks that I scarcely know which way to turn myself." Two months later, he lamented, "I am much burdened, for the poor blacks are running to me in droves from Maryland—men, women and children—to get out of the way of being sold

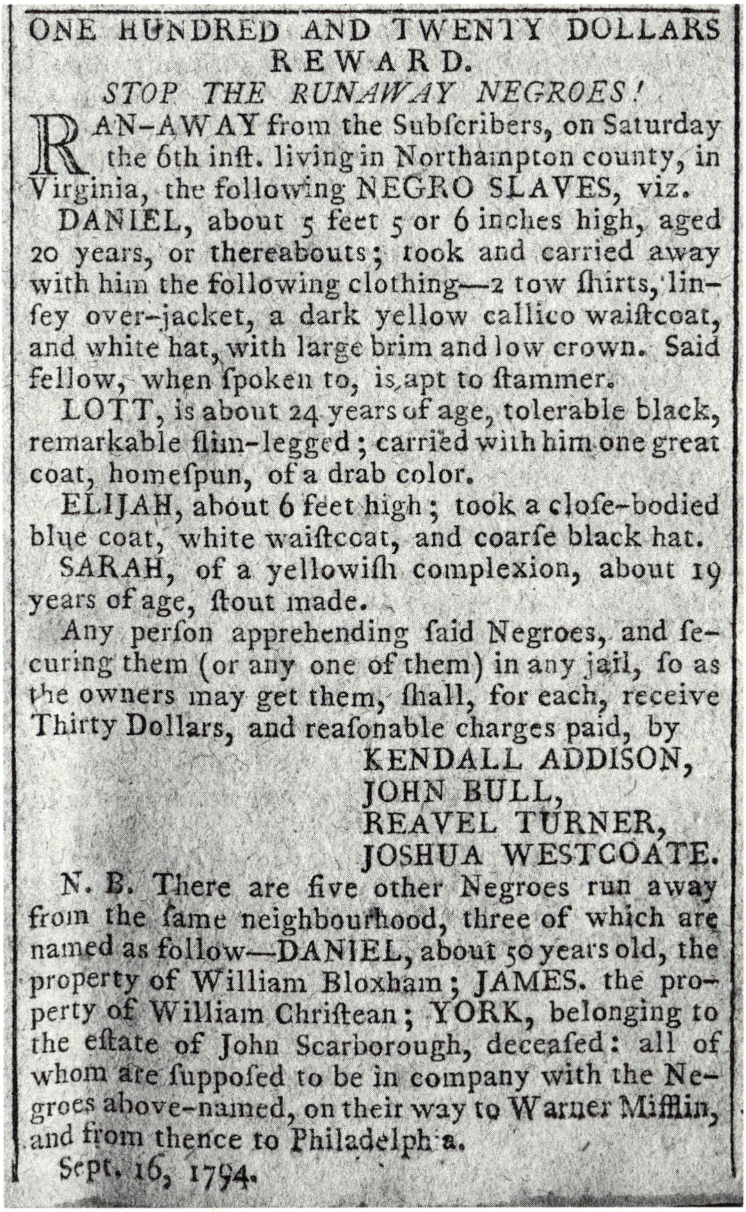

## ONE HUNDRED AND TWENTY DOLLARS REWARD.

### STOP THE RUNAWAY NEGROES!

RAN-AWAY from the Subscribers, on Saturday the 6th inst. living in Northampton county, in Virginia, the following NEGRO SLAVES, viz.

DANIEL, about 5 feet 5 or 6 inches high, aged 20 years, or thereabouts; took and carried away with him the following clothing—2 tow shirts, linsey over-jacket, a dark yellow callico waistcoat, and white hat, with large brim and low crown. Said fellow, when spoken to, is apt to stammer.

LOTT, is about 24 years of age, tolerable black, remarkable slim-legged; carried with him one great coat, homespun, of a drab color.

ELIJAH, about 6 feet high; took a close-bodied blue coat, white waistcoat, and coarse black hat.

SARAH, of a yellowish complexion, about 19 years of age, stout made.

Any person apprehending said Negroes, and securing them (or any one of them) in any jail, so as the owners may get them, shall, for each, receive Thirty Dollars, and reasonable charges paid, by

KENDALL ADDISON,
JOHN BULL,
REAVEL TURNER,
JOSHUA WESTCOATE.

N. B. There are five other Negroes run away from the same neighbourhood, three of which are named as follow—DANIEL, about 50 years old, the property of William Bloxham; JAMES, the property of William Christean; YORK, belonging to the estate of John Scarborough, deceased: all of whom are supposed to be in company with the Negroes above-named, on their way to Warner Mifflin, and from thence to Philadelphia.

Sept. 16, 1794.

*Figure 15.* Runaway ads such as this one from the *Delaware and Eastern Shore Advertiser,* September 17, 1794, show that slaves far down the Delmarva Peninsula knew how to reach Chestnut Grove. Mifflin's reputation as a friend of escaping slaves and free blacks in danger of kidnappers brought notice of him in runaway slave ads in Delaware, Maryland, and Pennsylvania newspapers. Courtesy Historical Society of Pennsylvania.

into Georgia and the Carolinas. Thinking I can do something for them, they fly to me."[64] In the same summer, he sighed again that hounded black Delawareans "are almost continually flying to me for succor, which is out of my power to yield them."[65] As the calendar moved forward, Mifflin found himself swamped. "I never was oppressed in mind more on account of the blacks," he wrote in planting time in 1792, "and I believe the inhumanity toward them never appeared more glaring than at this time in these parts of the country; the cruel trade to the southward have increased."[66] Two years later, nine slaves from Virginia's Northampton County coordinated a group escape from their masters to make "their way to Warner Mifflin and thence to Philadelphia."[67]

In another case that would soon become famous, Mifflin came to the aid of the long-suffering Abraham Johnstone, who had been born in Murderkill Hundred a few miles from Chestnut Grove. Sold from one master to another, Johnstone had been promised his freedom by a master whose life he had saved, only to end up in the Dover jail as a runaway slave after the master died. Then redeemed by a Kent County merchant, Johnstone was kidnapped by slave traders; escaping, he hurried to Mifflin to pursue a freedom suit in 1792. "Knowing the footing I was on," Johnstone wrote, "Mifflin stood my fast friend on the occasion, and obtained for me the manumission which I have got, as yet and which protected me." On the advice of Mifflin and others, Johnstone made his way north to Philadelphia and then across the Delaware to New Jersey. And there, on what may have been trumped up charges, he was convicted of murdering a fellow African. Little could Mifflin have known that the man he helped would salute him in 1797 from the gallows in Woodbury, New Jersey, where he wrote out his dying "confession," which was as much a declaration of racial injustice as a deathbed admission of a capital crime.[68]

Mifflin paid a price for helping fleeing slaves and supporting freedom suits. Trying to walk a fine line, he often was taken to court by Eastern Shore slaveowners. In the late spring of 1792, for example, he was indicted in the courts of Delaware, Maryland, and Virginia, in each case charged with abetting the flight of slaves. Mifflin apparently fended off these suits, probably for lack of evidence.[69] But while such attempts to intimidate him left him harassed and wearied, he never stood down. His letters are filled with the duress he felt. In 1793, he was "so bury'd under [helping] the poor blacks it seems sometimes as if I should be good for nothing in any [other] way or line." Nonetheless, he had come to believe that this was what the Almighty wanted of him: "If kind Providence will be pleased to make me what he pleases whereby his favour may be attained, I matter not what station I am in nor what I have to go through."[70] In November 1794, rising at dawn as winter approached, he wrote his friend Henry Drinker that he had four cases of fleeing blacks "to attend to before sunrise this morning." A month later, returning from Philadelphia: "I have had not less than five negroes, day and night, and sometimes as many as eleven for a night." Most were from nearby Maryland, "flying for fear of being carried to the [Lower] South." Sheltering refugees brought "many curses, reflections, sour looks, &c" from whites around him, making his life "exceed-ingly disagreeable even beyond description." Though sometimes yearning "to be rightly clear of this business," he struck his usual stoic stance: "to the Great Caretaker ... I desire to commit my cause, crave his Divine direction, succour and support, and that he may dispose of me as he pleases."[71] In 1795, returning from Annapolis, he wrote Drinker again that "I have now two men standing waiting for advice that have just escaped from the Chesapeake from the Caro-lina dealers. I believe I have not been without one or more almost every day since my return," sighing that "I am loaded thereby almost as much as I can stand under."[72]

What he could do without skirting the law was to encourage free blacks seized as purported slaves and scheduled for shipment to the Lower South to petition the Kent County Court of Common Pleas, where he promised to serve as "next friend." This was the case in spring 1791, when he worked to get Esther and her child released from jail where "her pretended master," claiming she was still his slave, had her confined. Such aid only widened the path blacks were beating to reach his doorstep. At least six times between 1791 and 1795, he did this. One of those coming to him as his best hope to escape the clutches of slave dealers gives a vivid sense of the terror that was never far from the small cabins of freed blacks. Jonathan, for whom Mifflin stood as "next friend," had been freed several years before and then strong-armed by a man claiming to be his slaveowner, who sold him to John Beauchamp, "a Negro trader," who intended to carry Jonathan to Kentucky.[73]

While Chestnut Grove served as a way station and temporary place of refuge in the 1790s, it also functioned as a clearinghouse for free black children whose parents' poverty obliged them to indenture them. Mifflin often sent young boys and girls from Kent County to Henry and Elizabeth Drinker in Philadelphia for placement in families where they might find a better life chance. The case of Peter Woodward, a boy about twelve, typifies Mifflin's efforts. Woodward "was ragged and lousey, having been for upwards of a week on board the vessel," diarist Elizabeth Drinker wrote in 1795, after Mifflin had arranged his trip north to be indentured. Drinker thought "his appearance at first was rather formidable," being "hard-favoured" in his tender years, but after being tubbed in soap and water, his head doused with rum mixed with larkspur, and dressed in cast-off clothes, he soon "looked like another creature." A few months later, Mifflin sent Rebecca Gibbs and her twelve-year-old daughter to Philadelphia to serve in the household of a Quaker friend.[74]

Nearly annual sojourns to Philadelphia for spring and fall Quaker meetings gave Mifflin opportunities to strengthen the pipeline from Chestnut Grove to the Henry Drinker house on North Front Street. In an especially moving case he placed a sixteen-year-old boy from Accomack County whose elderly father needed the money to complete the purchase of himself and his wife from slavery.[75] For Mifflin, it was a never-ending rescue operation. Not for many years would anyone else on the Delmarva Peninsula exert and endanger himself in this way.

## Consortship

Ann Emlen's marriage to Warner Mifflin had thrust her into a web of birth, maternal care, sickness, death, and plantation management, but it did not stop her from pursuing her own mission to spread the Quaker truth and engage as fully as possible in the work of Quaker meetings. She did this with an intensity that matched her husband's. Almost from her first arrival in Kent County, she folded herself into the Murderkill women's meetings; and by 1791, with her first child less than a year old, the Southern Quarterly Meeting recognized her calm demeanor and faithful service by appointing her as a delegate to the Philadelphia Yearly Meeting scheduled to convene that spring.[76] A few months later, she asked the meeting to authorize her "mindings" to visit the Nottingham and New Garden monthly meetings on the Maryland-Pennsylvania border. There, she joined hands, in what became an enduring bond, with Philena Lay, a devout Quaker minister who had grown up at Pharsalia with Warner Mifflin, after being orphaned as an infant. This led to Ann's first epistle—a moving plea to Friends to hold fast to their heritage of shunning "improper indulgence and vanity," and especially the "lavish and unnecessary use of indigo as a dye," which implicated them in the "bondage and misery [of] hundreds and thousands of poor Slaves."[77]

By the mid-1790s, leaving the brood of children in the care of hired house-keepers, Ann became Warner's nearly constant companion for the spring and fall meetings of the Philadelphia Yearly Meeting, and sometimes in between at monthly and quarterly meetings. On another trip of several weeks in late 1795 to Annapolis, just months after burying her infant daughter, she participated fully in women's meetings, helping to prepare a memorial to the Delaware legislature and organizing meetings of free black Marylanders across the peninsula.[78] The partnership of Ann and Warner grew even closer in the key roles they played in two landmark developments of the Society of Friends in 1796 and 1797.

The first could not have been closer to Warner, for it raised the touchy question whether Quakers truly played by the Golden Rule and believed that all mankind was of one blood. No one doubted that Quakers were the nation's first abolitionists and the first to compensate liberated slaves for unrequited labor. Equally commendable, Friends for years had visited the homes of freed people to counsel them, had since the late 1690s invited them to their religious meetings or facilitated meetings for the blacks themselves, and, led by Anthony Benezet, had set up schools to educate both enslaved and free blacks. But Friends would not admit people with dark skin to membership in the Society.[79] For African Americans who admired Quaker principles and their willingness to be martyred for them, this was a bitter pill to swallow.

The issue had been festering for years. Eventually in 1783 a brave mixed-race woman had raised the membership issue in Delaware County. When her application was referred to the Yearly Meeting, Ann Emlen reported that "mountains of opposition [were] . . . leveled before her."[80] Writing to James Phillips, the London Quaker printer who tirelessly published antislavery material, James Pemberton laid bare the opposition. All Friends agreed that God had made of one blood "all nations of men," but many pleaded that "unrestricted admission" would entitle black members "to the privilege of intermarriage." That is where the line was drawn. "There are few," Pemberton reported, "who would freely consent to introduce such a union in their families."[81]

Two years later, the issue resurfaced, "exciting much attention" according to James Pemberton. However, for another decade the issue lay dormant. Then in 1795, when Warner and Ann were both in attendance, the yearly meeting grasped the nettle. Forcing the issue was Cynthia Miers, a mulatto woman from Rahway, New Jersey, who had worshiped for many years at her local preparative meeting. When her request for membership was referred upward

from the monthly to quarterly and then the yearly meeting, the moving testimony of Joseph Drinker broke through the wall of resistance. A cooper of
modest means and lacking the leadership credentials of his brothers John and
Henry, Joseph's remarks carried weight. Christ died for all, he reminded his
Quaker friends, and how could Friends escape charges of hypocrisy when they
were the only denomination denying full membership to those with dark skin?
Was it not time for eminent Friends to set aside their opposition to admitting
black worshipers with the sugar-coated argument, cloaking repugnance for
interracial marriage, that black would-be Quakers should "fold by themselves
. . . that there should be one fold for black sheep and another fold for white
sheep"?[82]

Unable to reach consensus, the 1795 yearly meeting appointed a committee
to think deeply about the matter and make recommendations. In an unusual
move, the wavering committee opened its deliberations to Friends eager to
testify. As reported by committee member John Hunt, a New Jersey minister,
farmer, and pump maker, "a considerable number of other weighty, wise, solid
women" urged the Society to put its racial bias behind it. Among those testifying were Ann Mifflin and Mary Pusey Mifflin, the widow of Warner's father,
who had died in Accomack County just nine months before. Warner was among
the men who "were likewise strong and staunch in this cause," arguing there
"was never any discipline to prohibit any from being received into membership
amongst us on account of color or nation whatsoever."[83] This was enough to
sway resistant Friends. "It was a heart-tendering time, even to tears," Hunt
scribbled in his journal, and he "thought I never seen more love, nearness and
sweetness before amongst Friends." Hunt noted that the decision to admit the
mulatto woman to membership was agreed by mutual unity—"that monthly
meetings should be at liberty to receive all such where they were convinced of
their sincerity without distinction of nation or color."[84]

Mifflin's Duck Creek Monthly Meeting left no record of responding to
the yearly meeting decision, but it probably had no need to do so. Already,
preparative meetings had been conducting biracial worship, and Murderkill
meeting, which the Mifflin family attended, was certainly among them. When
Martha Routh, the English traveling minister, joined a Tuesday worship in
April 1796, she found "a very large mixed gathering in which were many black
people."[85]

A year after the wall of entrenched color bias tumbled down, Ann
and Warner became principal agents in the merging with the Quaker-like

Nicholites, who had pockets of worshipers in Delaware, Maryland, and North Carolina. Followers of Joseph Nichols, a charismatic small landowner and utterly inconspicuous man who was born near Dover in about 1730, the Nicholites shared much with the Society of Friends. Like the Quakers, they relied on the inward urgings of conscience rather than any external authority. Like the Quakers, they were pacifists, they refused to swear oaths, they practiced more gender equality than other churches, and they rejected all hierarchical religious institutions. Calling themselves "Friends," they were ultra-strict, eschewing dancing and music and emphasizing plain living and self-denial, to the point that they refused to grow ornamental flowers in their gardens or allow them in their houses. And like Quakers, they found slavery a cancerous disease that polluted spiritual and moral life.[86]

Nichols had gathered several hundred followers, mostly small farmers, both black and white; but after his death on the eve of the American Revolution, the Nicholites languished. Lacking a secure financial base to build meeting houses, and scattering as far south as the Carolinas, most of them by the mid-1790s had agreed to merge with the Quakers if this could be negotiated. When, in fall 1797, eighty Nicholites appealed for membership to a preparative meeting overseen by the Third Haven Monthly Meeting on Maryland's Eastern Shore, the Southern Quarterly Meeting appointed Ann and Warner, along with two of his married daughters, a son-in-law, and other relatives, to visit the Nicholite families "in order to feel after their growth and standing in the Truth." After visiting dozens of Nicholite families, the delegation reported positively on their findings. By early 1798 the merger had been approved, with the Mifflin family playing a key role.[87]

## The Flickering Candle

Even before Warner and Ann provided their devoted attention to these two issues, Mifflin had abundant reasons to throw in the towel on the slavery issue. The chances of moving Congress or the president on any aspect of the nation's festering problem were all but nil. Though state legislatures in the Upper South had yielded modestly by criminalizing the kidnapping of free blacks and the exporting of slaves across state boundaries, such laws were backed by little if any force. At the same time, Virginia and Maryland threw legal obstacles in the way of freedom suits that were usually brought by the small abolition societies.[88] In Delaware, the two abolition societies, having never recruited more than about sixty members, had disbanded by the late 1790s. Another discouragement came when the Methodist General Conference in 1796 withdrew its direct condemnation of slaveholding mandated in 1784.[89]

Yet there were reasons for hope. The number of free blacks grew rapidly between the federal censuses of 1790 and 1800, nearly doubling in the Upper South (though the number of slaves was growing as well). In Delaware, as the century drew to a close, free blacks exceeded the enslaved, and in Mifflin's Kent County three-fourths of the blacks were free (see Appendix 2). The slave rebellion in St. Domingue, which had sent thousands of white planters scurrying for refuge in the United States, spawned new plans for gradual abolition, raising the hope that Southerners would understand that they could avert black rebellion from leaping across the water only by phasing out the system of coerced labor. Terrified that an American St. Domingue was not far off, Vice President Jefferson, nearly frozen out of John Adams's presidential circle, sounded the alarm that "if something is not done and soon done, we shall be the murderers of our own children; ... The *murmura, venturos nautis prodentia ventos* [the breeze warning the sailors of the coming gale] has already reached us." A keen observer and incessant visitor in Philadelphia, Mifflin had easy access to the gazettes pulsing with news of the black revolt, frequently endorsed by commentators who saw in St. Domingue the striving for freedom built into the flesh and bone of all humankind.[90] Thus, as word coursed up and down the seaboard into the mid-1790s of the success of the black revolt engulfing St. Domingue, Miffllin had reason to believe that his first dream about black self-liberation had not betrayed him: as he told a friend, the subconscious rumblings convinced him that "the almighty" might well have ordained that "a kind of itching might be suffered to run through the blood of their [the slaves'] veins" such that they "had a craving for liberty, a little like the Americans had some years back."[91]

Now in his fifties, in his final antislavery labor, Mifflin focused on Maryland, Delaware, and North Carolina. In a two-week trip to Annapolis in December 1795, accompanied by his wife and the widely known traveling Quaker minister Mary Berry, he and four other Quakers again pressed Maryland's legislature to pass a gradual abolition bill. Working to rouse support, they conducted two public meetings in the state house and another at the Methodist meetinghouse "appointed principally for the blacks." Two addresses from the Friends, one of them from the women headed by Ann Mifflin and Mary Berry, were respectfully read by the clerk of the legislature. Despite "some violent opposers," they were sent to a committee for consideration—a sign in itself that the abolitionist cause was far from exhausted. The issue was held over until the next year, satisfying Mifflin that he had at least caught the attention of Maryland legislators. Modest progress occurred in 1796 when Maryland stiffened its penalties against importing slaves and cleared the way for voluntary manumission of slaves not more than forty-five years of age.[92]

Mifflin made one last effort in 1796 to obtain a Delaware gradual abolition law. Through the initiative of one lawmaker or another, usually a Methodist, the legislature had debated the issue several times in the early 1790s; repeatedly, it was turned aside, with Sussex County representatives staunchly opposed and those from Kent and New Castle counties divided. But in early 1796, with petitions coming from both New Castle and Kent county residents, gradual abolition came close to passage. Mifflin camped out in Dover for several weeks to attend the sessions. If passed, the law would have made "servitude for life ... utterly extinguished and forever abolished" for any child born after passage of the act, with such persons "deemed to be a servant" until reaching 26 if male and 22 if female (a less onerous twilight zone of half-freedom than prevailed in neighboring Pennsylvania). Any child born to a female serving 22 years as a servant would likewise serve 22 years.[93] It carried in the lower house, Mifflin reported, "by a large majority." However, the bill stalled in the Senate, which voted to publish it "for the consideration of the people," a dice throw tactic of proslavery representatives calculating that they would prevail in a vote of the electorate. When the lower house rejected this, the Senate tabled the House bill, and the matter was at an end.[94]

Mifflin now made a momentous decision. "I could have carried it [the gradual abolition act] through," he assured John Parrish, but instead decided to push the legislature to muscle Delaware's representatives in Congress "to bring before that body the case of the Negro trade in the Chesapeake by means whereof numbers are kidnapped from this state." His thinking was sound, that "no state laws are like to prevent it, they not having control over the navigation." The legislative resolution, he reported, "I got through both houses pretty readily in a few days."[95]

His decision to focus on combating the wave of kidnapping certainly addressed a grim and growing problem that was terrifying free blacks in the Chesapeake region. His letters in the 1790s were riddled with worries about the fragility of free black life, as man-stealers roamed the countryside in one of the most sorrowful chapters of American history. Free blacks, not slaves, were the primary targets of the human vultures, because white slaveowners could readily get satisfaction in court for the theft of their human property. That was not the case for free blacks. Barred from testifying against whites, their best chance of thwarting the kidnappers was white legal assistance. In Philadelphia, the Pennsylvania Abolition Society made this a priority, and sometimes it lent a hand for a Delaware victim. But Delaware's several abolition societies, struggling even to convene meetings, were of little help. In this situation, the odds for the man-stealers to escape arrest and conviction were enormously in their favor. As for the emancipated slave, hustled to the raw cotton frontier of the Deep South, the chances of ever seeing family again were faint.[96]

Why did Mifflin back off on the gradual abolition bill at a point when he believed it was close to passage? After all, Delaware legislators were acutely aware that black arsonists, inspired by the Haitian Rebellion, were leaving cities from Albany to Charleston in smoking ruins and thus fueling talk about universal freedom. Also, reviving discussions about the price of continued slavery, Virginia's St. George Tucker had just published his *Dissertation on Slavery; With a Proposal for the Gradual Abolition of It, in the State of Virginia* as the Delaware legislature took up the issue. Echoing Mifflin, Tucker argued that slavery was incompatible with republican government and was a monstrous stain on the national escutcheon, all the more urgent to deal with since the federal census of 1790 showed that, contrary to arguments that slavery would die out after slave importations ceased, the slave population was growing rapidly.[97] Had Mifflin decided to sacrifice those still enslaved in order to obtain Congressional remedies for closing down the sale of slaves out of state and stanching the wave of kidnapping that plagued Delaware's free blacks? Perhaps he was deluded in thinking he could push through the gradual abolition law. But if that was so, he made a puzzling, almost inexplicable, choice: while kidnapping pointed a dagger at free black families, its incidence did not compare to the plight of some seven thousand Delawareans and their progeny left enslaved for an unforeseeable duration.

Mifflin's hope that Congress would regulate the grim internal slave trade was illusory. He succeeded in convincing the Delaware legislature to petition Congress about this scourge, and even hoped for a complete federal ban on the interstate slave trade. After the Delaware lawmakers memorialized Congress—but only regarding kidnapping—Mifflin traveled to Philadelphia to take up his lobbying efforts, in company with a Pennsylvania Abolition Society committee. He believed the prospects "rather favourable," and was doubtless encouraged when the petition was referred to the Committee on Commerce and Manufactures, chaired by Pennsylvania's John Swanwick, a Jeffersonian with antislavery leanings. The committee's favorable report in May 1796 provided new reason for optimism.[98]

At that point, with Congress adjourning until December and the House committee deliberations hanging fire, Mifflin worked through the summer to take the printed page to Congress and the public at large. He titled his pamphlet *The Defence of Warner Mifflin Against Aspersions cast on him on Account of his endeavours to promote Righteousness, Mercy, and Peace among Mankind.* Published in Philadelphia, it was more than the title suggested. Tucked into thirty pages of autobiography, antislavery arguments with biblical backup, and an appeal to the nation's honor was a bloodcurdling account of kidnapped free blacks. It was aimed directly at the Congressmen scheduled to return for the second session of Congress on December 5.[99]

Though he expanded on the autobiographical material he had related three years before to the Archbishop of Canterbury, the purpose of the essay was to dislodge the federal government from its refusal to deal with any aspect of slavery. With "this nation … stained with the blood of the African slave trade" and 700,000 fellow humans continuing "to groan in a land of boasted liberty," he asked, how could the Americans escape "the hand of judgment [that] would be stretched out upon a guilty people"? "My heart has been aggrieved," he continued, "and my soul has lamented for this afflicted race, as well as for the condition of my country." The all-watching God "will assuredly recompence to all, according to the fruit of their doings—to nations as well as to individuals." It was in this belief, Mifflin averred, that he had spent years urging legislatures to remove obstacles to manumission and to protect free blacks.

Next, he addressed the matter awaiting Congressional action. Avoiding explicit mention of the abolition of slavery, he urged putting a stop to the "workers of iniquity" who were kidnapping free blacks, some in whole families, others individually, to be sold back into slavery. In Delaware and on the Eastern Shore of Maryland alone, Mifflin averred, more free blacks had been kidnapped and sold into slavery than American sailors had been captured by the Algerine pirates. Vivifying his appeal, he cited beastly actions against Eastern Shore blacks. When one Kent County black petitioned the court for his freedom, his "pretended master or his agents" seized the man, roped him to a horse, and set the horse to a gallop that so mangled the man he died the next day.[100]

In an indirect plea for ending slavery, Mifflin countered the assertion that freeing slaves would cast upon the land a society of inveterate pilferers. Deprived of liberty, the greatest of all property, should they not be excused for taking the necessaries of life, which "in equity their labour gives them some claim to from their possessors"? And "where do negro crimes exceed the crimes of white men?" he queried. Did stealing food to nourish their children compare to "selling tender babes from a fond mother, a beloved wife from an affectionate husband, or an aged father from his offspring with whom he lived from their early years"? Reaching for moral clarity, he asked the readers to consider just who were the ones at fault—"the poor, degraded blacks or . . . the nominal professors of the blessed name of Christ"?

Finally, Mifflin turned to the charges that he had encouraged slaves to flee their masters and come to him where they could obtain passes as free men and women. He denied he issued passes, calling it "beneath the uprightness of my profession to recommend any as free people, who are not such." What he would not deny was providing sustenance for fleeing slaves who found their way to Chestnut Grove. Though counseling escaping slaves to return to their masters, he would not send them away starving. Invoking a contemporary incident that would resonate with readers, he referenced the current excitement about the Algiers pirates capturing white American sailors and selling them into slavery. "Is there a white man among thousands," he asked, "who if captured by the Algerines, would not embrace his liberty, should opportunity present [itself]?" Could a white American citizen imagine himself as a humane Algerine finding at his door an enslaved American sailor, "informing that he had not eaten anything for several days" after slipping his shackles? "What then should be the conduct of the high professors of Christianity, in a similar case towards a people who differ from us by a few darker shades of the skin?" What part of the Christian religion "would authorize us to seize" escaped slaves and "drag them again into bondage"? God had created "of one blood all nations of men," he concluded, and he dreaded the "Divine displeasure" through a more vigorous application of the "gentle rod shaken over us" already through war on the frontier and the yellow fever pestilence. He was "a lover of his country and countrymen, a peaceable subject to its laws, and a universal friend of mankind," he concluded, by way of benediction.[101]

It is hard to say how widely read was Mifflin's last public appeal to his countrymen and government. Whatever its circulation, it did not convince more than a minority in the House of Representatives. Meeting only weeks after its publication, Deep South representatives, convinced that the Swanwick committee report was another "entering wedge" served up by antislavery advocates who hoped Congress would chip away at slaveholders' purported property rights, touched off a heated debate. In the early days of 1797, the matter was tabled, this time by a 46–30 vote. Mifflin and other Quakers, who had hoped Congress would move in a case where states had ceded authority to Congress on control of commerce in territorial waters and across state lines, again were rebuffed.[102] We can imagine how Mifflin's heart sank at the prospect that he had backed away from a gradual abolition law in Delaware while pursuing Congressional action on kidnapping and the internal slave traffic, only to see the latter fail.

Proslavery southern Congressmen (and many northern representatives) trusted that the nation's lawmakers would never be troubled again regarding the supposed power of Congress to regulate slavery. They found out how wrong they were on January 30, 1797, twelve days after disposing of the kidnapping and internal slave traffic issue. This time a petition arrived from an unlikely and unprecedented source—four black Americans. In the first petition of free black Americans to Congress, the four men, greatly assisted by John Parrish and Philadelphia's Meeting for Sufferings, pleaded that though North Carolina's Superior Court had confirmed their freedom after their Quaker owners liberated them, they were threatened with reenslavement by a law negating the Superior Court ruling and retroactively canceling their manumission. Along with a fifth man, who likewise had been liberated only to be reenslaved, the distraught black Carolinians had fled to the nation's capital with their lives in their hands. All four petitioners had lived in the city for several years, taking refuge in Absalom Jones's African Episcopal Church of St. Thomas, believing that man-stealers operating under the Fugitive Slave Act of 1793 were poised to seize them.[103]

The petition told sorrowful tales of the four black men and their families, capsule autobiographies of a hellish life in the boasted seat of global freedom. Restored to "our native right of freedom," they had been "hunted day and night, like beasts of the forest, by armed men with dogs, and made prey of as free and lawful plunder." They asked simply for "the public justice and protection which is the great object of government." Was it possible that the nation's legislative body could ignore the plight of men who had been emancipated "and tasted the sweets of liberty" only to be "again reduced to slavery by kidnappers and man-stealers"? Was this attempt to reenslave them not "a direct violation of the declared fundamental principles of the Constitution"? Was not "an evil of such magnitude highly worthy of the deep inquiry and unfeigned zeal of the supreme legislative body of a free and enlightened people"?

With George Thatcher, Mifflin's friend from the 1790 debate, taking the lead in supporting the petition, the southerners jumped into the fray with alacrity. Having just disposed of Delaware's plea for Congressional intervention in the bloody internal slave trade, they argued that even to consider the petition implied that Congress had the authority to tamper with slavery. The vote to refer the petition to a committee for study lost on a 50–33 vote. Nonetheless, the right to petition had been preserved.[104]

Eight months later, the Meeting for Sufferings, always alert to "the injured class of mankind, the black people," again took up the case of the black Carolinians. Even to meet in the city in September was testimony to the Quakers' dedication, for yellow fever had returned in August with almost the force of the 1793 biological onslaught. The flight of half the population by late August had hollowed out the city, but still Friends came to meet. By the time of the yearly meeting, about thirty Philadelphia Friends lay in their graves.[105]

Though his health was failing at fifty-two, Mifflin returned to ghostly Philadelphia for the 1797 Philadelphia Yearly Meeting, trusting that a merciful God would spare him. There, the meeting appointed him and fourteen others to prepare an address to Congress about "the enormous injustice & cruelty inflicted in some of the Southern States on free persons of the African Race." Their memorial argued that "national evils produce national judgments," and that just such a judgment—the "awful calamity" of yellow fever that had brought Philadelphia to its knees for the second time in five years—"ought to excite an inquiry in the cause and endeavors to do away those things which occasion the heavy clouds that hang over us." The address pointed to 134 black North Carolinians who had been seized and sold back into slavery after Friends had manumitted them. Would the Congress governing the land of liberty sit on its hands while many who had been free for as much as four years were reshackled?[106]

Mifflin returned to Philadelphia again in late November to join other Friends to present the memorial and lobby Congressmen. The Senate immediately ordered it to lie on the table, in effect neutering it.[107] In the House, an extended debate unspooled, with hardcore southerners rehearsing the 1790 arguments about the meddling Quakers roiling the waters of sectional controversy and inciting "a class of persons" (slaves) to bring "the most barbarous and horrid scenes" of St. Domingue to the United States. Hope rose in January 1798 when the petition was referred to a committee, which received a delegation from the Meeting for Sufferings that provided documents evidencing the reenslavement of black North Carolinians freed by Friends. But when the report was put before a Committee of the Whole, the House dismissed the matter by majority vote. The argument that prevailed was that Congress did not have jurisdiction over North Carolina's laws on manumission, which were a matter "exclusively of a judicial cognizance."[108] Mifflin may have sensed that this would be his last lobbying effort. Only a glimmer of satisfaction remained that Congress did not deny the First Amendment right of petition to the Quakers and to free black Americans as well.

## Endings

As Warner's body began to fail after his return to Chestnut Grove, Ann steeled herself for her husband's demise. At the same time, she prepared for the future. Already appointed a traveling minister, she expressed an inward calling to visit the few remaining Quakers on Barbados, where Friends had established their first foothold on the western strand of the Atlantic.[109] That Ann intended a trip to Barbados while Warner's grip on life was loosening is almost unaccountable. Nevertheless, she planned the trip with Mary Berry, the travel-hardened sixty-seven-year-old Public Friend and wife of the Maryland Eastern Shore's most active Quaker antislavery leader.[110] Her application through the usual procedures—preparative, monthly, quarterly, and Philadelphia's Meeting of Ministers and Elders—gives only the formulaic "I have soundings of my mind" to explain this seemingly reckless decision. But surely it indicates that she was determined to enlist in the Quaker church militant.[111] In the end, she deferred the trip, probably because of Warner's precarious health.

Come spring in 1798, when the Federalist-dominated Congress was poised to pass the Alien and Sedition acts to muzzle the Jeffersonian press and undercut the participation in politics of Irish immigrants, Mifflin was determined to go with his wife to the half-year meetings of the Philadelphia Yearly Meeting, though his body gave him every reason to do otherwise. "I have a very swelled face from violent pain in my teeth," he wrote his beloved friend Henry Drinker a few days before leaving Chestnut Grove. Nonetheless, he made it with Ann to Philadelphia for the spring meeting.[112]

Things got worse. He rallied enough by May to travel across the peninsula with his wife and Mary Berry to help ease the Maryland Nicholites into the Quaker fold. By month's end, he was struck again with fever and respiratory infections severe enough to put him to bed, nearly lifeless, for almost a month. Yet running through his head were "almost daily conflicts of mind on account of the poor blacks." "I have a great bodily weakness, a cough continues and my breast is disordered , . . and I have as great a debility of mind as of body," he penned Henry Drinker. At the end of June, still debilitated with hacking coughs, he spoke of his "great cause for humiliation and bowedness of soul." Feeling that many of his labors on behalf of African Americans had come to naught, he wrote dejectedly that "I have no ability scarcely to labour for a crumb." But he still believed that "the Master of our Assemblies has not forsaken us altogether in this degenerate and depraved age."[113]

On July 7, 1798, Mifflin lifted his pen with a heavy heart to say goodbye to Samuel and Lemuel, his young sons, and daughters Elizabeth and Sarah. Making a short trip with Ann and his son Warner Jr., probably to Chester County to see his daughter Susanna, he allowed that he "continues very poorly" and was "very weak" with "my breast considerably affected." He was "preparing for the final farewell to all things here below," but reminded "my dear children what a comfort it must be to a parent passing away to have a hope of their children preparing to do their day's work consistent with the mind of their Maker." He closed with professions that "my love is to you in farewell."[114]

Mifflin recovered sufficiently to reach Chestnut Grove in late July. Complaining again about "a sore conflict [of body] that has been my lot," he groaned that arriving home "I had eight [black] applicants and almost every day since." He asked Henry Drinker for help in buying the freedom of a seven-year-old girl whose father came to Chestnut Grove to plead the case of his daughter. Shortly after that, he arranged transportation by shallop to Philadelphia for a black boy and girl to be placed in service. These were the last free black juveniles he would send north in hope of a better life.[115]

Knowing his race was almost done, his last months measured out almost by the cup, Mifflin made the fateful decision once more to attend his beloved Philadelphia Yearly Meeting. From a distance of more than two centuries, one is tempted to consider this was tantamount to a death wish. Like everyone else up and down the seaboard, he knew the nation's capital was once again in the grip of a ferocious yellow fever epidemic even as it was recovering from the onslaught in 1797. Congress had decamped in mid-July; President John Adams had retreated to Quincy, Massachusetts; and by early August more than three-quarters of the population had emptied the city, leaving behind those without the means to find a place outside the city, along with a small number of dogged Quakers.[116]

It boggles the mind that Mifflin and other delegates to the yearly meeting persisted in convening in what had become a charnel house. By September's end, more than six weeks had passed since most Philadelphians had fled the "malignant scourge of mankind." The fever had spread to the city jail and the Pennsylvania Hospital, where most of the indigent contracting the gruesome disease had been taken. Arriving with his wife, Mifflin found handbills plastered on tavern doors and lampposts in bold capitals: "REFLECT BEFORE IT IS TOO LATE...WHY DO YOU PREFER FAMINE, SICKNESS, AND DEATH TO HEALTH AND PLENTY...GO BEFORE IT IS TOO LATE." The handbills warned that the fever was felling one hundred residents each day, sending half of them to their graves.[117]

No matter. Mifflin and a handful of fellow Quakers were determined to meet. From across the Delaware River in New Jersey, diarist John Hunt scribbled that "The sickness in town was so great and the town so disolate [sic] that divers Friends thought it was impracticable a Yearly Meeting could be held." Only one representative from the Philadelphia Quarterly Meeting was willing to enter the city. From Hunt's monthly meeting, only two dared go (one paying the ultimate price).[118] The redoubtable Rebecca Jones, the traveling minister who had braved many dangers during years of itinerant missions, took refuge with friends at a safe distance from the city. Miffed at the criticisms of some Friends for her decision to skip the yearly meeting, she grimly confided to a friend, "it is not for us who are absent to judge, and I much desire those who remain in the city may suspend their judgment of us who are out [of the city], remembering that 'The Lord knoweth all hearts.'"[119]

A few days before departing from Chestnut Grove, accompanied by Ann but leaving behind his children, Mifflin penned his will. It all but predicted his death. "Expecting in a few days to set off to attend our yearly meeting in Philadelphia, that city being at this time visited with an epidemic disorder of which great numbers dye, by accounts received, and great part of the inhabitants in consequence thereof have left the city," he was setting down his last will and testament. "It feels awful to undertake this journey," he spelled out in the first paragraph, "but believing it my duty to proceed therein, having nothing in view but to be found in the discharge thereof to Him who gave me a being, and whom I have faith to believe can preserve me even amidst the raging pestilence, if he is so pleased to do, however I desire to be resigned to his holy will therein."[120]

Arriving in the city on September 22, Warner and Ann huddled with the few who chose to defy the grisly odds against them. Among them was his old friend George Churchman, with whom he had traveled northward to New England for many weeks seventeen years before. Also present was James Emlen, Ann's younger brother, who had come from Chester County as a delegate from his monthly meeting. His old friend Jacob Lindley, another Chester County Public Friend, came as well. In a normal year more than one thousand would have gathered for the yearly meeting; this time, one reported, those assembled "was about as large as a Monthly Meeting"—some sixty to eighty. Most of them, having survived the 1797 epidemic, apparently believed they would endure. Moreover, they were convinced that a watchful God was testing them. But they stayed only for two sessions on September 23 and 24, when by consent they adjourned to reconvene in mid-December. One of Warner's friends recounted how he shook hands with Mifflin, who looked "very pleasant" and then sat between a Bucks County minister and his brother-in-law. Within days, all three were in their graves.[121]

While most of the other delegates headed home, Warner and Ann chose to stay to tend stricken Friends still in the city. Day by day the death toll mounted. Benjamin Franklin Bache, Benjamin Franklin's grandson, was dead. Samuel Pastorius, Germantown master builder and grandson of the German immigrant who had led the first protest against slavery in Pennsylvania 110 years before, was followed to the grave by his wife. Also lowered into the ground was Hannah Lindley, the wife of the Mifflins' valued friend Jacob Lindley. There were scores more. Of the twenty-one elders who attended, seven perished.[122]

On September 24, as Friends disbanded, Mifflin sat at his lodgings, took pen in hand, and composed the last letter he would ever write. To John Adams, the nation's second President, he poured out all his accumulated grief at the plight of black America and the sinfulness of white America, which had blood on its hands for enslaving 700,000 fellow creatures and oppressing 90,000 free blacks.

Starting with how "my mind has been deeply affected" as he gazed at "the awful judgments (as I believe) of an offended God now displayed conspicuously over this city through the grievous mortality suffered on its inhabitants," he confessed that "it has felt to me a little like taking my life in my hands to come hither, singly to endeavor in my small measure, to promote the cause of Righteousness in the Earth." He asked what the president might do about "the abominable trade carried on through [Delaware and Maryland] by Negro-Drovers, buying drove after drove of the poor afflicted Blacks, like droves of cattle for market; carrying them into the Southern States for speculation, regardless of the separation of nearest connections & natural ties." Perhaps the President "as prime Magistrate in the United States may be entirely without the knowledge of this atrocious & abominable crime." But surely he did. Who didn't know about the ballooning domestic slave trade that was betraying the promise of the American Revolution? Could not the president of the United States—a man who had been in the vanguard of the Age of Enlightenment, the intellectual heartbeat in the era of democratic revolutions, a constitution writer, a signer of the Declaration of Independence, a minister to England and France in the aftermath of the American Revolution—"do thy Duty [and] discharge thyself"?

Further, while recognizing "thou hast no constitutional power to do anything in this business and that the general government has none," was there no higher power which obliged Adams to speak out on the matter? How could a country withstand "divine displeasure" when it had "declared to all the world ... that 'it was self-evident all men were created equal; that they were endowed by their Creator with certain inalienable rights,'" and then "say nothing about withhold[ing] from so great a part of our fellow-man the unalienable rights with which they are endowed by their creator"? If barren of constitutional power, did not Adams have moral capital to draw upon? "Would to God our President might be animated ... to call the consideration of our legislature to this grievous ... oppression of our fellow-man, the Blacks in this land."

In a final stab, Mifflin charged that Adams had "fixed a stigma" on his presidency by "giving sanction" to the law that Congress had passed six months before to establish the Mississippi Territory, the last chance for the federal legislature to ban slavery east of the Mississippi River. Instead, it allowed a slave code that denied the slightest rights to blacks, even to owning a dog. Once more, the nation's leader had opened "a wide field to this infamous [slave] traffic," this time to a "new country back of Georgia."[123]

With the dreaded disease lurking in his body, Mifflin and his wife returned to Chestnut Grove.[124] They grieved at the word that her younger brother James, who had lost his wife in the 1793 yellow fever epidemic, had died shortly after returning home to Chester County from the yearly meeting, leaving six children parentless. Ann's brother had also believed "himself bound in duty to attend with the friends at the usual time and place, which was the third time he attended under such circumstances." Like Warner, he made "due provision for the settlement of his worldly affairs," penning a will and arranging for the guardianship of his young sons and daughters. The fever took him away in his thirty-eighth year.[125]

By October 10, the yellow fever was coursing through Mifflin's body. For the next six days, his family stood at his side. A year later, still distraught with grief, Ann recounted for her young sons the final moments:

> But oh! the imbittered pangs of separation . . . and . . . how doth mine eyes run down with tears . . . I was his steady nurse with your [half-] brother Warner [Jr.] and [half-]sister Susannah not very long before his departure, married with loss of sleep, grief, and attendance. I retired to another room to see if I could be sustained by a few moments rest, but sleep was far from me and when about to return I received a message that he wished to see me; I went and with a look filled with tenderness, he said he loved to have me bye him; a most affectionate embrace took place. . . . Not long after with much composure, though with some evident increase in pain (as he had laid in much quietness and without much apparent suffering for the greater part of his sickness) the solemn moment took place.

On October 16, 1798, Warner Mifflin passed away.

Writing of his death, Ann recounted her husband's worries about his young children. Then, "after repeated looks of inexpressible concern on my account, [he] desired me not to grieve for him." But how could she not after "agonies at seeing him die? . . . Ah! my dear children!" she counseled, "dwell as at the foot stool of Jesus, ask counsel of him the unerring guide and councillor. Delight to read instructive and good books. Don't pass over time in idleness and dissipation of mind that ought to be better applied."[126]

The next morning, on October 17, 1798, four African American men bore Mifflin's casket from a wagon to the Murderkill meetinghouse burial ground.

No record remains to tell us the names of the pallbearers, but it is likely that at least some of them were among the enslaved blacks Mifflin had liberated a quarter-century before. Grieving at the graveside was his widow, who would survive him for seventeen years. No doubt, his children were there to see their father buried, five days short of his fifty-third birthday. Warner, Jr., was twenty-one, Susanna was nineteen, Sarah was fourteen, Samuel and Lemuel were eight and six. Forbidden to attend were the area's enslaved men and women, whose masters feared the germ of freedom would spread.[127] Free black Kent Countians thronged the funeral to honor Mifflin and watch him lowered into an unmarked grave.[128]

Nathaniel Luff, a Quaker doctor from Dover and longtime friend of Mifflin, attended the funeral. He described how Mifflin's widow at the graveside "delivered some tender and interesting expressions of his respecting the black people, . . . he having been much concerned for their welfare in his illness." Mifflin "departed quietly and in resignation to the Divine will," the doctor noted. In a final salute, Luff confided to his journal that Mifflin was one of the Quakers "who hesitated not to venture their lives in that sickly place [Philadelphia] under a sense of their religious duty to their annual appointments [as delegates to the Philadelphia Yearly Meeting]."[129]

That black Delawareans carried Mifflin to his grave would have surprised nobody along the Atlantic Seaboard, for the deceased Quaker's efforts on their behalf had become widely known. The Kent County he left behind had become the locale, from New York south to Virginia, Pennsylvania excepted, where slavery had most rapidly yielded to free black life.[130] Ann Mifflin reminded her two young sons that their father's greatest mission was on behalf of black America:

> that which most engaged the uniform exercise of his mind for a number
> of years, as the top-stone of his religious concern, was a laborious travail
> of spirit and free disposal of his time & substance in advancing the
> liberation of the poor oppressed black people. A trumpet was given him
> on this subject with other brethren to spread the alarm within the
> borders of our Society that we might more and more arise and shake
> ourselves from the dust of the earth in a departure from this iniquity.
> And when our camp was in a good degree purged from this filthiness
> thereof, his commission was enlarged to go forth among the people
> and powers of the earth to labour and dissuade them from such an

unrighteous practice. . . . He patiently bore their contumely in the experience of that blessing devolving on those who are persecuted for righteousness sake. This laborious exercise on this subject . . . towards the latter part of his times had evidently a wasting effect on his frame, which hastened the period of a life much devoted to the self-denying path and close religious engagements of a faithful disciple of the Lamb. So that it might be truly said, he wore out his talents [but] did not rust out for want of use.[131]

"The wasting effect on his frame" had been a long time coming. It almost certainly figured in his grim insistence to confront the loathsome yellow fever storm that swept away Philadelphians and its visitors in the autumn of 1798. Was it a buried desire to end it all? We will never know. What is certain is that he was discouraged at the country he loved. Exuberant, materialistic, violent white America, unfaithful to its purported founding principles and turning self-interest into a virtue, had befouled the nation's promise and honored his treasured Golden Rule mostly in the breach. He could find little balm for his anguish about the plight of aggrieved blacks, and he trembled at what a troubled God would visit on a sinning nation.

# Chapter 6

## Mifflin's Long Shadow

*Mifflin's dedication to antislavery* could be ignored, muffled, lampooned, and deplored, but never could his cry to Christian humanity and universal freedom be silenced. For several decades after his death, no one so fully committed to hoisting the banners of abolition stepped into his shoes, though his cousin John Parrish and some of the leading members of the Pennsylvania Abolition Society and the Philadelphia Meeting for Sufferings did their best. Yet Mifflin's death cast a long shadow, and indeed the shadow reached across the Atlantic all the way eastward to the Russian-bound advances of Napoleon's army. This chapter delves into how his legacy influenced his extended family and others, Quakers and non-Quakers alike. They were the ones who tried to keep the lamps of antislavery burning in the early nineteenth century, creating a bridge to the radical abolitionists who emerged in the late 1820s. Though the fervor for purging the nation of its original sin declined during the presidencies of Jefferson and Madison, the early years of the nineteenth century were "hardly characterized by the collapse of revolutionary era antislavery and the triumph of proslavery and racism."[1] In Mifflin's Kent County, though out of the mainstream of seaboard politics, Quakers and Methodists were especially persistent in continuing his work, becoming important in funneling escaping slaves from the Upper South northward through the primitive network that prefigured the famous Underground Railroad of the antebellum decades.

Legacy is one thing; impact is another. Clearly, the antislavery activism of the revolutionary era embodied by Mifflin did not stop slavery's relentless growth, both in the numbers enslaved and in its march into immense new territories in the lower half of the new nation. From the time of his death in 1798 to the eve of the Civil War, the number of enslaved increased almost sevenfold, as the empire of liberty became the empire of slavery. In spite of the way the revolution had disrupted slavery, shattered the idea that it was a part of the natural order, inspired gradual emancipation in all the northern states, and given rise to the infrastructure of free black life, racial bondage endured in the region where it was most rooted and most deeply connected to a plantation economy. In the contest between human rights and property rights, the latter were, in the short run, the clear victor. In this sense, the impact of his work was limited. Yet, one can speculate that had he lived another decade, the diminishing energy that beset the abolition movement, partly because its strongest advocates soon followed Mifflin to their graves, might have been rekindled.

His residual effect, nonetheless, was substantial. For the generation that followed his death, he bequeathed the stubborn belief that slavery could be set on the road to extinction and that in the meantime the fight must go on to rescue from its clutches as many souls as possible. None of those who continued to believe that all humankind sprang from Adam's seed, none of those sure that God would punish America for its original sin of slavery, and none of those contending that the world was watching to see if the infant nation would fulfill its self-proclaimed boast that it was conceived as a demonstration of universal principles were willing to say they were on the wrong side of history. So, like Mifflin, they put discouragement aside to continue the labor of working for inalienable rights and racial justice. In their view, to decamp from a mission that framed their sense of moral, spiritual, and political obligation—in fact their definition of what it meant to be a good citizen in a nation where active citizenship was a prime criterion of excellence—was simply not possible. Our history books picture the early decades of the nineteenth century as the headlong decay of abolitionism.[2] Yet the efforts of Mifflin's descendants and admirers, though not stopping the juggernaut of chattel slavery, kept alive the idea of universal freedom and the vision of a biracial democracy, while inching toward the more radical abolitionism that emerged by the late 1820s.

And what of a million black Americans, eight out of every ten still in bondage? For them, Mifflin's legacy provided hope for the future and an impetus for grassroots activism. Of course the odds were stiffly against them; it had never been otherwise. But whatever the odds, free blacks overwhelmingly rejected the emerging plans for their colonization in Africa, choosing to stay the course in Young America, flocking to the northern cities for a better future, or, if enslaved, rubbing hard against their shackles and sporadically rising up to topple the house of slavery. This is what Mifflin bequeathed to black

Americans, who memorialized him as the early nineteenth century proceeded
through the presidencies of Jefferson, Madison, and Monroe.


## To Dishonor and Honor

Mifflin's body was hardly cold before his detractors resumed their attacks. The
day after his death, Thomas Rodney, his slaveowning Kent County neighbor
and younger brother of Caesar Rodney, signer of the Declaration of Independence and Delaware's governor from 1778 to 1781, ornamented his diary with
bitter comments that he no doubt shared with slaveocracy friends. Mocking
Mifflin's life, he scribbled that "his funeral was like his life—a piece of affecta-
tion. . . . He was opposed secretly to the American contest for freedom yet he
professed a great regard for Negro freedom & instead of teaching Negroes true
religion filled all slaves full of mischief toward their masters & has thereby
disturbed society more than any other person in it."[3]

More publicly, William Cobbett, arriving in Philadelphia in 1794, had been
ashore only months before attacking Mifflin. Concocting a dream of William
Penn, returning to Philadelphia in a post-death visit, Cobbett had Pennsylvania's founder blinking in dismay at those "precious hypocrites (these were his
words) Brissot and Warner Mifflin."[4] Then, within six weeks of Mifflin's death,
"Peter Porcupine" threw more quills. In a jaw-dropping gale of toxic rhetoric,
Cobbett pilloried Mifflin, who "will ever be looked on as the greatest fool or
the greatest hypocrite that God ever suffered to let live."[5] Crunching words
with spectacular alacrity, Mathew Carey replied in defense of Mifflin, returning venom with venom by deploring Porcupine's "cowardly and Billingsgate
attacks on . . . Warner Mifflin whose exemplary humanity had acquired him
the plaudits of all who knew him."[6]

Cobbett never let up. Called by his most recent biographer "the most effective, the most savage, and most satirical political journalist of his or any age,"
seven years after Mifflin's death Cobbett blasted the "crack-brained Anthony
Benezet and Warner Mifflin, surnamed in his country, THE HYPOCRITE."
Quakers and Methodists, "these new-fangl'd mongrel sects" should be "stig-
matized as reprobates; as men void of all religion, morality, and feeling." In
words that Mifflin's detractors from the Deep South must have relished, Cobbett asked, "shall we silently submit; to be told that we are not Christians and

to be threatened with perdition because we refuse to become followers of Benezet and Mifflin?"[7]

Though attacked in death as in life, Mifflin attracted laudatory notices up and down the seaboard and across the Atlantic soon after his demise. Death notices appeared in eastern newspapers from Baltimore to Providence. As the *Gazette of the United States and Philadelphia Daily Advertiser* reminded its readers, "Like the celebrated [John] Knox, the Scotch reformer," Mifflin "was a man that never feared the face of man." In devoting the last two decades of his life to the enslaved, "he begat hope in the minds of the miserable," while slaveholders "(by some of whom he was grossly insulted) trembled at his name." "The extent of the misery he lessened," the notice continued, "and of the good he did, will never be fully known till the great day when the righteous judge of Heaven and Earth, who has seen in secret his numerous labours of piety and benevolence, will reward them openly in the presence of an assembled world." *Claypoole's American Daily Advertiser* assured its readers that "Of the inestimable virtues of this amiable and truly valuable member of society, panegyric falls infinitely short. When we contemplate a whole life without one moment's interval to . . . the everlasting welfare of mankind, we have only to say that in him society has sustained an irreparable loss."[8]

Unsurprisingly, black Philadelphians mourned his death. Philadelphia's Richard Allen, minister of Mother Bethel, the African Methodist Episcopal Church, called him a "spiritual Moses." "Though he was rejected and despised by many who held our fellow creatures in bondage," wrote Allen, "like a good soldier he stood to his integrity, took up his cross daily, and despised the shame of befriending those despised people." For many years, Mifflin had been instrumental "in liberating hundreds, if not thousands of the African race," said Allen, who was sure the memory of "that great and good man . . . will not be forgotten for ages to come."[9]

Quakers too—some with reservations—memorialized Mifflin for his unceasing testimony to emancipationism and equality for free blacks. From Philadelphia, his friend Leonard Snowden wrote that "This day a Prince and Great Man is fallen in Israel. I have often had to say why is such a poor creature as I am spared when men that serve so eminently useful are taken."[10] George Churchman, his friend of so many years and so many thousands of miles astride horses, eulogized him as "a valuable standard bearer in the militant church" and a man incessantly striving for "the relief from oppression and distress of those he frequently called his brethren of the African race."[11] His beloved

Murderkill Meeting called him "exemplary in simplicity and moderation," "a Peace Maker [who] was frequently made use of in settling differences," and, above all, known for "his disinterested labours and dedication of his time and talents in advocating the cause and promoting the liberation of the oppressed black People."[12]

Across the Atlantic, Quakers in London quickly took notice of Mifflin's death. Within weeks, the London Quaker publishers Darton and Harvey printed a broadside where, beneath the notice of Mifflin's death, appeared "The Good Master and the Faithful Slave"—the account of how Mifflin and James, sitting in a field in Kent County, conversed to reach an agreement on James's liberation and how Mifflin would compensate him for eight and a half years of unpaid labor after James had reached twenty-one. Recycled as "Warner Mifflin and James: An American Anecdote," it ran in newspapers from Vermont to Virginia. Though retailed as an anecdote, it gave publicity to Mifflin's doctrine of reparations.[13]

Lifted from Crèvecoeur's Paris edition of *Lettres d'un cultivateur américain*, this embellished dialogue had since 1791 already reached school children. N. [Nicolas] Wanostrocht included the dialogue in his *Recueil choisi de traits historiques et de contes moraux: Avec la signification des mots en anglais au bas de chaque page* (Selected Historical Moral Stories), where English children learned French. So did Marie Elisabeth de la Fite in *Questions to be Resolved, or a New Method of Exercising the Attention of Young People Interspersed with Various Pieces Calculated for Instruction*. Thus thousands of children, their tutors, and their parents learned about "The Generous Quaker," alongside celebrations of storied figures such as Cincinnatus, Emperor Trajan, Brutus, Thomas More, William Tell, and Savonarola.[14]

On both sides of Atlantic, Mifflin's dedication to black humanity took on greater luster in 1808 with the publication of Thomas Clarkson's *History of the Abolition of the Slave Trade*. Internationally famous for his *Essay on the Impolicy of the African Slave Trade* (1788), Clarkson was the driving force in the long campaign to end the English slave trade. Like Mifflin, he was an agitator; like Mifflin, he devoted his life to the slavery issue.[15] Recognizing Mifflin's role as successor to John Woolman and Anthony Benezet, Clarkson, while lauding Quakers in general for their role in attacking slavery, singled out Mifflin not only as a leading manumitter of his own slaves but as a reparationist. In freeing their slaves, Clarkson wrote, some Quakers "gave the most splendid example in doing it, not only by consenting, as others did, thus to give up their property, and to incur the penalties of manumission, but by calculating and giving what was due to them, over and above their food and clothing, for wages from the beginning of their slaving to the day when their liberation commenced." He footnoted that encomium with "One of the brightest instances was that afforded by Warner Mifflin. He gave unconditional liberty to his slaves. He paid all the adults, on their discharge, the sum, which arbitrators, mutually chosen, awarded them."[16] With four thousand copies sold by subscription and thousands more within a few years, Clarkson's *History* made the patriarch of Chestnut Grove a familiar figure. Mifflin's persistence and courage were now secured for at least a generation.[17]

## The Widow's Ministry

Though anguished by Warner's death, Ann Mifflin put grief behind her to launch the life of a Quaker minister and activist, though in the latter role her options were constrained by the gender conventions of the day. She could not carry on his antislavery work, because the work of a lobbyist, writing petitions and memorials while haunting state and federal legislative chambers, was strictly a male prerogative. Nor could she act as "next friend" for blacks in freedom suits in the courts. Neither was there much opportunity to fill the public prints with remonstrances against a sinning, slaveholding nation. Also, in the decision to move to Philadelphia, Ann had left behind Chestnut Grove as a way station and place of counsel for refugee slaves. Yet she honored Warner's quarter-century crusade as best she could. Though giving priority to the plight of suffering Native Americans, she did not neglect the African American cause; and in her many sojourns to local and regional Quaker meetings, she followed her husband in pressing for stricter discipline. If he bore the cross, so did she.

But first, at forty-three, she had to deal with the complicated settlement of her husband's will while managing the distraught household at Chestnut Grove. Warner's will might have been straightforward. He struggled to make it so, but started too late, failing to complete it. With his body collapsing, he had wanted to think through its provisions with his wife's help. But since her husband had produced offspring by two mothers, Ann insisted she must leave it entirely to him.[18] This was a misfortune, though she claimed she was glad she did not participate in structuring such a complicated portfolio of property holdings.

The problem was not one of insufficient assets to provide for his large family, for Warner's real and personal property was ample to supply adequate legacies for widow Ann, the five children from his first marriage, and their two young sons. His mind clouded with thoughts of his demise, Mifflin scratched out a will on the eve of his departure to Philadelphia. It was badly drawn and ultimately declared invalid. He intended that the valuable Philadelphia properties Ann had brought to the marriage would revert to her. Ann would also get her dowry furniture, as well as "my best riding carriage," her choice of carriage horses, several work horses, a plow and harrow, six cows from the herd, a yoke of oxen and oxcart, three of the best beds with appurtenances, and most of the "mansion plantation" with its house and outbuildings. Their two young sons were also well provided for: Samuel, now eight, would inherit Chestnut Grove and the plantation at Cow Marsh, now at lease, when his mother died. Lemuel, now six, would have the "marsh plantation" of some 300 acres and two other properties when he reached twenty-one, the rents on it during his minority to support his education. Warner bequeathed the remainder of his estate in equal parts to the five living children from his first marriage. As executors of his estate he nominated his brother Daniel and his trusted brothers-in-law Jonathan Hunn and Samuel Howell, married to his half-sisters Patience and Elizabeth.[19]

The inexactitude and incompleteness of the will was so serious that Warner Mifflin, Jr., engaged Nicholas Ridgely, a foremost lawyer, to petition the Kent County Orphans Court to declare the will invalid insofar as it pertained to real estate spread over Murderkill, Mispillion, St. Jones, and Little Creek Hundreds. After the court declared that Warner died intestate "as to his real estate," the difficulty turned into a family squabble, with Ann's stepchildren unwilling to provide her support from leased properties until a welter of debts, both in favor of and against their deceased father, had been cleared and the court had ruled on the division of property. Court-ordered surveys of the many properties limped along. Finally, in 1806 the court ruled that Ann Mifflin would get the customary widow's third, with the other two-thirds split equally among seven living children.[20]

While this tangled estate settlement ran its course, widow Ann had two young boys to raise, as well as her fifteen-year-old stepdaughter. Nonetheless, an almost all-consuming desire to enlist in the army of the Quaker church militant led her from Chestnut Grove to Philadelphia. There, with her young sons and stepdaughter, she settled in under the roof of her aging mother, still hale at eighty.[21]

Returning to her Quaker city roots, Ann first moved to protect Warner's reputation. Writing as "An Observer" from Kent County, she grafted a corrective of what she regarded as misrepresentations in Brissot's lavishly positive portrayal of Mifflin onto a response to William Cobbett's acid-tongued attacks on her husband just after his death. It was an awkward piece, and she knew as much in seeking the advice and approval or two of Warner's most trusted friends—John Parrish and Moses Brown. She rejected Brissot's claim that in his conversation with Warner, her husband claimed "to exalt the character of the French Nation at the expense of the English." At a time of American disillusionment with the French Revolution, this needed correction. She knew his love "was universal," she wrote, and extended to "the whole bulk of mankind without respect to the nation or color." Cobbett's charges "to stamp him as a hypocrite" were more serious. Appealing to all who knew her husband as a man of great integrity, she invited subscribers to repay Peter Porcupine's attempt "to assassinate a character that . . . did honor to humanity" by canceling their subscriptions to Cobbett's newspaper.[22] Though it was never published, it at least satisfied Ann's devotion to keep the memory of her husband untarnished.

As guardian of Warner's legacy, Ann also had to bring to a conclusion the last letter he wrote. After drafting a plaintive missive to President John Adams in Philadelphia, with yellow fever victims dying around him, Warner had taken the letter back to Kent County to transcribe before dispatching it. Falling ill, he left it in his wife's hands. In her grief at his death, she left this unattended. Two years later, she asked Warner's lifelong friends George Churchman and Jacob Lindley to send the letter to Adams. This they did in January 1801, on the eve of Adams's completion of his presidential term. Picking up where Mifflin left off, they pointed to the increase in the "disgraceful traffick in human flesh." Sounding much like Mifflin, Churchman and Lindley asked, "Why should six hundred thousand fellow-creatures continue from year to year, and from age to age, to groan, many of them under more than Egyptian oppression, without the pity and compassion due from professed Christian rulers?" As Mifflin asked in his letter, would the president not lend his voice to stop "the engines of death and destruction" that insulted the Christian God and the land of professed liberty?[23]

Adams promptly replied in what Ann Mifflin could reasonably have interpreted as a defense of slavery, even a mockery of her husband's lifelong work.

With astounding dissimulation, Adams opined that "the practice of slavery is fast diminishing" and that "the condition of the common sort of white people in some of the southern states particularly in Virginia is more oppressed, degraded and miserable than that of the Negroes." Yes, slavery was an evil, he allowed, and ought in time to be gradually abolished. But Adams advised that Churchman and Lindley would better serve the country by focusing on "more serious and threatening evils" that promised "to bring punishment in our land, more immediately than the oppression of the blacks," such as "a general debauchery as well as dissipation produced by pestilential philosophical principles of epicures"—that is to say, deism and atheism. Offering no comfort, Adams warned that "inflammatory publications against the slavery of the blacks"—this was a thinly disguised reference to Mifflin's writings—would backfire, bringing more misery to the enslaved.[24] No letter in the surviving Adams correspondence tells us that Ann responded to Adams's feckless reply, but her subsequent concern for African Americans shows that she strongly disagreed.

Having reimplanted herself in Philadelphia Quaker circles in 1799 after an absence of eleven years, Ann took up housekeeping with her long-widowed mother in the Emlen mansion, across the street from the State House.[25] Sarah, now fifteen, forged an almost maternal bond with her two young stepbrothers. In 1800, when the Philadelphia Yearly Meeting opened the long-planned Westtown Friends boarding school in West Chester, Ann took her place on the female side of the governing board and enrolled Samuel and Lemuel. It did not go well for the boys, who lasted only a few semesters.[26]

While coping with her two struggling sons was difficult, Ann reestablished herself in Quaker affairs, becoming a familiar figure in the monthly, quarterly, and yearly Philadelphia meetings.[27] Also providing ballast in her personal travails, she involved herself in benevolent causes, busying herself with the education and poor relief of young white women, joining her second cousin Ann Parrish, who in her early twenties broke free of the traditional Quaker women's benevolence directed at needy Friends to found the Society for Relief of the Poor, which ministered to *non*-Friends. When Parrish founded the nonsectarian Aimwell School to educate poor girls, Ann joined that effort as well.[28]

However, dedicating herself to the life of a traveling minister became Ann Mifflin's raison d'être, a role she would play with quiet intensity for the remaining years of her life. For twelve years of marriage she had served on committees of preparative and monthly meetings in Kent County and as a delegate to quarterly and yearly meetings. But now, as the new century began, she launched a series of strenuous trips that took her thousands of miles, mostly on the back of a horse, to small Quaker communities on the fringes of white settlement and to Native American villages in western Pennsylvania and New York. Again and again, she went to the women's meeting with requests for traveling certificates: "she has had her mind drawn to visit divers meetings in remote parts of our Quarterly Meeting"; "her mind is investing with a religious concern"; "our beloved friend spread before the meeting a concern which has some time rested on her mind and of late with increasing weight." Each time the women's meeting approved and passed the recommendation along to the men's meeting, which in every case readily concurred. In the first five years of the new century six of these trips kept her on the road for about half of each year, and three of them would distinguish her as the first female missionary to the Brotherton, Stockbridge, Oneida, and Seneca peoples. In all of these trips, her frequent letters to her mother laid bare her concern, bordering on guilt, for leaving behind the two juvenile sons plagued with physical and emotional difficulties.[29]

Ann's initial trip in October 1800 took her for the first time west of the Appalachian Mountains, where Quaker farmers were taking up new land and building rude meetinghouses in the upper Susquehanna River settlements of Ceres-town, Munsy, and Half-Moon Valley. To undertake this by horse with the onset of winter, accompanied by the tanner and currier Arthur Howell and Ruth Richardson, wife of a wealthy Philadelphia silversmith, seemed to tempt disaster for three city dwellers; but they returned safely after about eight weeks, reporting "close unity" with the frontier-hardened Friends. A second long trip, northward to monthly, quarterly, and yearly meetings in New York, Connecticut, Rhode Island, and Nantucket Island from May to July in 1801 retraced the steps of Warner two decades before. Renewing her husband's warm interactions with Moses Brown of Providence and William Rotch of Nantucket kept alive old friendships.[30]

In 1802, toughened by travel, Ann turned to what she called "the laudable work of improving our brethren the natives."[31] For the next few years, this preoccupied her. Her interest in Quaker humanitarian aid to the Iroquois people reached back to the early 1790s, when Warner, her brother James Emlen, and close friends Jacob Lindley, William Savery, and John Parrish had taken up the cause of the bludgeoned native people struggling to adapt to reservation life after the American Revolution. Quakers had become unofficial observers and advisors at a series of treaty negotiations in the early 1790s, and their attempts to bring some stability and simple justice to the painful reduction of the Iroquois nations had earned them the respect of native people.[32] Then in 1795, the Philadelphia Yearly Meeting established an Indian Committee for Promoting the Improvement and Gradual Civilization of the Indian Natives. Its mission was to assist the federal government in promoting what was termed the "civilization" of native people by giving material aid and counsel that would nudge them toward taking up white ways, in particular plow agriculture, female domesticity, and literacy schooling. This, Friends hoped, would allow them to survive their encirclement by land-hungry post-revolutionary white Americans. Improving their lives, rather than converting native people to the Quaker faith, was at the heart of the efforts, and this made Friends more welcome in the villages of Iroquoia than the proselytizing Protestant missionaries who swarmed onto Indian lands in the 1790s.[33]

Appointed by the Indian Committee, Ann left Philadelphia in August 1802, for a three-month trip northward to "Upper Canady" to visit Oneida reservations, including the Brotherton and Stockbridge people domiciled within the Oneidas; others in villages on the vast land between Lakes Ontario and Simcoe; and still others on the Tonawanda and Tuscarora reservations. Before she returned to Philadelphia, she had covered more than twelve hundred miles by horse, foot, and canoe. The first white female to speak to the Brotherton and Stockbridge people, she explained her belief that they were part of the lost tribes of Israel, how she valued their Peacemakers who maintained community norms, and their vow to drive alcohol from their lives, and how she was gladdened by one of the speaker's promises that "we shall always remember what she said" about their origins, while imploring her to send other women instructors to live with them.[34]

The trip also afforded Mifflin a chance to play the role her deceased husband had performed for so many years on his traveling ministries—working to renew and revive the faith of Quaker meetings—but this time in the remote, newly settled gatherings that the Philadelphia Yearly Meeting was trying to bring closer under its disciplinary umbrella.[35]

In the following year, Ann was one of two women in the Friends delegation to the Allegany reservation of Seneca people just north of the Pennsylvania-New York border, where Quaker missionaries, at the invitation of Chief Cornplanter, had created a model farm in 1798 to demonstrate the advantages of plow agriculture, mills for grinding corn and sawing wood, frame houses, blacksmithing, and education in English and American ways.[36] Until 1803, this Quaker project had been entirely a male affair, though from the beginning the Friends understood that without changing the gendered division of labor their reform plan was doomed. More than a decade before, Cornplanter had asked for white women to teach spinning and weaving.[37] But for five years, since setting up their demonstration farm, no woman had come to the Allegany Seneca to instruct and inspire the women. That is where Ann Mifflin became an agent of change. She set out with three Friends—Penrose Wiley, John Letchworth, and Mary Bell—she and Mary were the first white women to reach the model farm at Genesinguhta (Old Town), about nine miles upriver from Cornplanter's village, just north of present-day Warren, Pennsylvania.[38] Over rutted and stony roads, through rugged low mountain country, and across deep, swift-running river fords, Ann's horse took her more than three hundred miles to reach Genesinguhta.[39] Elk, wolves, mountain lions, and bears were more her daily companions than the sparsely encountered hardscrabble frontier settlers.[40] Along the way she communed with scattered Quaker families only beginning to form into preparative meetings.

To judge by reports sent back to the Indian Committee, Seneca women listened attentively to Ann Mifflin and Mary Bell, who urged that they adopt "branches suited to our sex"—spinning and weaving—rather than "drudging alone in the labors of the field." This realignment of gender roles did not happen quickly or without resistance, though it was encouraged by Seneca leaders, including Cornplanter, his half-brother Handsome Lake, and even the less assimilation-inclined Red Jacket. But upon returning to Philadelphia, Mifflin found no women willing to join the Quaker men who had taken up residence in the villages.[41] This would change in 1805 with the arrival of two Quaker women. From then on, the instruction of Seneca women continued, though by no means as rapidly as hoped by Ann and other Quaker reformers.[42]

Ann Mifflin's last effort to add her voice to the new republic's discourse on creating "a more perfect union" aligned her with Warner's grand obsession of aiding the oppressed black Americans. After his death, she had brooded about the plight of the enslaved Americans she saw in her journeys down the Eastern Shore and across the Chesapeake Bay to Virginia.[43] By 1806, she was proposing a new colony for the "colonization of the black people on the coast of Africa."[44] It was far from a new idea. Since the late revolutionary period supporters of abolition, both white and black, had floated schemes for finding a New Jerusalem for those who had broken slavery's chains but found little promise for genuine freedom. The sites of possible relocation ranged from Louisiana to the trans-Mississippi West to coastal West Africa, and the motives varied from group to group, including those eager to empty the United States of all its black citizens. The Sierra Leone colony, established in 1789 by English abolitionists, had already attracted several thousand African Americans, most of whom had gained their freedom with the British during the American Revolution. However, only a handful of free blacks in the United States had joined this now floundering colony. Some Virginians had discussed such a plan a few years before, with no results. That a Quaker woman would try to jump-start the back-to-Africa movement was in itself a remarkable display of Ann's determination to play a role on the national stage.

The first woman to become involved in the colonization movement, Ann discussed her idea of state-based "returning societies" with Paul Cuffe, when the mixed-race New Bedford Quaker sea captain and merchant spent several weeks in December 1807 in Philadelphia, where he met with black leaders and members of the Pennsylvania Abolition Society.[45] President Jefferson's embargo, a response to French and British attacks on neutral American shipping, blocked any chance at that time to mount an emigration of American free blacks. But Mifflin revived the idea in 1809 when she asked Democratic Pennsylvania Senator George Logan, grandson of James Logan, to present the idea to Thomas Jefferson.[46] Jefferson chose not to respond.

If Jefferson would not reply to her, she would go to him. Or try. Traveling with Sarah Zane, a Philadelphia Quaker with deep Virginia connections, Mifflin made a last attempt in 1810 to rally support among Virginia political leaders, while still hoping to enlist Jefferson. Incorporating her husband's ideas about reparations, she proposed state-based societies that would underwrite the cost of shipboard passage to Africa and provide six months of provisions for former slaves wanting to return to Africa.[47] Her hope—distinct from what would become a main goal of the American Colonization Society, founded a year after her death in 1815 to rid the nation of troublesome free black people— was to induce slaveowners to free their slaves. As she explained to her mother, the goal was "the releasement of this country from the cloud of slavery that hangs over it" and the chance for "such of them [liberated slaves] as were disposed to go to the ancient bounds of their habitation."[48]

From bayside Maryland to tidewater Alexandria to interior Richmond and Lynchburg, Virginia, Mifflin and Zane met with every slaveholder who would give them a hearing, arguing that they should free their slaves and help those

who wished to return to Africa—"and not empty handed." Former governor
James Wood, who had freed his slaves, promised to promote the idea. So did
John Tyler, the present governor. All along the way in this two-month mission,
the two women found many receptive Virginians. However, when Jefferson
found it inconvenient to meet her, Ann was left to send the retired president
her request for support though John Lynch, Quaker former slaveowner, pros-
perous businessman, and founder of Lynchburg. Jefferson, supportive in
principle (though by now backing away from his former support for gradual
abolition), replied that he had long wished "for gradually drawing off this part
of our population most advantageously for themselves as well as for us," hoping that liberated slaves "would thus carry back to the country of their origin
the seeds of civilization, which might render their sojournment and sufferings
here a blessing in the end to that country."[49] As for participation in such an
endeavor, Jefferson silently declined.

After this last effort honoring Warner's decades-long efforts, Ann Mifflin
began to fall into decline, never again leaving Philadelphia as a traveling minister. Seeing her end, she lined out a will in 1811, making her older son sole
executor of her extensive estate and guardian of his nineteen-year-old brother
until he reached twenty-one.[50] Four years later, heartbroken for reasons soon
to be discussed, she died on March 21, 1815, just short of her sixtieth birthday.
She did not rust, as she had said about Warner; she wore herself out. Rather
than having her remains interred in Delaware alongside those of her husband,
she chose as her last resting place the burial ground of the Friends Arch Street
meetinghouse, where she had communed for so many years. A year later, her
mother died at ninety-five, having outlived her husband by forty years and
leaving substantial legacies to her grandsons Samuel and Lemuel.


## Samuel and Lemuel


It was a matter of great torment to Ann Mifflin that her two sons, fathered by
Warner, had health issues, few prospects for useful careers, little interest in
Quaker humanitarian affairs, and an indifference to the Society of Friends
itself. In their early years, their half-sister Sarah, who had come to Philadelphia
with her stepmother, was devoted to the boys. She, along with their grandmother Ann Emlen, provided much of the emotional support they needed
when their mother was away on her frequent missions. Samuel, the older boy,

developed signs of emotional disorders as well as physical difficulties from an early age. Though he seemed to acquire no gainful occupation, he made a tentative entry in 1812 into urban charitable work as a member of the Philadelphia Society for Free Instruction of Indigent Boys.[51] But by this time, at twenty-two, Samuel had become unhinged, caused in the view of his younger brother by "excessive studiousness and intense application."[52] A year later, drawing on the vast Mifflin network of cousins, Ann tried—to no avail—to get cousin Joseph Mifflin, Jr., who had opened a school in western Pennsylvania, to take her troubled son under his wing.[53]

Remaining in Philadelphia, Samuel lapsed into strange ruminations about his family's history. In 1814, inexplicably turning against the Society of Friends, he wrote two rambling, incoherent letters to Jefferson, retired at Monticello. The letters exalted General Thomas Mifflin, his father's second cousin, who was disowned by the Society of Friends, and tried to salvage the reputation of Joseph Galloway, his Loyalist great-uncle. If his mother had read the letters before they were posted to Jefferson, she would have nearly collapsed with grief at scanning the tangled, syntax-mangled sentences. "Whether the valour of Thomas Mifflin did not shine conspicuous before the eternal spirit and whether his fame has not been injured by the indigence of the Quaker Society," one passage stumbled along, "whether the little want of principle of virtue of intelligence of liberality in the State of which he was a member has not or whether the envy and enmity of private families have not infringed upon his right and glory and whether the vanity of others, Virginians as well as Pennsylvanians." A second letter continued in this vein: "The Mifflin family and the Mifflin name is the greatest in the world as by the authority of the word of God it is testified. The Mifflin family are inspired by the Holy Ghost to protect man from the vanity of the Quakers, to protest America from the contempt of Devils."[54]

Samuel's insanity disfigured the rest of his life. By 1815, the executorship of his mother's estate was transferred by court order to his younger brother. A Committee of Lunacy appointed by the court managed his affairs, while his uncle Samuel Mifflin, a doctor trained in Philadelphia and London, did his best to ease his nephew through the six remaining years of his life.[55]

While his older brother Samuel suffered recurring attacks of derangement, Lemuel tried to find his life's purpose through contacts with the family of William Jackson, the Chester County farmer and Quaker elder with whom his father had made the momentous New England trip in 1781. Briefly a schoolmate of Jackson's nephew, Lemuel spent summers as a teenager at the Jackson home in Chester County, and maintained a correspondence with the younger Jackson.[56] Surely his mother was encouraged when at eighteen Lemuel was elected secretary of the Philadelphia Hose Company, the pride of young men from some of the city's oldest Quaker families. This forecast a bright future.[57]

It was not to be. Accompanying his mother to the Eastern Shore on her traveling ministry journeys, by age eighteen he began distancing himself from the inbred circle of old-family Philadelphia Quakers. Tiring of the city, and utterly uninterested in his father's dreams of a better America, he lurched from one scheme to another. First, he planned to purchase a farm in Chester County; scuttling that plan, he made his way to Pittsburgh and from there down the Ohio River to find a new purpose in life.[58]

The journey to the Ohio country, in the summer of 1812 when the war with Great Britain was under way, almost proved his undoing. A month after he left Philadelphia, his mother received an alarming letter, recounting his journey through "the back countries," where he saw settler families in full flight. "Children that was big enough to travel," he wrote, "has a bundle to carry, and that some they met would flee into the woods and hide and could hardly be persuaded that their fears were groundless and the alarms false, although it appeared it really was so." This was the backwash of the Battle of Detroit, where the British and their native allies under Tecumseh overwhelmed the Americans at Fort Detroit. Lemuel described some 1,600 Ohio militia, paroled after capture by the British, fleeing southward in disarray.[59]

Ann Mifflin must have been thankful to see her son return safely to Philadelphia, only to be horrified when he enlisted in 1815 to fight in the 1st Regiment of Pennsylvania Volunteers, officered by John R. Mifflin, one of his many Mifflin relatives.[60] Unscathed after four months, he mustered out on New Year's Day in 1815. Four days later, after several months of admonishing Lemuel for violating "our peaceable testimony," the Philadelphia Monthly Meeting declared him "separated" from the Society of Friends.[61] Three months later he saw his mother buried in the Arch Street Quaker cemetery. Hearing of her death, John Hunt, one of Warner's close friends, inscribed in his journal a chilling benediction to her life: "Heard of the death of our worthy Friend Anna Mifflin and some think she died of a broken heart. One son went crazy and the other, worse, into the wars. . . . These were the sons of that worthy elder Warner Mifflin." Six weeks later, unable to dislodge sorrowful thoughts from his mind,

Hunt scrawled in his journal that "some thought the conduct of her sons short-ened her days," then quoted Genesis 34:30: "Ye have made me to stink amongst the inhabitants of the land, among the Canaanites and Perizzites, said good old Jacob."[62]

After their mother and grandmother died, Samuel and Lemuel, amply supported by their inheritances, lived only a few more years, plagued by physical and mental disorders.[63] When Samuel died in 1821, unmarried and intestate at thirty-one, his estate, virtually all of it inherited from his mother, was adjudicated by the Pennsylvania Supreme Court, which awarded part of the estate to his surviving brother and half-sister.[64] Lemuel for several years established a dry goods business in Philadelphia, outlived his brother by three years, and died in 1824 at thirty-two. The Quaker interment records report the cause of death as *mania a potu* (madness from drinking; delirium tremens; insanity).[65] One wonders who was at the grave for the burial. Only two of Warner's twelve children were still alive—Warner, Jr., and Sarah.

## The Abolitionist Strain

Along with the loss of historical memory of Warner Mifflin's life work has been the disappearance in the record of the mark he made on his descendants. This is partially explained because it was through the female branch of the Mifflin family tree that the abolitionist impulse made its appearance. If there is such a thing as an abolitionist gene, it passed from Mifflin to the female line of his family while bypassing the male line, which in any event died out with the death of his three sons. Losing their birth surname through marriage, the sisters and daughters have lost their place in the annals of antislavery. But without doubt, Mifflin's imprint on his half-sisters and daughters was a mat-ter of pride for the way they lived their lives while influencing the men they married.

It must have been a source of consternation and grief among the Mifflin kinfolk that Warner's sons by his second marriage fell away from their father's life-long hope to reform Young America. As for his only son from his marriage with Elizabeth Johns, the story was not much better.

Warner Mifflin, Jr. (1777–1840), only son of Warner and Elizabeth Johns Mifflin, was only six months old when his father rode into the camp of General Howe at Germantown after the ferocious battle on October 5, 1777. He surely grew up with this story and came of age to witness his father's unremitting campaigns against slavery and Quaker backsliding. But the son never had the temperament of a reformer. Though he was a member of the Murderkill Preparative Meeting, though he sometimes accompanied his father to quarterly and yearly meetings, and though he became a valued member of the Mifflin family network, he had little appetite for supporting Eastern Shore blacks and none for tangling in the politics of the new republic. At heart he was an ordinary Kent County farmer. Not until he inherited a portion of his father's extensive landholdings could he strike out on his own, and no traces remain of any abolitionist activity. He married late, at thirty-three, to Sarah Ann Newlin, from a staunchly Quaker family in Chester County. After her death, in 1825 he married Elizabeth Laws, who gave him four children, the first of whom was Warner Mifflin, III, born in 1826 and dying at age seven.

When the Delaware Abolitionist Society was revitalized a few years after his father's death, Warner, Jr., remained on the sidelines. As far as he would go to honor his father's lifetime work was to add his name in 1816 and 1817 to petitions sent to the legislature to stiffen the penalties for convicted man-stealers.[66] We can infer that he remained an abolitionist at heart, joining the abolition-minded Hicksite separatists in 1827–1828, but he rarely entered the fray.[67]

In a particularly regrettable incident, Warner Mifflin, Jr., was unable, through passivity or reasons buried in history, to save Elijah Morris, son of Sampson, one of the slaves his father had freed in 1775. Sampson had taken the name Morris, and, as in so many cases of freedmen in this era, he thought it advisable—or likely straitened circumstances compelled it—to indenture his young son. Perhaps he considered it a blessing that Warner Mifflin, Jr., agreed to take Elijah and provide him with skills equipping him for adult life. One can only imagine Sampson Morris's horror when he learned in about 1808 that Warner had sold the remaining years of his son's indenture to Charles Hazzard, captain of a Delaware Bay coasting vessel. Hazzard promptly sold the boy's time to another master, who consigned Elijah to a Maryland agent of a Virginia slave trader. Hustled to Fredericksburg, Virginia, and chained among seventy in a slave coffle headed for Nashville, Elijah escaped, only to be captured and thrown in the Clarksville, Tennessee, jail. The Pennsylvania Abolition Society tried to rescue the boy, hiring a lawyer in Clarksville, who insisted that "Old Warner Mifflin of Pennsylvania" had liberated Elijah's father. Though he was asked urgently for proof of Elijah's freeborn status, Warner did not comply in time to save the boy, not yet twenty, from shipment farther south. At that point, Elijah Morris disappeared into the maw of the cotton boom of the Mississippi Territory, with only the mournful comment of the Clarksville attorney that "justice could not be served."[68]

Much different from that of his son were the lives of most of the women in Warner Mifflin's immediate family—five half-sisters and four daughters. A majority were abolitionists, some to the core, others with restrained commitment; only a few remained indifferent. Many of the men they married figured in Delaware antebellum abolitionism after Warner died, and some, as we will see, became legendary figures in the Underground Railroad. How much of their abolitionist fervor can be attributed to the imprint of Mifflin cannot be exactly measured; but their marriage choices and the trajectories of their lives surely reflect Warner's strong convictions and self-sacrificing career.

Among Warner's half-sisters, the two oldest, Mary and Patience, were born when Warner was entering adulthood, so they knew him as a much older brother who seems to have shone in their eyes. They married to his great satisfaction and sent their offspring into the nineteenth century with impeccable abolitionist credentials. Part of this passing of the torch involved the connections between the Mifflin and Hunn families, for Mary and Patience Mifflin married Hunn brothers—Nathaniel and Jonathan—in the 1780s.[69]

Preceding the Mifflins to Kent County, the Hunns were a formidable Quaker clan with many property holdings and deep involvement in the abolition-minded Murderkill and Little Creek preparative meetings.[70] In 1781, Mary Mifflin (1760–1785) married Nathaniel Hunn (1759–1795), a prospering farmer, but Mary's death severed the marriage four years later, leaving Nathaniel a quiet antislavery supporter. If Mary could not live long enough to play any role in her half-brother's black liberation crusade, her father enjoined her children to do so. Only a toddler when her mother died, daughter Ann learned in 1795 that she was included in grandfather Daniel Mifflin's will, in which he instructed his children and grandchildren to ensure that the blacks he had freed were supported if they were unable to do so themselves.[71]

Daniel and Warner, father and son, welcomed another Mifflin-Hunn connection when Patience Mifflin (1766–1817) married Jonathan Hunn (1764–1820) in 1789. An avid abolitionist and friend of free blacks, Jonathan became one of the founders and funders of the Camden School for Colored Children, the first school for free blacks in Kent County. Meanwhile, he joined the efforts in the early nineteenth century to get legislative action to suppress the kidnapping of free blacks. In a memorable case in 1811, he came to the aid of Aaron Cooper, a free black man living near Dover who had fallen prey to white man-stealers. Snaring him at night, the kidnappers carried Cooper off to a slave dealer headed south. For three years, Cooper toiled in the cotton fields, subject to the whip like all other slaves, before he was rescued through the efforts of Hunn and others providing interrogatories to the Mississippi Territorial Court. Swearing they had known Cooper from the time he and his parents had been freed by a fellow Quaker, they testified that Cooper, whose father had worshiped with Quakers, had become an upstanding man in his community. When the Mississippi Superior Court of Law and Equity finally conducted a jury trial in 1814, Cooper was adjudged a falsely enslaved free man, now at liberty to return to his Kent County family.[72]

Though not marrying into the Mifflin family, Ezekiel Hunn, the youngest brother of this numerous clan, was the most inspired by Warner Mifflin and became the progenitor of an even more famous abolitionist family. He too was active in defending Kent County's free blacks, and worked with his brother Jonathan to stem the tide of kidnapping that was feeding them into the flourishing slave markets in Nashville, New Orleans, and Natchez. When Aaron Cooper was snatched from his family in 1811, Ezekiel saddled up with a posse of Quakers to pursue the kidnappers. Galloping across the peninsula into Maryland to find their abducted black neighbor, they found they were too late, for Cooper had been herded aboard a ship carrying its human cargo to Norfolk for trans-shipment to New Orleans.

From then on, the brothers Jonathan and Ezekiel patrolled mid-Kent County, watching for "slave catchers and dealers who snatched up the colored children on the high road and from the cabin doors to sell them." "Devoted to [Warner Mifflin's] cause," they helped escaped slaves across to the Jersey shore in the early days of the Underground Railroad. "[Great] Uncle Jonathan was evidently a man of resolution to ferret out wrong," wrote his grand-niece many years later. "This hatred of slavery passed on to the next generation."[73] The brothers died a year apart, Jonathan in 1820, Ezekiel the next year. If not remembered in the history books, they were etched in the annals of American novelistic literature when George Alfred Townsend (1841–1914), later to become a famed Civil War correspondent, published *The Entailed Hat; or Patty Cannon's Times* in 1884.[74]

If the spirit of Warner Mifflin hovered over Ezekiel Hunn and his brothers, it did so even more emphatically with Ezekiel's son, John (1818–1894). After youthful wandering, John Hunn became one of the most notable conductors of the Underground Railroad—a friend and collaborator of Harriet Tubman, William Still, Robert Purvis, and other committed abolitionists.[75] Hated by proslavery Delawareans, he experienced his moment of conviction in November 1845, just after sunrise with six inches of snow on the ground. Hunn saw an approaching horse-drawn covered wagon with four black men and their black "pilot," Samuel D. Burris, a Delaware-born free black man, walking alongside, directed to seek refuge with Hunn while trying to get north of the Mason-Dixon Line. Tumbling from the wagon was a black family headed by Samuel Hawkins, a free black man from Maryland's Eastern Shore. Hawkins had tried to buy his family, a wife and six children, out of slavery, only to be refused by their several masters, to whom they had been parceled out. Knowing that his wife and children were likely to be torn from him and dispatched to the rice swamps and cotton fields of Georgia and Mississippi, Hawkins made his break for his family's freedom. "This was the first time I had ever been called upon to assist fugitives from the hell of American slavery," Hunn recounted, thus beginning a career that earned him a place in history. "They were gladly welcomed," related Hunn, "and made as comfortable as possible until breakfast was ready" for the nearly frozen fugitives.[76] Soon seized by slave traders, the family ended up in the New Castle jail, there to be rescued by Thomas Garrett, the Maryland-born Quaker already famous as a principal Eastern Shore conductor in the Underground Railroad. Obtaining a decision from Delaware's Chief Justice to free the family, Garrett had them ferried northward to Philadelphia.

This far from ended the matter. Owners of the Hawkins family brought suits against John Hunn and Thomas Garrett for abetting runaway slaves under the Fugitive Slave Act of 1793. Winding its way through the courts, the case climaxed three years later when Roger B. Taney, Chief Justice of the U.S. Supreme Court, impaneled a jury in Sussex County packed with proslavery Delawareans. Two years before the Dred Scott case, the jury found for the claimants. Determined to derail the Underground Railroad, Taney levied penalties against Hunn and Garrett so severe that John Hunn was obliged to sell at sheriff's auction the land he had inherited from his father and grandfather. Garrett's penalty was even more draconian, amounting to what today would be half a million dollars. Family history recorded Hunn's reply to Taney on May 26, 1848, a few months after the Treaty of Guadalupe Hildago ended the Mexican-American War: "Roger Taney, I will never refuse thee bread and meat if thou asks me for them." Taney replied: "You are a very dangerous young man." Taney's decision set a precedent, putting a new flourish on the Fugitive Slave Act of 1793: those convicted of aiding fugitive slaves were liable for $500 for *each* slave aided rather than a blanket fee of $500 for such an incident.[77]

If Taney thought he had given the Fugitive Slave Act of 1793 sharper teeth, he was wrong, at least in the case of John Hunn. Stripping him of most of his assets to satisfy the court's decision did nothing to temper Hunn's abolitionism. In fact, it spurred him on. He proudly claimed that the Hawkins family were the first group of several hundred black Americans he steered northward, following the North Star.[78] Appointed a minister by the Southern Quarterly Meeting in 1854, Hunn rode the circuits preaching against the evils of slavery.[79] After the outbreak of the Civil War, he joined Philadelphia's Port Royal Relief Association, going to the South Carolina Sea Islands to work among newly freed slaves. Accompanying him was his daughter, who taught freed men and women at the William Penn School with Charlotte Forten, daughter of James Forten, the celebrated black sail maker of Philadelphia. Hunn served as a store keeper and farm manager for two decades in the service of radical reconstruction. Known as "Father Hunn," he returned to Delaware in 1893, his health broken, to finish out his life among his children. Writing to William Still, he sounded very much like Warner Mifflin: "I ask no other reward for any efforts made by me in the cause, than to feel that I have been of use to my fellow-men."[80] John Hunn and his wife died in 1894 and were buried in the Murderkill meeting burial ground, a few yards from Warner Mifflin's grave.

Among the four daughters of Warner Mifflin who survived childhood, all wove their father's dedication to black Americans into their lives. Elizabeth (1771–1807), the oldest, at twenty-one married Clayton Cowgill, son of one of her father's closest Kent County friends. Like so many of Warner's children, her life was short, lasting only thirty-six years.[81] Her husband was a pillar of his monthly meeting and frequently a delegate from the Southern Quarterly to the Philadelphia Yearly Meeting. Penning his will, Warner favored Cowgill as one of the executors of his estate. Cowgill passed on his abolitionist beliefs to two sons, Warner Mifflin Cowgill (1799–1852) and Daniel Cowgill (1802–1877). The latter, in 1825, purchased what is now the Delaware governor's house and became a station master in the Underground Railroad.[82]

Warner's second surviving daughter was sickly from her infancy and rarely in full health, suffering, like so many of the family, with the chronic sickness that plagued Kent County. Nonetheless, the short life of Ann Mifflin (1774–1799) was intensely principled and indelibly marked by her father's fervor. In marrying Warner Raisin [Rasin] in 1795, she joined a notable Quaker abolitionist family across the peninsula in Kent County, Maryland, where members of the Cecil Monthly Meeting had been freeing their enslaved people since the early 1770s.[83] Fourteen months after Warner's death, his widow wanted Friends up and down the Atlantic seaboard to know of her stepdaughter's dedication to Quaker foundational principles and her father's cause. In a two-page closely written testimonial, nested in the Raisin family Bible for more than two centuries, Ann Mifflin recounted the tragically brief life of Warner and Elizabeth Johns Mifflin's third daughter. "Through many tribulations," wrote widow Ann, "the righteous enter the Kingdom of God": and thus, "being ranked among the redeemed and prepared for the White Robe," daughter Ann had anticipated an early death "for some time before her departure." Even so, she had played an important role at Chestnut Grove, teaching the young blacks who lived there. At eighteen, the Murderkill Women's Monthly Meeting appointed her clerk, a leadership role rarely conferred on a teenager. After she married Raisin when she was twenty, the Cecil Monthly Meeting appointed her an overseer, a position full of responsibilities for monitoring marriage intentions, discipline, and other affairs.

In September 1798, twenty months after the birth of her first child, Ann Raisin tempted fate by attending the Philadelphia Yearly Meeting "from a settled sense of religious duty," though warned that this was foolhardy and even presumptuous, with yellow fever ravaging the city. There she saw her father for the last time. A few months later, sick and several months pregnant, she insisted on journeying to the Southern Quarterly Meeting, where she silenced her critics, standing before them to ask whether they would not place their "eternal all" before worldly concerns as she had done.[84] The next year Ann delivered her second child. Three weeks later, she expired in her twenty-fifth year. "She was a dutiful and affectionate daughter," wrote her stepmother, "a loving and faithful wife, an attentive and careful parent, a tender and kind mistress." Shedding light on the texture of life at Chestnut Grove, she continued that "the old family blacks where her lot was cast, lamenting over her, professed they had lost a mother in her; and the young ones have cause to mourn the loss they will sustain for want of her great daily attention to their school education." "Though but young in years," concluded Ann Mifflin, "[she was] matured and old in wisdom."[85]

Susanna, born in 1779 during the height of the Revolution, was the second daughter to marry a Cowgill. At twenty, on the last day of the eighteenth century, she exchanged vows with John Cowgill, son of Warner's bosom friend, at the Murderkill meetinghouse.[86] It was a brief, painful marriage, severed when she died in 1801 at twenty-two, only months after giving birth to a son.

If Warner Mifflin could have smiled from his grave, it might well have been occasioned by hearing that his fourth son-in-law was to be Daniel Neall (1784–1846), the polymathic son of dedicated Bucks County, Pennsylvania, Quaker abolitionists. Warner's last daughter, Sarah Mifflin (1784–1837), had been a near-mother to Samuel and Lemuel after Warner's death. In 1810, at twenty-six, she exchanged vows with Daniel Neall in the Murderkill meeting-house, before a joyous gathering of the extended Mifflin family.[87] By marrying Neall, who regarded himself as a disciple of her father, Sarah yoked herself to a distinguished dentist (after a career as carriage maker, printer, farmer, and inventor), who became as dedicated an emancipationist as his deceased father-in-law. She lived to see him become vice president of the Pennsylvania Abolition Society and president of the Pennsylvania Hall Association, a largely Quaker organization formed to build a free-speech tabernacle for reformist lecturers, especially those committed to women's rights and antislavery. Her death in 1837 spared her one of Philadelphia's darkest moments. Three days after the opening of the hall in May 1838, Neall, with John Greenleaf Whittier at his side, faced a churning mob determined to destroy the building. "I am here, the president of this meeting," he told the crowd, "and I will be torn in pieces before I leave my place at your dictation. Go back to those who sent you. I shall do my duty." Defiant, the mob shattered the windows and doors, then torched the building, leaving it in ashes as they moved on to burn churches and the black orphanage.[88]

Daniel Neall and Sarah Neall endured their share of the Mifflin curse—death in the cradle. Their first child, Sarah, born in May 1813, died after seven weeks. The second, Warner Mifflin Neall, died after three months in 1815. The third child, Daniel, was the first to survive infancy. However, it was the fourth and last child, Elizabeth, born in 1819, who was to loom large in abolitionist and feminist history and carry the legacy of Warner Mifflin deep into the nineteenth century. Elizabeth's mother, Sarah Mifflin Neall, had never known her mother, Elizabeth Johns Mifflin, who had died when she had not yet reached her second birthday. But she kept the memory of her mother alive by naming her only daughter to survive the cradle Elizabeth Johns Neall (1819–1907). Sarah Mifflin Neall died in 1837 when daughter Elizabeth was eighteen, so she did not live to see her daughter marry Sydney Howard Gay (1814–1888), destined to become one of the foremost abolitionists of the antebellum era and the man, along with John Hunn, who best advanced Warner Mifflin's cause. That he married Warner Mifflin's feisty abolitionist granddaughter made for a politically charged partnership.[89]

Though she bore the name of her grandmother Elizabeth Johns, Elizabeth Johns Neall was more like her stepgrandmother, Ann Emlen Mifflin. Brought up in the Philadelphia Quaker community that had been fractured by the 1827–1828 Hicksite Separation, she became intensely dedicated to antislavery and the vibrant women's rights movement gaining momentum in the 1830s. Only twenty, she was the youngest by far in a quartet of women, including Lucretia Mott, who crossed the Atlantic as delegates of Philadelphia's Female Anti-slavery Society at the World Anti-Slavery Convention in London. Founded in 1833, the society was the first integrated antislavery organization in the country; but in London, they found that gender integration was as unwelcome as interracial marriages. Refused seats on the delegate benches, they endured "the insults and scoffings of a whole nation . . . where drunkards and gamblers were welcomed & honest women . . . rejected and insulted."[90] Here was a baptism of fire for the work ahead with the man she would marry.

Sydney Gay, whose ancestors traced back to the first wave of Puritan immigrants to the Massachusetts Bay Colony, did poorly in school, but at age twenty-four found his life's work as an antislavery writer. Joining the swelling ranks of William Lloyd Garrison's antislavery immediatists, those who had given up on gradualism and moral suasion in favor of confrontational and unconditional demands for removing the cancer of slavery blighting the nation, Gay traveled with Frederick Douglass, Abby Kelley, and Charles Lenox Remond to carry the antislavery message to points west from the Eastern Seaboard.

When in 1844 Gay assumed the editorship of the *National Anti-Slavery Standard*, an arm of the Garrisonian antislavery crusade, he had all but earned the love of Elizabeth Johns Neall, for she had admired the *Standard*'s resolute language for several years and hoped it would continue until slaveowning was "utterly annihilated and the recollection of the accursed system only handed over to the scorn and contempt of coming generations."[91] They were married in 1845, when Gay described Warner Mifflin's granddaughter as "fresh, eager, pretty, and graceful."[92]

After her husband became the chief of operations of New York City's Underground Railroad depot, funneling absconding men and women from the Upper South northward through Philadelphia to Canada, Elizabeth Gay became an energetic member of the New York female antislavery auxiliaries—a sisterhood that held bazaars and fairs to support the cause.[93] Though never becoming a public antislavery and feminist speaker such as Lucy Stone, Frances Watkins Harper, and Lucretia Mott, she pulled her weight through the 1850s while mothering her small brood of children at her home on Staten Island. Out-living her husband by nineteen years, she died in 1907.[94] With her death, the reform-minded lineage of Warner Mifflin more or less came to an end. However, it was Elizabeth Johns Neall Gay's great-niece, Hilda Justice (1874–1940), who heard many stories about her great-great-grandfather and decided in 1905 to preserve the memory of his convictions and courage. A graduate from Bryn Mawr College in 1896 and about to embark on a career as a faculty member at the Pennsylvania School of Horticulture for Women, founded through a Quaker bequest of land, she stitched together Warner's two published essays with family stories, wills, and marriage certificates; Quaker meeting minutes, Friends' memorials to legislative bodies, and her translation of Crèvecoeur's pages on Mifflin from *Lettres d'un cultivateur américain*.[95]

## Echoes in Europe

While many of Mifflin's descendants remembered him by their own commitments to a true empire of liberty and a biracial democracy, his reputation slowly declined in the nineteenth century. But Germans, Austrians, and Russians came to know him at least briefly through the artistry of August von Kotzebue, Germany's most prolific playwright. The author of hundreds of plays, many promoted by Johann Wolfgang von Goethe in Weimar, Kotzebue was almost a household name as the Napoleonic Wars swept across Europe. Chased out of Berlin by Napoleon's army in 1806, Kotzebue, after reaching Russia where he had previously served in the diplomatic corps, became a vocal critic of Bonaparte. Mifflin likely caught Kotzebue's attention when Napoleon's massive army prepared in 1810–1811 for what the emperor believed would be the final, crushing blow to crown his control of Europe. Kotzebue was already an admirer of Quakers through his visits to Bad Pyrmont in northern Germany. It was here that German mercenaries who had fought alongside the British in the American Revolution had returned with admiration of Quaker principles. Moved by Quaker traveling ministers, including Mifflin's close friends John Pemberton and Sarah Harrison, the German veterans formed a small community of Friends at Pyrmont. Three years before his death, Warner had learned of Pemberton's death and burial there.[96]

With mounting opposition to what many viewed as Napoleon's endless wars, Kotzebue put a pacifist Quaker on the stage as his contribution to the cause of peacemaking. He was probably influenced as well by his close association with Czar Alexander I, who was such an admirer of the Society of Friends that he called himself a Quaker at heart. Thus, as Napoleon was strong-arming Prussia and Austria to furnish thousands of troops and much matériel to his Grande Armée in late 1811, *Die Quaker*, in one act with eleven scenes, opened first in Vienna in September 1811, then in Mannheim in mid-January 1812, and finally in Berlin and St. Petersburg at the end of the month. Helping himself to Crèvecoeur's account of Mifflin's peacemaking efforts during the American Revolution, Kotzebue dressed up Warner's encounter with General Howe, turning it into a suspenseful account of "Walter Mifflin," cast as "an old Quaker" whose son Edward, trying to protect his betrothed from the rape-minded son of General Howe, thinks he has killed the general's son and will have to pay for it with his own life. Kotzebue did nothing to convince Napoleon to end his intended conquest of Russia—what playwright could ever sway a megalomaniac?—but he lodged the peace-loving Quaker in the consciousness of German, Austrian, and Russian theatergoers.[97]

## Forgotten Tribune

Quakers decry monuments, regarded as pretentious emblems inappropriate to the quiet cultivation of the Light Within, so there is no reason to lament the scanting of Mifflin in metal, marble, and plaster—and even street names and schools. But why did word monuments decay and disappear? One group that did not forget him was Philadelphia's African Americans. Almost two decades after his death, the city's large free black community expressed its gratitude for Mifflin's labors by founding the African Warner Mifflin Society. "The objects of our association," announced the charter, "are to diffuse knowledge to suppress vice and immorality and to encourage benevolence, charity and brotherly love."[98] Thus Mifflin took his place among the Philadelphia black benevolent societies named for Anthony Benezet, Benjamin Rush, and William Wilberforce. After that, only the *Colored American*, the nation's second black newspaper, recognized Mifflin when it included a small part of his 1793 *Expostulations* in the editors' screed on "American Inconsistency," where they insisted "that slavery and American prejudice are at war with the laws of God and the republican principles of man."[99]

By the time Mifflin's children had met their Maker, only a handful of Quaker writers and editors believed that keeping the memory of Mifflin intact might serve the abolitionist cause, possibly inspiring a new generation of crusaders. Even though the early 1830s marked the advent of radical abolitionism, where Mifflin's brand of nonviolent moral suasion had given way to confrontational emancipationism, they did their best to remember the man whose perseverance was worth emulating. In 1832, the editors of *Friends' Miscellany*, monthly reading for Friends with historical and literary interests, published the moving "Testimony concerning Warner Mifflin" by his close friend George Churchman. Two years later, they reprinted Mifflin's *A Defence Against Aspersions*, along with "Anecdotes and Memoirs of Warner Mifflin" that included encounters with George Washington. More widely read was abolitionist and feminist Abigail Mott's *Biographical Sketches and Interesting Anecdotes of Persons of Color*, where she translated Wanostrocht's moral lesson for youngsters about "The Good Master [Mifflin] and His Faithful Slave [James]."[100]

In Philadelphia in the 1840s the Quaker editor Robert Smith did more. With radical abolitionism running high, he exhumed Mifflin's *A Defence against Aspersions* and *Serious Address to the House of Representatives*, interspersed them with letters he obtained from the Drinker and Parrish families, added a few of the legislative memorials bearing Mifflin's stamp, and wove it all together as an eighteen-part account of Mifflin's life and labors. Probably few Americans read any of this, because Smith ran "Relics from the Past" in *The Friend: A Historical and Literary Journal* whose circulation was very narrow. Yet Quakers surely savored the remembrance of Mifflin after Smith tempted them in the first issue: "It is really refreshing in this day of excitement, of eloquent speaking, and of abundance of professions on the subject of slavery, to be able to look back to the past century, and to witness the calmness, the sweetness, the dedication of spirit which characterized the labours of those practical friends of the slave, the Woolmans, the Benezets, and the Mifflins; three men, who having bowed to the cross of our Lord Jesus Christ, did what they did for the slave, in obedience to what they believed their Master required at their hands."[101] But other than Friends, few were ready to be refreshed with the likes of Warner Mifflin.

Apart from Quaker publicists such as Smith who catered to the shrinking population of American Friends, antebellum annalists of American history left Mifflin moldering in his grave.[102] After the Civil War even readers of Quaker journals found only morsels to remember him by. Why? War was hardly out of fashion, and Quaker peace witnessing was not out of fashion either. But a restless, violence-prone, triumphalist white-dominated America had other heroes in mind—expansionists, Indian haters, military leaders, captains of industry, and racial purity spokesmen. An inward-dwelling man who was certain that history was on his side and that God would not forget if he proved a disappointment hardly fit this mold. As boisterous nationalism, genocidal wars against Native Americans, and segregationist dicta gripped the country, he became nearly an anti-hero best left unmentioned.[103]

Mifflin appeared briefly in several late nineteenth-century biographical encyclopedias, though by now his name was receding into the misty past, beyond the recollection of the vast majority of Americans. At the end of the century, the president of Haverford College bravely bowed to forgotten Quaker abolitionists in a forlorn requiem. In the last sentence at the end of a book on Quaker government in colonial and revolutionary Pennsylvania, Isaac Sharpless, stretching to get readers to see the continuing relevance of the Society of Friends, wrote: "And when [civil] war came, a war on an evil against which they [Quakers] were committed by every item of their history and every instinct of their religion, they could not join in it, but they could thankfully say, in the spirit of Southeby, Woolman, Benezet, and Mifflin, and in the words of their own poet [John Greenleaf Whittier]":

> It is done!
> Clang of bell and roar of gun,
> Send the tidings up and down
> How the belfries rock and reel;
> How the great guns, peal on peal,
> Fling the joy from town to town!
>
> Ring, O bells!
> Every stroke exultant tells
> Of the burial hour of crime.
> Loud and long, that all may hear;

Ring for every listening ear,
Of eternity and time!

   Let us kneel!
God's own voice is in that peal,
And this spot is holy ground.
Lord forgive us! What are we
That our eyes this glory see,
That our ears have heard the sound![104]

# Appendix 1

### Crèvecoeur and Mifflin

In the preceding pages, readers have met the famous St. John de Crèvecoeur (born Michel-Guillaume St. Jean de Crèvecoeur) and how he celebrated Warner Mifflin as "the good Quaker," a man who personified Enlightenment principles of universal freedom, equality, and social justice.[1] I offer evidence here of the Crèvecoeur-Mifflin connection, along with undiscovered details on how the Frenchman came to know the Kent County plantation owner. Until Marie-Jeanne Rossignol touched on it in her recent work on French abolitionists of the revolutionary era, the Mifflin-Crèvecoeur relationship has never been explored, and to this day much remains unexplained about this fascinating putative friendship between a very well-known Frenchman and a very obscure American.[2]

Europeans first met Mifflin through Crèvecoeur's writings after the Frenchman became a fervid abolitionist in the closing years of the American Revolution. An emigrant from Caen, Normandy, in 1754 to French Canada, where he served in the Seven Years' War as a surveyor and cartographer, Crèvecoeur resigned his French commission and moved in 1759 to New York. Here he acquired English citizenship and an American wife. Always an adventurer, always a scribbler in his journals, he toured much of the northern interior—trips reaching all the way to the Great Lakes and the Mississippi would provide grist for a book to become famous—while establishing himself as a successful farmer.

Then came the American Revolution. Despite his Loyalist sympathies, the British arrested and imprisoned Crèvecoeur for three months after he entered occupied New York City in early 1779. Negotiating his release, he left New York as part of an eighty-ship British convoy in September 1780, with charges of Loyalism following him across the Atlantic. Debarking in Dublin, Crèvecoeur soon reached London; there for ten months in 1781 he pulled together many of his loosely written travel accounts and autobiographical fragments—he called himself "no author but a plain scribbler"—into a manuscript loosely grouped as *Letters from an American Farmer*. In the opportunity of a lifetime, he found publishers willing to gamble on printing the volume—the stroke of good fortune that soon propelled him onto the international literary scene in 1782. By the time the book came off the press, Crèvecoeur had already reached his ancestral home in Caen.[3]

With its celebration of the sturdy, liberty-loving Americans, the *Letters* was an unlikely success because English taxpayers were tired of paying for a costly war to smother the American struggle for independence and tired of hearing about universal natural rights from colonists building their economy on slave labor. But the book sold beyond all expectations, leading quickly to Dutch and German translations. Soon to be acclaimed as a paean to American character, the *Letters* had not a word on Warner Mifflin, though Crèvecoeur lavishly praised the Quakers on Nantucket Island as a people with Enlightenment principles worth emulating. The book also ended with a bone-chilling description of man's inhumanity to man—an account of a slave hanging in a cage from a tree near Charleston, South Carolina with his body torn by birds of prey and biting insects. Though he had owned one or more slaves in New York, Crèvecoeur made clear his distaste for slavery in other parts of the book and by its dedication to Abbé Raynal, whose *Histoire philosophique des deux Indes* (1770) had become a compendium of Enlightenment thinking on the blight of slavery disfiguring societies throughout the western world.[4]

Such antislavery probes foreshadowed Crèvecoeur's decision, as he began to prepare a greatly expanded French edition of *American Farmer*, to introduce readers to Warner Mifflin. Indeed, as if to make sure this did not escape notice, he would open the first volume of what would become the two-volume *Lettres d'un cultivateur américain* with twelve pages on Mifflin. "I have never in my life made an acquaintance who made such an impression on me," Crèvecoeur enthused; "I spent nearly a month with this worthy farmer; during this time, the fertility of his mind raised a thousand new and informative things that I should never have thought of." Further, "the great reputation which he enjoys is less founded on his great fortune than on the eminence of his virtue, his humanity, that we can truly call the essence of the Gospel. His candor, his affability, and his knowledge makes him in my eyes as well as the public's eyes, one of the touching and venerable men who honor his homeland and their century." Then came details about Mifflin's marriage to a fabulously wealthy

Kent County young woman (misnamed Phoebe). Crèvecoeur finished with a flourish about how Mifflin had freed all his thirty-seven slaves in a single day, along with a lengthy discussion with Jacques, who was reluctant to accept freedom when continued service to his master seemed to be a better life strategy. Appended was the manumission document for Jacques. This dialogue, Crèvecoeur told his readers, came to him from Guillaume Roberts, Mifflin's nephew, who had witnessed the liberation of Jacques and thirty-six other Mifflin slaves.[5]

No literary scholar or historian has inquired into the question of Crèvecoeur's claim about how he captured the details of Mifflin's early married life, the liberation of his slaves, and his dialogue with the enslaved Jacques through a visit to Delaware when Guillaume Roberts was at Mifflin's plantation home. In fact, no trace of such a journey to mid-Delaware has ever been found. And who was "Guillaume Roberts"? If he indeed existed, when and where did he provide Crèvecoeur with the rich details about Mifflin? His identity as Crèvecoeur's confidant has remained a mystery for more than two centuries, and I had great doubts about his existence after searching Kent Country, Delaware, records, finding only a simple farmer named William Roberts, who had no connection whatsoever to Warner Mifflin. But further research revealed that William Roberts indeed existed, not Mifflin's nephew but his second cousin, the son of Ann Eyre Mifflin Roberts and a youth whose life had intersected with that of Warner and his family for many years, as chronicled in Chapter 3. By the time he arrived in London in late 1780, Roberts was in possession of a mental archive of information about Mifflin and his wife. As a youth, he had traveled back and forth between his Northampton County home at the tip of Virginia's Eastern Shore and Philadelphia, where he had been enrolled as a young boy at the Philadelphia Academy since 1770. This gave him frequent occasions to visit his Mifflin kinfolk, uncle and cousin, both living along the King's Highway leading to Philadelphia, and to learn about the emancipation of Daniel and Warner's slaves in 1774–1775 as well as the details of his cousin's marriage to the dower-rich Elizabeth Mifflin. Then in 1777, fleeing conscription into the American army, he spent about three months with his uncle Daniel and cousin Warner from late 1777 to early March 1778. It was surely then that Roberts garnered Warner's account about his peace testimony to Generals Howe and Washington when he crossed the blood-soaked battlefield at Germantown in October 1777, just months before Roberts took refuge with him.[6]

That William Roberts was Crèvecoeur's key informant on the early married life of Mifflin, his transforming moments when he turned his life to abolition-ism, the story of liberating James, his slave; and his battlefield peace mission in 1777 cannot be proven by direct evidence of their face-to-face meeting or by a surviving exchange of letters. But the indirect evidence is compelling that the two men met in the spring or summer of 1781 and that the place where they met was in London.[7] That is where Crèvecoeur spent the months from May to August after his return from the war-torn United States, while Roberts, having taken refuge as a Loyalist, lived in the British capital from late December 1780 to June 28, 1782.[8]

It was a propitious time for Crèvecoeur to hear about the enlightened Quaker from Kent County, Delaware, for he was already drawing on the volu-minous scribblings he had brought from New York for a new much enlarged, French edition. The inspiration for this was his sojourn in Paris after leaving London in September 1781. Happily joining the salons of Madame Sophie d'Houdetot, Crèvecoeur soaked up the antislavery writings of Raynal, Diderot, and others. With the encouragement and help of Madame d'Houdetot, he translated *The American Farmer* into French, while bulking it up with new material designed to please a pro-American audience. The stories of Mifflin, by way of William Roberts, were tailor-made for this.

By late 1782, Crèvecoeur was ready to float some of his accounts of Mifflin in the January 4, 1783, issue of *Mercure de France*, the distinguished literary journal widely read in pre-Revolutionary France.[9] When the two-volume *Lettres d'un cultivateur américain* reached the book stalls in Paris in December 1784, those who snapped it up (including Benjamin Franklin and other Americans in Paris) found the same material but were in for another helping of Mifflin dialogue.[10] Again noting William Roberts as his source, Crèvecoeur spooled out the embellished dialogue between Mifflin and Generals Howe and Wash-ington (partially provided in Chapter 3). Mifflin the abolitionist and Mifflin the pacifist had reached the French reading public.[11]

It is impossible to know how much William Roberts contributed to the emotional dialogue between Mifflin and his slave or the tension-filled repartee between Mifflin and General Howe. Some of it may have come from Roberts's conversations with Crèvecoeur, for Warner Mifflin's cousin had literary preten-sions and was apparently fond of dramatizing the scenes he related to the Frenchman.[12] But, as many Crèvecoeur scholars have noted, the American Farmer was a man who delighted in embellishing almost anything he wrote about. Some scholars have judged Crèvecoeur as more a novelist than a sharp-eyed observer of colonial America.[13] In the end, perhaps it matters little because, however he exaggerated and added flourishes to his accounts of Mifflin, Crèvecoeur was true to the basic facts of the Quaker's dedication as an aboli-tionist and pacifist, sealing the reputation of Mifflin, not only in France but throughout Europe, where tales of the "Good Master and the Faithful Slave" resonated for generations as related in Chapter 6.

The Crèvecoeur-Roberts-Mifflin connection continued sporadically. In 1786, Roberts and Crèvecoeur met again in London, where the Frenchman introduced Roberts to Jefferson, the American minister to France.[14] Four years later, after the Frenchman had returned to the United States as consul to the city, Mifflin met Crèvecoeur, almost certainly for the first time, for a two-hour dinner in New York. Less than two months later, Crèvecoeur returned to France, never to see Mifflin or Roberts again.

# Appendix 2

## Slavery's Decline in Delaware 1790–1830

Although apparently no censuses for Delaware were taken in the colonial period or in the 1780s, and the federal censuses between 1790 and 1810 are incomplete and sometimes in error, it is clear from the surviving data that Kent County manumission by slaveowners outpaced those in New Castle and Sussex counties, making Warner Mifflin's county an unusually important region of free black life in the Early Republic.

The manuscript of the Delaware census of 1790 was lost but reconstructed from tax records and other sources, including the Report of the Delaware Abolition Society to the American Convention of Abolition Societies, 1796, which gave the total number of free blacks for the state in 1792 Papers of the Pennsylvania Abolition Society, Microfilm edition, Reel 28. See Leon De Valinger, "Reconstructed Census of Delaware," *National Genealogical Society Quarterly* (Sept. 1948–Dec. 1953); and Essah, *A House Divided*, Table 1, p. 7; Table 7, p. 79. For further discussion of county variations, see Essah's deft analysis on pp. 75–84. For comparison, Talbot County, Maryland, on the other side of the peninsula, where Quakers and Methodists were thickly settled, had 1,076 free and 4,777 slaves in 1790, 1,591 and 4,775 in 1800; Carroll, "An Attack on the Manumission of Slaves," *Maryland Historical Magazine* 80 (1985): 141.

|  | White | % White | Free Black | Slave | Total Black | % Free | Total |
|---|---|---|---|---|---|---|---|
| **New Castle** | | | | | | | |
| 1790 | 16,487 | 83.7 | 639 | 2,562 | 3,201 | 20.0 | 19,688 |
| 1800 | 20,769 | 88.0 | 2,754 | 1,838 | 4,592 | 60.0 | 25,361 |
| 1810 | 19,463 | 80.0 | 3,919 | 1,047 | 4,966 | 79.0 | 24,429 |
| **Kent** | | | | | | | |
| 1790 | 14.050 | 74.3 | 2,570 | 2,300 | 4,870 | 52.9 | 18,920 |
| 1800 | 13,823 | 70.7 | 4,246 | 1,485 | 5,781 | 74.0 | 19,544 |
| 1810 | 14,151 | 69.0 | 5,516 | 728 | 6,244 | 88.3 | 20,395 |
| **Sussex** | | | | | | | |
| 1790 | 15,773 | 77.0 | 690 | 4,025 | 4,715 | 14.6 | 20,488 |
| 1800 | 15,260 | 78.8 | 1,268 | 2,830 | 4,098 | 31.0 | 19,358 |
| 1810* | *21,747* | *78.5* | *3,601* | *2,402* | *6,003* | *60.0* | *27,750* |
| *1810 corrected estimates* | | | | | | | |
| 1810 | 16,900 | 79.0 | 2,100 | 2,402 | 4,502 | 46.6 | 21,402 |
| 1820 | 18,732 | 77.9 | 3,081 | 2,244 | 5,325 | 57.9 | 24,057 |
| 1830 | 20,721 | 76.4 | 4,476 | 1,918 | 6,394 | 70.0 | 27,115 |
| **Total** | | | | | | | |
| 1790 | 46,310 | 78.4 | 3,899 | 8,887 | 12,786 | 30.5 | 59,096 |
| 1800 | 49,852 | 77.6 | 8,268 | 6,153 | 14,421 | 57.3 | 64,273 |
| 1810 | 55,361 | 76.2 | 13,136 | 4,177 | 17,313 | 75.9 | 72,674 |

*The numbers in italics are unreliable and surely mistaken. This is evident in looking at the recorded data from 1790 to 1830.

# *Notes*

≈

## Introduction

1. Notice of Warner Mifflin's death, *Gazette of the United States*, Oct. 23, 1798.

2. By "first wave," I mean the abolitionist advocates stepping forward at mid-century to usher in the period of antislavery action, initiated primarily by the Society of Friends. An earlier set of Quaker spokesmen witnessing for abolishing slavery, beginning in 1688, are covered briefly in "The First Emancipators," chapter 2 of my book with Jean R. Soderlund, *Freedom by Degrees: Emancipation in Pennsylvania and Its Aftermath* (New York: Oxford University Press, 1991). Among these lonely voices whose bold pronouncements against slavery had no immediate effects, the greatest was Benjamin Lay, the subject of Marcus Rediker's *The Fearless Benjamin Lay: The Dwarf Quaker Who Became the First Revolutionary Abolitionist* (Boston: Beacon, 2017).

3. Benezet to George Dillwyn [1783], in George S. Brookes, *Friend Anthony Benezet* (Philadelphia: University of Pennsylvania Press, 1937), 374; Henry Cadbury, "Anthony Benezet as a Friend," *The Friend: A Historical and Literary Journal* 107 (1934): 350, cited in Maurice Jackson, *Let This Voice Be Heard: Anthony Benezet, Father of Atlantic Abolitionism* (Philadelphia: University of Pennsylvania Press, 2009), 220. The Overseers of the Press was a standing committee of the yearly meeting whose imprimatur on writings from the pen of Friends was required for publication. Since the yearly meeting saw itself representing Friends to the world at large, the Overseers often refused to sanction essays they deemed radical and therefore likely to endanger the Society's reputation for probity. Working to regain acceptance into civil society at the end of the revolution, the Philadelphia Quaker leaders were not ready to endorse a bold essay on the immediate abolition of slavery.

4. Pemberton to John Pemberton, May 14, 1784, in Brookes, *Friend Anthony Benezet*, 458–60, quote 460. Benezet put his hopes on Nicholas Waln and John Parrish as well. Formerly a brilliant lawyer, Waln had become a devout and effective traveling minister, and that is the role he would play, spending much of the next few decades in England and Europe. Parrish, a second cousin of Mifflin and a close friend, became almost coequal with Warner as an abolitionist torch bearer, but his commitment to Native Americans absorbed even more of his remarkable energy until his death in 1807. Note: For ease of reading I have used conventional dating rather than the Quaker avoidance of what they regarded as "pagan" month and day names. Thus, rather than the Quaker "first day" or "fourth day," I have used Sunday and Wednesday; rather than "first month," I have used the conventional January, and so on. Also, I have silently modernized punctuation, capitalization, and spelling.

5. *Gazette of the United States*, Oct. 23, 1798; Thomas Rodney Diary, Oct. 17, 1798, Brown Collection, DHS.

6. In "The Psychology of Commitment: The Constructive Role of Violence and Suffering for the Individual and for His Society," Silvan S. Tomkins denotes common features in the early lives of four antebellum abolitionists he put on the couch. These do not correspond to Mifflin's formative years; however, Mifflin perfectly fits Tomkins's overreaching judgment about his subjects—Weld, Garrison, Phillips, and Birney—that "their Christianity required that they save others if they would save themselves," Tomkins, in Martin Duberman, ed., *The Antislavery Vanguard: New Essays on the Abolitionists* (Princeton, N.J.: Princeton University Press, 1965), 270–98, quote 281. Mifflin certainly did not suffer from status decline or as part of "a displaced class," as David Donald described the abolition immediatists of the antebellum period, "Toward Reconsideration of Abolition," in Donald, *Lincoln Reconsidered: Essays on the Civil War Era* (New York: Knopf, 1956), 19–36.

7. "Memorial for Warner Mifflin," Southern Quarterly Meeting and approved by the Philadelphia Yearly Meeting Meeting for Sufferings, Miscellaneous Mss, Haverford (hereafter PYM-MS); "Testimony concerning Warner Mifflin, by his intimate friend and survivor, George Churchman," *Friends Miscellany* 2 (Philadelphia, 1832): 328, 330.

8. Quoted in Frederick B. Tolles, *Quakers and the Atlantic Culture* (New York: Macmillan, 1960), 21.

9. Fox is quoted in ibid., 77; Penn is quoted in Rufus M. Jones, *The Faith and Practice of the Quakers* (London: Methuen, 1927), 77. For more on plainness, see Emma J. Lapsansky, "Plainness and Simplicity," in Stephen W. Angell and Ben Pink Dandelion, eds., *The Oxford Handbook of Quaker Studies* (Oxford: Oxford University Press, 2013), 335–46.

10. Cutting somewhat against the Quaker grain, they took on the color of a spiritual elite. As their name implied, most elders were mature in years—described by the nineteenth-century historian of the Philadelphia Yearly Meeting as "those of riper years and more knowledge and experience in conducting the affairs of the Church." Ezra Michener, *A Retrospect of Early Quakerism: Being Extracts from the Records of Philadelphia Yearly Meeting* (Philadelphia: T. Ellwood Zell, 1860), 169.

11. Tolles, *Quakers and Atlantic Culture*, 25; Tolles calls the itinerating ministry "the bloodstream of the transatlantic Society of Friends" (29).

12. Rebecca Larson, in *Daughters of Light: Quaker Women Preaching and Prophesying in the Colonies and Abroad, 1700–1775* (New York: Knopf, 1999), ch. 2, explains the unpredictable development of women's spiritual "gifts" and how female Quaker ministers received their appointments. The Quakers' female ministry set the Society of Friends sharply apart from almost every other Christian body in the world.

13. Stephen Crane, *Puritan Tolerance and Quaker Fanaticism Briefly Considered* (New York, 1848). On the title page, Crane inscribed "Oh prejudice, where is thy reason; Oh bigotry, where is thy blush?"

14. Patrick Rael, *Eighty-Eight Years: The Long Death of Slavery in the United States* (Athens: University of Georgia Press, 2016), 19.

15. Robert McColley, *Slavery and Jeffersonian Virginia* (Urbana: University of Illinois Press, 1964), 157.

16. Writing a half-century ago, Fawn Brodie deplored the general view of the abolitionist: "Except in the eyes of the Negro and a small minority of whites he has never been accepted as hero. Far from being applauded for his compassion and courage in combating a corrosive national blight, he is assailed for his fanaticism and 'pertinacious meddling.'" "Who Defends the Abolitionist?" in Duberman, *Antislavery Vanguard*, 52–53. Brodie was speaking mostly of antebellum abolitionists,

but her characterization rings true for late eighteenth-century emancipationists as well. Brodie describes how attempts at one psychiatric evaluation of the abolitionists concluded that they suffered from "a kind of collective neurosis" (65). I have argued against the notion that slavery could not have been abolished gradually after the Revolution in *The Forgotten Fifth: African Americans in the Age of Revolution* (Cambridge, Mass.: Harvard University Press, 2006), ch. 2.

17. Important recent work includes Christopher Brown, *Moral Capital: Foundations of British Abolitionism* (Chapel Hill: University of North Carolina Press, 2006); Charles Rappleye, *Sons of Providence: The Brown Brothers, the Slave Trade, and the American Revolution* (New York: Simon & Schuster, 2006); Jackson, *Let This Voice Be Heard*; Thomas Slaughter, *The Beautiful Soul of John Woolman, Apostle of Abolition* (New York: Hill & Wang, 2008); Richard Newman and James Mueller, eds., *Antislavery and Abolition in Philadelphia: Emancipation and the Long Struggle for Racial Justice in the City of Brotherly Love* (Baton Rouge: Louisiana State University Press, 2011); John Craig Hammond and Matthew Mason, eds., *Contesting Slavery: The Politics of Bondage and Freedom in the New American Nation* (Charlottesville: University Press of Virginia, 2011); Geoffrey Plank, *John Woolman's Path to the Peaceable Kingdom: A Quaker in the British Empire* (Philadelphia: University of Pennsylvania Press, 2012); Brycchan Carey and Geoffrey Plank, eds., *Quakers and Abolition* (Urbana: University of Illinois Press, 2014); Brycchan Carey, *From Peace to Freedom: Quaker Rhetoric and the Birth of American Antislavery, 1657–1761* (New Haven, Conn.: Yale University Press, 2012); Maurice Jackson and Susan Kozel, eds., *Quakers and Their Allies in the Abolitionist Cause, 1754–1808* (London: Routledge, 2015); Ira Berlin, *The Long Emancipation: The Demise of Slavery in the United States* (Cambridge, Mass.: Harvard University Press, 2015); Rael, *Eighty-Eight Years*; James J. Gigantino II, *The Ragged Road to Abolition: Slavery and Freedom in New Jersey, 1775–1865* (Philadelphia: University of Pennsylvania Press, 2015); Manisha Sinha, *The Slave's Cause: A History of Abolition* (New Haven, Conn.: Yale University Press, 2016); Rediker, *The Fearless Benjamin Lay*.

## Chapter 1. The Making of a Quaker Reformer

1. *A Defence of Warner Mifflin Against Aspersions cast on him on Account of his endeavours To promote Righteousness, Mercy, and Peace Among Mankind* (Philadelphia: Samuel Sansom, 1797), 3. Hilda Justice included *Defence* in Hilda Justice, *Life and Ancestry of Warner Mifflin: Patriot—Philanthropist—Humanitarian* (Philadelphia: Ferris & Leach, 1905) (hereafter, *Mifflin*), but her transcription has small errors and important omissions. Hereafter, the original edition is used and cited as *Defence of Mifflin*. Warner was probably referring to the Cool Springs Meeting in Sussex County, Delaware, or the Third Haven Meeting in Easton on Maryland's Eastern Shore.

2. Amelia Mott Gummere, *The Quaker: A Study in Costume* (Philadelphia: Ferris & Leach, 1901) provides illuminating insights into the plain dress of Quakers.

3. Jean R. Soderlund, *Lenape Country: Delaware Valley Society Before William Penn* (Philadelphia: University of Pennsylvania Press, 2015), ch. 6 for immigrant relations with the Lenape. For the Swede-dominated colony, see Gunlog Fur, *Colonialism in the Margins: Cultural Encounters in New Sweden and Lapland* (Leiden: Brill, 2006). Aside from London, County Wiltshire was Penn's most important recruiting ground. In the far south of England, Wiltshire contributed one-tenth of the "First Purchasers" of land in Philadelphia in the first years of settlement. Mary Maples Dunn and Richard Dunn, eds., *The Papers of William Penn*, 5 vols. (Philadelphia: University of Pennsylvania Press, 1981–1987), 3: 633.

4. Quoted in Amy C. Schutt, *Peoples of the River Valleys: The Odyssey of the Delaware Indians* (Philadelphia: University of Pennsylvania Press, 2007), 42.

5. Petition in *New Jersey Archives, First Series*, 42 vols. (Newark, 1880–1949), 1: 289; Andros grant in *Documents Relative to the Colonial History of the State of New York*, 15 vols. (Albany: Weed, Parsons, 1853–57), 12: 623–24; Soderlund, *Lenape Country*, 144–49. The site was close to where William Penn would soon build his country home at Pennsbury.

6. Soderlund, *Lenape Country*, 147 quoting Inhabitants of Crewcorne to Governor Andros, April 12, 1680, in *Colonial History of New York*, 12: 645–46.

7. "An Account of the Mifflin Family written by Jonathan Mifflin, Senior, on the Fifteenth of September 1770," in Justice, *Mifflin*, 34. Mifflin had been charged in June 1680 with taking a pair of shoes and five small locks from a fellow immigrant. He was acquitted in a jury trial. H. Clay Reed and George J. Miller, eds., *The Burlington Court Book: A Record of Quaker Jurisprudence in West New Jersey, 1680–1709* (Washington, D.C.: American Historical Association, 1944), 1–2. Jean Soderlund brought this case to my attention.

8. Justice, *Mifflin*, 31. Justice was a descendant of Warner Mifflin; in her late twenties she began to unearth documents that would memorialize her all-but-forgotten ancestor.

9. "Germantown Friends' Protest Against Slavery, 1688," in Roger Bruns, ed., *Am I Not a Man and a Brother: The Antislavery Crusade of Revolutionary America, 1688–1788* (New York: Chelsea House, 1977), 3–5.

10. Philadelphia Monthly Meeting Minutes (hereafter PMMM), 1682–1714, April 30, 1714, 329; PMMM, Arch St., Certificates of Removal, 1686–1758, #53, accessed Ancestry.com, Jan. 3, 2015. Quaker preparative meetings for worship brought together those in a particular locale. Such local meetings—three, four, or more—reported to the monthly meeting, the basic unit for conducting business such as providing for the poor, supervising marriages, disciplining wayward Friends, and disowning them for violating the Society's code of behavior. Women's Monthly Meetings paralleled those of the men.

11. James H. Marshall, Northampton County, Virginia: Abstracts of Wills and Administrations, 1632–1802, Personal Papers Collection, Library of Virginia, 223, cited in Virginia Eastern Shore Public Library, MilesFiles15.0 Online, accessed April 18, 2015.

12. Occupied with his hurried marriage and the birth of his first child, Mifflin was absent at his father's death in Philadelphia in June 1714. In her "Mifflin Genealogy," Hilda Justice listed Ann as the third child, without birth and death dates. But Ann was the firstborn of Edward and Mary [Eyre Littleton] Mifflin's six children. For documentation, see MilesFile15.0/Edward Mifflin Online.

13. Matthew M. Wise, *Littleton Heritage: Some American Descendants of Col. Nathaniel Littleton (1605–1654) of Northampton County, Virginia, and His Royal Forebears* (West Columbia, S.C.: Westworth, 1997), 5–8.

14. Will of Southey Littleton, Dec. 31, 1712, easternshoreheritage.com/processions/Accomack/acc/htm, accessed Oct. 24, 2014. The meetinghouse was never built, for reasons hidden to history.

15. Quoted in Kenneth Carroll, "Quakerism on the Eastern Shore of Virginia," *Virginia Magazine of History and Biography* 74 (1966): 174–75.

16. Near present-day Cheriton, Virginia, Eyre Hall was designated a National Historic Landmark in 2012. It has been in the family since 1668; today its gardens are open to the public.

17. The exact date of the marriage that united Edward Mifflin with Mary Eyre is elusive, because the civil government of Virginia did not recognize marriages outside established churches,

and the Quaker records, such as might have been set down, are not extant for the Virginia Eastern Shore.

18. T. H. Breen and Stephen Innes, *"Myne Owne Ground": Race and Freedom on Virginia's Eastern Shore, 1640–1676* (New York: Oxford University Press, 1980).

19. Some of the Mifflin plantation is now part of the Virginia State Magothy Bay Natural Area Preserve, which encompasses 140 acres of songbird habitat.

20. MilesFile15.0 Online lists Ann, Mary, and John, born about 1714, 1718, and 1720.

21. Fothergill made his first American traveling odyssey in 1705 when he was twenty-nine; *An Account of the Life and Travells in the Work of the Ministry of John Fothergill* (London, 1754). He was the father of the famous physician and botanist who became a friend and science-minded compatriot of Benjamin Franklin.

22. Manuscript Journal of Samuel Bownas, vol. 4, Quaker Collection, Swarthmore College Library (hereafter FHLSC), cited in Carroll, "Quakerism on Eastern Shore of Va.," 185–86; thanks to Chris Densmore for pdf of pages from the manuscript journal of Bownas. In a small gesture of thankfulness and Quaker generosity, Mifflin lent his small boat to Bownas to cross eight miles across the Chesapeake Bay to its western shore.

23. Because she and her first husband had no children in their short year of marriage, Mary Eyre Littleton derived the benefits from some of her inherited land after remarrying, but only until her deceased husband's sisters married or reached the legal age of eighteen. Then, because the wills of his grandfather and uncle had entailed the land to the male heirs or heirs at common law, some of Southey Littleton's land was his widow's to use only into the 1720s. Sister Esther married in 1722; sister Sarah died unmarried in 1720. Edward and Mary had negotiated an agreement with Mary's sisters-in-law from her first marriage to split Pharsalia, with Edward and Mary taking 840 acres facing the Atlantic Ocean. Deed from Joshua Chapman to Edward Mifflin, June 17, 1735, Somerset County Land Records, liber AZ, 228–29, digital image,http.//mdlandrec.net, accessed Dec. 14, 2014. It is possible the Mifflins spent some time at Pharsalia earlier than this. Justice, *Mifflin*, without documentation, says their son Daniel was born there in 1722.

24. A third plantation called Nadua was part of Ann Eyre Littleton's dowry; it no doubt included many slaves who were not mentioned in Southey Littleton's will because they were understood, in Virginia legal language, to be included in "the appurtences" of a plantation or "all the benefits thereof."

25. Will of Edward Mifflin, Oct. 7, 1740, in Justice, *Mifflin*, 15–16, 207–9; the extraordinarily detailed eight-page inventory is in Accomack County Wills, 1743–1749, 57–65, Library of Virginia. Southey Mifflin, named for his mother's first husband, was about thirteen at his father's death; his brother Samuel was about fifteen. Their inheritance was held in trust until they reached twenty. Widow Mary was given the profits on the properties left to the younger sons until they reached adulthood, and Daniel was given the right to exchange bequests with either of his younger brothers.

26. Justice, *Mifflin*, 132–33 for marriage certificate with list of attendees, including the bride's father; Samuel Mifflin, Daniel's younger brother; and a brace of cousins, aunts, and uncles on both sides of the family; Kenneth Carroll, *Quakerism on the Eastern Shore* (Baltimore: Maryland Historical Society, 1970), Appendix, Part III: Cecil Monthly Meeting records, 274 for birth and parentage of Mary Warner.

27. Only "a few isolated Quaker families," writes Kenneth Carroll, lived south of the Maryland border on the Eastern Shore in the 1740s; "Quakerism on the Eastern Shore of Virginia," 170.

Warner was undoubtedly schooled on the books his grandfather bequeathed to his sons, including some of the key building blocks of Quaker doctrine and history: William Penn's *No Cross, No Crown* (1669), George Fox's *Journal* (1694), Robert Barclay's *Apology for the True Christian Divinity* (1676), James Nayler's *Tracts of Nayler* (1716), Edward Burrough's *A Vindication of the People Called Quakers* (1660), William Sewel's *History of the Rise, Increase, and Progress of the Christian People Called Quakers* (1722), and Latin and English dictionaries.

28. "Testimony concerning Warner Mifflin, by his intimate friend and survivor, George Churchman," *Friends Miscellany* 2 (1832): 328.

29. One such home marriage, when Warner was eight, united his Aunt Sarah, his mother's widowed sister, with Ezekiel Nock, one of the leading Quakers in Delaware's Kent County and a man with whom Warner would work in the years ahead. Carroll, *Quakerism on the Eastern Shore*, 97–98 and n17 for the marriage of Sarah [Warner] Maxfield, widow of Joseph Maxfield, to Ezekiel Nock of Kent County, Delaware in 1753; witnesses included Daniel and Mary Mifflin (Daniel's mother) and two other unidentified Mifflins, Mary, Jr., and Hannah.

30. It is possible that Mary Warner Mifflin, Daniel's wife, died during the birth of Joshua in 1756. Both mother and child apparently died within months of the birth. Mifflin Family Tree (by Mifflin consulting) website. Mary Warner Mifflin was almost certainly buried in the family cemetery at Pharsalia, where many slaves must also have been buried. No archaeological work has been done in this area, to my knowledge. Hilda Justice noted that Daniel Mifflin's third wife, Mary Pusey Mifflin, was buried in the "Family Burying Ground, Accomac," Justice, *Mifflin*, 15.

31. For Phillip Mongon's 99-year lease on the Mattapony Hundred acreage and its passing into white hands, see Ralph T. Whitelaw, *Virginia's Eastern Shore: A History of Northampton and Accomack Counties*, 2 vols. (Gloucester, Mass.: Peter Smith, 1968), 2: 1216, 1329, 1332, 1353. Many years later, Daniel Mifflin willed this land to the son of his second marriage, Jonathan Walker Mifflin. Daniel Mifflin's will is in Justice, *Mifflin*, 218–22. For the life of Phillip Mongon/Mongum and demise of free black land ownership, see Breen and Innes, *Myne Owne Ground*, 80–83.

32. Duck Creek Monthly Meeting Minutes (hereafter DCMMM), Sept. 19, 1757; Minute book transcription, HSP, 201.

33. "Marriage Certificate of Daniel and Ann (Walker) Mifflin," Justice, *Mifflin*, 134–35. Fox's advice on marriage ceremonies is on most Quaker marriage websites.

34. msa.maryland.gov/stager/s1400/s1437/html, accessed Jan. 27, 2015. These purchases are documented in Whitelaw, *Virginia's Eastern Shore*, 2: 1384. Mifflin's will is in Justice, *Mifflin*, 218–22.

35. Worcester County, Md., Land Records, Deed Book F, 410; digital image, http://mdlandrec .net, accessed Jan. 25, 2015. Worcester County, Md. Tax Records, 1783 Assessment: msa.maryland .gov/msa/stagser/s1400/stagser1437, accessed Jan. 27, 2015.

36. After Edward Mifflin died in 1743, the disposition of his slaves, left unmentioned in his will, became a source of dispute between Daniel and his two brothers. Edward's widow was appointed by the Accomack County Court to serve as guardian of them and ruled that the many slaves should be equally distributed among the four children. JoAnn Riley McKey, *Accomack County, Virginia Court Order Abstracts, 1737–1744*, vol. 17 (Berwyn Heights, Md.: Heritage Books, 1996), 372.

37. "Anecdotes and Memoirs of Warner Mifflin," in Justice, *Mifflin*, 70–71; Ezekiel may have first told this story in 1825, a half century after he had been freed. It was first published, so far as I can determine, in "Anecdotes and Memoirs of Warner Mifflin," *Friends Miscellany* 5 (1834):

217–18. It is unlikely that they ate and slept together, probably the romanticized recollection of a very old man.

38. Mifflin to the Archbishop of Canterbury, June 30, 1787, Society Autograph Collection, HSP; *Defence of Mifflin*, 4.

39. The first quote is from the letter to the Archbishop of Canterbury; the second from *Defence of Mifflin*, 4–5.

40. The spelling of Murderkill in eighteenth-century sources, and even today, varies: Murderkill, Murtherkill, Motherkiln, and Motherkill.

41. "Brief Account of Warner Mifflin," Emlen Family Papers, HSP. The account was written for her two orphaned sons.

42. Hilda Justice may have gotten this from "Anecdotes and Memoirs of Warner Mifflin," 217, but it is curious that the venerable and proud Mifflin family would pass this down the line. It was repeated in John Houston Merrill, "Memoranda, Relating to the Mifflin Family" (Philadelphia: Privately Published, 1890) and many genealogical websites.

43. www.pennock.ws/surnames/fm or Pennocks of Primitive Hall website is the only genealogical website I've found that gets Elizabeth's parentage right. That Elizabeth Johns was the daughter of Samuel Johns and sister of Joseph Galloway is confirmed in land records of Kent County; Daniel Boorstin, ed., *Delaware Cases, 1792–1830* (St. Paul, Minn.: West Publishing, 1943), 82–85; Samuel Johns and Elizabeth Galloway were married about 1745; their second daughter, Elizabeth Johns, was born about 1748 or 1749.

44. Mifflin's mother-in-law, Elizabeth Galloway Hilliard, made him co-executor of her estate, and he carried out this responsibility in April 1790, four years after his first wife died. Probate File of Elizabeth Hilliard, Kent County Register of Wills RG 3545.000, Delaware Public Archives, Dover (hereafter DPA).

45. Bruce Lively, "Toward 1756: The Political Genesis of Joseph Galloway," *Pennsylvania History* 45 (1978): 117–38. The land acquisitions of Peter Galloway and Samuel Johns in Kent County can be followed in Mary Marshall Brewer, *Kent County, Delaware Land Records*, vol. 3 *(1723–1734)*, vol. 4 *(1735–1743)* (Westminster, Md.: Heritage, 2008, 2009) (hereafter *KCDLR*).

46. The marriages of Elizabeth Johns Hilliard and her inherited properties are detailed in a deed of May 17, 1765, *KCDLR*, vol. 8 *(1764–1768)*, 24; Indenture of July 21, 1769; vol. 9 *(1768–1772)*, 53; and Indenture of May 13, 1771, 130–31. The deeds are silent on inherited slaves, but there certainly were many of them.

47. Charles Hilliard's father stood atop the Kent County economic and social hierarchy; see Richard L. Bushman, *The Refinement of America: Persons, Houses, Cities* (New York: Knopf, 1992), 17 for Hilliard's estate, exceeding one thousand pounds at his death in about 1755.

48. PYMM, Oct. 1, 1762, quoted in Jack D. Marietta, *The Reformation of American Quakerism, 1748–1783* (Philadelphia: University of Pennsylvania Press, 1984), 66, where he discusses how the 1762 directive on enforcing a strict marriage discipline quickly led to an upsurge of disownments (67–70). The Philadelphia Yearly Meeting was the policy-making body for all Friends meetings in New Jersey, Pennsylvania, Delaware, and Maryland's Eastern Shore. As many as several thousand Quakers would gather for its week-long assemblies, making the yearly meeting a place to do business, meet old friends and relatives, find or pursue a romantic relationship, and attend fellowship services in the city's three Quaker meetinghouses, where traveling Quaker ministers from abroad could be counted on to furnish spiritual inspiration. The yearly meeting's Epistles or Advices defined what it meant to be a Friend in good standing.

49. DCMMM, June 23, 25, Aug. 27, 1763.

50. Thomas Rodney, a young blade from the famous Rodney family, noted Elizabeth Johns's wealth and believed she was to be matched with Vincent Loockerman, son of one of the wealthiest Delaware merchant-planters; but two months later Warner swept her off her feet. Thomas Rodney to Sally Ridgely, April 20, 1767, Ridgely Papers, Box 10, file 1, DHS. If one is to believe St. John de Crèvecoeur, the dowry was more than considerable, indeed it was mountainous. Crèvecoeur fixed the amount at 327,000 livres, the equivalent of nearly 23,000 pounds in Pennsylvania and Delaware currency. Crèvecoeur, *Letters from an American Farmer*, translation in Justice, *Mifflin*, 58 from 1787 expanded Paris edition. Nobody in Kent County had that kind of fortune.

51. Why the marriage occurred in Philadelphia, on May 14, 1767 (according to Hilda Justice) is unknown, but it seems likely that a home wedding was conducted by one of Philadelphia's Anglican ministers in the Bucks County mansion of Elizabeth's uncle, Joseph Galloway, or in his Philadelphia house. No record is in the marriage records of Philadelphia's three Anglican churches. How Hilda Justice knew the exact wedding date more than 230 years later suggests a family record of the marriage. It is possible that Richard Peters, minister of Philadelphia's Christ Church, conducted the private wedding, just as Robert Janney had done for Warner's uncle George Mifflin in 1753 when Anne Eyre, a non-Quaker, was the bride. Janney's eight-line certification of the marriage is in Mifflin Family Papers, Box 1, Franklin and Marshall College Special Collections (hereafter, FMCSP).

52. Ann Emlen Mifflin, "Brief Account of Warner Mifflin," 1799, Emlen Family Papers, Box 1, HSP; the "supposed difficulty" was almost certainly the Murderkill meeting's disownment of Elizabeth Galloway Johns Hilliard and her membership in Dover's Anglican church.

53. DCMMM, March 26, 1768, included in Justice, *Mifflin*, 138. I have not been able to determine why the Murderkill meeting waited ten months after the wedding to issue the challenge to his membership. It is likely that Elizabeth, like her mother and stepfather, was a member of Christ Church.

54. Ann Mifflin, "Brief Account of Warner Mifflin," Emlen Family Papers, HSP.

55. DCMMM, Feb. 27, 1768.

56. DCMMM, June 24, 1769; Feb. 22, Mar. 23, Apr. 27, May 26, June 22, July 27, Aug. 25, Sept. 30, Oct. 28, Nov. 23, Dec. 28, 1782.

57. Paul Clemens, *The Atlantic Economy and Colonial Maryland's Eastern Shore: From Tobacco to Grain* (Ithaca, N.Y.: Cornell University Press, 1980), 45–46, 195–96 and map 46 for weak soil conditions on much of the bayside Eastern Shore of Maryland; see also Gregory A. Stiverson, *Poverty in a Land of Plenty: Tenancy in Eighteenth-Century Maryland* (Baltimore: Johns Hopkins University Press, 1977), 85–103. It was all the more advantageous to forsake Maryland's Eastern Shore for Delaware because of the pernicious way tobacco had exhausted the soil after generations of planting. To maintain the soil's fertility, tobacco farmers had to rest it seven of every eight years; for grain farmers two harvests of winter wheat required only one year in fallow.

58. Bushman, "The Gentrification of Rural Delaware," in *Refinement of America*, 3–29; Bushman takes no notice of Quakers.

59. The Maryland family of Warner's mother were Joseph and Ann (Coale) Warner. Crèvecoeur claimed that Warner received thirty-seven slaves from his father—an exaggeration that makes no mention of his wife's dowry slaves. Crèvecoeur, *Letters from American Farmer*, trans. Hilda Justice from the 1787 Paris edition in *Mifflin*, 59–60. In his letters to the Archbishop of Canterbury

and Alexander Huston, Mifflin claimed he owned twenty-seven slaves, five more than he later manumitted.

60. Clemens, *Atlantic Economy*, 174–83, 195–98. For an elaborate analysis of the final stages of the transition from tobacco to grain in Delaware see Brooke Hunter, "The Rage for Grain: Flour Milling in the Mid-Atlantic, 1750–1815," Ph.D. dissertation, University of Delaware, 2001. James Tilton, writing in response to queries from the French agronomist Abbé Alexandre Henri Tessier (1745–1822), who was producing an agricultural encyclopedia in the midst of the French Revolution, provided detailed answers about agriculture in Delaware that were published by Mathew Carey in 1789 in his *American Museum*. They are reprinted with editorial comments in R. O. Bausman and J. A. Munroe, "James Tilton's Notes on Agriculture in Delaware in 1788," *Agricultural History* 20 (1946): 176–87. Tilton explained that Kent County exported grain through Wilmington to the West Indies and "even to Europe," but much more passed through Philadelphia. "James Tilton's Notes on Agriculture," 185.

61. "James Tilton's Notes on Agriculture," 185, 196. For a succinct picture of Delaware agriculture, see John Munroe, *Federalist Delaware, 1775–1815* (New Brunswick, N.J.: Rutgers University Press, 1954), 114–25.

62. Harold B. Hancock, "Description and Travel Accounts of Delaware, 1700–1740," *Delaware History* 10 (1962): 150.

63. *Memoirs and Recollections of Count Segur, Ambassador from France to the Courts of Russia and Prussia* (Boston: Wells and Lilly, 1825), 257. "James Tilton's Notes on Agriculture," 185. The deeds of land transactions in Kent County testify to the heavily forested land of mid-Delaware, left in their prime after thousands of years of native occupancy.

64. Quoted in Emil G. Winslow and Don O. Winslow, eds., *Dover: The First 250 Years* (Dover, Del.: City of Dover, 1967), 11.

65. *Journal of the Life of Nathaniel Luff, M.D. of the State of Delaware, Written by Himself* (New York: Clark & Sickels, 1848), 26, 41.

66. Tilton submitted a long letter on climate and disease in Delaware to Philadelphia's eminent physician William Currie, published as *An Historical Account of the Climates and Diseases of the U.S.* (Philadelphia, 1792). Tilton's extended comments, titled "The Account of the Situation, Climate, and Diseases of the State of Delaware," were sent to Currie from Dover on April 20, 1791. They can be found in Currie, *Historical Account*, 203–24. The correspondence of Dover's affluent Ridgely family is littered with complaints of Kent County's lethal climate, especially during summer months, even to the extent that it was difficult to engage the services of a female servant who "would object to the unhealthiness of Kent" (Ann Ridgely to Henry Ridgely, Dec. 29, 1794, 134) or an overseer: "Dover's reputation for unhealthiness makes people unwilling to go there." Henry M. Ridgely to Ann Ridgely, Dec. 20, 1794, 132. Leon deValinger, Jr., ed. and comp., *A Calendar of Ridgely Family Letters, 1742–1899*, 3 vols. (Dover, Del.: Public Archives Commission, 1948–1961), 1: 25, 126, 134, 160, 169, 185, 209, 237, 253, 264, 279, 328, 337–38, 347. Refugees from Philadelphia's 1797 yellow fever epidemic poured into Wilmington but avoided Dover as simply another death sentence. Ann Ridgely to Henry M. and George W. Ridgely, Sept. 3, 1797, *Calendar*, 169.

67. Ann Warder Diary, *PMHB* 18 (1894): 62.

68. "Return of the division of the lands of Samuel Johns, deceased," Aug. 4, 1766, Kent County Orphans Court, RG 3840.006, Delaware Public Archives. Resource Specialist Margaret Dunham, Delaware Public Archives, provided this survey. The survey included a detailed map. Elizabeth

Hilliard, Warner's mother-in-law, lived with her husband near Dover. The marriage of Ann Johns to the widower Richard Holliday is detailed in Duck Creek Women's Monthly Meeting Minutes, 1711–1830 (hereafter DCWMMM), Aug. 28 and Oct. 4, 1764. Deeds in *KCDLR*, vol. 8:57, 76; vol. 9:25, 29, 116, make it clear that the couple lived in Duck Creek Hundred, leaving the Gainsborough plantation house to sister Elizabeth and Warner. The buyout occurred two years after the marriage, when Warner paid 850 pounds on July 24, 1769, for title to all of Gainsborough. *KCDLR*, vol. 9: 53–54. Mike McDowell provided a copy of the survey.

69. PYM-MME, Ancestry.com, frames 431, 453, 467; by 1775 Mifflin was appointed by his monthly meeting to inquire into the qualifications of others proposed as elders, "to visit and treat . . .in love" with a young man intent on training for the army, and in investigating an irregular marriage; DCMMM, Mar. 28, 1772; Aug. 28, 1773; Feb. 25, 1775; Aug. 6, 1775. Seven quarterly meetings, each embracing three to five monthly meetings, discussed weighty issues such as ridding the Society of slave trading and slaveholding. Each quarterly meeting sent its most respected men and women as delegates to the Philadelphia Yearly Meeting, some of them traveling hundreds of miles to reach Philadelphia in late September.

70. The amount of time Mifflin was devoting to yearly, quarterly, monthly, and preparative meetings, as well as to committee visits to individual families, could not have been less than eighty days a year.

71. Ann Emlen, "Brief Account," HSP.

72. *KCDLR*, vol. 9: 94; vol. 10 *(1772–1775)*, 9; Justice, *Mifflin*, 110 for the record of appointments. Mifflin held the justice of the peace office through 1774, and was appointed justice of the Kent County Court of Quarter Sessions and Common Pleas in that year.

73. *Defence of Mifflin*, 6–7.

74. The major acquisitions can be followed in *KCDLR*, vol. 9, 44, 53, 122; vol. 10, 46–47.

75. Befitting a member of the county elite, Mifflin was often called to oversee or witness land transactions or serve as the executor or guardian of the estates of collateral kin and others. This involved him with such eminences as Dr. Samuel McCall of Dover, lawyer and politician; and Philadelphia's Joseph Galloway, who maintained a large estate in Kent County. *KCDLR*, vol. 9, 124, 131; vol. 10, 33, 68. Mifflin's involvement in the administration of estates is detailed in Leon deValinger, Jr., *Calendar of Kent County Delaware Probate Records, 1680–1800* (Dover, Del.: Public Archives Commission, 1944): named administrator of estate of John Jackson, March 15, 1771 (258); executor of estate of Joseph Goodfellow, Nov. 29, 1772 (272); named as guardian with others in will of Govey Emerson, March 5, 1773 (278); made executor of estate of his kinsman and neighbor Jabez Jenkins, June 26, 1773 (280); made executor of estate of George Melchop, Feb. 9, 1774 (288); made executor of Jonathan Emerson estate, Apr. 3, 1784 (359); and so forth. In his *Defence against Aspersions* he refers to two estates for which he was appointed executor and had to deal with slave property.

76. Among 600–700 taxpayers in Murderkill Hundred in the decade before the American Revolution, Mifflin consistently ranked in the top five to eight. Kent County Tax Assessments, DPA, Microfilm #2 (1743–1767); #3 (1768–1784).

77. The births and deaths of Warner and Elizabeth's children are detailed in Justice, *Mifflin*, 18–19; the years of birth for slave children were included in Mifflin's manumission deeds of 1774 and 1775.

78. David L. Crosby, ed., *The Complete Antislavery Writings of Anthony Benezet, 1754–1783* (Baton Rouge: Louisiana State University Press, 2013), 8. For a stirring biography of Benezet see

Maurice Jackson, *Let This Voice Be Heard: Anthony Benezet, Father of Atlantic Abolitionism* (Philadelphia: University of Pennsylvania Press, 2009); for Benezet's editing of Woolman's draft, see 53.

79. Thomas E. Drake, *Quakers and Slavery in America* (New Haven, Conn.: Yale University Press, 1950), 51.

80. *Defence of Mifflin*, 4–5.

81. The oft-told Quaker antislavery campaign has been dissected by Sydney James, *A People Among Peoples: Quaker Benevolence in Eighteenth-Century America* (Cambridge, Mass.: Harvard University Press, 1963), ch. 7–9, 12; and Jean R. Soderlund, *Quakers and Slavery: A Divided Spirit* (Princeton, N.J.: Princeton University Press, 1985), ch. 1–2, 4; quotes 87 (hereafter Soderlund, *Quakers and Slavery*).

82. Soderlund, *Quakers and Slavery*, 93–95; the Wilmington manumission book is not extant.

83. Ferris to James Rigby, April 7, 1766 in J. William Frost, *The Quaker Origins of Antislavery* (Norwood, Pa.: Norwood Editions, 1980), 182.

84. Western Quarterly Meeting Minutes (hereafter WQMM), Nov. 18, 1765, 118; Marietta, *Reformation of American Quakerism*, 125–27; Phillips Moulton, ed., *Journal and Major Essays of John Woolman* (Richmond, Ind.: Friends United Press, 1971), 145. For Woolman, see Thomas P. Slaughter, *The Beautiful Soul of John Woolman, Apostle of Abolition* (New York: Hill and Wang, 2008) and Geoffrey Plank, *John Woolman's Path to the Peaceable Kingdom* (Philadelphia: University of Pennsylvania Press, 2012).

85. Quoted in Jackson, *Let This Voice Be Heard*, 28.

86. Soderlund, *Quakers and Slavery*, 90, 95, citing Wilmington Monthly Meeting minutes, Sept. 16, 1761 and July 16, 1766. The Nicholites, a small group sharing most Quaker principles, started freeing slaves in Kent County in 1766. Kenneth Carroll, *Joseph Nichols and the Nicholites: A Look at the "New Quakers" of Maryland, Delaware, North and South Carolina* (Easton, Md.: Eastern Publishing, 1962), 20–21, 25–26.

87. *Defence of Mifflin*, 5.

88. WQMM, Aug. 17, 1767; Aug. 15, 1768; Aug. 21, 1769; Aug. 20, 1770; quotes from Aug. 17, 1767, and Aug. 20, 1770.

89. Among them were Benezet's *Some Historical Observations of Guinea* (1771); Benjamin Rush's *An Address to the Inhabitants of the British Settlement in America* (1773); George Dillwyn's *Brief Considerations on slavery and the expediency of its abolition, with some hints on the means whereby it may be gradually effected* (1773); and David Cooper's *A Serious Address to the Rulers of America on the Inconsistency of their Conduct Respecting Slavery* (1773).

90. WQMM, Aug. 16, 1773, 229–30; May 16, 1774, 243–44.

91. Justice, *Mifflin*, 210 for an abbreviated will of Mary Mifflin. When his grandmother died in 1775, the manumission took effect. Equally remarkable, Mifflin had been a regular representative from his monthly meeting to the quarterly meetings in Chester County from 1770 to 1774, where he was party to the insistent calls for action on purging slaveholding. Mifflin's attendance at seven quarterly meetings is noted in the WQMM, Aug. 20, 1770; Aug. 19, 1771; Aug. 17, Nov. 16, 1772; May 17, Nov. 15, 1773; Aug. 15, 1774.

92. WQMM, Aug. 15, 1774.

93. Mifflin to John Pemberton, Sept. 22, 1774, Pemberton Papers, Box 26/155b, HSP. What Mifflin described as "a bilious fever" was most likely the malarial fever that frequently struck Kent County in late summer.

94. Manumission in Justice, *Mifflin*, 111–12. Mifflin said he had manumitted James "some time back," though he left no record of this.

95. Mifflin to Huston, Jan. 17, 1779, Emlen Family Papers, Box 2, HSP. I am indebted to Mike McDowell for a transcription of this lengthy, difficult-to-read letter.

96. *Defence of Mifflin*, 5–6; I have conflated statements in *Defence* with those in the letter to the Archbishop of Canterbury. These conversion narratives, presented as a *cri de conscience*, an internal, soul-cleansing rehabilitation from slaveowning ways, omit the external pressure from the yearly meeting that surely was part of his moral rehabilitation. In her *Teach Me Dreams: The Search for Self in Revolutionary America* (Princeton, N.J.: Princeton University Press, 2000), 220–21, Mechal Sobel notes the significance of lightning in the conversion experiences of many early modern figures.

97. Added to the twenty-two slaves he manumitted were several others he had sold before 1774. Several probably died between 1767 when he acquired them and 1774–1775.

98. *Defence of Mifflin*, 6.

99. The manumission deed, recorded in the Duck Creek Manumission Book, is transcribed in Justice, *Mifflin*, 112–13. It is not clear why Mifflin called himself "merchant" rather than "farmer." Transcriptions of the manumission book are at HSP.

100. Daniel Mifflin's deeds of manumissions, April 8, 1775 are in Justice, *Mifflin*, 116–21. Eva S. Wolf, *Freedom and Slavery in the New Nation* (Baton Rouge: Louisiana State University Press, 2006), 45n7, 55, counts 91 manumissions. Daniel Mifflin re-recorded the deed in the Accomack County Deed Books in 1782 after the legislature legitimized private manumissions. As customary, the final release of minors took effect when they reached their majority. For Daniel Mifflin's abolitionist work, see Wolf, *Freedom and Slavery*, 55–56, 61–62.

101. Nomination as elder and clerk is in Justice, *Mifflin*, 139–40, from DCMMM.

102. Mifflin to Huston, Jan. 17, 1779. Mifflin related that he had paid one hundred pounds for one slave and pledged (four years after his second deed of manumission) to renew the offers to reclaim others whose masters had declined Mifflin's entreaties.

103. Deed of manumission, Feb. 6, 1777, Kent County Bills of Sale, Liber DD #3, Folio 37, quoted in Carroll, *Quakerism on the Eastern Shore*, 139.

104. Mifflin to John Parrish, Aug. 27, 1784, Coxe-Parrish-Wharton Papers, Series I, Box 1, folder 10, HSP (hereafter, C-P-W). In an embellished (and erroneous) account, Crèvecoeur celebrated Mifflin for trying to rescue a slave he had sold for obstinacy to a man who then "sent [the slave] to Jamaica, where the fever soon made him more docile and well-behaved." After receiving a "touching letter" from his former bondsman describing "his misery and repentance," the guilt-ridden Mifflin "set sail for this island, from whence, after buying back his former slave, he brought him to Philadelphia and gave him his liberty." Justice, *Mifflin*, 63.

105. If these ages are correct, or nearly so, they confirm modern research that enslaved women conceived children very early, often by fourteen or fifteen.

106. For example, WQMM, Aug. 18, 1765; Aug. 17, 1767; Aug. 15, 1768. Every year thereafter similar "advices" were sent to the monthly and preparative meetings. The deed of manumission included Mifflin's vow that "it [is] my duty to take upon myself the power and authority of the young ones to raise and educate them till they arrive to lawful age."

107. George Thatcher to Thomas B. Wait, Nov. 6, 1790, Linda Grant DePauw et al., eds., *Documentary History of the First Federal Congress*, 21 vols. (Baltimore: Johns Hopkins University Press, 1974–2017), hereafter *DHFFC*, 21: 52.

108. Ezekiel's narrative was apparently first published in Abigail Mott's *Biographical Sketches and Interesting Anecdotes of Persons of Color* (New York: Mahlon Day, 1826; 2nd ed. 1837); Justice included it in *Mifflin* (69–71).

109. Nineteen of the first 62 members were black; Lewis V. Baldwin, *Mark of a Man: Peter Spencer and the African Union Methodist Tradition* (Lanham, Md.: University Press of America, 1987), 11, citing John D. C. Hanna, ed., *Centennial Services of Asbury Methodist Episcopal Church* (Wilmington, Del.: Delaware Printing, 1889), 141; William Henry Williams. *Garden of American Methodism: The Delmarva Peninsula, 1769–1820* (Wilmington, Del.: Scholarly Resources, 1984), 116. Coston may have moved first to New Castle, then to Wilmington, Delaware. The 1800 Census listed a free black family of four headed by E. Cosdon in New Castle. African Union Church was the first independent black church in the U.S. completely free of white authority, preceding Richard Allen's Mother Bethel African Methodist Episcopal Church in Philadelphia.

110. I have not found the initial manumission deed for James, but a copy of the "Certificat de Manumission" was published in *Mercure de France*, Jan. 4, 1783.

111. Justice, *Mifflin*, 59–62, translating from a 1787 Paris edition of Crèvecoeur's *Letters from an American Farmer*. Justice mistranslates the dowry as 270 pounds a year or 2,295 pounds. The widely circulated story, as given in a London broadside ("Warner Mifflin and James: An American Anecdote," London, 1798) says 21 pounds, 5 shillings per year or 95 pounds, 12 shillings, sixpence. This broadside may be the first English translation of the story first told by Crèvecoeur in 1784. The Society of Friends recycled the Mifflin-James dialogue as a part of its abolitionist crusade in the antebellum era. For example, *The Friend* 6 (1833): 143–44; *Friends Miscellany* 5 (1834): 217–18; and Henry W. Wilbur, *The Life and Labors of Elias Hicks* (Philadelphia: Friends General Conference, 1910).

112. Justice, *Mifflin*, 70.

113. Patience Essah's examination of wills and deeds shows that "hundreds of slaves . . . listed Warner Mifflin and other Kent County Quakers as friend or advocate in their freedom suits," and the deeds of manumission frequently bore the name of Mifflin as a witness. *A House Divided: Slavery and Emancipation in Delaware, 1638–1865* (Charlottesville: University Press of Virginia, 1996), 81. See her chapter 3 for an analysis of the many complicated arrangements imbedded in the deeds of manumission.

114. The Duck Creek Monthly Meeting embraced meetings for worship throughout Kent County, part of Sussex County, and southern New Castle County.

115. Essah, *A House Divided*, 47, citing DCMMM, Jan. 28, 1775. Jean Soderlund's survey of Quaker records in the mid-Atlantic region shows the great variation in how local preparative and monthly meetings responded to the advisories of the Philadelphia Yearly Meeting. Coordinating a trans-Atlantic campaign with the London Yearly Meeting, the Philadelphia Yearly Meeting set the agenda. Yet much depended on "the dynamics of leadership and the enforcement of discipline within local meetings." Soderlund, *Quakers and Slavery*, 90–92. The Duck Creek Monthly Meeting Minutes are littered with reports of Mifflin's family visits, almost always with women as part of the committee and often with his close friends and relatives—John and Ezekiel Cowgill, Isaiah Rowland, and Robert Holliday.

116. DCMMM, April 25, 1778; this was one of a number of especially difficult cases because the wife was a Quaker but the husband was not. DCMMM, Aug. 23, 1777. For last holdout, DCMMM, July 24, 1779.

117. DCMMM, Oct. 26, 1776; Feb. 28, 1778; May 25, 1778.

118. For the case of Mary Morris: DCMMM, Sept. 27, Oct. 25, Nov. 22, Dec. 27, 1782; Jan. 1, Feb. 28, Mar. 27, Apr. 24, May 22, June 26, 1783; and DCWMM for same dates.

119. Carroll, *Quakerism on the Eastern Shore*, 140.

120. Delaware's Anglican clerics derived their salaries from the profits of the vast Codrington slave plantations in Barbados and owned slaves themselves, rendering them immune to Mifflin's preachments. For a brief view, see "Slavery in Delaware: Report Produced by the Committee on Slavery of the Diocese of Delaware" (2009).

121. Thomas Rodney, manuscript essay on slavery, Brown Collection, B23, F24, Historical Society of Delaware. After Mifflin withdrew from Kent County civil appointments in 1773, Rodney continued his trajectory upward in the Delaware political elite. Elected to the General Assembly of Delaware in 1775, he rose to Judge of the Admiralty Court (1778–1785), and House of Assembly (1786–1787), where he was chosen as speaker. Later, almost a broken man, he was chosen by Jefferson to establish and lead the judiciary in the Mississippi Territory. For his biographer's description of him as "a financially broken, paranoiac delusional figure," see William Baskerville Hamilton, *Thomas Rodney: Revolutionary and Builder of the West* (Durham, N.C.: Duke University Press, 1953), vii–viii and passim.

122. For a history of Chew's slave operations at Whitehall and Cliveden, see Phillip Seitz, *Slavery in Philadelphia: A History of Resistance, Denial, and Wealth* (Philadelphia: n.p., 2014). One family of slaves Chew sold to Stokely Sturgis, his neighbor, included Richard Allen, who was to become founder of the African Methodist Episcopal Church in Philadelphia.

123. Dickinson maintained about sixty slaves at Poplar Hall in Kent County. For Dickinson's oscillation between birthright Quakerism and Anglicanism, see Jane E. Calvert, *Quaker Constitutionalism and the Political Thought of John Dickinson* (New York: Cambridge University Press, 2009), 189–95; and Milton E. Flower, *John Dickinson, Conservative Revolutionary* (Charlottesville: University Press of Virginia, 1983), 285–87. Dickinson's highly inflated claim that he sacrificed eight to ten thousand pounds by freeing his slaves was reported many years later by a Quaker friend. James Bringhurst to Elizabeth Coggeshall, Oct. 8, 1799, Bringhurst Papers, FHLSC.

124. "Committee Draft of the Articles of Confederation (1776)," Papers of the Continental Congress, RG360, National Archives, Washington, D.C., quoted in Jane Calvert, "An Expansive Conception of Rights: The Abolitionism of John Dickinson," in William R. Jordan, ed., *In the Course of Human Events: 1776 in America and Beyond* (Macon, Ga.: Mercer University Press, 2017). Calvert portrays Dickinson as singular among the Founding Fathers who liberated their slaves.

125. Deed of conditional manumission, May 12, 1777, Logan Papers, HSP. Dickinson's Quaker wife and mother-in-law badgered him on other matters and probably on slave keeping.

126. The 1781 deed of manumission is in Logan Papers, May 11, 1786, HSP and in Kent County Deed Book Y1, 217, reprinted in *KCDLR*, 1785–1789, pp. 32–33.

127. Mifflin to Dickinson, Aug. 11, 1786, R. R. Logan Collection, Box 1, folder 31, HSP.

128. Mifflin to Huston, Jan. 17, 1779, Emlen Family Papers, Box 2, HSP.

129. Dee Andrews, *The Methodists and Revolutionary America, 1760–1800: The Shaping of an Evangelical Culture* (Princeton, N.J.: Princeton University Press, 2000), 60–61, 125–32 (quoted passages 125–26), 159–60, 192–94; Williams, *The Garden of American Methodism*, 161–65; Kenneth Carroll, "Religious Influences on the Manumission of Slaves in Caroline, Dorchester, and Talbot Counties," *Maryland Historical Magazine* 56 (1961): 187–97, details the release of 1,833 slaves, mostly by Methodist slaveowners.

## Chapter 2. Trial by Fire

1. *Defence of Mifflin*, 14–16.

2. Jack D. Marietta, *The Reformation of American Quakerism, 1748–1783* (Philadelphia: University of Pennsylvania Press, 1984), 88–89. In this vein, the Meeting for Sufferings in Philadelphia, six years into the long war, worked to keep steady the moral compass of the Friends with the advice that "It is through tribulation that the righteous in every age enter the Kingdom." PYM-MS, Nov. 15, 1781, quoted in Marietta, *Reformation*, 89. The Philadelphia Meeting for Sufferings, modeled on the London-based Meeting for Sufferings that had recorded persecutions against Quakers since the 1660s, was a standing committee of the Philadelphia Yearly Meeting. The action arm of the yearly meeting, it corresponded with the five other yearly meetings in British North America as well as the London Meeting for Sufferings.

3. By mid-July 1776, Warner and Elizabeth Johns Mifflin's daughters were eight, five, and one. Two infant daughters had died in 1770 and 1773 before reaching six months. Justice, *Mifflin*, "Children of Warner and Elizabeth (Johns) Mifflin," 18.

4. John Adams to Abigail Adams, Sept. 8, 1777, in L. H. Butterfield, ed., *The Adams Papers: Adams Family Correspondence*, vol. 2 (Cambridge, Mass.: Harvard University Press, 1965), 337–38.

5. Jane Calvert, "Thomas Paine, Quakerism, and the Limits of Religious Liberty During the American Revolution," in Ian Shapiro and Jane E. Calvert, eds., *Selected Writings of Thomas Paine* (New Haven, Conn.: Yale University Press, 2014), 606.

6. For an account of the Free Quakers, see Arthur J. Mekeel, *The Relation of the Quakers to the American Revolution* (Washington, D.C.: University Press of America, 1979), ch. 16. Mekeel estimates that about 11 percent of Quaker males of military age in Pennsylvania were disowned for joining or assisting the Patriot military (333, 336).

7. Marietta, *Reformation of American Quakerism*, 232. The September 28, 1776, advice from the Philadelphia Yearly Meeting is in Isaac Sharpless, *A History of Quaker Government in Pennsylvania*, vol. 2, *The Quakers in the Revolution* (Philadelphia: T.S. Leach, 1899), 138–42. Sharpless's long-forgotten account of the agonizing deliberations of the yearly meeting presents many of its epistles on involvement in the revolution.

8. *Defence of Mifflin*, 7; "Testimony concerning Warner Mifflin, by his intimate friend and survivor, George Churchman," *Friends Miscellany* 2 (1834): 329. For Wilson's meetings with Mifflin, Wilson Diary, 1768–1769, QCHC. The warmth of Wilson's reception during her months-long itinerating tour of the Atlantic seaboard is treated in Rebecca Larson, *Daughters of Light: Quaker Women Preaching and Prophesying in the Colonies and Abroad, 1700–1775* (New York: Knopf, 1999), passim.

9. Marietta, *Reformation of American Quakerism*, 246–48, discusses the rancor between the Society of Friends and Free Quakers in Philadelphia.

10. Ibid., 203.

11. Quoted in Mekeel, *Relation of the Quakers*, 134; see also Jack D. Marietta, "Wealth, War, and Religion: The Perfecting of Quaker Asceticism, 1740–1783," *Church History* 43 (1974): 237–38 for a consideration of the Patriots' arguments. For Philadelphia-area documents on tax resistance see David M. Gross, *American Quaker War Tax Resistance*, 2nd ed. (n.p., Picket Books, 2011).

12. Sydney V. James, "The Impact of the American Revolution on Quakers' Ideas About Their Sect," *WMQ* 19 (1962): 360–82; Marietta, *Reformation of American Quakerism*, 221–27. The Meeting for Sufferings kept exact records detailing sheriffs' seizure of goods, usually sold at auction

or turned over to the patriot forces. Those extant are found in PYM-Meeting for Sufferings, Miscellaneous Manuscripts, QCHC. Mekeel provides an overview in his *Relation of the Quakers*, passim.

13. *Defence of Mifflin*, 19.

14. The Western Quarterly Meeting first appointed Mifflin to the Philadelphia Yearly Meeting in 1774; Mifflin to John Pemberton, Sept. 22, 1774, Pemberton Papers, HSP. 26 f155b. Mifflin regretted that he could not go, confined for eight days with bilious fever and tending "one of our children, [who] being very ill, fell into a convulsion fit."

15. "The Ancient Testimony & Principles of the People Called Quakers," Jan. 20, 1776, published in *Pennsylvania Ledger*, Jan. 27, 1776, and available in Sharpless, *A History of Quaker Government in Pennsylvania*, 2: 125–28.

16. Peter Brock, *Pacifism in the United States From the Colonial Era to the First World War* Princeton: Princeton University Press, 1968), 204–5. On Quaker oath-taking doctrine see Ezra Michener, *Retrospect of Early Quakerism Being Extracts from the Records of the Philadelphia Yearly Meeting* (Philadelphia: T. Ellwood Zell, 1860), ch. 23. Friends also objected to taking oaths because it implied that an individual might not tell the truth in court, whereas Quaker religious principles required truth-telling at all times.

17. After the war moved south in 1780, the frequent trips to Philadelphia from Delaware became less precarious.

18. This paragraph and those following on Brandywine lean heavily on the accounts in Stephen R. Taaffe, *The Philadelphia Campaign, 1777–1778* (Lawrence: University Press of Kansas, 2003), ch. 3; and Thomas J. McGuire, *Campaign for Philadelphia*, vol. 1, *Brandywine and the Fall of Philadelphia*, 2 vols. (Mechanicsburg, Pa.: Stackpole, 2006), ch. 4.

19. For the capture of John McKinly, a Wilmington physician and ardent Whig, see G. S. Rowe, "The Travail of John McKinly, First President of Delaware," *Delaware History* 17 (1976): 21–36. A year later, McKinly was released in a prisoner exchange for William Franklin, Benjamin Franklin's son, who had enraged Patriots as royal governor of New Jersey.

20. Mifflin had previously been appointed in 1771 and 1772; Mifflin to John Pemberton, Sept. 22, 1774, Pemberton Papers, 26/155b.

21. Churchman's wife, refusing to avoid the Kennett Square Monthly Meeting scheduled for September 11, sat in the meetinghouse as the battle raged around her, returning the next day convinced she "was in the way of her duty in giving up to go." Churchman Diary, Sept. 1777, QCHC.

22. Churchman Diary, Sept. 1777.

23. Churchman Diary, Sept. 1777; John Hunt Diary, Sept. 26, 1777, FHLSC, on New Jersey delegates unable to cross the Delaware since all boats were "sent away" to prevent river crossings, while Quaker wagons were impressed by the Americans; PQMM, 1772–1826, 70–71, on those "northward in the country" blocked by American forces.

24. For Galloway's extensive powers over almost all local governmental functions, see John M. Coleman, "Joseph Galloway and the British Administration of Philadelphia," *Pennsylvania History* 30 (1963): 272–300.

25. A few months later, back in occupied Philadelphia, Mifflin had dinner with Elizabeth Drinker on the same day she agreed to provide Galloway with house furnishings. Elaine Forman Crane, ed., *The Diary of Elizabeth Drinker*, 3 vols. (Boston: Northeastern University Press, 1991), Dec. 2, 1777 (1:260) (hereafter *Drinker Diary*); for Galloway's frequent contacts with prominent Quakers, all friends of Mifflin, see ibid., Nov. 22, Dec. 19, 1777 (1:260, 266).

26. Some of the most energetic Quaker leaders of the self-cleansing reform movement, such as George Churchman and Anthony Benezet, believed that many of the exiles, having abandoned true Quaker virtue and simplicity in favor of a lavish lifestyle, were now paying for it beneath the gaze of a frowning God. Marietta, *Reformation of American Quakerism*, 253–54.

27. Thomas Gilpin, *Exiles in Virginia: With Observations on the Conduct of the Society of Friends During the Revolutionary War* (Philadelphia: C. Sherman, 1848), for an extensive account of one of the Revolution's most blatant violations of civil liberties. The author was the grandson of one of the exiled Philadelphians. A modern account is Robert Oaks, "Philadelphians in Exile: The Problem of Loyalty During the American Revolution," *PMHB* 96 (1972): 298–325.

28. John W. Jackson's discursive *With the British Army in Philadelphia, 1777–1778* (San Rafael, Calif.: Presidio Press, 1979) is the fullest account of the occupying army. More incisive is Aaron Sullivan, "'In But Not of the Revolution': Loyalty, Liberty, and the British Occupation of Philadelphia," Ph.D. dissertation, Temple University, 2014.

29. PYM-MME, Ancestry.com, frames 499–500, 521.

30. Testimony from the Philadelphia Yearly Meeting, in Justice, *Mifflin*, 159–61. In an early form of massive leaflet distribution, the yearly meeting ordered 4,000 copies of their "Epistle or Testimony" printed, along with 200 translated into German.

31. Colonel Elias Dayton described "the thickest fog known in the memory of man, which, together with the [gun] smoke, brought on almost midnight darkness, [so] it was not possible . . . to distinguish friend from foe five yards distance." Quoted in Philander D. Chase, ed., *The Papers of George Washington: Revolutionary War Series*, 23 vols. (Charlottesville: University Press of Virginia, 1995–2009), 11: 400n7.

32. Across the river in New Jersey, John Hunt recorded in his diary, "There was a most dreadful noise of guns and roaring of cannon over in Pennsylvania, the most violentest firing of guns that I believe that was ever heard in our parts." Hunt Diary, Oct. 4, 1777. Elizabeth Drinker, the grieving wife of Henry Drinker, one of the Virginia exiles, took note of the first sketchy reports of the battle reaching the city late on October 4, the day of the battle. *Drinker Diary*, 1:239–40.

33. Gilpin, *Exiles in Virginia*, 57–61 for approval of the testimony on Oct. 2, the appointment of the delegation on Oct. 3; the testimony itself; and the report of the delegation when returning to Philadelphia on Oct. 11.

34. William L. Smith to Edward Rutledge, Feb. 28, 1790, *DHFFC*, 18:674.

35. *Defence of Mifflin* 17.

36. Mifflin to Greene, Oct. 21, 1783, QCHC, printed in Richard K. Showman, ed., *The Papers of Nathanael Greene*, 13 vols. (Chapel Hill: University of North Carolina Press, 1980–2005), 13:155–60.

37. Mifflin confessed "there was not much in prospect" for convincing the generals and feared "that our necks must pay" for passing into the military encampments, nonetheless "believing it was for his Name and Truth we were called to appear on behalf of and if even our lives were to go for it, they could not be too much." Mifflin to Greene, Oct. 21, 1783, in Showman, *Papers of Greene*, 13:156–57.

38. Ibid., 155–60. Mifflin's was no idle thought. The disposition of the Americans can be imagined from the diary entry that day of Lieutenant James McMichael of the Pennsylvania State Regiment: "I had previously undergone many fatigues, but never any that so much overdone me as this. Had it not been for the fear of being taken prisoner, I should have remained on the road all night. I had marched in twenty four hours 45 miles, and in that time fought four hours, during

which we advanced so furiously thro' buckwheat fields, that it was almost an unspeakable fatigue." "Diary of Lieutenant James McMichael of the Pennsylvania Line, 1776–1778," *PMHB* 16 (1892): 129–59, quote 153; thanks to Tom McGuire for this reference.

39. Report to Philadelphia Yearly Meeting, in Justice, *Mifflin*, 162–64, quote 162; Armstrong to Thomas Wharton, Oct. 8, 1777, quoted in Alfred C. Lamdin, "The Battle of Germantown," *PMHB* 1 (1877): 393n2.

40. The officer was probably Colonel Ludwig von Wurmb, who commanded the Vanderin Mill outpost. He had good reason to suspect the Quakers, for Washington's spies were legion and some may have donned Quaker dress to appear as disinterested persons passing through. Several Jäger patrols had been ambushed and were taking no chances. I am indebted to Tom McGuire for this reference.

41. Report to Philadelphia Yearly Meeting, in Justice, *Mifflin*, 162–64, quote 164.

42. *Drinker Diary*, Oct. 11, 1777 (1:242) for return to Philadelphia. For the enhancement of Fountain Green in the hands of Warner's uncles and cousins, see Mark Reinberger and Elizabeth McLean, *The Philadelphia Country House* (Baltimore: Johns Hopkins University Press, 2015). Elizabeth Drinker described how the British destroyed the house of Jonathan Mifflin, another of Warner's cousins, not far from Fountain Green, on November 26, 1777. *Drinker Diary*, Nov. 22, 1777 (1:256).

43. Gay Wilson Allen and Roger Asselineau, *St. John de Crèvecoeur: The Life of an American Farmer* (New York: Viking, 1987), 93. Jefferson acquired both the 1784 and 1787 editions of *Lettres*; he had probably met Mifflin in Philadelphia before this.

44. Edith Phillips, *The Good Quaker in French Legend* (Philadelphia: University of Pennsylvania Press, 1932), especially ch. 3, "The Utopia of Penn." Working from Crèvecoeur's Paris edition of 1787, Hilda Justice included the Mifflin dialogue with Generals Howe and Washington for her book of documents on Mifflin published in 1905. See Justice, *Mifflin*, 41–63.

45. The dialogue took up sixteen pages in Crèvecoeur's 1784 Paris edition; Justice's translation is in Justice, *Mifflin*, 41–56. For those of the Paris salons who did not read Crèvecoeur's *Lettres d'un cultivateur américain* in 1784, a second, slightly amended edition in 1787 repeated much the same story. It was eagerly consumed as the French Revolution erupted. Many obvious errors occur in this constructed dialogue; for example, Crèvecoeur had Mifflin carrying the peace testimony of Delaware Quakers rather than the epistle written by the Philadelphia Yearly Meeting, that the meeting occurred in Philadelphia, not Germantown; and that Mifflin then traveled to Valley Forge to meet with Washington.

46. Edwin G. Burrows, *Forgotten Patriots: The Untold Story of American Prisoners During the Revolutionary War* (New York: Basic, 2008), 119. Military protocol dictated that prisoners were to be supplied by civilians or their own army. This led to a complicated system of commissary attention to the Virginia 9th and charges and counter-charges between the American and British officers. With both armies requisitioning foodstuffs from farmers or plundering the countryside, general food shortages during the first five months of the Philadelphia occupation put the prisoners of war at terrible risk. Several hundred of the Virginia prisoners were buried in unmarked trenches in Washington Square. For grisly details on this, see Burrows, *Forgotten Patriots*, 118–20, and Joseph Lee Boyle, *"Their Distress is almost intolerable": The Elias Boudinot Letterbook, 1777–1778* (Bowie, Md.: Heritage Books, 2002). Soon to become president of the Continental Congress, Boudinot did his best to relieve the starvation of the American prisoners.

47. James Morris, "Memoirs of a Connecticut Patriot; Life Story of James Morris," *Connecticut Magazine* 11 (1907): 452. I thank Lee Noble for this reference. The grave was in Washington Square, where commemorative plaques make little mention of these burials of the starving and diseased American prisoners.

48. *Drinker Diary*, 1: 241 (Oct. 9); 242 (Oct. 11); 246 (Oct. 18). Some Quakers took food and drink to wounded Hessian soldiers as well. See Nicholas B. Wainwright, ed., "A Diary of Trifling Occurrences: Philadelphia, 1776–1778," *PMHB* 82 (1958): 454–57 for severe shortages and Sarah Logan Fisher's delivery of "a tub of broth" for wounded Hessians.

49. "Abolition—The Quakers," *Delaware Register and Farmers' Magazine* 2 (1837–38): 146. The account was republished after it appeared in the *United States Gazette* in 1837. The editorial note in the *Delaware Register* reported that the account was written "by a member of the Society of Friends, lately a citizen of our state [Delaware], and now of the city of Philadelphia." The body of the article, written as the abolitionist crusade grew more intense, was intended to convince readers that Quaker abolitionists regarded "the master as much the object of their tender sympathy and love, as the slave is of their affectionate concern." John Woolman and Warner Mifflin were singled out as examples of the Quaker doctrine that "Quaker abolition is founded in love; love and good will to master and slave." Mifflin was back in Philadelphia for the spring meeting of the Philadelphia Yearly Meeting from about March 24–27, 1778. *Drinker Diary*, 1: 290–91. The brother mentioned would have been Daniel, his younger brother.

50. George Churchman Diary, 10 vols., QCHC. The paragraphs below are based on Churchman's diary entries.

51. In his letter to Smallwood, Aug. 31, 1786, Mifflin recounted his many "remembrances" of Smallwood's leniency "while thou had the command of the American troops at Wilmington." Gilder Lehrman Collection, New York City, #GLC06508.09.

52. Churchman noted that "the sight of country friends coming in being rather uncommon for near two months past because of the British Army having possession of the city."

53. As was customary, Mifflin dined at the Drinker house (*Drinker Diary*, 1:260. Dec. 2, 1777). Henry Drinker was still exiled in Winchester, but his wife Elizabeth carried on at their handsome house. From Churchman's point of view, "we were favoured with a degree of courage and strength to revive and impress on the mind of friends in the city at each meeting the concern adopted by the Philadelphia Yearly Meeting for a close inspection regarding inconsistencies and deviations from the purity of our profession."

54. Gilpin, *Exiles in Virginia*, 276–77, 281. Washington ordered the men released in April 1778. For the travail of Elizabeth Drinker, wife of one of the most prominent Philadelphia exiles, see Wendy Lucas Castro, "'Being Separated from My Dearest Husband, in This Cruel Manner': Elizabeth Drinker and the Seven-Month Exile of Philadelphia Quakers," *Quaker History* 100 (2011): 40–63. Mifflin's participation in this mission is recorded in Churchman Diary, Feb. 24, 1778.

55. "This is an intercourse that we should by all means endeavour to interrupt," directed Washington, "as the plans settled at these meetings are of the most pernicious tendency." Anticipating that Quakers would come on horses, Washington ordered that any horses fit for military service should be seized and sent to the quartermaster general. Washington to Brigadier General John Lacey Junior, March 20, 1778, in *The Writings of Washington from the Original Manuscript Sources, 1745–1799*, ed. John C. Fitzpatrick, 39 vols. (Washington, D.C.: Government Printing Office, 1931–1944), 11: 114. Probably General Smallwood, commanding a Patriot regiment

at Wilmington, allowed a small delegation, including Mifflin and his wife, to pass through the American lines. Churchman Diary, Feb. 24, 1778, records that he was also able to attend the meetings, where he met Mifflin and his wife during the last week of February.

56. PYM-MME, Ancestry.com frames 555, 559, 574, 583–84. The advisory of the Ministers and Elders on March 24, 1778; PWMMM, 1772–1821, March 25, 1778.

57. William H. Nelson, *The American Tory* (New York: Oxford University Press, 1961), 108; Harold Hancock, "The Kent County Loyalists," *Delaware History* 6 (1954): 3–24. Hancock argues that in Delaware Loyalists were proportionately more numerous than in almost any other state, explained by the "proximity of loyalist sections in Maryland, in the opportunity to trade with the enemy in Delaware River and Bay, and in the stronger ties of common interests between the inhabitants and England" (3).

58. In the most extensive exploration of Clow's insurrection, Wayne Bodle suggests that foraging parties sent by Washington from Valley Forge into Delaware may have triggered the insurrection by requisitioning food supplies from the small farmers on the western shore of Kent County. Wayne Bodle, 'The Ghost of Clow': Loyalist Insurgency in the Delmarva Peninsula," in Joseph S. Tiedemann, Eugene R. Fingerhut, and Robert W. Venables, eds., *The Other Loyalists: Ordinary People, Royalism, and the Revolution in the Middle Colonies, 1763–1787* (Albany, N.Y.: SUNY Press, 2009), 19–44, especially 27–28.

59. Harold B. Hancock, *The Loyalists of Revolutionary Delaware* (Newark: University of Delaware Press, 1977), 80–88. Hancock writes that "Kent County continued to be infested with the disaffected in the spring of 1778" (87). I have treated what I call "radical loyalism" in Maryland and Delaware in Nash, *The Unknown American Revolution: The Unruly Birth of Democracy and the Struggle to Create America* (New York: Viking, 2005), 238–45, drawing heavily on Ronald Hoffman's *A Spirit of Dissension: Economics, Politics, and the Revolution in Maryland* (Baltimore: Johns Hopkins University Press, 1971).

60. Mifflin to [President Nicholas Van Dyke], July 16, 1783, Mifflin Papers, William Clements Library, University of Michigan (hereafter WCLUM). Clow escaped, was recaptured, and was executed five years later. Hancock, *Loyalists of Revolutionary Delaware*, 80–81, 87; "History of Cheney Clow," *Delaware Register* (1838): 220–36.

61. Nathan Bangs, *The Life of the Rev. Freeborn Garretson, compiled from his printed and manuscript journals . . .* , 4th ed. (New York: G. Lane and C. C. Tippett, 1845). Garretson wrote of preaching in September 1778 "at Mr. S's." I believe "Mr. S." was Stockley Sturgis, the owner of Richard Allen's family. Garretson related preaching to hundreds in Dover, where he was accused by an inflamed crowd of being a Loyalist and "one of Clowe's men," enough to make him fit for hanging. Robert Drew Simpson, ed., *American Methodist Pioneer: The Life and Journals of Freeborn Garretson, 1752–1827* (Rutland, Vt.: Academy Books, 1984), 74.

62. Richard S. Newman's *Freedom's Prophet: Bishop Richard Allen, the AME Church, and the Black Founding Fathers* (New York: New York University Press, 2008) is an engaging biography of Allen. Garretson as a spearhead of Methodism on the Eastern Shore is explored in William H. Williams, *The Garden of American Methodism: The Delmarva Peninsula, 1769–1820* (Wilmington, Del.: Scholarly Resources, 1984), 30–35 and Dee E. Andrews, *The Methodists and Revolutionary America, 1760–1800* (Princeton, N.J.: Princeton University Press, 2000), 127–29, 140–41.

63. Churchman Diary, May 10–26, 1778, for many details of the trip. Mifflin and Churchman may not have heard about the profligate farewell extravaganza to General Howe, called the

Meschianza, on May 18, but they surely heard what was on everyone's lips—the British were already destroying everything of military use in Philadelphia and preparing to evacuate the city.

64. "Diary of Grace Growden Galloway," *PMHB* 58 (1934): 141. By late 1779, deeply depressed and despairing, she wrote: "I am wrapped in impenetrable darkness; . . . can it ever be removed and shall I once more belong to somebody? . . . Now I am like a pelican in the desert" (164).

65. Grace Galloway's diary notes some of Mifflin's visits while the Patriots were confiscating her house, carriage, and other properties. See ibid., *PMHB* 55 (1931): 32–94; 58 (1934): 152–89 (diary entries, July 1, Aug. 4, Sept. 31, 1778). In her letters to her daughter, Galloway noted Mifflin's visits throughout the fall of 1778: Grace Galloway to Elizabeth Galloway, Oct 1; same to same, Oct. 4; same to same, Nov. 27, 1778, Galloway Papers, LC. In September 1778, Mifflin was in the city for the yearly meeting, accompanied by his wife's sister, Nancy Johns Holliday Rowland, as noted in a Oct. 4 letter from Grace Galloway. As early as 1776, Mifflin became Galloway's agent, along with Isaiah Rowland (who married Elizabeth Johns Mifflin's sister Ann after she lost her first husband, Richard Holliday).

66. Samuel Emlen, Jr., was remembered in Grace Galloway's will; Will of Grace Growden Galloway, Dec. 20, 1781, Galloway Papers, LC; for Ann Emlen's visits, and presence at the funeral, Deborah Morris to Elizabeth Galloway, May 29, 1782, ibid.

67. Mifflin to McKean, Nov. 5, 1781, C-P-W, Box 12, folder 61.

68. Mifflin to John Parrish, May 13, 1784, C-P-W, Box 1, folder 10. In May 1777 the Western Quarterly Meeting asked each monthly meeting to watch over and assist those whose goods were distrained and "to preserve and transmit a faithful account of all such suffering, agreeably to the advice of the [Philadelphia] Yearly Meeting." Michener, *Retrospect of Early Quakerism*, 372–73, from Western Quarterly Meeting minutes. Duck Creek Monthly Meeting reported to the Meeting for Sufferings that from 1778 to 1785 grain, cattle, and other property had been seized in the amount of 1,590 pounds, by far the most of any monthly meeting. "Report of the Friends appointed to inspect the accounts of sufferings," PYM-MS, Sept. 15, 1785.

69. Marian Balderston, "The Real Passengers on the *Welcome*," *Huntington Library Quarterly* 26 (1962): 40–41.

70. Brock, *Pacifism in the U. S.*, 207; Cowgill's daughter recounted the painful incident almost a half-century later. Mary Corbit to John Cowgill, June 18, 1835, Corbit, Higgins, Spruance Papers, DHS; Harold Hancock, "The Kent County Loyalists: Documents," *Delaware History* 6 (1954): 122–26, for the Committee of Inspection's resolution condemning Cowgill. The other quotes are from his daughter's letter.

71. *Defence of Mifflin*, 12.

72. "Warner Mifflin's Piece on Continental Currency," August 1779, Miscellaneous Manuscripts, FHLSC. Mifflin repeated this nighttime reading of Revelation, ch. 13, in his *Defence of Mifflin*, 11–13. He added that he found "my wife so far united with me, as to refuse it [Continental currency] likewise, saying, though she did not feel that matter as I did, yet through fear of weakening my hands, she was most easy not to touch it."

73. Ibid.

74. Ibid.

75. "Relics of the Past, #4," *The Friend* 17 (1844): 158.

76. "John Hunt's Diary," *Proceedings of the New Jersey Historical Society* 52 (1934): 235.

77. Waln was far from dead. Perhaps this was an unconscious death wish Mifflin never would have wanted to admit.

78. Mifflin to Nicholas Waln, December 1780, Mifflin Family Papers, WCLUM. See Carla Gerona, *Night Journeys: The Power of Dreams in Transatlantic Quaker Culture* (Charlottesville: University of Virginia Press, 2004), 195–97 for a fuller interpretation of Mifflin's dream. Gerona shows how the tortured question of dealing with tainted Continental currency entered the dream life of many Quakers.

79. For two accounts of Fort Wilson, see Steven Rosswurm, *Arms, Country, and Class: The Philadelphia Militia and the "Lower Sort" During the American Revolution* (New Brunswick, N.J.: Rutgers University Press, 1987), ch. 7; and John K. Alexander, "The Fort Wilson Incident of 1779: A Case Study of the Revolutionary Crowd," *WMQ* 31 (1974): 589–612.

80. Marietta, *Reformation*, 242–45; *Drinker Diary*, 1: 361 (Oct. 4, 1781). Drinker noted that John Drinker and many others were slated for a second exile of Quakers from the city in the late summer of 1779, when the runaway depreciation of Continental currency and food shortages led to a fiery debate on price controls.

81. *Drinker Diary*, 1: 393 (Oct. 24, 1781); Marietta, *Reformation*, 245.

82. G. S. Rowe, *Thomas McKean: The Shaping of an American Republicanism* (Boulder: Colorado Associated University Press, 1978), 129–31. Appointing a Friend as a wartime constable was a deliberate attempt to corner a principled Quaker, judicially embarrass, and financially injure him.

83. For an analysis of the treason trials and execution of Abraham Carlisle and John Roberts see David W. Maxey, *Treason on Trial in Revolutionary Pennsylvania: The Case of John Roberts, Miller* (Philadelphia: American Philosophical Society, 2011).

84. Mifflin to McKean, Nov. 5, 1781, C-P-W. See Rowe, *Thomas McKean*, ch. 8: for an evaluation of McKean's court and his attempt to create an "independent and moderate" court. For the outcry of the Philadelphia Meeting for Sufferings, see its lengthy address, Nov. 22, 1781, with long excerpts in Sharpless, *A History of Quaker Government in Pennsylvania*, 2: 201–3.

85. Philadelphia Meeting for Sufferings, "To the President and Executive Council, the General Assembly of Pennsylvania. . .," Nov. 15, 1781, quoted in Marietta, *Reformation*, 256; the meeting printed and distributed 5,000 copies of the address.

86. Quoted in Marietta, *Reformation*, 41 from George Crosfield, ed., *Memoirs of the Life and Gospel Labours of Samuel Fothergill* (Liverpool: D. Monples, 1858).

87. DCMMM, Jan. 22, and LCMMM, Oct. 28, 1780, in Justice, *Mifflin*, 145.

88. LCMMM, March 24, 1781, in Justice, *Mifflin*, 146; Mifflin delayed his mission northward, returning for a new traveling certificate in late April. Duck Creek Monthly Meeting minutes, April 24, 1781, 335. The Meeting of Ministers and Elders in Philadelphia in late March 1781 approved Mifflin's intention to travel to the New York and Rhode Island yearly meetings. PYM-MME March 26, 1781, Ancestry.com, frame 680.

89. Rebecca Larson, *Daughters of Light*, 95ff. Deep into the nineteenth century, an early chronicler of the Philadelphia Yearly Meeting reminded readers that "the most efficient preachers which the world has ever witnessed were illiterate fishermen, obscure husbandmen, and mechanics taken from the lower walks of life." Michener, *Retrospect of Early Quakerism*, 159–60.

90. Michener, *Retrospect of Early Quakerism*, 155.

91. The following pages on the pilgrimage are based on the accounts of George Churchman and David Cooper. In sixty-eight pages, making entries almost daily for three months, Churchman provided one of the most illuminating Quaker travel journals of the eighteenth century. George Churchman Diary, 4: 28–96, QCHC. The entries in Cooper's diary, also in QCHC, cover fifteen

pages. Churchman's East Nottingham home was on the Maryland-Pennsylvania border, soon to be bisected by the Mason-Dixon line. Michael Churchman, *The Churchman Family of Nottingham Lots* (Baltimore: Otter Bay, 2013).

92. The leader of the Nottingham Monthly Meeting in Chester County, Pennsylvania, Churchman was a gentle critic of the urbane affluence of Philadelphia Quakers such as Henry and Elizabeth Drinker. See Churchman to Drinker, Nov. 5, 1779, *The Friend* 32 (1859): 138–39 for criticism of the Drinkers' sumptuous living.

93. In his letter to John Pemberton, July 1, 1781, in "Relics of the Past, #5," *The Friend*, 17 (1844), 167, George Churchman recounted the names of the traveling group. The third was Thomas Carrington, whose identity I have not found.

94. For a brief account of Cooper's journey, see Henry J. Cadbury, "A Quaker Travelling in the Wake of War, 1781," *New England Quarterly* 23 (1950): 396–400. For the understudied David Cooper, another of the early abolitionists history has left behind, see the biographical appreciation of one of his closest friends' son, W. J. Allinson, in "Notices of David Cooper," *Friends Review* 15 (1861–62): 466ff.; and the undergraduate honors thesis of Kristin DeBusk, "An Ordinary Man in Extraordinary Times: David Cooper's Fight Against Slavery," Texas Tech University, 2004.

95. A shocked Baron Ludwig von Closen, a Bavarian-born young officer who served as translator for Washington-Rochambeau negotiations, wrote, "It was really painful to see these brave men, almost naked with only some trousers and little linen jackets, most of them without stockings, but, would you believe it? Very cheerful and healthy in appearance. A quarter of them were negroes, merry, confident, and sturdy." Evelyn M. Acomb, "The Journal of Baron von Closen," *WMQ* 10 (1953): 90–91.

96. Several weeks before, Washington had fended off a mutiny of his generals and field officers with his storied emotional speech at Newburgh.

97. Washington's Continental Army units controlled the Hudson Highlands, while British units occupied the area south to New York City. For an analysis of the two armed bodies, engaging in a stand-off producing irregular, predatory "banditti," see Harry M. Ward, *Between the Lines: Banditti of the American Revolution* (Westport, Conn.: Praeger, 2002).

98. The mayhem in Westchester County, where neither side was willing to mount an offensive, made an indelible imprint on the American consciousness after James Fenimore Cooper published *The Spy: A Tale of the Neutral Ground* in 1821. Cooper had nothing to say about the Quakers' travails in Westchester County. His interest in the bloody neutral ground was more than casual after he married James DeLancey's granddaughter. Likewise, in the copious literature on DeLancey's Westchester County Cowboys, lost in the telling is the Quakers' nightmarish odyssey, as documented in the diaries of David Cooper and George Churchman. For a trenchant account of Westchester County's terrified inhabitants, so traumatized that they were unwilling to support either side of the war, see Sung Bok Kim, "The Limits of Politicization of the American Revolution: The Experience of Westchester County, New York," *Journal of American History* 80 (1993): 868–89; and Catherine S. Crary, "Guerilla Activities of James DeLancey's Cowboys in Westchester County," in Robert A. East and Jacob Judd, eds., *The Loyalist Americans: A Focus on Greater New York* (Tarrytown, N.Y.: Sleepy Hollow Restorations, 1975), 14–26. See also Lincoln Diamant, "When a Black Unit Battled the British," *New York Times*, May 12, 1996.

99. William Cooper Nell, *The Colored Patriots of the American Revolution* (Boston: R.F. Wallcat, 1855), quoted in Nash, *The Unknown American Revolution*, 230. Washington's diary entries of May 14 and 16 provide details but make no mention that the Rhode Island First Regiment was composed of blacks and Native Americans. See Donald Jackson and Dorothy Twohig, eds., *The Diaries of George Washington*, vol. 3, *1771–75, 1780–81* (Charlottesville: University Press of Virginia, 1978), 364–65.

100. Churchman recorded in his journal that the group agreed to split up so they could cover all the "first day" meetings for "public worship," quote 41. The mild-tempered Brown, a striking figure in his flowing white shoulder-length hair, had freed his slaves in November 1773, before he became a Friend. Thereafter, he became one of Rhode Island's most dedicated abolitionists. See Mack Thompson, *Moses Brown: Reluctant Reformer* (Chapel Hill: University of North Carolina Press, 1962) and Charles Rappleye, *Sons of Providence: The Brown Brothers, the Slave Trade, and the American Revolution* (New York: Simon & Schuster, 2006).

101. Robert E. Leach and Peter Gow, *Quaker Nantucket: The Religious Community Behind the Whaling Empire* (Nantucket: Mill Hill Press, 1999). Churchman noted that after "some pertinent sentences were dropped to those present in a loving closeness by Warner [Mifflin] and Moses Brown, they became very serious, the men's wife especially being much tendered. Thus we see the kindness of our heavenly Father sometimes extended towards those who have not sufficiently abode in his fear, whilst dwelling in outward affluence with a brilliant show of grandeur."

102. Churchman estimated 1,000 on June 22, 1,200 on June 23, and 1,500 on June 24, Diary, 52, 53, 56. Churchman was also pleased that "their Grave-yard was kept in a plain way with no marks of distinction [in tombstones]," Diary, 56–57.

103. Cooper Diary, July 15, 1781. At the outset of the odyssey, Cooper had written that "My feeble state of health, without a steady companion, . . . exceedingly discouraged me [to] undertake this journey."

104. Mifflin to French officers in "Relics of the Past #18," *The Friend*, 17 (1844), 278. For French interactions with Newport Quakers, see T. Cole Jones, "'Displaying the Ensigns of Harmony': The French Army in Newport, Rhode Island, 1780–1781," *New England Quarterly* 85 (2012): 430–67.

105. Churchman Diary, July 16, 1781, 78–79.

106. Ibid., 85–87. More intense engagement occurred when a man along the way offered a defense of the long war, prompting a lengthy rehearsal of the Quaker peace testimony.

107. Ibid., Aug. 2, 1781, 92; Aug. 6, 1781, 93.

108. Mifflin to James Pemberton, [late] August, 1781, Mifflin to John Pemberton, Aug. 26, 1781, Pemberton Papers, Box 35 f. 173, 180, HSP; Mifflin to Moses Brown, Oct. 3, 1781, Moses Brown Papers, RIHS.

109. Mifflin to Moses Brown, Oct. 3, 1781, Moses Brown Papers.

110. Mifflin to John Pemberton, Aug. 26, 1781, Pemberton Papers, Box 35, f173. On the same day, Mifflin wrote to Henry Drinker that he had returned home "under a measure of a thankful sense of the renewed kindness of the Father of Mercies conferred on me a poor unworthy creature." Moreover, "I still feel my mind engaged to press forward for the mark set before us, believing it is many times cause of encouragement to the honest-hearted to feel that they have companions therein." "Relics of the Past, #5, *The Friend* 17 (1844): 167.

111. Mifflin to Moses Brown, Oct. 3, 1781, Moses Brown Papers.

112. Ibid.

## Chapter 3. To Reform a Nation

1. *Defence of Mifflin*, 20.

2. Much earlier, after his arrival in Philadelphia in 1731, the irrepressible Benjamin Lay, a vegetarian hunchback living in a cave in Abington, north of Philadelphia, had adopted an ascetic life in its more extreme form. For a full treatment of the much vilified Lay, see Marcus Rediker, *The Fearless Benjamin Lay: The Quaker Dwarf Who Became the First Revolutionary Abolitionist* (Boston: Beacon, 2017).

3. Jack D. Marietta, "Wealth, War, and Religion: The Perfecting of Quaker Asceticism, 1740–1783," *Church History* 43 (1974): 230–41. For antecedents of the Free Produce movement see Julie L. Holcomb, "Rejecting the Gain of Oppression: Quaker Abstention and the Abolitionist Cause," in Maurice Jackson and Susan Kozel, eds., *Quakers and Their Allies in the Abolitionist Cause, 1754–1808* (London: Routledge, 2015), 99–110; for an extended treatment see Holcomb, *Moral Commerce: Quakers and the Transatlantic Boycott of the Slave Labor Economy* (Ithaca, N.Y.: Cornell University Press, 2016).

4. Robert Oaks, "Big Wheels in Philadelphia: Du Simitiere's List of Carriage Owners," *PMHB* 95 (1971): 351–63. Though composing only one-seventh of the city's householders, Friends owned 40 percent of the carriages. Among them were Mifflin's merchant cousins John, Jonathan, and George Mifflin.

5. Drafted in 1763–1764, a *Plea for the Poor* was not published until 1793, two decades after Woolman's death; nonetheless, the word was on the street. Thomas Slaughter discusses *Plea for the Poor* in his *The Beautiful Soul of John Woolman, Apostle of Abolition* (New York: Hill & Wang, 2008), 269–71.

6. One of the irritated was Israel Pemberton, "King of the Quakers," as he was dubbed. Benezet found Pemberton's bequest of a huge fortune to his children "the corruption of his off-spring;" Pemberton wearily said, "It is tiresome to hear Anthony always saying the same thing." Benezet to George Dillwyn, Nov. 11, 1779, in George S. Brookes, *Friend Anthony Benezet* (Philadelphia: University of Pennsylvania Press, 1937), 337.

7. Benezet to Israel, John and James Pemberton, John Hunt, Henry Drinker, Samuel Pleasants, Edward Penington, et al., Jan. 28, 1778, in Brookes, *Friend Anthony Benezet*, 325–27.

8. *Mercure de France*, Jan. 4, 1783; incorporated in the expanded Paris, 1784 edition, x–xii of *Letters of American Farmer*, first published in London in 1782. Justice, *Mifflin*, 58, translated these passages from Crèvecoeur, *Lettres* (Paris, 1787), 197–222. See Appendix 1 for Crèvecoeur's alleged visit to Chestnut Grove.

9. Roberts Vaux, *Memoirs of Benjamin Lay and Ralph Sandiford, Two of the Earliest Public Advocates for the Emancipation of the Enslaved Africans* (Philadelphia: Solomon W. Conrad, 1815), 24. For more on Lay's consumer boycott, including the smashing of his wife's tea cups as a protest against the exploitation of tea and sugar workers, see Rediker, *The Fearless Benjamin Lay*. Offended by his dramatic public displays of slavery's cruelties and his vehement prose, Quaker Overseers of the Press would not authorize Lay's *All Slave-Keepers that Keep the Innocent in Bondage, Apostates pretending to lay claim to the pure & holy Christian religion . . .* (Philadelphia, 1737). Benjamin Franklin, at thirty-one, published it without his imprint. It is unlikely Mifflin had read Lay's *All Slave-Keepers*.

10. Quoted in Geoffrey Plank, *John Woolman's Path to the Peaceable Kingdom* (Philadelphia: University of Pennsylvania Press, 2012), 111. Even Woolman sold sugar and rum in his store until the late 1760s.

11. For the spectacular explosion see William James Morgan, ed., *Naval Documents of the American Revolution*, vol. 8 (Washington, D.C.: Naval History Division, 1980), 321–22, 335–36, 379. Mifflin was misinformed about or misremembered the *Morris* cargo. The ship was bringing 2,500 muskets, 2,100 barrels of gunpowder, and a vast quantity of clothing from France. The captain of the ship lost his life in ordering the demolition of the ship to prevent the weaponry and gunpowder from falling into the enemy's hands.

12. *Defence of Mifflin*, 19–20. Not until a few years after Mifflin's abstinence from slave-grown sugar would Joseph Wood's *Thoughts on the Slavery of Negroes*, published anonymously in London in 1784, launch the Free Produce movement in England. It reached Philadelphia in 1785, apparently with little effect. See Holcomb, *Moral Commerce*, 39–44.

13. For bottle and bowl, *Defence of Mifflin*, 10–11, 19–20.

14. Ezra Michener, *A Retrospect of Early Quakerism: Being Extracts from the Records of Philadelphia Yearly Meeting* (Philadelphia: T. Ellwood Zell, 1860), 205–10 for examples of family visit routines.

15. "Report of Committee on Reformation," Jan. 24, 1778, DCMMM, published in Justice, *Mifflin*, 165–66, quote 165.

16. Rebecca Larson, *Daughters of Light: Quaker Women Preaching and Prophesying in the Colonies and Abroad, 1700–1775* (New York: Knopf 1999); Sarah Crabtree, *Holy Nation: The Transatlantic Quaker Ministry in an Age of Revolution* (Chicago: University of Chicago Press, 2015), Part I.

17. Jean R. Soderlund, "Women's Authority in Pennsylvania and New Jersey Quaker Meetings, 1680–1760," *WMQ* 44 (1987): 722–49.

18. Soderlund's canvassing of many monthly meetings within the compass of the Philadelphia Yearly Meeting has uncovered women on a few visiting committees as early as 1764, though most meetings relied on male committees until the late 1770s. Email from Soderlund to author, March 2, 2015.

19. One of the four women was Elisabeth Cowgill, the mother of Clayton Cowgill, who would marry one of Warner Mifflin's daughters in 1792.

20. Report of Committee on Reformation, Jan. 24, 1778, in Justice, *Mifflin*, 165–66; Mifflin's name led the nine signers, suggesting his authorship.

21. Jean Soderlund distinguishes conservative Friends with a limited interest in going beyond freeing their slaves as part of a "tribalistic reform tradition," while activist reformers, or "progressives," cleaved to a "humanitarian reform tradition," *Quakers and Slavery*, 173–75.

22. PYMM, Sept. 26, 1778, quoted in Soderlund, *Quakers and Slavery*, 180. In examining four monthly meetings in New Jersey and eastern Pennsylvania, Soderlund shows that visiting committees were performing much the same tasks in visiting black families. See also James J. Gigantino II, *The Ragged Road to Abolition: Slavery and Freedom in New Jersey, 1775–1865* (Philadelphia: University of Pennsylvania Press, 2015), ch. 3.

23. Assuming that most of the 210 attending were adults, at least three-quarters of those freed by Kent County Quakers made it their business to gather with the visiting committee. From 1775 to 1783, Duck Creek Monthly Meeting members freed 424 slaves; William H. Williams, *Slavery and Freedom in Delaware, 1639–1865* (Wilmington, Del.: Scholarly Resources, 1996), 147.

24. Report of Committee for Visiting Free Negroes, WQMM, Aug. 17, 1778; DCMMM, Sept. 19, 1778, in Justice, *Mifflin*, 141–44.

25. DCMMM, Aug. 17, 1778. As Clerk of Duck Creek Monthly Meeting, Mifflin also presided over these business meetings.

26. The February 1779 report noted ten families that had established their own households, while about thirty individuals, both single and married, lived with white families, one of whom was Warner and Elizabeth Mifflin's.

27. WQM report, Aug. 18, 1778.

28. William Dunlap, *Quaker Education in Baltimore and Virginia Yearly Meetings with an Account of Certain Meetings of Delaware and the Eastern Shore Affiliated with Philadelphia* (Philadelphia, n.p., 1936), 472–76.

29. DCMMM, Nov. 16, 1778; Feb. 15, 1779; May 17, 1779.

30. Mifflin self-reported the accusation many years later in his *Defence of Mifflin*, 9–10. In 1779, he wrote the nearby Presbyterian minister that he had arranged for the committee to recommend a restitution plan "within a few months after I discharged them." Mifflin to Alexander Huston, Jan. 17, 1779, Emlen Family Papers, Box 2, HSP. The quoted words at the end of the paragraph are from this letter.

31. Since the founding of the National Coalition of Blacks for Reparations in America in 1987, the issue has filled news media. For the last quarter century, John Conyers has introduced a bill (HR 40) for Congress to study the issue and propose "appropriate remedies" for the damaging effects of slavery and institutionalized racism over four centuries. The bill has never reached the floor for debate. For a recent review and examples of reparations before the Civil War, see Ta-Nehisi Coates, "The Case for Reparations," *Atlantic*, Aug. 23, 2014.

32. Roy Finkenbine cites the case of Belinda in 1783 as a precedent-setting case of reparations in "Belinda's Petition: Reparations for Slavery in Revolutionary Massachusetts," *WMQ* 64 (2007): 94–104. The court awarded the aged and infirm Belinda a pension from the estate of a deceased Loyalist, formerly Medford, Massachusetts' wealthiest slaveowner. Among the work of many historians deploying the term "reparations," see especially Hilary Beckles, *Britain's Black Debt: Reparation for Caribbean Slavery and Native Genocide* (Kingston: University of the West Indies Press, 2012) and Finkenbine, "Historians and Reparations," *OAH Newsletter* 34, 1 (2006): 3.

33. Kenneth Carroll, "Maryland Quakers and Slavery," *Quaker History* 72 (1983): 28. For similar cases in the Philadelphia region, see Gary B. Nash and Jean R. Soderlund, *Freedom by Degrees: Emancipation in Pennsylvania and Its Aftermath* (New York: Oxford University Press, 1991), 61–73. Leaving land or money by will cost the manumitting master nothing in his or her lifetime, though diminishing the inheritance.

34. Ferris to Samuel Field and Wife, Sept. 20, 1767, in Martha Paxson Grundy, *Resistance and Obedience to God: Memoirs of David Ferris (1707–1779)* (Philadelphia: Friends General Conference, 2001), 69–73, quote 72. Ferris wrote to Robert Pleasants, as the Virginia Quaker was preparing to free his many slaves in 1774, "Those in their prime, give to them a full discharge from all future service, and to those of them who have served thee after they were of age, pay them for that service honestly, and thereby put them into a way of getting their living. This will be just, and is undoubtedly thy duty" (73–77, quote 76).

35. Quoted in Plank, *Woolman's Path to the Peaceable Kingdom*, 171–73; Woolman's *Plea for the Poor* was regarded by the Overseers of the Press as too radical to publish.

36. Sharp, "Extract of a Letter from the Author to a Gentleman at Philadelphia, July 18, 1775," in *The Just Limitation of Slavery in the Laws of God . . . , Appendix (No. 1)* (London: B. White and

E.&C. Dilly, 1776), 57–58. Dee Andrews has tracked the exchange of antislavery pamphlets in 1775–1776 to reach the conclusion that the "Gentleman in Philadelphia" was Anthony Benezet (email to author, July 20, 1016). See also Jonathan D. Sessi, "With a Little Help from the Friends: The Quaker and Tactical Contexts of Anthony Benezet's Abolitionist Printing," *PMHB* 135 (2011): 33–71. Benezet hinted at reparations in *Some Historical Account of Guinea* (1771), where he proposed "a small tract of land [be] assigned to every Negro family, and they obliged to live upon and improve it (when not hired out to work for the white people)." Benezet was silent on who would assign the tracts of land and where it would be located, but the inference is that it would be a state-sponsored program. The passage quoted is in David L. Crosby, *The Complete Antislavery Writings of Anthony Benezet, 1754–1783* (Baton Rouge: Louisiana State University Press, 2013), 182.

37. James Swan, *A Dissuasion to Great Britain and the Colonies from the Slave Trade to Africa* . . . (Boston, 1772), in Roger Bruns, *Am I Not a Man and a Brother: The Antislavery Crusade of Revolutionary America, 1688–1783* (New York: Chelsea House, 1977), 205.

38. "Some Thoughts on the Subject of Freeing the Negroe Slaves in the Colony of Connecticut . . ." (c. 1775), discussed in detail by Joanne Pope Melish, *Disowning Slavery: Gradual Emancipation and "Race" in New England, 1780–1840* (Ithaca, N.Y.: Cornell University Press, 1998), 57–62. While he believed slavery would continue to poison the white bloodstream, Hart was convinced free blacks would be a failure in society.

39. Soderlund, *Quakers and Slavery*, 177; Soderlund documents several cases of restitution in the Philadelphia region, but the vast majority of Quaker manumitters made no such commitment (178–79). Even David Ferris, the foremost advocate of restitution, admitted that "I look upon slave keepers, to be in a much greater bondage than their poor Negroes are; and in a far worse condition because inward bondage is of a more dismal and fatal consequence than outward can be." Ferris to James Rigby, April 7, 1766, in Grundy, *Resistance and Obedience to God*, 79–80.

40. DCMMM, Sept. 18, 1778.

41. WQMM, Report of Committee for Visiting Free Negroes, May 17, 1779. Mifflin signed the report on behalf of the committee, indicating his pivotal role.

42. Mifflin to Huston, Jan. 17, 1779. Quoting scripture, Mifflin directed Huston to Isaiah 33:15 on "the gain of oppression."

43. *A Brief Statement of the Rise and Progress of the Testimony of the Society of Friends Against Slavery and the Slave Trade* (Philadelphia, 1843), 38, quoted in Thomas E. Drake, *Quakers and Slavery in America* (New Haven, Conn.: Yale University Press, 1950), 77. Drake believed that membership for all Quakers in the verge of the New England, New York, and Baltimore yearly meetings "became contingent on one's compensating his former slaves," but I have found no evidence of this and doubt its accuracy.

44. WQMM, Aug. 31, 1780. Sometimes, mixed gender committees visited Friends; other times all-female committees made the visits.

45. DCMMM, May 26, 1781; WQMM, Aug. 20, 1781.

46. The Duck Creek Women's Meeting Minutes were by early 1780 reporting "obstructions" to their reparationist visits to Quaker manumitters and "too great a backwardness in Friends making restitution to that injured people." DCWMMM, 1711–1830, Feb. 26, 1780; May 27, 1780.

47. DCMMM, Mar. 27, Dec. 25, 1779; Jan. 22, Feb. 26, March 25, April 22, May 27, June 24, July 22, Aug. 26, 1780.

48. DCMMM, Dec. 23, 1780. The two brothers and a sister of the Nock family split the cost of the reparations. The agreement also provided that two other slaves owned by their father, who

had been promised freedom but were bound to serve until twenty-five, be freed at eighteen if female and twenty-one if male.

49. DCMMM, June 23, 1781.

50. DCMMM, June 23, Aug. 25, Sept. 22, 1781.

51. WQMM, Aug. 18, 1783; Aug. 1784, II: 38, 72, 88; the latter minute mentioned that it was recommended by the Philadelphia Yearly Meeting. The Women's Meeting Minutes for Camden, Duck Creek, and Murderkill Monthly Meetings, 1711–1830, are filled with references to women's participation in the Committee for Visiting Free Negroes in the 1780s.

52. In examining the monthly meeting records for four meetings, two in New Jersey and two in Pennsylvania, Jean Soderlund found only scattered reparation payments, and almost all of them were not negotiated by appointed committees but through the volition of individual slave emancipators. Soderlund, *Quakers and Slavery*, 179–81.

53. Mifflin to Henry Drinker, Jan. 11, 1781, Quaker Collection #851, Box 13, QCHC.

54. For a lively account of Arnold's exploits, see Michael Kranish, *Flight from Monticello: Thomas Jefferson at War* (New York: Oxford University Press, 2010). Jefferson's flight anguished him for the rest of his life and became political capital for his enemies.

55. DCMMM, Feb. 18, 1782 for a report on the visit. Cropper noted in his diary that he had bought the boy "attached by the sheriff to pay Mr. Mifflin's assessment." Barton Haxell Wise, *Memoir of General John Cropper* (Richmond: Eastern Shore of Virginia Historical Society, 1892), 21. Mifflin and Lindley also used the visit to talk with other slaveowners on the Eastern Shore and particularly at the Accomack County Court House about "the iniquity of enslaving our fellow men." Though they met with "some abuse . . . intended us by some who through a desire of outward gain was induced to oppose this concern," their labor was rewarded with manumissions of "upwards sixty slaves."

56. Mifflin to John Parrish, Jan. 6, 1783, C-P-W, Box 1, f 9. In the "Battle of the Barges," Nov. 28, 1782, the last naval action of the American Revolution, one of Cropper's former slaves who had fled to the British saved his life.

57. The *U. S. Gazette* (1823–1847) was a premier newspaper in the second quarter of the nineteenth century and predecessor of the *North American*. The article, titled "Abolition—the Quakers," appeared first in the *Gazette* in 1837 and a year later in *Delaware Register* 2 (1838–1839): 145–48.

58. The marriage, on March 12, 1732, in Northampton County, was probably at Golden Quarter, the Eyre plantation at the tip of the Delmarva Peninsula. For the marriage, see Jean M. Mihalyka, *Northampton County, Virginia Marriages, 1660–1854* (Bowie, Md.: Heritage Books, 2000), 167. Neech Eyre was the son of Thomas Eyre, III, one of the most important land and slaveowners in Northampton County. Eyre left the plantation, with its uncounted slaves, to his only son. Ralph T. Whitelaw, *Virginia's Eastern Shore: A History of Northampton and Accomack Counties*, 2 vols. (Gloucester, Mass.: Peter Smith, 1968), 1:64.

59. Neech Eyre married widow Isabel Harmanson on March 21, 1734; within three years she too died. Details on Eyre's ill-fated marriages are available at "Neech Eyre," MilesFiles16.1 (subsequently 17.1) Online.

60. Neech's will, leaving most of his estate to his only child, is abstracted in "Neech Eyre," MilesFiles 16.1 online. Edward Mifflin's will, probated May 31, 1743, is in Justice, *Mifflin*, 207–9. Grandfather Edward left Ann "a young Negro girl," probably Ann's age or a bit older.

61. JoAnn Riley McKey, *Accomack County, Virginia, Court Order Abstracts, 1737–1744*, vol. 17 (Bowie, Md.: Heritage Books, 1996), 372.

62. Her grandmother, given guardianship of Daniel Mifflin's minor brothers and Ann Eyre, was paid £21-0-2 out of the estate for "keeping and schooling the said orphan" from Sept. 1745 to Nov. 16, 1747. "Account of expenses in keeping orphan Ann Eyre," Mifflin Family Papers, WCLUM.

63. For George Mifflin I's eight slaves, see *PMHB* 14 (1890): 101–4.

64. George Mifflin II died in 1755; his will, dated Jan. 1, 1755, is in Mifflin Papers, FMCSC.

65. The Mifflin Family Papers at WCLUM include an invoice to George Mifflin I for "disbursements made on behalf of" his grandson, Charles Mifflin, from late 1760, when the boy was six, through his eleventh year. The disbursements covered clothes, schooling, and sundries.

66. Under Wharton's guardianship, Charles was sent to the Ephrata Cloister in Bethlehem to learn German, an important skill in Philadelphia's Atlantic-wide mercantile circles. Charles Mifflin's diary entry about schooling there can be found in *PMHB* 33 (1909): 365. His mother and Thomas Wharton enrolled him in the Germantown Academy by 1762 when he was nine, and he was there two years later when Pelatiah Webster, to become a noted political economist, was the tutor. After attending the Academy of Philadelphia, Mifflin furthered his mercantile career by marrying Mary Waln (1755–1786), daughter of wealthy Philadelphia Quaker Richard Waln (1717–1764), in 1777; the marriage certificate is in PMMMM, 1772–1778.

67. The marriage, which took place in Northampton County, Virginia, probably occurred at Golden Quarter. Marriage license in Stratton Nottingham, *Marriage License Bonds of Northampton Co., Virginia from 1707 to 1854* (Baltimore: Genealogical Publishing, 1994), 79.

68. Most of what is known about the early life of Humphrey Roberts and his immigration to Virginia is found in his Loyalist Claims Commission depositions cited below.

69. I am indebted to James Duffin, Head of University of Pennsylvania Archives, for data from the Academy and College tuition books and lists of students who were schoolmates of Roberts (among whom were Benjamin Franklin's two grandsons, William Temple Franklin and Benjamin Franklin Bache; others included teenagers who would figure prominently in the Revolution: Moses Levi, Jonathan Mifflin, Benjamin Chew, Jr., Edward Shippen, Jr., William Biddle, Tench Coxe, Moses Franks, and several Maryland Tilghmans). For life at the Academy and College see Ann D. Gordon, *The College of Philadelphia, 1749–1779: Impact of an Institution* (New York: Garland, 1989).

70. William Roberts Travel Notebook, Galloway Papers, LC.

71. Virginia House of Burgesses, address to Governor Dunmore, June 19, 1775, quoted in Woody Holton, *Forced Founders: Indians, Debtors, Slaves, and the Making of the American Revolution in Virginia* (Chapel Hill: University of North Carolina Press, 1999), 141.

72. Ibid., 156–61 for a vivid account of Dunmore's Proclamation.

73. William James Van Schreeven and Robert L. Scribner, comps. and eds., *Revolutionary Virginia: The Road to Independence*, 8 vols. (Charlottesville: University Press of Virginia, 1973–1983), vol. 1 (1763–1774), 78–84. Roberts was one of the first merchants signing the document, an agreement to stop importing a long list of articles, from beer to looking glasses to boots and saddles (see 82–83 for the list of signers). Mike McConnell, University of Sydney, called this to my attention.

74. Alan Gilbert, *Black Patriots and Loyalists: Fighting for Emancipation in the War for Independence* (Chicago: University of Chicago Press, 2012), 26; Adele Hast, *Loyalism in Revolutionary Virginia: The Norfolk Area and the Eastern Shore* (Ann Arbor, Mich.: UMI Omohundro Institute of Early American History Research Press, 1982), ch. 3 for a detailed account of Loyalists in Norfolk and Portsmouth. For the exodus of most declared Loyalists in late 1775

and early 1776, see H. J. Eckenrode, *The Revolution in Virginia* (Boston: Houghton Mifflin, 1916), 119–20.

75. AO13/32/484, 486, Public Record Office, UK, available at Ancestry.com, American Loyalist Claims (hereafter ALC). Two Norfolk Whigs reported to the president of the Virginia Revolutionary Convention on Dec. 17 that Roberts, "a noted Tory," had "removed with his family" to the Eastern Shore. Pierce and Smith to Edmund Pendleton, in Van Schreeven and Scribner, *Revolutionary Virginia*, 5: 170.

76. Humphrey Roberts noted the leasing of Golden Quarter and the slaves, his wife's property, in several schedules of his losses submitted to the Claims Commission, where he also noted that his wife "was deprived about five years [of her property] when they were restored to her by the laws made in favour of absentee wives and children." AO12/54/130 and AO13/134/717, ALC.

77. "Schedule of Losses . . . ," AO12/54/131, ALC.

78. "An Estimate of the real and personal estate belonging to Humphrey Roberts," which included Roberts's testimony citing a letter from Ann in December 1779 with this disclosure. AO13/32/140, ALC. Whether the property of suspected loyalists was seized legally or otherwise, Eckenrode claims that an act in 1777 put the property of British subjects living in Virginia under the control of commissioners to "manage in the interest of the State" but then in May 1779 confiscated these properties. *Revolution in Virginia*, 187–91.

79. "Evidence on the foregoing Memorial of Humphrey Roberts," AO12/54/118–20, ALC.

80. The smallpox epidemic that had erupted in North America in late 1774 reached Virginia in January 1776, with devastating effects. See Elizabeth A. Fenn, *Pox Americana: The Great Smallpox Epidemic of 1775–82* (New York: Hill & Wang, 2001), 55–61; and Philip Ranlet, "The British, Slaves, and Smallpox in Revolutionary Virginia," *Journal of Negro History* 84 (1999): 217–26.

81. Detailed accounts are in Hast, *Loyalism in Revolutionary Virginia*, ch. 3; and Gilbert, *Black Patriots and Loyalists*, 30–37.

82. For a recent biography of Lord Dunmore, see James C. David, *Dunmore's New World: The Extraordinary Life of a Royal Governor in Revolutionary America* (Charlottesville: University Press of Virginia, 2013).

83. Roberts Travel Notebook, where William noted that he traveled with Samuel Inglis (a wealthy Philadelphia merchant with Virginia ties and Loyalist sympathies).

84. William Roberts, Memorial to the Lords of the Treasury, July 7, 1781, AO13/32/490, ALC. Dunmore testified to the account and spoke favorably on behalf of father and son.

85. Roberts gave testimony to the Loyalist Claims Commission that his son escaped incarceration at the hands of the Patriots in the summer of 1778. "The Memorial of Humphrey Roberts," March 31, 1779, AO13/32/408. For the effort to conscript Virginians into the Continental Army in 1777–1778 and the draft resistance that followed, see Michael A. McDonnell, *The Politics of War: Race, Class, and Conflict in Revolutionary Virginia* (Chapel Hill: University of North Carolina Press, 2007), ch. 9. I have not been able to document Roberts's imprisonment; it is possible that he contrived this in his Loyalist Claims Commission memorial, but this seems unlikely, especially since he was currying the favor of important Londoners in his efforts to gain admission to the Middle Temple.

86. In his travel notebook he scribbled, "traveled by land to my uncle Mifflin in Accomack and from there to my cousin Warner's near Dover." Roberts Travel Notebook, March 6–August 18, 1778, LC. In his pleas to the English Lords of the Treasury, he recounted his "fruitless attempts

to get to Philadelphia when the British troops were there." Memorial to the Lords of Treasury, July 7, 1781, AO13/32/490, ALC.

87. AO13/32/484, ALC. For the early attempts to relieve the penury of Loyalists reaching England before the Loyalist Claims Commission began its work in 1783, see Gregory Palmer, *Biographical Sketches of Loyalists of the American Revolution* (London: Meckler, 1984), x–xii.

88. "Estimate of the real and personal estate belonging to Humphrey Roberts, late of Portsmouth in Virginia . . ." AO13/32/401, ALC. William Roberts, on reaching England, provided testimony that his mother and siblings were "turned out of their habitations." AO13/32/490, ALC.

89. H. R. McIlwaine, ed., *Journals of the Council of the State of Virginia*, vol. 2 (Richmond: Virginia State Library, 1932), 212 for appointment of Capt. Paul Loyall as Commissioner for the Estate of Humphrey Roberts and others. Roberts claimed in his petitions to the Loyalist Claims Commission that his family was denied access to Golden Quarter but it was "restored to her by the laws made in favour of absentee wives and children" after "about five years." AO13/134/566, ALC. Warner Mifflin confirmed this in 1786 when he wrote that Humphrey Roberts was "deemed by the laws of Virginia a refugee and by their laws as though he was dead." Thus the state authorities "were so honorable . . . as not to confiscate the estate of any person who had gone off in that way that left wife or children [behind]." Mifflin to James Pemberton, Dec. 12, 1786, Pemberton Papers, 47/57, HSP.

90. Duck Creek Manumission Book, HSP transcript, 89–90.

91. Mifflin recorded the deed in the Duck Creek Manumission Book, knowing that Virginia did not permit manumissions without legislative approval. Four years later he recounted how he drew up the manumission deed for Ann Roberts. Mifflin to James Pemberton, Dec. 12, 1786, Pemberton Papers, 47/57.

92. Duck Creek Manumission Book, HSP transcript, 89–90, #441–70. The deed was signed in the presence of Warner Mifflin, Edward Roberts (Ann's second son by her second marriage), her daughter Ann Roberts, and two neighboring Northampton County friends. Warner carried it to Philadelphia, where Charles Mifflin signed it two months later on March 3, 1782.

93. The two youngest slave children listed in the deed of manumission had been born in October 1780 and June 1781, so it is reasonable to conclude that there were adult males at Golden Quarter as late as September 1780—a year before she signed the deed. Possibly the fathers were from neighboring plantations, but the absence of any adult males is very unusual. I have no explanation for the puzzling disproportion of fourteen boys and four girls. Roberts's claim of 53 slaves entirely lost to the war is in "An Estimate of the real and personal estate belonging to Humphrey Roberts, late of Portsmouth in Virginia," Feb. 18, 1783, AO13/32/401; "Evidence on the foregoing Memorial of Humphrey Roberts," June 13, 1785, AO12/54/234; "Memorial of Humphrey Roberts, late of Portsmouth in the County of Norfolk, Virginia Dec. 13, 1783," AO 13, 134/564–67, ALC.

94. In one case, according to the petition of Ann Roberts in 1786, Jim was seized by the Patriot Col. Edward Lynch and sent to the public mines in Bedford County, where he labored for a decade. Legislative Petitions to the General Assembly, Nov. 20, 1786, Virginia State Library, Richmond.

95. McDonnell, *Politics of War*, 292, quoting *Journals of the Council*, 1: 483.

96. In his memorial requesting compensation, London, Oct 7, 1779, Roberts groaned that "General [Edward] Mathews expedition burned his ship on the stocks" which was to carry "near 500 hhds of tobacco so I was ruined even by our own side" AO12/54/231; AO12/109/256; "Memo-

rial of Humphrey Roberts." AO13/32/565–67, ALC. For the Mathews expedition, see Hast, *Loyalism in Revolutionary Virginia*, 99–102.

97. Sylvia R. Frey, *Water from the Rock: Black Resistance in a Revolutionary Age* (Princeton, N.J.: Princeton University Press, 1991), 150–59; Frey estimates that about 1,500 slaves were carried off by the British, "some of them apparent victims of British or Tory kidnapping" (150); Hast, *Loyalism in Revolutionary Virginia*, ch. 7, especially 139–43.

98. When Mifflin and John Parrish passed through Northampton County in May 1782, only a few miles from Golden Quarter, they found the Patriots "much alarmed on account of people [called] barge men who often come on shore." Parrish, "Notes on a Journey to Virginia," Journal Books: Parrish Family, FHLSC.

99. Mifflin to John Parrish, Aug. 18, 1782, C-P-W, Box 1, f7.

100. Mifflin to James Pemberton, Dec. 12, 1786, Pemberton Papers, 47/57.

101. Ibid. Without mentioning dates, Mifflin reported that Humphrey Roberts had returned to Virginia and tried to reclaim the women and children listed in the manumission deed of January 6, 1782. I date Roberts's arrival in late 1785 or early 1786. In sworn testimony before the Loyalist Claims Commission on June 13, 1785, Roberts claimed he arrived in England from New York in March 1779 and "has been here ever since." "Evidence on the foregoing Memorial of Humphrey Roberts," AO12/54/235, ALC. On April 15, 1786, Humphrey and Ann Roberts deeded "half of the present dwelling house [in Portsmouth, Va.] wherein the said Humphrey Roberts now dwells" to their daughter Ann Roberts Taylor. Norfolk County Deed Book Db30, 122. Mike McDowell provided this information.

102. *Thomas, a Negro vs Roberts*, Oct. 18, 1793, Stratton Nottingham, *Accomack County Virginia Land Causes, 1728–1825* (Baltimore: Genealogical Publishing, 1999), 53–57; the testimony declared that Humphrey Roberts returned "soon after the peace concluded on a treaty between Great Britain & America" and "took possession of the whole of the said negroes in the said deed mentioned." When Thomas reached twenty-one in 1793, he sued for his freedom in what became a landmark case in determining the boundaries between slavery and freedom. See Christopher Doyle, "Judge St. George Tucker and the Case of *Tom v. Roberts*: Blunting the Revolution's Radicalism from Virginia's District Courts," *Virginia Magazine of History and Biography* 106 (1998): 410–42.

103. The will he wrote on Nov. 24, 1788 and the proving of the will on Dec. 19, 1791, both in Norfolk County, Virginia, indicates that Roberts blocked most of Mifflin's efforts to secure the freedom of the Golden Quarter slaves. Roberts apparently eased his way back into Portsmouth society, for he left land and houses, as well as a plantation outside the town, "with all my Negroes that I may have at my decease" to his second son, Edward Roberts. To Mary Roberts, his youngest child, he left £1,000 sterling. Widow Ann was the beneficiary of "all the [silver] plate and household furniture." Norfolk County Will Book 1788–1802, Library of Virginia.

104. *Defence of Mifflin*, 17.

105. Quoted in James H. Kettner, "'Persons or Property? The Pleasants Slaves in the Virginia Courts, 1792–1799," in Ronald Hoffman and Peter J. Albert, eds., *Launching the "Extended Republic": The Federalist Era* (Charlottesville: University Press of Virginia, 1996), 140. For efforts in 1769 and 1770, see William F. Hardin, "Litigating the Lash: Quaker Emancipator Robert Pleasants, the Law of Slavery, and the Meaning of Manumission in Revolutionary and Early National Virginia," Ph.D. dissertation, Vanderbilt University, 2013, 66.

106. Kettner, "Persons or Property," 138. For the complex construction of the will and the quasi-freedom that it offered a few of the slaves, see Hardin, "Litigating the Lash," 11–22.

107. Eva Shepherd Wolf, *Race and Liberty in the New Nation: Emancipation in Virginia from the Revolution to Nat Turner's Rebellion* (Baton Rouge: Louisiana State University Press, 2006), 31–33; Wolf quotes the petition on 32. See Hardin, "Litigating the Lash," 88–92, for efforts of Robert Pleasants in 1778 to get the anti-manumission law repealed. For the role of the Virginia Yearly Meeting in pushing the manumission bill, see A. Glenn Crothers, *Quakers Living in the Lion's Mouth: The Society of Friends in Northern Virginia, 1730–1865* (Gainesville: University Press of Florida, 2012), 58–60. In a letter to Anthony Benezet, Pleasants described the near-passage of the bill in 1780, when many legislators were shaken by the flight of hundreds of slaves to the invading British army, including about forty of the most valuable slaves owned by the speaker of the House of Assembly. Pleasants to Benezet, February 1781, in Brookes, *Friend Anthony Benezet*, 436–38.

108. Parrish, "Notes on a Journey to Virginia," Parrish confided in his notebook that he "was made hourly thankful to the father of mercy in providing me so good a companion so well qualified to hold up the hands of so weak and feeble an instrument." Parrish's bow to his friend, sixteen years his junior, reflects the growing respect for Mifflin.

109. The Virginia Yearly Meeting gathering is detailed in the biographical sketch of Parrish in *Friends Intelligencer* 27 (1870–71): 131. The lobbying effort was described briefly by Stabler in his letter to Henry Drinker [?], June 26, 1782, *The Friend* 5 (1834): 172; John Parrish's journal provides a day-by-day colorful account of the proceedings.

110. "The Memorial of a Committee of the People called Quakers," House of Delegates Petitions, May 29, 1782, Archives Division, Library of Virginia.

111. Parrish, "Notes on a Journey to Virginia." The three most recent historians to assay the 1782 manumission law agree that Quaker lobbying made a crucial difference. See Anthony A. Iaccarino, "Virginia and the National Contest over Slavery in the Early Republic, 1780–1833," Ph.D. dissertation, University of California, Los Angeles, 1999, 4–5; Wolf, *Race and Liberty*, 9, 28–35; and Hardin, "Litigating the Lash," 61–62, 125–26. Hardin gives Robert Pleasants much of the credit for the victory. However, Pleasants was a sick man, fearing death was nigh, struggling at his plantation many miles from Richmond. The loss of the legislative journal for 1782 has clouded the issue, making it impossible to distinguish those who spoke for or against the bill.

112. The 1782 manumission law is reprinted in Bruns, *Am I Not a Man and a Brother*, 470–71.

113. Quoted in ibid., 470.

114. *Defence of Mifflin*, 18; Mifflin to Archbishop of Canterbury, June 30, 1787, Society Collection.

115. Stephen B. Weeks, *Southern Quakers and Slavery: A Study in Institutional History* (Baltimore: Johns Hopkins University Press, 1896), 210–13; Wolf, *Race and Liberty*, ch. 2.

116. St. George Tucker, *A Dissertation on Slave with a Proposal for the Gradual Abolition of It, in the State of Virginia* (Philadelphia: M. Carey, 1796), 70.

117. Parrish, "Notes on a Journey to Virginia."

118. Mifflin told the Archbishop of Canterbury that a gradual abolition bill had been discussed by the Virginia legislators and "was lost but by a small majority." Mifflin to Canterbury, June 30, 1787, HSP.

119. "Some Remarks proposed for the Consideration of the People of Virginia and particularly of those in the Legislature and Executive Powers of Government." Bringhurst, Shipley, Hargraves Family Papers, Box 3 F30, University of Delaware Library.

120. Benezet to George Dillwyn, c1783, in Brookes, *Friend Anthony Benezet*, 374. Henry Cadbury believed it was Benezet's intention at the end of his life to push for immediate emancipa-

tion in this last essay. Cadbury, "Anthony Benezet as a Friend," *The Friend* 107 (1934): 350, cited in Maurice Jackson, *Let This Voice Be Heard: Anthony Benezet, Father of Atlantic Abolitionism* (Philadelphia: University of Pennsylvania Press, 2009), 220.

121. Mifflin to John Parrish, Oct. 31, 1782, Jan. 6, 1783. C-P-W, Box 1, f8. His essay was apparently never published.

122. Ibid.

123. Mifflin to [John Parrish], March 10, 1783, "Relics of the Past, #17, *The Friend* 17 (1844): 181.

124. The yearly meeting's decision was inspired in part by the decision of the usually timid London Yearly Meeting in June 1783 to lay before Parliament a petition pleading the case of enslaved Africans. John Pemberton, Philadelphia's persuasive traveling minister, had been instrumental in coordinating efforts of the London Yearly Meeting and Philadelphia Yearly Meeting. Christopher Leslie Brown, *Moral Capital: Foundations of British Abolitionism* (Chapel Hill: University of North Carolina Press, 2006), ch. 7.

125. "To the United States in Congress Assembled," in Justice, *Mifflin*, 167–69; Bruns, *Am I Not a Man and a Brother*, 493–502, where the signatures are reproduced. Jay Worrall, Jr., *The Friendly Virginian: America's First Quakers* (Athens, Ga.: Iberian, 1994), 237–38 believes Mifflin read the address, but David Cooper and James Pemberton remembered it differently; William Dillwyn to John Pemberton, Dec. 6, 1783, Pemberton Papers, 40/5, HSP; David Cooper Diary, Oct. 8, 1783, QCHC.

126. Cooper recounted that his fellow Quaker delegates had opportunities to talk with members of the Congress, dining with a number of them who listened civilly to the Quakers' arguments. *Friends Review* 15 (1862): 738 from Cooper Diary.

127. The yearly meeting tried again in the next several years. In 1784, they pressed the London Yearly Meeting's *The Case of Our Fellow-Creatures, the Oppressed Africans* on each member of Congress and on the lawmakers in Pennsylvania and New Jersey as well. They petitioned again to stop the slave trade the next year with no success. Maurice Jackson, *Let This Voice Be Heard*, 164–65, 221.

128. Mifflin to Greene, Oct. 21, 1783, QCHC and in *Greene Papers* 13:155–58.

129. Greene to Mifflin, Nov. 1783 in *Greene Papers* 13:191–93. Greene counted himself among most Patriots who believed that while the pacifism of many Friends dictated their neutrality during the war, many others were pro-British and hid behind their principles. Greene's defense of slaveholding skipped over the possibility that he could have freed the slaves while offering a sharecropping arrangement.

130. Brookes, *Friend Anthony Benezet*, 156–75 provides a full account of Benezet's death and legacy; see also Jackson, *Let This Voice Be Heard*, 226–30.

131. Roberts Vaux, *Memoirs of Anthony Benezet* (Philadelphia: James P. Parke, 1817), 147, quoted in Brookes, *Friend Anthony Benezet*, 160.

Chapter 4. Widening the Circle

1. Mifflin to Parrish, Aug. 18, 1782, C-P-W, Box 1, f7.

2. Introduction to "Relics of the Past"—an eighteen-part series of letters and documents on Warner Mifflin, *The Friend* 17 (1844): 135.

3. Kristin Sword, "Remembering Dinah Nevil: Strategic Deceptions in Eighteenth-Century Antislavery," *Journal of American History* 97 (2010): 315–43, quote 317. Though not mentioned,

Mifflin fits Sword's argument that after the Revolution "a tiny subset" of "an intercolonial and transatlantic network of white and black activists" "engineered most antislavery actions on both sides of the Atlantic."

4. Pemberton also became an important officer of the Pennsylvania Abolition Society after its reorganization in 1787. With its devoted platoon of lawyers, working pro bono, and a structured committee system, the abolition society was busy rescuing blacks from masters trying to circumvent Pennsylvania's 1780 gradual abolition act, but it also became important to Mifflin as it tried to "chip away at bondage's legal sanction in individual states." Richard S. Newman, *The Transformation of American Abolitionism: Fighting Slavery in the New Republic* (Chapel Hill: University of North Carolina Press, 2002), 61. When Henry Drinker, also a Winchester exile, became clerk of the Philadelphia Yearly Meeting, he became another valued source of advice and support for Mifflin.

5. J.-P. Brissot de Warville, *New Travels in the United States of America, 1788*, trans. and ed. Mara Soceanu Vamos and Durand Echevarria (Cambridge, Mass.: Harvard University Press, 1964), 300.

6. Essah, *A House Divided*, 38–40. The sister of Mifflin's wife, Ann Holliday, was among those who were reluctant to free their slaves because of the "oppressive law in force relative to the freeing of Negroes." Duck Creek MM Minutes, 1774–1792, 16, HSP transcripts, quoted in William H. Williams, *Slavery and Freedom in Delaware, 1639–1865* (Wilmington, Del.: Scholarly Resources, 1996), 143.

7. Mifflin to James Pemberton Dec. 9, 1783, Pemberton Papers, 40/11, HSP.

8. Mifflin to James Pemberton Dec. 9, 1783, Pemberton Papers, 40/11.

9. PYM-MME, Sept.–Oct. 1784.

10. Mifflin to James Pemberton, Nov. 12, 1784, Pemberton Papers, 42/112.

11. Essah, *A House Divided*, 37–38, provides a concise treatment of the final stages of the transition from tobacco to grain in Delaware. For an elaborate analysis, see Brooke Hunter, "The Rage for Grain: Flour Milling in the Mid-Atlantic, 1750–1815," Ph.D. dissertation, University of Delaware, 2001.

12. For the Methodist recruitment of Delawareans, see William H. Williams, *The Garden of American Methodism: The Delmarva Peninsula, 1769–1820* (Wilmington, Del.: Scholarly Resources, 1984).

13. Delaware's constitution of 1776 included a ban on importing slaves, but it was mostly honored in the breach, for no enforcement mechanism had been legislated. Mifflin to James Pemberton, Feb. 16, 1785, Pemberton Papers, 43/30. Mifflin included a copy of the Maryland law in his letter to Pemberton. Claudia L. Bushman et al., eds., *Proceedings of the Assembly of the Lower Counties on Delaware, 1770–1776, of the Constitutional Convention of 1776, and of the House of Assembly of the Delaware State, 1776–1781*, 2 vols. (Newark: University of Delaware Press, 1986–88), 2:288 for introduction of the bill.

14. Mifflin to James Pemberton, Jan. 16, 1785, Pemberton Papers, 42/166. Mifflin recounted to John Pemberton that he had been distributing Quaker antislavery pamphlets on Maryland's Eastern Shore in the summer of 1784; Mifflin to John Pemberton, Aug. 17, 1784, Pemberton Papers, 41/171.

15. "Message from the President of the State of Delaware to the General Assembly," *Pennsylvania Packet*, Nov. 7, 1782, Dickinson also recommended repeal of the security law on manumitting slaves; address in *Minutes of Council of Delaware State from 1776 to 1792* (Wilmington: Historical Society of Delaware, 1887), 749–50.

16. The bill is in Charles J. Stille, *Life and Times of Dickinson, 1732–1808* (Philadelphia: Lippincott, 1891), 424–31, from manuscript in Dickinson's hand at HSP; drafts are in the Logan Papers, HSP; thanks to Jane Calvert for copies of these.

17. Address, dated Dec. 27, 1785, in PYM Minutes, 3:19–20; original in Legislative Papers, Petitions, Negroes, and Slavery, Delaware State Archives; entered in PYM-MS, March 26, 1786, and endorsed after revisions; reprinted in *The Friend* 17 (1844): 188–89, where authorship of the petition was attributed to Mifflin. On drawing up memorials from Mifflin and the Duck Creek Monthly Meeting, sent to the Philadelphia Yearly Meeting for Sufferings, which approved both for presentation to Assembly, see Robert Holliday to James Pemberton, Dec. 12, 1785 and Meeting for Sufferings to Holliday, Dec. 17, 1785, PYM-MS Miscellaneous Papers, 1792 file, QCHC. The presentation of the petition is recorded in *Proceedings of the House of Assembly*, 288, 305; DCMMM, vol. 2, Feb. 24, 1787, HSP.

18. *Proceedings of the House of Assembly*, 305, 308–9, 314, 325, 330, 333, 338, 340–41.

19. Dickinson to James Pemberton, June 21, 1792, Gratz, Old Congress Collection, HSP. It is not clear when Dickinson reintroduced the bill.

20. Mifflin to Daniel Mifflin, June 6, 1786, Mifflin Papers, DPA. J. P. Brissot de Warville, whom Mifflin was about to meet in Philadelphia, wrote movingly about the composure of Quakers when they lost their closest relations: "It is the fruit both of their religious principles and of right conduct constantly maintained. After a death the survivors seem either to abandon themselves to grief less than do most people or else to contain it within themselves. They hold Heaven their home and do not believe that death, which leads to it, can be a misfortune." Brissot de Warville, *New Travels*, 305.

21. Mifflin to John Parrish, Feb. 9, 1787, C-P-W Box 1, f13; Mifflin to Moses Brown, Dec. 3, 1787, Moses Brown Papers, RIHS. Mifflin repeated his inner conflict—reluctant "to leave my dear babes in their motherless condition" but "favoured to be preserved in a state of resignation to the divine will."

22. PYM-MS, 1785–1802 (Oct. 19, 1786).

23. *Friends Intelligencer* 27 (1870–1871): 131 for names of the delegation, which included some of the weightiest leaders of the Philadelphia Yearly Meeting: James Pemberton, Isaac Zane, Samuel Emlen, Nicholas Waln, William Savery, Henry Drinker, Joseph Gibbons, and Jacob Lindley. For the committee report to the yearly meeting see PYM-MS, Dec. 21, 1786.

24. PYM-MS, 1785–1802, Nov. 16, 1786. Jay Worrall, *The Friendly Virginians: America's First Quakers* (Athens, Ga.: Iberian, 1994), 238 suggests the influence of the Quaker petition on the clause in the Northwest Ordinance that banned bringing slaves into the territory. See also Thomas E. Drake, *Quakers and Slavery in America* (New Haven, Conn.: Yale University Press, 1950), 94–95.

25. Mifflin had spent much of December 1786 visiting monthly and quarterly meetings in the Western Quarter; Mifflin to John Parrish, Feb. 9, 1787, C-P-W, Series 1, Box 1, f13. In 1786 and 1787 the Western Quarter appointed him a delegate to the yearly meeting. WQMM, Aug. 21, 1786; Aug. 20, 1787.

26. Mifflin to Parrish, Feb. 9, 1787, C-P-W, Box 1, f13; Mifflin to James Pemberton, Feb. 3, 1787, Pemberton Papers, 47/124.

27. This and the next paragraph are from Mifflin to John Parrish, Feb. 9, 1787, C-P-W, Box 1, f13.

28. Additional laws in 1789 strengthened the bill, requiring approval of five justices of the peace, adding slightly to the fine of convicted offenders, and adding Virginia and Maryland to the interstate ban. In 1793, aware of how the law was flouted, the legislative passed an additional law providing that slave masters charged with violating the 1789 law post bond or remain in

custody until their case was adjudicated. If convicted, the offending slaveowners could expect the court to declare the unconditional freedom of the enslaved persons scheduled for sale out of state. In addition, public whippings and ear cropping were to be inflicted on manstealers. Essah, *A House Divided*, 40–41, 50–52, 84–85, 110, 121–23, citing *Laws of the State of Delaware*, 2 vols. (New Castle: Samuel and John Adams, 1797), 2:884–88, 941–44, 1093–95; *Proceedings of the House of Assembly*, 398–400, 428–29, 438.

29. Essah, *A House Divided*, 50–51, cites several freedom suits in Slavery Material, Indentures, Petitions for Freedom, 1701–99, Box 5, DPA.

30. Mifflin to John Parrish, Feb. 9, 1787, C-P-W, Box 1, f13. Mechal Sobel, *Teach Me Dreams: The Search for Self in the Revolutionary Era* (Princeton, N.J.: Princeton University Press, 2000) shows how Quaker dreams reflected how they sorted through nettlesome concerns about race relations.

31. Mifflin to Ann [?] Parrish, wife of John Parrish, May 13, 1787, C-P-W, Box 1, f13. Daniel Mifflin's second wife, who had been Warner's stepmother during his teens, died in spring 1787. His father would remarry the next year.

32. John Parrish to William Dillwyn, Oct. 9, 1787, Slavery Collection, New-York Historical Society.

33. Mifflin to William Smallwood, Aug. 31, 1786, Gilder Lehrman Collection #GLC06508.09. I have been unable to find any response from Smallwood.

34. Mifflin to Parrish, June 19, 1787, C-P-W, Box 1, f12.

35. Samuel Chase represented Baltimore in the legislature. The petition from Baltimore Yearly Meeting was read on December 10, 1787, http://aomol.msa.maryland.gov/megafile/msa/speccol/sc4800/sc4872/003197/html/m3197-0818.html. I thank Emily Huebner, Research Archivist for the Study of the Legacy of Slavery, Maryland State Archives for assistance on this. For the vote, see Jeffrey R. Brackett, *The Negro in Maryland: A Study of the Institution of Slavery* (New York: Negro Universities Press, 1969 [orig. 1889]), 52.

36. Mifflin to John Parrish, June 19, 1787, C-P-W, Box 1, f12.

37. Mifflin to Henry Drinker [?] Oct. 14, 1787, "Relics of the Past #9," *The Friend* 17 (1844): 199.

38. Drake, *Quakers and Slavery*, 83–84; Michael J. Crawford, *The Having of Negroes Is Become a Burden: The Quaker Struggle to Free Slaves in Revolutionary North Carolina* (Gainesville: University Press of Florida, 2010) provides primary documents showing Quaker efforts to free slaves and the determination of the state to thwart these efforts.

39. Steven B. Weeks, *Southern Quakers and Slavery: A Study in Institutional History* (Baltimore: Johns Hopkins University Press, 1896), 209–10, 217. Weeks believed the law "paralyzed the hands of Friends" for several years, but this overstates the case. Some Quaker owners freeing their slaves, reckoning with the likelihood that the enslaved person would end up in the hands of a more severe master, offered free-wage or tenant agreements to stay on the land.

40. Hiram H. Hilty, "North Carolina Quakers and Slavery," Ph.D. dissertation, Duke University, 1968, 45, concludes that the state's legislature "suspected that the Quakers had really freed their slaves in order to embarrass the Revolution." Hilty provides copious details on the Quaker running battle with sheriffs and the relaxing of the "meritorious service" clause, 53–64, 68–70.

41. In her eleven-month sojourn, Harrison oversaw the release of some two hundred slaves held by Quakers. "Memoirs of the Life and Travels of Sarah Harrison," *Friends Miscellany* 11 (1837–1838): 97–216, 102–3 for meeting with Mifflin. Mifflin reported on the many meetings he visited in a letter to Moses Brown, Dec. 3, 1787, Moses Brown Papers, RIHS.

42. By 1790, free blacks in North Carolina numbered about five thousand; Ira Berlin, *Slaves Without Masters: The Free Negro in the Antebellum South* (New York: New Press, 1974), 31, 46–47.

43. Mifflin to Moses Brown, Dec. 3, 1787, Moses Brown Papers. For the account of the North Carolina Yearly Meeting to the Philadelphia Yearly Meeting's Meeting for Sufferings of about 134 manumitted slaves who had been seized and reenslaved between 1777 and 1797, see Crawford, *The Having of Negroes*, 101–5. The meeting believed many more were reenslaved that they could not document. Seizing freed blacks and auctioning them back into slavery is covered by Larry Tise, "'Taking Up' Quaker Slaves: The Origins of America's Slavery Imperative," in *Varieties of Southern Religious History*, ed. Regina D. Sullivan and Monte Harrell Hampton (Columbia: University of South Carolina Press, 2015), 35–50.

44. *A Narrative of Some of the Proceedings of North Carolina Yearly Meeting on the Subject of Slavery Within its Limits, Published by order of the Meeting for Sufferings of North Carolina Yearly Meeting* (Greensborough, 1848), 16–18. A similar petition submitted the next year is in Crawford, *The Having of Negroes*, 133–34. Philadelphia Yearly Meeting Meeting for Sufferings and leaders of the Pennsylvania Abolition Society were in close touch with North Carolina antislavery Quaker leaders as part of the emerging interstate abolitionist coalition.

45. Mifflin to Pemberton, Dec. 21, 1787, Pemberton Papers, 49/34.

46. Mifflin to John Parrish, Dec. 13, 1787, C-P-W, Box 1, f13; Mifflin to James Pemberton, Dec. 21, 1787, Pemberton Papers, 49/34.

47. Mifflin to Moses Brown, Dec. 3, 1787, Moses Brown Papers, RIHS.

48. The North Carolina Yearly Meeting remonstrance and the 1788 law are in Crawford, *The Having of Negroes*, 133–36. Whether the 1788 law had its intended effect awaits further investigation.

49. Thomas Lloyd, *Proceedings and Debates of the General Assembly of Pennsylvania . . .*, 4 vols. (Philadelphia, 1787–1788), 3: 219–25, 231.

50. Jacob Cox Parsons, ed., *Extracts from the Diary of Jacob Hiltzheimer* (Philadelphia: Wm. F. Fell, 1893), 144.

51. Mifflin to James Pemberton, May 4, 1788, Pemberton Papers, 50/153.

52. Ibid.; Mifflin was back home by early May; Mifflin to Hannah Moore, May 9, 1788, Howland Collection, Box 9, QCHC.

53. For a report on forming a constitution and installing a slate of officers in June 1788, see [Philadelphia] *Independent Gazetteer*, Aug. 23, 1788. Mike McDowell provided this citation. For the Pennsylvania Abolition Society's reorganization in 1787, which brought in nearly one hundred new members, tilted toward genteel Philadelphians, see Gary B. Nash and Jean R. Soderlund, *Freedom by Degrees: Emancipation in Pennsylvania and Its Aftermath* (New York: Oxford University Press, 1991), 123–25, 130–31.

54. Never attracting more than sixty members and poorly financed, the societies had modest results in convincing slaveholders to release their chattel property. Both societies limped along before folding their tents just after Mifflin died in 1798. Essah, *A House Divided*, 59–61.

55. *Proceedings*, 539–40, 548; Philadelphia Yearly Meeting, Meeting for Sufferings Minutes, 1775–1802, pp. 84–86 (May 22, June 19, 1788); the petitions are in Record Group 1111.0000, Legislative Papers, 1788–89, DPA. Drafts from the Philadelphia Yearly Meeting are in PYM-MS, Miscellaneous Papers, 1792 file, QCHC. Essah, *A House Divided*, 51–52.

56. The five petitions are in Legislative Papers, 1788–89, RG 1111.0000, DPA. In a letter to Moses Brown, May 17, 1788, James Pemberton described the British ship's activity. Gilder Lehrman Collection #GLC04980.

57. Mifflin to John Parrish, April 5, 1788, C-P-W, Box 1, f14. Mifflin had put into the hands of each legislator Thomas Clarkson's *Essay on the Slavery and Commerce of the Human Species, Particularly the African* (London, 1786), which may have helped turn the tide. *Proceedings of the House of Assembly*, 583–85, 589–90, 594–95, 612–13, 623–24; *Laws of Delaware*, 2:941–44.

58. Essah, *A House Divided*, 40–41; "An Additional Supplementary Act . . . to Prevent the Exportation of Slaves," *Laws of Delaware* 2: 941–44, 1093–95; *Proceedings of the House of Assembly*, 428–29, 438.

59. "Anecdotes and Memoirs of Warner Mifflin," *Friends Miscellany* 5 (1834): 218–19. Writing in 1834, the editors of *Friends Miscellany*, hinting that Mifflin was held back for petty reasons, regretted that he "was prevented from prosecuting his visit."

60. By this time the London Meeting for Sufferings, in close contact with its Philadelphia counterpart, was emerging from its shell of indifference to public policy and political advocacy, adopting a more vigorous stance as the sentinels of freedom and the trumpet of abolitionism. Christopher Leslie Brown, *Moral Capital: Foundations of British Abolitionism* (Chapel Hill: University of North Carolina Press, 2006), ch. 7, is the indispensable source for how the London Society of Friends charged to the front of the abolitionist cause, leaving behind its unwillingness to try to influence national legislation.

61. Epistle to London Yearly Meeting, May 18, 1786, composed by committee appointed March 25, 1786, Philadelphia Yearly Meeting, Meeting for Sufferings, May 16, 1786. Brown's *Moral Capital*, 434–50 analyzes how "organized abolitionism finally crystallized in Britain in 1787." The other members of the Philadelphia Yearly Meeting committee—Nicholas Waln, James Thornton, David Evans, and John Drinker—were also intimates of Mifflin.

62. The petition had first been made to Parliament in 1783, printed in 1784, and widely circulated as *The Case of our Fellow-Creatures, the Oppressed Africans, respectfully Recommended to the Serious Consideration of the Legislature of Great-Britain, by the People Called Quakers*, and resubmitted to Parliament almost annually.

63. Mifflin to Archbishop of Canterbury, June 30, 1787, Society Autograph Collection, HSP. The autobiographical account he sent the archbishop formed the basis of Mifflin's *Defence of Warner Mifflin Against Aspersions*, published nine years later. In 1792, Mifflin reported to President Washington that the archbishop had been asked "if he had any exception against the contents" of the letter. The archbishop replied: "We never take exception to things well meant." Mifflin to Washington, Oct. 12, 1792, *Papers of George Washington, Presidential Series* 11:505.

64. DCMMM, Dec. 22, 1787, Jan. 26, Feb. 23, April 26, May 24, July 26, 1788, in Justice, *Mifflin*, 150–52; Mifflin to John Parrish, May 11, 1788, C-P-W, Box 1, f14; John Drinker to James Thornton, July 26, 1788, Howland Collection, QCHC; In his letter to John Parrish, Nov. 19, 1788, Mifflin said that his monthly meeting had finally given its blessing and the travel certificate was now before the Western Quarterly Meeting. C-P-W, Box 1, f14. Two days before this letter, the Western Quarterly Meeting appointed a committee, including his close friends Jacob Lindley and George Churchman, to consider the case. WQMM, Nov. 17, 1788. By then, Mifflin had another matter close at hand, one so intimate that he abandoned his effort to cross the Atlantic.

65. De Lormerie to Mifflin, undated but probably in the late 1780s, in Justice, *Mifflin*, 102–3. For identification of de Lormerie, see *Papers of George Washington, Presidential Series* 2:401–2; de Lormerie to Jefferson, May 29, 1801, April 14, 1809, Founders Online. In the later letter, de Lormerie

noted he had been in the U.S. for almost fifteen years, most of it in Philadelphia. While minister plenipotentiary in Paris, Jefferson had facilitated de Lormerie's purchase of 5,277 acres of land in Kentucky in 1787.

66. Brissot wrote of "having read the touching tribute to him [by Crèvecoeur]." Brissot de Warville, *New Travels*, 165. For new scholarship on Brissot and his connections with Crèvecoeur, see Marie-Jeanne Rossignol, "Jacques-Pierre Brissot and the Fate of Atlantic Antislavery During the Age of Revolutionary Wars," in Richard Bessel et al., eds., *War, Empire and Slavery, 1770–1830* (London: Palgrave Macmillan, 2010), 139–56; Rossignol, "The Quaker Antislavery Commitment and How It Revolutionized French Antislavery Through the Crèvecoeur-Brissot Friendship, 1782–1789," in Brycchan Carey and Geoffrey Plank, eds., *Quakers and Abolition* (Urbana: University of Illinois Press, 2014), 180–93. For the broader context of French visitors and émigrés to Philadelphia, see François Furstenberg, *When the United States Spoke French: Five Refugees Who Shaped a Nation* (New York: Penguin, 2014).

67. Quoted in Rossignol, "Jacques-Pierre Brissot," 146. In close contact with London Quaker abolitionists such as Thomas Clarkson and Granville Sharp, Brissot had joined the Society for Effecting the Abolition of the Slave Trade in 1787, just after its founding in London. Rossignol, "Jacques-Pierre Brissot," 141.

68. Brissot de Warville, *New Travels*, 166–67, 245. Years later, John Greenleaf Whittier, the celebrated Quaker poet, claimed that Brissot's "intimacy with Warner Mifflin . . . profoundly affected his [Brissot's] whole after life." *Prose Works of John Greenleaf Whittier*, 3 vols. (Boston: Houghton Mifflin, 1899), 3: 342–43. This probably goes too far, for Brissot was already a committed abolitionist by the time he met Mifflin. But the measured intensity of Mifflin figured importantly in the Frenchman's assessment of the Quakers, who played the star role in his *New Travels*.

69. Brissot de Warville, *New Travels*, 165.

70. For English language editions and others in German, Dutch, and Swedish, see ibid., xxvi–xxvii. The quoted phrases are on 166.

71. Ibid., 167.

72. Mifflin's remarriage after 28 months of the widower's life was much sooner than usual. See Robert V. Wells, "Quaker Marriage Patterns in a Colonial Perspective," *WMQ* 39 (1972): 424–25, where 3.6 years was the average for males.

73. Bruce Dorsey, *Reforming Men and Women: Gender in the Antebellum City* (Ithaca, N.Y.: Cornell University Press, 2001), 39–49 explains the role of divinely inspired young unmarried Quaker women in the Philadelphia area.

74. Her father's death may have initiated the transformation. See ibid., 45–46 for the near-death experience that led to a similar change of life for her cousin Anne Parrish.

75. Emlen Family Papers, Box 1, HSP. Ann must have spent countless hours at the High Street Great Meetinghouse, where she could consult the mounting correspondence between the Philadelphia Yearly Meeting and the London Yearly Meeting.

76. "On Politicks," Emlen Family Papers, Box 1.

77. Ann Emlen to "a delegate in Congress" [Thomas Burke of North Carolina], March 3, 1779, C-P-W, Ser. 4, Box 10, f51. Sarah Fatherly, *Gentlewomen and Learned Ladies: Women and Elite Formation in Eighteenth-Century Philadelphia* (Bethlehem, Pa.: Lehigh University Press, 2008), 170 for Emlen's exchange of poems with Burke. See Fatherly, ch. 6 for the struggles of elite women in Philadelphia, mostly Quakers, during the Revolution.

78. Ann Emlen to John Dickinson, undated, "Submitted by I. S. [Isaac Sharpless]," *Bulletin of Friends Historical Association* 1 (1906): 36. That she refers to herself as a girl indicates she was a teenager.

79. "Some Account of My Religious Progress," Emlen Family Papers, Box 1.

80. Ann Emlen to Sally Fisher, June 12, 1781, Corbit, Higgins, Spruance Papers, Box 91, f7, DHS.

81. "Notes on Religion," Nov. 1779, Emlen Family Papers, Box 1. For analysis of the dream see Carla Gerona, *Night Journeys: The Power of Dreams in Transatlantic Quaker Culture* (Charlottesville: University of Virginia Press, 2004), 173–76, 193–95.

82. "Notes on Religion," November 1779.

83. Ibid., March 18,; April 13, 1781. Her friends' dismay was noted in the diaries of Sally Logan Fisher and Anne Rawle, HSP, quoted in Mary Beth Norton, *Liberty's Daughters: The Revolutionary Experience of American Women, 1750–1800* (Boston: Little, Brown, 1980), 128.

84. John Pemberton to Ann Emlen, June 6, 1781, Pemberton Papers, 35/143.

85. Ann Emlen to John Pemberton, June 12, 1781, in Pemberton Papers, 35/144.

86. Emlen's intended marriage to Jacob Lindley (1744–1814), a Chester County Quaker minister who was to become a good friend of Warner Mifflin, was broken off in about June 1781. Sally Fisher (Kent County) to [cousin] Sally Fisher (Philadelphia), Spring 1781, in John A. H. Sweeney, ed., "The Norris-Fisher Correspondence: A Circle of Friends, 1779–82," *Delaware History*, 6 (1955), 221. Ann dwelled on this in her letter to Sally Fisher, June 12, 1781, Corbit, Higgins, Spruance Papers, Box 9, f7, DHS. Mike McDowell provided this letter. For female Quaker traveling ministers see Rebecca Larson, *Daughters of Light: Quaker Women Preaching and Prophesying in the Colonies and Abroad, 1700–1775* (New York: Knopf, 1999), and Sarah Crabtree, *Holy Nation: The Transatlantic Quaker Ministry in an Age of Revolution* (Chicago: University of Chicago Press, 2015).

87. "Notes on Religion," undated but probably 1782, Emlen Papers, Box 1.

88. Warder described "a dark snuff-colored tabareen [that] looked old and so awkward-made that if her person was not so agreeable it would be disgusting—I mean her dress." Ann Warder Diary, QCHC, excerpts in *PMHB*, 17 (1893), 444–61 (445–47 for dress descriptions); 18 (1894), 51–63. Obsessed with her next tea or dinner appointment, Warder traded in gossip, but her keen eye on the Quaker social scene after the war is of unusual interest.

89. Ann Emlen to John Pemberton, Jan. 15, 1785, Pemberton Papers, 42/162.

90. Drinker to James Thornton, July 26, 1788, Richard Cadbury Collection, QCHC. Drinker noted that Mifflin's Duck Creek Monthly Meeting had approved his trip to England and he was to go the Western Quarterly Meeting for final approval.

91. Mifflin requested a certificate from the Philadelphia Monthly Meeting to marry Ann Emlen, a member of that meeting. DCMMM, July 26, 1788. Ann Emlen, "Notes on Religion," October 1788.

92. "Diary of Ann Warder," *PMHB* 18 (1894): 62. James Pemberton, Mifflin's friend and mentor, was more generous, reporting that after more than a week in Philadelphia, "Mr. Mifflin, with his prize, set off . . . for his habitation in Kent" after a marriage found "less reconcilable" by many friends who had come to value Ann's "improving in experience and usefulness." James Pemberton to John Thornton, Oct. 21, 1788, Richard Cadbury Collection, QCHC.

93. *Memorials of Rebecca Jones*, Robert J. Allinson, comp. (Philadelphia: Henry Longstreth, 1849), 174. For Bank Meeting, torn down the following year, see Ezra Michener, *A Retrospect of Early Quakerism: Being Extracts from the Records of Philadelphia Yearly Meeting* (Philadelphia:

T. Ellwood Zell, 1860), 52; for the meeting as the site of black worshippers, see Henry Cadbury, "Negro Membership in the Society of Friends," *Journal of Negro History* 21 (1936): 153.

94. Marriage vows between Ann Emlen and Warner Mifflin and the Elizabeth Brookes account are in Mifflin Family Papers, Box 1, f24, FMCSC.

95. Mifflin to Parrish, Nov. 19, 1788, C-P-W, Box 1, f14. Hilda Justice exhumed a story of how no sooner had Warner taken his bride home than he shattered the blue china she brought with her by throwing it against the house at Chestnut Grove "as too worldly." Hilda Justice, "Notes on trip to Dover, Smyrna, and Camden, Nov. 5, 1932," American Friends Letter Collection, QCHC. Justice searched for fragments of the china set without success.

96. Murderkill Monthly Meeting, Women's Minutes, 1788–1845, 3, 5, 8, 9, 10, 11, 12, 18, 25, 28, 29, 30, 39 for her appointments to committees between February 1789 and December 1791. The Southern Quarterly Meeting, comprising Maryland's Eastern Shore meetings and Delaware's meetings, was carved out of the Western Quarterly Meeting in 1789.

97. Mifflin to Parrish, Nov. 29, 1788, C-P-W, Box 1, f14. The "mulatto law" was a perennial issue in Maryland, tracing back more than a century when Lord Baltimore's indentured servant Irish Nell had married an enslaved African and bore a child that was deemed free. In *Mary Butler v. Adam Craig*, the General Court in 1787 revisited the slave system based upon patrilineage for African descendants and matrilineage for biracial children whose maternal ancestor was European. See Patricia Reid, "Between Slavery and Freedom," Ph.D. dissertation, University of Iowa, 2006, 60–66. A gradual abolition act was introduced the next year by the newly established Maryland Abolition Society, along with an appeal to repeal the law prohibiting manumission of slaves by will, with substantial support, including that of William Pinkney, whose speech must have given Mifflin encouragement when Mathew Carey printed it in his *American Museum*, 6 (1789), 74–77. The florid "Speech in the House of Delegates in Maryland" was published separately in Philadelphia in 1790. Brackett, *The Negro in Maryland*, 53–54; Mary S. Locke, *Antislavery in America from the Introduction of African Slaves to the Prohibition of the Slave Trade, 1619–1808* (Cambridge, Mass.: Radcliffe College Monographs, 11, 1901), 120–21.

98. Allinson, *Memorials of Rebecca Jones*, 179.

99. PYM-MME, March 23, 1789; Oct. 2, 1789; Jan. 28, 1790. In a letter to John Thornton, Mar. 30, 1789, James Pemberton gave details of the imbroglio; Richard Cadbury Collection, QCHC; Mifflin to Henry Drinker, April 11, 1789, "Relics of the Past, #9, *The Friend* 17 (1844): 199 for Mifflin's ritualistic bow to his elders. Pennsylvania Abolition Society General Meeting Minutes, 1784–1824, pp. 68–69, PAS Papers, HSP, Microfilm edition, Reel 1 for Mifflin's election to the Pennsylvania Abolition Society.

100. I have discussed this in *The Forgotten Fifth: African Americans in the Revolutionary Age* (Cambridge, Mass.: Harvard University Press, 2006), ch. 1.

101. Albert Matthews, "Notes on the Proposed Abolition of Slavery in Virginia in 1785," *Colonial Society of Massachusetts Publications* 6 (1904): 170–80; James Madison to George Washington, Nov. 11, 1785, *The Papers of James Madison*, William T. Hutchinson and William M. E. Rachal, eds., 17 vols. (Chicago: University of Chicago Press, 1962–1991), 8: 403.

102. Jefferson to Richard Price, Aug. 7, 1787, Julian Boyd et al., eds., *The Papers of Thomas Jefferson*, 42 vols. (Princeton, N.J.: Princeton University Press, 1950–2016), 8: 357; Brissot, *New Travels*, 238.

103. David Waldstreicher, *Slavery's Constitution: From Revolution to Ratification* (New York: Hill and Wang, 2009), 150. In ch. 3 Waldstreicher discusses the antislavery position of many

antifederalists who opposed ratification of the Constitution. However, some antislavery activists in the Society of Friends supported ratification of the Constitution despite its distinctly pro-slavery clauses (120).

104. For a persuasive counter-argument to conventional wisdom, see Nicholas Perry Wood, "Considerations of Humanity and Expediency: The Slave Trades and African Colonization in the Early National Antislavery Movement," Ph.D. dissertation, University of Virginia, 2013, 79–82.

105. Marcus Rediker, *The Slave Ship: A Human History* (New York: Viking, 2007), ch. 10, 308 for the quoted passage and 311–15 for the first English edition and Carey's Philadelphia edition. Pemberton to London Yearly Meeting, June 24, 1789, PAS, Committee for Correspondence, Letter Book, 1789–1794, 18. James Green, Librarian, Library Company of Philadelphia called my attention to this letter.

106. William G. diGiacomantonio, "'For the Gratification of a Volunteering Society': Antislavery and Pressure Group Politics in the First Federal Congress," *Journal of the Early Republic* 15 (1995): 169–97. The appointment of Mifflin to the delegation charged with presenting an antislavery petition to the First Congress is in PYM-MS, 1785–1802, Oct. 15, 1789. Writing from his father's home in Accomack County, where he, his wife, and twelve-year old son were visiting, he acknowledged his willingness to serve in a letter to James Pemberton, Dec. 28, 1789, Pemberton Papers, 53/65.

107. Mifflin to Drinker, Feb. 1790, Vaux Collection, QCHC.

108. "Names of Friends appointed to attend the application to Congress respecting slavery …", Pemberton Papers, in *DHFFC*, 18:497n3. The editors of *DHFFC* call Mifflin "unquestionably the most active of these early lobbyists." *DHFFC*, 19:1686–87n2. This brilliantly edited publication of a wide array of primary sources related to the first federal Congress has been used for the House and Senate debates discussed below instead of the *Annals of Congress*, published without annotation in the 1830s.

109. Memorial of the Philadelphia Yearly Meeting, Oct. 3, 1789, *DHFFC*, 8:322–23.

110. The New York Yearly Meeting memorial is in *DHFFC*, 8:323–24. The New York legislature had rebuffed Quaker attempts to address the issue with a state law, claiming that only the federal government had the power to regulate trade.

111. Burke and Jackson's speeches in ibid., 12: 286–87. In the first of a series of on-the-scene accounts to his brother James Pemberton, John Pemberton reported on the events of Feb. 11, 1790: PAS Papers, in *DHFFC*, 18:496; Especially infuriating to the Georgians and South Carolinians was the Pennsylvania Abolition Society broadside of the slave ship *Brooks* that had been sent south for distribution, packed with tobacco in a hogshead according to Jackson. John Pemberton to James Pemberton, Feb. 11, 1790, *DHFFC*, 18: 496 for hogshead allegation and Jackson's language as "violent and abusive."

112. For variant analyses of the petition controversy, see diGiacomantonio, "'For the Gratification of a Volunteering Society,'"; Howard A. Ohline, "Slavery, Economics, and Congressional Politics, 1790," *Journal of Southern History* 46 (1980), 335–60; Richard Newman, "Prelude to the Gag Rule: Southern Reaction to Antislavery Petitions in the First Federal Congress," *Journal of the Early Republic* 16 (1996): 571–99; and Robert G. Parkinson, "'Manifest Signs of Passion': The First Federal Congress, Antislavery, and Legacies of the Revolutionary Era," in John Craig Hammond and Matthew Mason, eds., *Contesting Slavery: The Politics of Bondage and Freedom in the New American Nation* (Charlottesville: University Press of Virginia, 2011), 49–68.

113. "Memorial of the Pennsylvania Abolition Society," Feb. 3, 1790, *DHFFC*, 8:324–26. The editors of *DHFFC* provide a brief discussion and calendar of events related to the petitions in ibid., 314–21.

114. *DHFFC*, 12:295, 306 (Tucker); 296, 308 (Jackson); 300 (Burke); 303 (Jackson). Though not confirmed by John Pemberton in his detailed accounts to his brother James, South Carolina's William Loughton Smith claimed that Mifflin and his delegation "had the impudence to express a wish to be admitted within the house but were told it would not be granted" and therefore occupied the galleries. Smith to Edward Rutledge, Feb. 28, 1790, in *DHFFC*, 18:673.

115. *DHFFC*, 3: 295–96 lists the representatives' ayes and nays. *DHFFC*, 12: 312 for Madison's argument that "there were a variety of ways by which they [Congress] could countenance the abolition [of the slave trade], and they might make some regulations, respecting the introduction of [slaves] into the new states, to be formed out of the Western Territory, different from what they could in the old settled states."

116. Donald Robinson provides a keen analysis of the committee report and the debate over it in *Slavery in the Structure of American Politics, 1765–1820* (New York: Norton, 1971), 304–12.

117. Edgar S. Maclay, ed., *Journal of William Maclay: United States Senator from Pennsylvania, 1789–1791* (New York: D.A. Appleton, 1890), 196; and Adams to Thomas Crafts, May 25, 1790, Adams Papers, Massachusetts Historical Society, both quoted in Ohline, "Slavery, Economics, and Congressional Politics," 344. For Adams's long-standing resentment of Quakers, see diGiacomantonio, "'For the Gratification of a Volunteering Society,'" 178–79. While remaining in Philadelphia, James Pemberton coordinated the distribution of copies of the Pennsylvania Abolition Society petition to members of the House and Senate. See Pemberton's letters to Speaker of the House Frederick Muhlenberg and John Adams, in *DHFFC*, 8:328–29, 332.

118. John Pemberton to James Pemberton, Feb. 16, 1790, PAS Papers, for departure of seven Friends. When their carriage overturned during a violent rain storm, several barely escaped with their lives. John Pemberton to James Pemberton, Feb. 23, 1790, PAS Papers, in *DHFFC*, 18:615–16.

119. "Books sent to the Committee of the House of Representatives in Congress, Feb. 15, 1790," *DHFFC*, 8: 328; "Mem[orial] respecting Negro Affair Before the Congress at New York," Feb. 15, 1790, Pemberton Papers, HSP, in *DHFFC*, 8:327–28. The editors note the Memorial was in Mifflin's hand.

120. Ibid. Recounting this many years later, the editor of *The Friend* noted that Mifflin "was suffering under severe indisposition of body." "Relics of the Past, # 9," *The Friend* 17 (1844), 199. DiGiacomantonio, "'For the Gratification of a Volunteering Society,'" 181 notes the near uniqueness of this oral testimony by Mifflin.

121. John Pemberton to James Pemberton, Feb. 23, 1790, *DHFFC*, 18:615–16; Miers Fisher to Brissot de Warville, May 1, 1790, *DHFFC*, 19:1063–64.

122. Smith to Edward Rutledge, Feb. 28, 1790, *DHFFC*, 18:674. "Warner seldom misses their breaking up to catch opportunity as well as in visits to their apartments," reported John Pemberton as the Foster committee was completing its report. "Warner is . . . the most laborious, he is fitted for it, not easily daunted & very persevering & yet with prudence." John Pemberton to James Pemberton, March 2, 1790, *DHFFC*, 18:710–11.

123. "Warner Mifflin's Queries to the Committee," *American Museum* 8 (Aug., 1790), 61, *DHFFC*, 8:334–35; John Pemberton to James Pemberton, March 2, 1790, *DHFFC*, 18:710 for Fisher obtaining copy of Foster committee report and Mifflin's visit to the committee.

124. Mifflin to Abiel Foster, c. March 3, 1790, *American Museum* 8 (August 1790), 65, *DHFFC*, 8:331–32.

125. *DHFFC*, 8:810; John Pemberton to James Pemberton, Mar, 2, 1790, *DHFFC*, 18:711 for dinner meeting on March 1.

126. Ohline, "Slavery, Economics, and Congressional Politics," 346–47; Foster Committee report, *DHFFC*, 8:335–37.

127. John Pemberton to James Pemberton, Mar. 2, 1790, *DHFFC*. 18:710–12, quote 711.

128. *DHFFC*, 8:320–21 for details of the motions and counter-motions that led to an agreement to make the Foster report the order of the day for March 16. Newspaper reports of the fracas are in 12: 639–50.

129. Mifflin to [William Smith], Mar. 10, 1790, *DHFFC*, 18:818–22. Mifflin arranged to get the letter published five months later in Mathew Carey's Philadelphia *American Museum*, Aug. 1790. A year later, Brissot excerpted a large portion of the letter in his *New Travels*.

130. Mifflin's "Address to Members of Congress, March 16, 1790," *DHFFC*, 8:337–38. For copying and distributing it, see Mifflin to Benjamin Rush, June 19, 1790, *DHFFC*, 19:1872. It is possible the fourteen copies went to the Virginia and Maryland representatives, thought by Mifflin to be the most likely supporters.

131. Mifflin paved the way for this visit in a letter to Washington, March 12, 1790, where he referred to "the short interview we had with thee, when I a little opened the nature of our embassy." This earlier visit is not recorded in the Washington diaries. W. W. Abbot, Dorothy Twohig et al., eds., *The Papers of George Washington, Presidential Series*, vol. 5 (Charlottesville: University Press of Virginia, 1996), 222–24.

132. Washington's reply is quoted in Paul F. Boller, Jr., "George Washington and the Quakers," *Bulletin of the Friends Historical Association* 49 (1960): 78.

133. Donald Jackson, ed., *George Washington Papers, The Diaries of George Washington*, 6 vols. (Charlottesville: University of Virginia Press, 1976–79), 6: 47. Shortly after Mifflin's visit, Washington wrote a relative that "the memorial of the Quakers (and a very mal-apropos one it was) has at length been put to sleep, and will scarcely awake before the year 1808." Washington to David Stuart, March 28, 1790, in John C. Fitzpatrick, ed., *The Writings of George Washington*, 39 vols. (Washington, D.C.: Government Printing Office, 1931–1944): 31, 28–30. As explained in the next chapter, Washington underestimated the perseverance of Mifflin and his fellow emancipationists.

134. DiGiacomantonio, "'For the Gratification of a Volunteering Society,'" 183.

135. The bombastic rhetoric of Jackson, Smith, and Burke can be followed in *DHFFC*, 12:719–22, 725–34 (Jackson); 738–39, 744, 746–49 (Burke); 739–46, 749–61 (Smith).

136. *DHFFC*, 12:752.

137. *DHFFC*, 12:741, 745, 752 (Smith); 728, 733 (Jackson).

138. Ibid., March 16, 1790, 12: 731; John Pemberton recounted this attack on Mifflin in a letter to his brother, March 16, 1790, in *DHFFC*, 19:884. Mifflin had related his thunderstorm conversion to abolitionism to William L. Smith during his lobbying visit to his lodgings and in his letter to Smith of Mar. 10. The Deep South delegates gleefully retailed this account, turning Mifflin into a God-obsessed, guilt-ridden fanatic.

139. *DHFFC*, 12: 720–21, 733; Madison to Benjamin Rush, Mar. 20, 1790, *DHFFC*, 19:933.

140. "A Citizen of the Union to Mr. Greenleaf," *New York Journal*, Mar. 18, 1790, *DHFFC*, 19:913–19. Mifflin suspected the essay of more than 2,500 words had been written by Abraham Baldwin of Georgia. Only in Baldwin's home district was it printed in the South.

141. John Pemberton to James Pemberton, March 23, 1790, *DHFFC*, 19:971; diGiacomantonio, "'For the Gratification of a Volunteering Society,'" 193; final action of House in *DHFFC*, 12:844.

142. "We dare not flatter ourselves with anything more than a very gradual work," James Pemberton wrote the London Society for the Abolition of the Slave Trade, Feb. 28, 1790, PAS Letterbook, 1: 27–29, quoted in Wood, "Considerations of Humanity and Expediency" 92.

143. Chapter 5 treats how this protection of the right to petition led to Congressional action on the outfitting of slave ships.

144. James Pemberton, summarizing the debates in New York for overseas supporters, stressed how the debates "served to disseminate our principles," and that "it is generally acknowledged that the cause of humanity has been advanced by its being agitated in that public body whose powers are too restricted to do what many of the members are disposed to promote." Pemberton to Société des Amis des Noirs, Aug. 30, 1790, and Pemberton to Robert Pleasants, April 20, 1790, both quoted in Wood, "Considerations of Humanity and Expediency," 87. Wood challenges the view that the 1790s debates were a setback for the abolitionists and a clear-cut victory for southern slaveholding interests (87–103).

145. "Historicus" to the editor of *Federal Gazette*, March 23, 1790, *DHFFC*, 19:974–76. For a general treatment of the Barbary Coast pirates, see A. G. Jamieson, *Lords of the Sea: A History of the Barbary Corsairs* (London: Reaktion, 2012).

146. For Franklin's advance toward an emancipationist position, see variant analyses in David Waldstreicher, *Runaway America: Benjamin Franklin, Slavery, and the American Revolution* (New York: Hill & Wang, 2010), ch. 9; Gary B. Nash, "Franklin and Slavery," *American Philosophical Society Proceedings* 150 (2006): 620–37; and Emma J. Lapsansky-Werner, "At the End, an Abolitionist?" in Page Talbott, ed., *Benjamin Franklin in Search of a Better World* (New Haven, Conn.: Yale University Press, 2005), 273–97.

147. Emlen Family Papers, Box 1.

## Chapter 5. Finish Line

1. Warner Mifflin, *A Serious Expostulation with the Members of the House of Representatives . . .* (Philadelphia: T. Lawrence, 1793), in Justice, *Mifflin*, 191–92.

2. "These events," writes James Alexander Dun, "reverberated in America because of their capacity to provoke self-reflection . . . and raised questions about Americans' own revolutionary pasts and their current realities." Dun, *Dangerous Neighbors: Making the Haitian Revolution in Early America* (Philadelphia: University of Pennsylvania Press, 2016), 4.

3. James Bringhurst to William Almy, March 30, 1790, Bringhurst Family Papers, FHLSC.

4. Thatcher to Mifflin, June 12, 1790, responding to Mifflin's letter to the antislavery Massachusetts representative on May 4. Both in *DHFFC*, 20:1429, 1793–94.

5. Parrish to Madison, May 28, 1790; Madison to Parrish, June 6, 1790, *Papers of James Madison*, Charles F. Hobson and Robert A Rutland, eds., vol. 13 (Charlottesville: University Press of Virginia, 1981), 232–33, 240. Available online at FoundersOnline. Madison expressed surprise at the number of American bottoms involved in the African slave trade, and believed that "should the evil still go on, . . . the interposition of the General Government ought to be applied as far as constitutional."

6. "Warner Mifflin to Members of the House of Representatives," c. May 20, 1790, *DHFFC*, 19:1683–87. The quoted passages in next paragraph are from his open letter to House members.

7. Ibid.

8. Since he knew Congress was about to adjourn for the season, it is almost certain that Mifflin wrote this for public consumption. Mifflin to Henry Drinker, June 3, 1790, Vaux Papers, QCHC excerpted in "Relics of the Past, #9," *The Friend* 17 (1844): 200. The editor of *The Friend* believed Mifflin obtained the approval of the Philadelphia Meeting for Sufferings for the message in May and then sent it to two Friends in New York for distribution to those he believed were supporters, including Virginia's John Page. By early July, the debate over moving the nation's capital from New York to Philadelphia as a temporary home (until the ultimate seat on the Potomac had been prepared) showed that hard-shelled proslavery southern delegates had been unmoved. "Everyone in New-York knows the behavior of Mifflin and the other deputies from the Quakers," decried Aedanus Burke. The South Carolinian vowed he would rather "pitch my tent beneath a tree in which was a hornet's nest as I would . . . vote for placing the government in a settlement of Quakers." Getting more particular, he attacked Mifflin and his friends for hovering in the gallery during the debates over slavery and continuing "their incessant teasing and obtrusion on the members at their houses, in the streets, and in the lobby." To move to Philadelphia would only embolden Mifflin and his Quaker friends to press "the business of an emancipation in the southern states." *New-York Daily Gazette*, July 6, 1790, report on House deliberations in *DHFFC*, 13:1663.

9. Mifflin to Rush, June 19, 1790, *DHFFC*, 19:1871–72. Mifflin assured Rush that southern charges that he meant to destroy the constitutional edifice were malevolently mistaken. "I was for preserving the harmony of government," he wrote, "though I might conceive there was some rotten pillars, therein. I was not for pulling them out at once in such manner as to endanger the building." I have discussed Rush's involvement with Philadelphia's black community and the antislavery cause in *Forging Freedom: The Formation of Philadelphia's Black Community, 1720–1840* (Cambridge, Mass.: Harvard University Press, 1988), 70–71, 104–5, 123–25.

10. *American Museum* 8 (August 1790), 61–65; 8 (October 1790): 156–58. Fernando Fairfax, "Plan for Liberating the Negroes within the United States," *American Museum* 8 (December 1790): reprinted in my *Race and Revolution* (Madison, Wis.: Madison House, 1990), 146–50.

11. Mifflin to Rush, June 19, 1790, *DHFFC*, 19:1872. Trying to paint Mifflin as facilitator of runaway slaves, Arthur Bryan added to his runaway slave advertisement offering a reward for capturing Phill, who had fled Maryland's Eastern Shore four years before, referring to Phill as among others obtaining a pass from "a certain public disturber W. M. _____ 's infamous band of Runaway Pensioners." The ad was placed in the *Delaware Gazette*, Feb. 20, 1790, just as the fulminations against Mifflin and the other Quaker petitioners reached their height at the first Federal Congress.

12. First published in the Boston *Argus*, "Rights of Black Men" appeared in Philadelphia's *Federal Gazette*, Dec. 3, 7, 17, 1791; and in *American Museum* 12 (November, 1792). The quoted passage is in *Federal Gazette*, Dec. 3, 1791. On Bishop's growing reputation as an abolitionist spokesman, see David Waldstreicher and Stephen R. Grossbart, "Abraham Bishop's Vocation: or, the Mediation on Jeffersonian Politics," *Journal of the Early Republic* 18 (1988): 616–57.

13. For the swelling support for the abolition of slavery and universal freedom in public discourse of the early 1790s, see Seth Cotlar, *Tom Paine's America: The Rise and Fall of Transatlantic Radicalism in the Early Republic* (Charlottesville: University Press of Virginia, 2011), ch. 1 and 55–67. Cotlar argues that Paine's *Rights of Man*, published in May 1791, inspired much of the "rights talk."

14. Rice, *Slavery Inconsistent with Justice . . .* (Philadelphia: Parry Hall, 1792). Rice had worked among slaves for many years in Virginia; as a member of the Kentucky constitutional convention, he proposed a plan for the gradual abolition of slavery. For other expressions of support for the self-emancipation of enslaved St. Dominguans into the mid-1790s, see Dun, "Atlantic Antislavery, American Abolition: The Problem of Slavery in the United States in an Age of Disruption, 1770–1808," in Andrew Shankman, ed., *The World of the Revolutionary American Republic: Land, Labor, and the Conflict for a Continent* (New York: Routledge, 2014), 228–31 and at greater length in chapter 2 of Dun's *Dangerous Neighbors.*

15. Timothy Whelan, "William Fox, Martha Gurney, and Radical Discourse of the 1790s," *Eighteenth-Century Studies* 42 (2009): 397–411, esp. 402–3, 409n22. Whelan estimates that, going through more than twenty printings, some 250,000 copies of Fox's *Address* rolled off the presses in 1791–92. For more see Julia L. Holcomb, *Moral Commerce Quakers and the Transatlantic Boycott of the Slave Labor Economy* (Ithaca, N.Y.: Cornell University Press, 2016), 42–60.

16. J. R. Oldfield, *Transatlantic Abolitionism in the Age of Revolution: An International History of Anti-Slavery, c.1787–1820* (Cambridge: Cambridge University Press, 2013), 96; quote from Whelan, "William Fox, Martha Gurney, and Radical Discourse of the 1790s," 409n22.

17. Mifflin to Parrish, April 10, 1790, C-P-W, Box 1, f15, HSP.

18. Warner Mifflin, "To the General Assembly of the Delaware State," Jan. 18, 1791, General Assembly, Legislative Papers, RG1111, DPA; accessible on Slavery and Law Petitions Project, Petition #10379101; and (Phila.) *American Daily Advertiser*, Feb. 10, 1791.

19. Accounts of the Maryland lobbying are in WQMMM, May 23, Aug. 22, 1791, Feb. 27, 1792; report of Third Haven Monthly Meeting to Philadelphia Meeting for Sufferings, June 6, 1791, PYM-MS, Miscellaneous Papers, 1791; Mifflin to Henry Drinker, July 14, 1791, PYM-MS, Miscellaneous Papers, 1791 folder, QCHC.

20. Mifflin, "To the Citizens of the Delaware State, and more particularly to the members of the convention now sitting at Dover," Dec. 22, 1791, in Claudia L. Bushman et al., eds., *Proceedings of the Assembly of the Lower Counties on Delaware, 1770–1776, of the Constitutional Convention of 1776, and of the House of Assembly of the Delaware State, 1776–1781* (2 vols.; Newark: University of Delaware Press, 1986–98), 2:844–46.

21. Ibid., 846–53.

22. "The Memorial and Address of the Religious Society called Quakers," *The Friend*, "Relics of the Past, #9," 17 (1844), 200. The memorial also strenuously objected to the cloudy language on militia duty, which did not adequately protect Friends "who, from a conviction of religious duty, are conscientiously restrained from being active in warlike measures." Pemberton to Dickinson, June 6, 1792, R. R. Logan Collection of Dickinson Manuscripts, LCP.

23. Dickinson to James Pemberton, June 21, 1792, Simon Gratz Autograph Collection, Old Congress Collection Correspondence, Case 1, Box 5, HSP. Mifflin to Drinker, June 27, 1792 in Justice, *Mifflin*, 105–6. For the ban on slave trafficking, see *Proceedings of the House of Assembly*, 917.

24. Dickinson to Pemberton, June 6, 1792, and Dickinson to Pemberton, Oct. 22, 1792, quoted in Milton Flowers, *John Dickinson, Conservative Revolutionary* (Charlottesville: University Press of Virginia, 1983), 258; see also Jane Calvert, "An Expansive Conception of Rights: The Abolitionism of John Dickinson," in William R. Jordan, ed., *In the Course of Human Events: 1776 in America and Beyond* (Macon, Ga.: Mercer University Press, 2017).

25. Dickinson to James Pemberton, June 21, 1792, HSP.

26. Pemberton to Dickinson, Oct. 22, 1792, R. R. Logan Papers, Box 3, f3; Dickinson to Pemberton, Nov. 1, 1792, Etting Collection, Members of Congress, vol. 1, 52, HSP.

27. *Proceedings of the House,* 879, 880–82 for Dickinson's bill and its defeat. I have not found Mifflin's letter to Dickinson, but Warner described it in a letter to Henry Drinker, June 27, 1792, in Justice, *Mifflin,* 104–7. The voluminous Dickinson papers at HSP and LCP include no letter of reply to Mifflin.

28. Reflecting his ability to recapture his dream life, Mifflin wrote, "I sometimes have a hope from some sensations that have accompany'd my mind both sleeping and waking respecting thee that a measure of the favour of the Almighty was yet toward thee." Mifflin to Washington, Feb. 20, 1791, Founders Online, Mifflin to Washington, Dec. 12, 1792, note 9 where the Feb. 20, 1791, letter is given in full. Mifflin held the letter back through "diffidence," but enclosed it in his December 12, 1792, letter to Washington.

29. Quakers to President Washington and Congress, December 16, 1791. The memorial was signed by Mifflin and forty other Friends. It was printed in *National Gazette* (Philadelphia), Dec. 29, 1791, at Founders Online. *Annals of Congress,* 2nd Cong., 1st Sess., 278.

30. Quakers to the President, Senate, and House of Representatives, Nov. 17, 1792, Founders Online, founders.archives.gov/documents/Washington/05-11-02-0226, accessed June 14, 2014. The editors of the *Papers of George Washington, Presidential Series,* note that the representation was in Mifflin's hand.

31. In a letter of Dec. 4, 1792, James Pemberton wrote Moses Brown about how Mifflin floated his plan to submit a memorial to Congress, how "divers friends after deliberate consideration concurred" with this, and how a "small number of friends selected by himself to assist him" suggested small alterations. The letter is in Moses Brown Papers, RIHS.

32. Mifflin to the President, Senate, and House of Representatives of the United States, Nov. 23, 1792, *Papers of George Washington, Presidential Series,* 11:427–31, Founders Online, founders .archives.gov/documents/Washington/05/11/02/0243, accessed May 27, 2014.

33. Ibid.

34. *Annals of Congress,* 2nd Cong., 2nd Sess., 730–31; on the gag rule, see William G. diGiacomantonio, "'For the Gratification of a Volunteering Society': Antislavery and Pressure Group Politics in the First Federal Congress," *Journal of the Early Republic* 15 (1995): 196–97. In a moment of bitterness, Mifflin later wrote George Thatcher, complaining he did nothing to help. Mifflin to Thatcher, July 10, 1793, Foster Autograph Collection, Massachusetts Historical Society, Boston. Chuck diGiacomantonio brought this letter to my attention.

35. *Baltimore Evening Post,* Nov. 30, 1792; *Providence Gazette,* Dec. 22, 1792. John Carter, the *Gazette*'s editor, printed abolitionist material, often prompted by John and James Pemberton in Philadelphia and Moses Brown in Providence. See Oldfield, *Transatlantic Abolitionism in the Age of Revolution,* 56–57; and Charles Rappelye, *Sons of Providence: The Brown Brothers, the Slave Trade, and the American Revolution* (New York: Simon & Schuster, 2006), 260.

36. Mifflin to Washington, Dec. 12, 1792 *Papers of Washington, Presidential Series,* vol. 11:502–8. The site of the President's House is now the Liberty Bell Center with outside exhibits on Washington's presidency. Mifflin refers to meeting Washington in the evening, probably around November 20: "I was much pleased with the freedom thou used with us," he averred, that is, "speaking frankly about the Indian situation." Mifflin tried to placate Washington on his Indian policy, convinced by Washington's earlier discussion that he was favorably disposed to the legitimate grievances of the western Indian peoples. Mifflin hoped for peaceable negotiations, "can thou but devise means to keep in order the lawless whites."

37. Mifflin to John Parrish, Jan. 21, 1793, C-P-W, Box 1, f17. "I have patched up something to send up . . . after I got my thoughts on paper," he wrote Parrish, asking his kinsman to share the still uncompleted draft with James and John Pemberton, Nicholas Waln, and John and Henry Drinker. He was willing to incorporate their revisions but content to have it published with or without them. Mifflin admitted that "I did feel much oppressed when I left the city more than I can tell thee, and that on account of some others besides Congressmen." This probably referred to Friends who believed pushing Congress again was hopeless.

38. Dated January 21, 1793, *Serious Expostulation* was published in Philadelphia within a week or so by Daniel Lawrence, a Quaker printer of abolitionist material, including Benjamin Banneker's famous letter to Thomas Jefferson. Lawrence moved the next year to Dutchess County, New York, and may have arranged to have *Serious Expostulation* printed there. Appended to the Poughkeepsie edition was Mifflin's four-page Memorial to the President and Congress of November 23, 1792. Dunlap's (Phila.) *American Daily Advertiser* reprinted *Serious Expostulation* on Feb. 19, 1793, giving it a much wider audience.

39. For convenience, the page numbers for quoted material in this and the next paragraph are in the Hilda Justice reprinting of *Serious Expostulation*. Justice, *Mifflin*, 190–93.

40. The interstate conflict between Virginia and Pennsylvania that forced the issue involved a free black man who had been seized in Pennsylvania and carried back to Virginia, where his former master claimed legal ownership. Warner's second cousin, Thomas Mifflin, was Pennsylvania's governor at the time; acting at the behest of the Pennsylvania Abolition Society, he had asked for extradition of the three alleged kidnappers and restoration of the kidnapped man to freedom. See Don E. Fehrenbacher, *The Slaveholding Republic: An Account of the United States Government's Relations to Slavery* (New York: Oxford University Press, 2001), 209–13.

41. In *Dangerous Neighbors*, ch. 3, "The Negrophile Republic: Emancipation and Revolution," Dun explores in detail how these events, all following Mifflin's *Expostulation* by a few months, raised the prospect of a surging global crusade for universal freedom, while at the same time raising the specter of the French Revolution careening out of control.

42. PYM-MME, Sept. 21, 1793, for names of those present and absent from each quarter. Mifflin was one of only three of the eleven appointed by the Southern Quarterly Meeting to attend. In a long account of the devastating epidemic, James Pemberton tallied the sixty delegates who dared to come and detailed the deaths of a number of elders and ministers. Pemberton to Moses Brown, Dec. 4, 1793, Moses Brown Papers, RIHS. The history of the 1793 yellow fever epidemic is very large. For an incisive recent account, see Billy G. Smith, *Ship of Death: A Voyage That Changed the Atlantic World* (New Haven, Conn.: Yale University Press, 2013).

43. From August 1 to the end of the year, 385 Friends were buried, and probably more than one hundred others carrying the fever home were buried in their local burying grounds. The numbers are from the mortality bills published in Mathew Carey, *A Short Account of the Malignant Fever. . .* (Philadelphia: M. Carey, 1793).

44. Mifflin to Parrish, Jan. 24, 1794, C-P-W, Box 1, f17. Mifflin penned his letter to Parrish on the day the pamphlet by Allen and Jones was published. The copyright was issued and was the first for a black publication.

45. American Convention, Minutes and Committee reports, Jan. 1–7, 1794, in PAS Papers, Microfilm edition, Reel 28; the memorial is in *The American Convention for Promoting the Abolition of Slavery and Improving the Condition of the African Race: Minutes, Constitution, Addresses, Memorials, Resolutions, Reports, Committees and Anti-Slavery Tracts*, 3 vols. (New York: Bergman, 1969), 1. Mary Locke, *Anti-Slavery in America* (Boston: Ginn & Co., 1901), 101–9, 199–201, provides an

overview of the American Convention. Also see Richard S. Newman, *The Transformation of American Abolitionism* (Chapel Hill: University of North Carolina Press, 2002), 19–20, 33–34.

46. Mifflin to Moses Brown, Jan. 24, 1794, Moses Brown Papers, RIHS. Mifflin vowed to stay the course—"to travel on through good report and bad report, neither to err to the right hand nor the left, to do all my duty and no more."

47. *Annals of Congress*, 3rd Cong, 1st Sess., 36, 38–39, 64, 72, 249, 253, 455, 469, 483, Appendix, 1425; Fehrenbacher, *Slaveholding Republic*, 140–41. The Pennsylvania Abolition Society and other bodies prosecuted a Rhode Island merchant the next year and many others in the years that followed. Nonetheless, Rhode Island slave trade merchants frequently eluded the law, even after Congress, six years later, stiffened the penalties and authorized the U.S. Navy to seize slave ships as prizes. Under the obliging eye of Jefferson's appointee as customs officer for Bristol, who had grown up in the slave trade, the Rhode Island slave trade reached illegal heights by 1805, with about fifty slave ships sailing for Africa. See Rappleye, *Sons of Providence*, 336–38. For a corrective to historians' inattention to the Foreign Slave Trade Act, see Nicholas Perry Wood, "Considerations of Humanity and Expediency: The Slave Trades and African Colonization in the Early National Antislavery Movement," Ph.D. diss., University of Virginia, 2013, 108–16.

48. Ann Emlen to Susanna Mifflin, Aug. 4, 1788, Mifflin Letters, DPA. Mike McDowell brought this letter to my attention. Lisa Wilson's *A History of Stepfamilies in Early America* (Chapel Hill: University of North Carolina Press, 2014) provides insights into "The Wicked 'Stepmother'" (ch. 3) and "Through the Eyes of a Stepchild" (ch. 4).

49. Mifflin to John Parrish, Oct. 10, 1791 C-P-W, Box 1, f16. Two years later, in December 1793, Mifflin again wrote Parrish that he was not well—"I am but weakened," Dec. 2, 1793, C-P-W, Box 1, f17.

50. "Notes on Religion," Emlen Family Papers, Box 1. There are many other verses.

51. Mifflin to Henry Drinker, Aug. 6, 1792, Charles Evans Papers, 1681–1860, Box 2, QCHC. Ann, second oldest of Mifflin's living daughters, was married in May 1795 to Warner Raisin, a Maryland Eastern Shore Quaker.

52. Mifflin to Susanna Mifflin, Nov. 2, 1794, Cowgill-Mifflin Letters, DPA. Mike McDowell provided this letter. It is apparent from Mifflin's affectionate letter to his daughter that the decision was not hers. "I think it no disparagement to any girl to do this," he wrote, "but to their credit so that by this, while thou art getting thy school learning thou may be improving as to the management of a family, and I do think it a benefit for a person to be brought up to business."

53. Will of Daniel Mifflin, in Justice, *Mifflin*, 218–22.

54. The census of 1800 showed five free blacks at Chestnut Grove.

55. Mifflin to John Parrish, undated but probably 1783, C-P-W, Box 1, f16.

56. Mifflin to Parrish, Oct. 10, 1791, C-P-W, Box 1, f17.

57. Georgia's James Jackson claimed that Mifflin "made his boasts" to this. *DHFFC*, 12:733.

58. Brooke Hunter, "Creative Destruction: The Forgotten Legacy of the Hessian Fly," in Cathy Matson, ed., *The Economy of Early America: Historical Perspectives and New Directions* (University Park: Pennsylvania State University Press, 2006), 236–62. Hunter analyzes the havoc visited on the wheat fields of Benjamin Chew, a few miles north of Warner Mifflin's properties. By the time mid-Atlantic wheat producers had learned to manage "an environmental and commercial crisis," Mifflin was in his grave (253–56, 261–62). To my knowledge, nobody has measured how the

Hessian fly infestation affected the livelihoods of the free black smallholders recently released from slavery, but surely they suffered as well.

59. *KCDLR, 1785–1789*, 9–10, 68–69, 99. Even after disposing of these properties, Mifflin remained one of Kent County's largest landowners. Levy lists of 1798 at Delaware Public Archives show property in four locations totaling 3,208 acres.

60. Worcester County Deed Book Liber N, folio 254–57, in Justice, *Mifflin*, 214–17; Indenture of October 1791 for leasing lots owned by Ann Emlen Mifflin in Philadelphia and Darby, Emlen Family Papers, Box 2.

61. David W. Maxey, "Samuel Hopkins, the Holder of the First U.S. Patent: A Study in Failure," *PMHB* 122 (1998), 3–37 tells the full story of Hopkins's debacle as a potash manufacturer and his chastisement from the Philadelphia Yearly Meeting. Hopkins was the grandson of Margaret Johns and thus a distant relation to Mifflin's first wife. Living a stone's throw from Drinker's Front Street house and an active Quaker heavily involved in yearly meeting affairs until 1789, he was almost certainly well known to Mifflin.

62. Drinker was appalled that Mifflin rashly signed a contractual agreement with Hopkins in 1797, warning that the crafty Quaker was so poorly circumstanced "as to forbid an expectation of restitution" of Mifflin's investment. Drinker to Mifflin, Nov. 15, 1797, Henry Drinker Letterbook, 1796–1800, Drinker Papers, HSP; Samuel Hopkins to Mifflin, July 29, 1798; Mifflin to Drinker June 16, 1798; and Mifflin to Drinker and Ann Mifflin to Henry Drinker, June 26, 1798, Vaux Collection, QCHC. Mifflin's letters to Hopkins have not been found, but his distress is echoed in his letters to Drinker.

63. *Defence Against Aspersions*, 27; Mifflin to William L. Smith, March 10, 1790, *DHFFC*, 18:818–22. Mifflin sent a copy of his letter to Smith to Benjamin Rush, who probably arranged to have it published in *American Museum* (August 1790); *DHFFC*, 18:822 editorial note; Brissot included an excerpt of the letter to Smith in his *New Travels*, 245.

64. Mifflin to Parrish, April 10, 1790, C-P-W, Box 1, f15; Mifflin to Henry Drinker? June 15, 1790, "Relics of the Past #9," *The Friend*, 17 (1844), 200; Mifflin to Parrish, Oct. 10, 1791, C-P-W, Box 1, f16.

65. Miffin to Henry Drinker, July 14, 1791, PYM-MS, Miscellaneous Papers, 1791, QCHC. In common law, "next friend" was a person representing someone unable to bring a suit on his or her own behalf.

66. Mifflin to Parrish, May 6, 1792, C-P-W, Box 1, f16. By the end of the year, James Pemberton confirmed Mifflin's view, telling Moses Brown that "the continuance of the affliction of the poor blacks in two adjacent states, Delaware and the eastern part of Maryland, is very great, and attended with the enormous cruelties of African slave traders, and our men in power remain deaf to all entreaties to redress their grievances." Pemberton to Brown, Dec. 4, 1793, Moses Brown Papers, RIHS.

67. *Delaware and Eastern Shore Advertiser*, Sept. 17, 1794. The group included one woman, age nineteen; five young males; a man age fifty; and two others with gender and age unspecified.

68. *Address of Abraham Johnstone, A Black Man, Who was Hanged at Woodbury in the ... State of New Jersey ...* (Philadelphia: n.p., 1797). The case and the pamphlet are discussed at length in Jeannine Marie DeLombard, *In the Shadow of the Gallows: Race, Crime, and American Civic Identity* (Philadelphia: University of Pennsylvania Press, 2012), ch. 3, "The Ignominious Cord: Crime, Counterfactuals, and the New Black Politics."

69. Mifflin to Parrish, May 6, 1792, C-P-W, Box 1, f16. I have not been able to track the Maryland and Virginia cases in the courts; in the case tried in Kent County, where he was charged with "harbouring and concealing a Negro who ran in consequence of his expecting to be carry'd off," the claimant had to pay all the costs of the suit.

70. Mifflin to Henry Drinker, Aug. 6, 1792, Charles Evans Papers, QCHC; Mifflin to Moses Brown, June 15, 1793, Moses Brown Papers, RIHS.

71. Mifflin to Drinker, Nov. 12, 1794, Henry Drinker Correspondence, FHLSC; Mifflin to Drinker, Dec. 14, 1794, *The Friend* 17 (1794): 230.

72. Mifflin to Drinker, Dec. 20, 1795, Henry Drinker Correspondence, FHLSC.

73. Race and Slavery Petitions Project, Petition #20379405. For other cases brought by Mifflin before the Court of Common Pleas in Dover see Petition #20379104, 20379511, and #20379409, the later two involving Anteaguea Handy, illegally held as a slave by Peggy Handy, a white woman; and Amy, a free woman seized and "transported as a slave into the most Algerine parts of this Continent."

74. *Drinker Diary*, Dec. 6, 1794 (1:624); April 28, 1795 (1:674).

75. Mifflin to Henry Drinker, Nov. 12, 1794, Henry Drinker Correspondence, 1760–1806, FHLSC; Mifflin to Drinker, Jan. 21, 1795, Vaux Papers, QCHC for three blacks needing opportunities in Philadelphia, including a twelve-year-old girl, well read in the Bible, whose father "wants her further improved in learning and to be brought up to work." Elizabeth Drinker noted in her diary many other placements of young free blacks in Philadelphia through Mifflin's conduit: *Drinker Diary*, Dec. 6, 1794 (1:624); March 29, 1795 (1:651); Jan. 2, 1798 (2:993); Feb. 23, 1798 (2:1014–15); April 2, 1798 (2:1018).

76. SQMM, in PYM-MME, March 1, 1791. She was often reappointed to this important office; ibid., Aug. 24, 1794.

77. "Epistle from Philena Lay and Anne Mifflin to Friends of New Garden Monthly Meeting, [July] 1791," Miscellaneous Papers, FHLSC. Philena Lay's devotional life is recounted in "Testimony of Murtherkill Monthly Meeting concerning Philena Lay," in *Memorials to Deceased Friends: Being a Selection from the Records of the Yearly Meeting for Pennsylvania from 1788 to 1819*, 3rd ed. (Philadelphia: Joseph Rakestraw, 1850), 72–75.

78. For Ann's visits to the home of Elizabeth and Henry Drinker, *Drinker Diary*, Oct. 4, 1795 (1:737), March 27, 1796 (2:803), May 17, 1796 (2:808), April 5, 1797 (2:904). Mifflin to Moses Brown, Jan. 24, 1794, Moses Brown Papers, RIHS for Mifflin's account from Brandywine on the way home about his and Ann's meeting with Brown; Mifflin to Henry Drinker, Dec. 30, 1795, Henry Drinker Correspondence, 1760–1806, FHLSC for the Annapolis trip.

79. For numerous examples from New England to the Carolinas that Quakers organized and promoted separate meetings of black worshipers, see Henry J. Cadbury, "Negro Membership in the Society of Friends," *Journal of Negro History* 21 (1936): 156–60. However, since the 1750s blacks had attended "first day" worship in many meetinghouses, including Philadelphia's Great Meetinghouse at Second and High Streets and the Bank Street Meetinghouse (167–69).

80. Emlen to Hannah Townsend, Oct. 4, 1783, quoted in Cadbury, "Negro Membership," 172; the woman was half white, one-eighth black, and three-eighths Indian.

81. Pemberton to Phillips, Nov. 18, 1794, Gilder Lehrman Collection #GLC04237.

82. *Drinker Diary*, Oct. 4, 1795 (1:737) for the Mifflins' attendance. Joseph Drinker's memorandum, January 1795, is quoted in Cadbury, "Negro Membership," 172, printed in its entirety in Thomas E. Drake, "Joseph Drinker's Plea for the Admission of Colored People to the Society of Friends, 1795," *Journal of Negro History* 32 (1947), 110–12.

83. Committee report in Pemberton Papers, 55/42, cited in Cadbury, "Negro Membership," 174n72. Cadbury, 172–76, provides details on the case as it made its way from the preparative meeting through the monthly and quarterly meetings and finally to the Philadelphia Yearly Meeting, where the final decision was made in September 1796.

84. John Hunt Journal, *Proceedings of the New Jersey Historical Society* 53 (1935): 208–9. In its first printed "Discipline," the Philadelphia Yearly Meeting affirmed and emphasized the historic decision. Cadbury, "Negro Membership," 176.

85. *Memoir of the Life, Travels, and Religious Experiences of Martha Routh* (London: W. Alexander and Son, 1822), 180.

86. Kenneth Carroll, *Joseph Nichols and the Nicholites: A Look at the "New Quakers" of Maryland, Delaware, North and South Carolina* (Easton, Md.: Easton Publishing, 1962); and "Another Look at the Nicholites," *Southern Friend* 5 (1983), 3–26. Mifflin's good friend, Joshua Evans, provided comments on the Nicholites in his 1797 tour of the South. *Friends Miscellany, Containing Journals of the Lives, Religious Exercises, and Labours in the Work of the Ministry of Joshua Evans and John Hunt, Friends Miscellany*, 10 (Philadelphia: John and Isaac Comly, 1837), 165–72, 193–97. For the ban against flowers, see a pre-Civil War account of the Nicholites and their merger with the Society of Friends in "Relics of the Past, 17," *The Friend* 17 (1844), 268–69.

87. SQMM, 1759–1822, 59–64.

88. Ira Berlin, *Slaves Without Masters: The Free Negro in the Antebellum South* (New York: New Press, 1974), 81–83; laws holding whites assisting blacks in freedom suits subject to court costs affected Mifflin and other emancipationists. Berlin avers that the small abolition society in Maryland "never recovered from the shock of legislative censure and new repressive legislation."

89. Essah, *A House Divided*, 59–60; William H. Williams, *Slavery and Freedom in Delaware, 1639–1865* (Wilmington, Del.: Scholarly Resources, 1996), 126–27. By the 1790s, Methodism was the dominant church in Kent County, attracting by far the most numerous black worshipers.

90. Jefferson to St. George Tucker, Aug. 28, 1797, Founders Online. For detailed analysis of the Philadelphia press see Dun, *Dangerous Neighbors*.

91. Mifflin to John Parrish, Oct. 10, 1791, C-P-W, Box 1, folder 5.

92. Mifflin to Henry Drinker, Dec. 30, 1795, Henry Drinker Correspondence, 1760–1806, FHLSC; Locke, *Anti-Slavery in America*, 121. The sharp increase in free blacks between 1790 and 1800, greater than in Virginia and even Delaware, suggest the effect of the new manumission law. See Table 2 in Berlin, *Slaves Without Masters*, 46.

93. The operative clause is given in *Journal of the Senate of the State of Delaware* (Wilmington, Del.: Samuel and John Adams, 1796), 54. This was a more generous version of Pennsylvania's gradual abolition act, which held children born after its passage, both female and male, to 28 years of servitude.

94. *Journal of the House of Representatives*, 46, 65, 69, 108–11; *Journal of the Senate*, 31, 40, 47, 53–55, 63, 65, 77.

95. Mifflin to Parrish, Feb. 13, 1796, C-P-W, Box 1, f21.

96. Essah, *A House Divided*, 122, points out that in the early nineteenth century the Delaware courts, "on a case-by-case basis," allowed free blacks to testify against accused kidnappers. Other cases of such kidnapping "in the neighborhood of Camden (the new name for Mifflin's Crossroads)" were recorded in "Statement of a few Cases of Kidnapping free Negroes . . . ," 1801, C-P-W, Box 10. Mifflin detailed one case of a Kent County plantation owner living seven miles from him who was prosecuted for carrying three free black children out of state to be sold to a Carolina slave trader. Several hundred people waited outside the courthouse until ten at night to hear the jury's

verdict of guilty. Mifflin to Parrish and Thomas Stewardson, Dec. 3, 1797, C-P-W, Box 1, f23. Slaveholders such as Kent County's Thomas Rodney deplored the "savage, barbarous, and cruel law that would have disgraced even the reign of Nero" and lambasted Quakers who "have been seen prosecuting to conviction under that law and have [been] seen viewing the whipping, pillowering [pillorying] and cropping of the criminals with all that anxious and malignant satisfaction which a tyrant feels at the execution of those they order to destruction, and all for only conveying Negroes out of one state and into another." Rodney Diary, Dec. 8, 1797, DHS.

97. I have discussed Tucker's *Dissertation on Slavery* in *Race and Revolution*, 43–47. Not until after Mifflin was in his grave did the Delaware legislature again debate a gradual abolition bill. Essah, *A House Divided*, 154–61 for eleven legislative debates on a gradual abolition between 1803 and 1849, lacking only one vote for passage on several occasions. Nor would Delaware ratify the Thirteenth Amendment abolishing slavery in the United States, earning the dubious distinction of becoming the first nonseceding state to reject ratification. Kentucky and New Jersey also rejected ratification. In 1901, the Delaware legislature unanimously ratified the Thirteenth, Fourteenth, and Fifteenth Amendments.

98. Mifflin to Moses Brown, Philadelphia, March 26, 1796, Moses Brown Papers, RIHS; Wood, "Considerations of Humanity and Expediency," 130–33; David Lightner, "The Founders and the Interstate Slave Trade," *Journal of the Early Republic* 22 (2002): 35–51; Donald Robinson, *Slavery in the Structure of American Politics* (New York: Norton, 1994), 286–88; Carol Wilson, *Freedom at Risk: The Kidnapping of Free Blacks, 1780–1865* (Lexington: University Press of Kentucky, 1994), 68–69. For introduction of the petition and referral to committee, see *Annals of Congress*, 4th Cong., 1st Sess., 1025, 1299–1300.

99. *Defence Against Aspersions* came off the press of Samuel Sansom in November 1796. Philadelphia Quaker leaders with whom Sansom was connected may have facilitated the printing and distribution of the pamphlet. Mifflin probably arranged this when he was in Philadelphia for the yearly meeting in September.

100. *Defence Against Aspersions*, 23–25 for the quotations in this and next two paragraphs. About 130 American sailors had been captured by Algerine pirates by this time; a recent treatment is Lawrence A. Peskin, *Captives and Countrymen: Slavery and the American Public, 1785–1816* (Baltimore: Johns Hopkins University Press, 2009).

101. Mifflin's use of the Algerine parallel was obviously inspired by Franklin's final philippic against slavery six years before.

102. *Annals of Congress*, 4th Cong., 2nd Sess., 1692, 1730–37, 1740–41, 1895–96 (Jan. 18, 1797).

103. The blacks' petition is in *Annals of Congress*, 4th Cong., 2nd Sess., 2015–18. It is reprinted in Nash, *Race and Revolution*, 185–89; and Michael J. Crawford, *The Having of Negroes Is Become a Burden: The Quaker Struggle to Free Slaves in Revolutionary North Carolina* (Gainesville: University Press of Florida, 2010), 143–48. The fifth refugee, freed by a Quaker master, had lived free for eleven years, had a wife and four children, and committed suicide after a North Carolinian planter, reenslaving him, placed a bounty on his head, offering $10 in silver for his return and $50 silver with proof he had been killed. In "A 'Class of Citizens': The Earliest Black Petitioners to Congress and Their Quaker Allies," *WMQ* 74 (2017), Nicholas P. Wood shows the "interstate and interracial collaboration and political boldness" of the petition placed before Congress and excavates new evidence documenting the crucial role of John Parrish and the Philadelphia Meeting for Sufferings in working with Absalom Jones and other Philadelphia black leaders to generate the petition.

104. Robinson, *Slavery in American Politics*, 288–90; Michael J. Crawford, *The Having of Negroes*, Part 3 for the background; Part 4 for the petitions and parts of the Congressional debates. The debate and vote can be followed in *Annals of Congress*, 4th Cong., 2nd Sess., 1895–96, 2015–24. Philadelphia's *American Universal Magazine* put the petition before the public on Feb. 6, 1797.

105. Richard Folwell, *Short History of the Yellow Fever that Broke Out in the City of Philadelphia in July 1797 with a List of the Dead*... (Philadelphia: Richard Folwell, 1797); *Drinker Diary*, Sept. 16–26 (2:964–67). Drinker believed that by early September more Philadelphians had succumbed to the disease than in the 1793 holocaust. Suggestions that the yearly meeting should meet across the Delaware River in Burlington, New Jersey, were dismissed, so the Friends, defying the gruesome disease, went forward with their meeting. John Hunt noted in his diary that the meeting "was but about one quarter as large as usual on account of the pestilential fever then prevailing, of which by accounts from 15 to 20 have died a day latterly. But this day they say 28, and it is said more than one half, some say 3 fourths, of the people of the city are removed into the country." Hunt Diary, Sept. 23, 1797.

106. Justice, *Mifflin*, 198–202 for charge to the committee and "The Memorial and Address of the People called Quakers...," Sept. 29, 1797. A copy is in PYM-MS, Miscellaneous Manuscripts, QCHC. Most of the committee members were longtime friends of Mifflin—Nicholas Waln, Jacob Lindley, George Churchman, John Parrish, and Henry Drinker, for example.

107. Mifflin and John Parrish, his constant companion, were on both the yearly meeting committee that presented the petition to Congress and the Meeting for Sufferings committee that oversaw its progress. PYMM, Sept. 28, 1797 and Dec. 15, 1797. Nicholas Wood provided this information, which is fully covered in "'A Class of Citizens'."

108. Crawford, *Having of Negroes*, 162–81 for part of the Congressional debates from *Annals of Congress*. For additional debate see *Annals of Congress*, 5th Cong, 2nd Sess., 1306, quotation from *Annals*, 659. As part of their continuing effort to rally public support, Philadelphia Yearly Meeting distributed five hundred copies of their *Memorial and Address* (Philadelphia: J. Crukshank, 1798).

109. In June 1798, John Parrish wrote that "Ann Mifflin has a certificate of Friends' full concurrence in joining Mary Berry, on the like occasion of a concern to visit the West Indies." Parrish to Phoebe Speakman, June 16, 1798, *Friends Miscellany* 6 (1835): 262. For the dissolution of the once thriving Quakers in Barbados and Parrish's involvement in settling the meetinghouse properties, see C. Dickinson Sturge, "Friends in Barbados," *Journal of the Friends Historical Society* 5 (1908): 43–46; and Larry Gragg, *The Quaker Community on Barbados* (Columbia: University of Missouri Press, 2009).

110. Mary Berry, married to James Berry, an ardent antislavery leader in Talbot County, Maryland, was a close friend of Warner and Ann. At one of her visits to Murderkill meeting in 1790, she was described by Job Scott as "lift[ing] up her voice like one of the sweetest singers of Israel" and "as much set on things from above, as anyone I ever saw without exception and she shines accordingly." Quoted in Kenneth Carroll, *Quakerism on the Eastern Shore* (Baltimore: Maryland Historical Society, 1970), 156.

111. Sarah Crabtree, *Holy Nation: The Transatlantic Quaker Ministry in an Age of Revolution* (Chicago: University of Chicago Press, 2015), ch. 2 on "Lamb-Like Warriors: The Quakers' Church Militant." After Ann presented travel certificate endorsements from her monthly and quarterly meetings to the Ministers and Elders, they authorized her trip to the island. Nicholas Waln to "Friend in Baltimore," March 28, 1798, *Friends Miscellany* 5 (1834), 141. Waln spoke of Mary Berry's "advanced age and infirmities."

112. Mifflin to Drinker, April 1, 1798, Vaux Family Papers, QCHC. Warner and Ann communed at the Drinker house on March 25 and 28 and April 2. *Drinker Diary*, II:1016–18.

113. Mifflin to Drinker, May 4, 1798; June 16, 1798; June 26, 1798, Vaux Family Papers, QCHC.

114. Mifflin to "dear Children," July 7, 1798, Cowgill-Mifflin Letters, DPA; Mike McDowell provided this letter.

115. Mifflin to Henry Drinker [c. late July], 1798, Drinker Papers, QCHC.

116. Benjamin Rush, *Account of the Yellow Fever Epidemic of 1798* (Philadelphia: Thomas Dobson, 1798); Thomas Condie and Richard Folwell, *History of the Pestilence Commonly Called Yellow Fever, Which Almost Desolated Philadelphia in the Months of August, September & October 1798* (Philadelphia: R. Folwell, 1799).

117. Ibid., 9, 79; about one-third of those who remained paid with their lives.

118. John Hunt Diary, Sept. 23, Sept. 30, Oct. 8, 1798, FHLSC.

119. Jones to Leonard Snowden, Sept. 21; same to same, Sept. 29, 1798, Rebecca Jones Letterbook, QCHC.

120. Will of Warner Mifflin, Justice, *Mifflin*, 223–28, quote 223.

121. Leonard Snowden to Rebecca Jones, Oct. 21, 1798, Rebecca Jones Letter Book, QCHC. Snowden sent a series of reports on the situation in Philadelphia to Jones through the late summer and early fall of 1798.

122. Noted in the death notice of Mifflin in *Baltimore Daily Advertiser*, Oct. 24, 1798.

123. Mifflin to John Adams, Sept. 24, 1798, Adams Papers, MHS; available at FoundersOnline. As detailed in Chapter 6, Mifflin carried his letter to Adams home with him, later to be delivered to Adams. For the debate in Congress on the Mississippi Territory, opposed by George Thatcher and eleven other northern Congressmen, see Robinson, *Slavery in the Structure of American Politics*, 387–92; George van Cleve, *A Slaveholders' Union: Slavery, Politics, and the Constitution in the Early American Republic* (Chicago: University of Chicago Press, 2010), 213–14; and Adam Rothman, *Slave Country: American Expansion and the Origins of the Deep South* (Cambridge, Mass.: Harvard University Press, 2005), 24–26. It was cold comfort for abolitionists that the legislation forbade the importing of slaves from abroad, because the internal slave trade was an assured source of slaves for the new cotton fields, while the ban on smuggling of slaves from Africa and the West Indies went unenforced.

124. One report said that after taking off the coat he had worn in the city, he donned it again after several days at Chestnut Grove, and in this way the infection inhabited his body on about October 10. *Drinker Diary*, Oct. 29, 1798 (2:1103). George Churchman and Jacob Lindley to John Adams, Jan. 17, 1801, Adams Papers, Massachusetts Historical Society, describes how Mifflin lasted six days after the yellow fever infection made its appearance.

125. "Memoir of James Emlen, late of Delaware and Pennsylvania," *The Friend: A Religious and Literary Journal* 54 (1881): 161–62.

126. "A Brief Account of the late Warner Mifflin, Signed by A. Mifflin Kent 10 mo 25th 1799," Emlen Family Papers, Box 1, HSP. Ann wrote this account for her sons to be read when they grew up; she appended "A Testimony of Mother Kiln Monthly Meeting concerning Warner Mifflin deceased."

127. Thomas Rodney Diary, Oct. 17, 1798, DHS. Mike McDowell provided a transcription of the diary entries. There were still about 1,500 enslaved blacks in Kent County, though the number was dropping rapidly, falling to 728 in 1810.

128. All early grave sites in the Murderkill Meeting cemetery, just north of present-day Magnolia, were marked with plain stones barren of names or dates. The cenotaph commemorating Mifflin's life, erected in 2005, is at the approximate site of his burial.

129. Nathaniel Luff, *Journal of the Life of Nathaniel Luff, M.D. of the State of Delaware* (New York: Clark & Sickels, 1848), 91–92.

130. The federal census of 1800, taken less than two years after Mifflin's death, showed that only a quarter of Kent County's blacks were still enslaved, compared to 40 percent in New Castle County and 69 percent in Sussex County. In New York and New Jersey, two-thirds of black people were still enslaved (see Appendix 2).

131. Ann Mifflin, "Short Account," Emlen Family Papers, Box 1.

Chapter 6. Mifflin's Long Shadow

1. Nicholas Perry Wood, "Considerations of Humanity and Expediency: The Slave Trades and African Colonization in the Early National Antislavery Movement," Ph.D. dissertation, University of Virginia, 2013. Wood's arguments and extensive documentation for antislavery activism in the early republic provide a major corrective for standard accounts.

2. In her comprehensive history of American abolitionism, Manisha Sinha in *The Slave's Cause: A History of Abolition* (New Haven, Conn.: Yale University Press, 2016), agrees that "Contrary to conventional wisdom, the abolition movement persisted and broadened its reach in the early Republic" (105), but she only begins to explore the terrain, which is better covered in Wood's "Considerations of Humanity and Expediency." Patrick Rael, *Eighty-Eight Years: The Long Death of Slavery in the United States, 1777–1865* (Athens: University of Georgia Press, 2015) gives slight attention to antislavery in the 1790s and opening years of the new century.

3. Thomas Rodney Diary, Oct. 17, 1798, Brown Collection, DHS. Five years after Mifflin's death, Jefferson appointed Rodney as a justice and land commissioner of the Mississippi Territory. He died in Natchez, owner of many slaves, some of them Delaware-born. William Baskerville Hamilton, Rodney's biographer, describes him as "a toothless old failure living on romantic and mystic dreams, rescued from the grave by an unusual, and temporary, access to patronage by the Democratic-Republican party in Delaware." *Thomas Rodney: Revolutionary and Builder of the West* (Durham, N.C.: Duke University Press, 1953), vii.

4. Cobbett, *A Bone to Gnaw for Democrats* (Philadelphia: Thomas Bradford, 1795), 36–37. In the fourth edition of *Bone to Gnaw* (Philadelphia: Thomas Bradford, 1796), 36–37, Cobbett added to his attacks on Mifflin and Brissot.

5. This was in response to John Parrish's letter to Cobbett, Nov. 17, 1798, which referred to Warner Mifflin, Daniel Mifflin, and Jonathan Hunn calling attention to an imposter, Henry Penn Wharton, in *Porcupine's Works Containing Various Writings and Selections by William Cobbett* (London, 1801), 10: 33–35, a selection from *Porcupine's Gazette*, Nov. 1798–June 1799.

6. Carey, *Plumb Pudding for the Humane, Chaste, Valiant, Enlightened Peter Porcupine* (Philadelphia: M. Carey, 1799), dated Dec. 22, 1798.

7. Cobbett, "Slave Trade," March 9, 1805, *Political Register* 7–8, 64–66., in Richard Ingrams, *The Life and Adventures of William Cobbett* (New York: HarperCollins, 2005), 2. It is unclear why Cobbett attacked Benezet and Mifflin, though his targets were so diverse—Paine, Rush,

McKean, and many others—that one presumes his acidic flourishes were meant to sell newspapers.

8. *Gazette of the United States,* Oct. 23, 1798; *Claypoole's Advertiser,* Oct. 23, 1798; copied from *Philadelphia Gazette and Universal Daily Advertiser,* Oct. 22, 1798, and again in *Federal Gazette and Baltimore Daily Advertiser,* Oct. 24, 1798; *Porcupine's Gazette,* Oct. 23, 1798; *Deutsche Porcupein,* Oct. 31, 1798; *Providence Gazette,* Nov. 3, 1798.

9. Allen had grown up in slavery about ten miles north of Chestnut Grove, and it is probable the two men met in Philadelphia, where Allen was closely connected with Quaker leaders after moving there in 1778 to begin his ascent as a leader of the black community. Quotes from Allen are in *Articles of Association of the African Episcopal Church of the City of Philadelphia . . .* (Philadelphia: John Ormrod, 1799), 17. Richard Newman, *Freedom's Prophet: Bishop Richard Allen, the A.M.E. Church, and the Black Founding Fathers* (New York: New York University Press, 2008), 142–44 for Allen's connections with Mifflin.

10. Snowden to Rebecca Jones, Oct. 21, 1798, Rebecca Jones Letter Book, QCHC.

11. "Testimony concerning Warner Mifflin, by his intimate friend and survivor, George Churchman," *Friends Miscellany* 2 (Philadelphia, 1832): 328–33. The eulogy was probably written for one of the monthly meetings where Mifflin was involved.

12. "A Testimony of Murtherkill Monthly Meeting concerning Warner Mifflin, deceased," QCHC.

13. Broadside at HSP; the story appeared in the *New York Mercantile Advertiser,* Dec. 8, 1798; *Federal Gazette and Baltimore Daily Advertiser,* Dec. 8, 1798; [New Bedford, Mass.] *Columbia Courier,* Nov. 21, 1800; *Alexandria* [Va.] *Advertiser and Commercial Intelligencer,* Dec. 11, 1800; *Trenton Federalist and New Jersey State Gazette,* Dec. 23, 1800; [Peacham, Vt.] *Green Mountain Patriot,* Jan. 15, 1801, [Hudson, N.Y.] *The Bee,* Aug. 17, 1802; and other seaboard newspapers.

14. First published in London, Wanostrocht's primer went through dozens of printings, including ones in Boston in 1805, Baltimore in 1810 and 1813, and Philadelphia in 1813; it was reprinted into the 1850s. Madame de la Fite's *Questions to be Resolved* was published in London in 1791.

15. Coleridge called Clarkson "the moral steam-engine, or the Giant with one idea." Quoted in Ellen Gibson Wilson, *Thomas Clarkson: A Biography* (London: Macmillan, 1989), 1.

16. Clarkson, *The History, Rise, Progress & Accomplishment of the Abolition of the African Slave Trade, of the British Parliament,* 2 vols. (London, 1808). I have used the Philadelphia reprinting, published by James Parke in 1808, 146. Clarkson erred that restitution was paid for the entirety of a liberated person's life; rather, Mifflin and virtually all others who followed him, reckoned the restitution from age twenty-one for males and eighteen for females. For a recent view of Clarkson, see Dee E. Andrews and Emma Jones Lapsansky-Werner, "Thomas Clarkson's Quaker Trilogy: Abolitionist Narrative as Transformative History," in Brycchan Carey and Geoffrey Plank, eds., *Quakers and Abolition* (Urbana: University of Illinois Press, 2014), 194–208.

17. Wilson, *Clarkson,* 117 on initial sales. Wilson notes that a condensed version for Sunday school children was published in Augusta, Maine, in 1830.

18. In her "Brief Account of Warner Mifflin," Ann recounted how she would not participate in framing the will. See Lisa Wilson, *Life after Death: Widows in Pennsylvania, 1750–1850* (Philadelphia: Temple University Press, 1992), 32–33, where Ann's reasoning on this is quoted.

19. Will of Warner Mifflin in Justice, *Mifflin*, 223–28. Mifflin reckoned his wife's real estate, with principal, interest, and rents, at 2,000 pounds—equivalent today of nearly half a million dollars.

20. Petition of Warner Mifflin, [Jr.] to the Kent County Orphans Court, Dec. 4, 1799; RG 3840.006, DPA. For unknown reasons, the court did not make a ruling until February 21, 1803, when it appointed five freeholders to survey the properties. A year later, the court reordered the survey. In despair, Ann Mifflin pleaded for help from Nicholas Ridgely. Ann Mifflin to Ann Ridgely, Dec. 11, 1804, Ridgely Collection RG9200.R09.0000, DPA. Ann Ridgely's brother, Nicholas Ridgely, was by this time Chancellor of the State of Delaware. It took the Orphans Court years to settle the case.

21. On May 5, 1799, Ann Ridgely, her Kent County neighbor, wrote her daughter that Ann "has, it seems, left this county entirely." Ridgely to Ridgely, Ridgely Collection, DPA. The Murderkill Monthly Meeting sent the customary recommendation of meeting transfer to Philadelphia's Women's Meeting. PWMMM, 1783–1802, July 15, 1800.

22. The defense of Mifflin from "An Observer," C-P-W, Box 9, f7; Ann sent it to Moses Brown for his comments and to Parrish for advice on the advisability of publishing it; Mifflin to Brown, Oct. 3, 1801, Moses Brown Papers, RIHS; Mifflin to Parrish, c1799, C-P-W, Box 1, f25.

23. Churchman and Lindley to Adams, Jan. 17, 1801, Adams Papers, Mass. Hist. Soc., available on Founders Online.

24. Adams to George Churchman, Jan. 24, 1801, Adams Papers, Mass. Hist. Soc. available at Founders Online. Churchman renewed his appeal to retired President Adams in 1804, again taking up Mifflin's work. Full of deference in the first half of the letter, he breathed fire thereafter, reminding Adams that illegal slave traders operating out of Massachusetts and Rhode Island were hauling in their "filthy lucre" by transporting enslaved men and women from West Africa to the west side of the Atlantic. How could Adams, with his reservoir of political capital, not act, like Solomon, to "open thy mouth for the dumb"? How could a man of "thy age, experience, and character" stand by watching this "antichristian cruelty" that was adding "to the ponderous weight of guilt already incurred in our land, through the iniquity attending that detestable traffick"? Churchman to Adams, July 13, 1804, Adams Papers, Massachusetts Historical Society, available at Founders Online.

25. Her mother, Ann Emlen, is listed in city directories at 179 Chestnut Street, the address from which the letters of Ann Mifflin and her son Lemuel were written over the next decade.

26. Chronic sickness probably contributed to the problem. I am indebted to Mary Brooks, Westtown School Archivist, for information on Samuel and Lemuel's brief enrollments; personal communication, Nov. 23, 2015. *Drinker Diary*, Mar. 31, 1801 (2:1396) for Ann's report to the Drinkers "that her son's lame foot was put to rights lately by a Powwow Doctor or one of that sort."

27. Warner Mifflin was one of 47 men appointed to the first governing board of the school in 1794 and served on it until his death; Watson W. and Sarah B. Dewees, *Centennial History of Westtown Boarding School, 1799–1899* (Philadelphia: Sherman and Co., 1899), 27. Elizabeth Drinker's diary has many notations about Ann's eleven-year involvement in Westtown School. *Drinker Diary*, 2:1322, 1336–38, 1346, 1360, 1386.

28. Margaret Morris Haviland, "Beyond Women's Sphere: Young Quaker Women of Charity in Philadelphia, 1790–1810," *WMQ* 54 (1994): 419–46; Bruce Dorsey, *Reforming Men and Women: Gender in the Antebellum City* (Ithaca, N.Y.: Cornell University Press, 2002), 46–47 on the Society for the Poor and Aimwell School.

29. Arch Street Monthly Meeting minutes (hereafter ASMMM); PWMMM, 1793–1805, 268–69, 276, 283, 297, 320, 323. Mifflin's frequent letters to her mother provide copious details on the trips. Emlen Family Papers, Box 2, HSP.

30. Arch Street Men's Monthly Meeting Minutes, Letters to her mother on June 3, 8, 26, 30, and July 21, 1801 give rich details such as visiting the inmates of the state prison and poor house in New York. Emlen Family Papers, Box 2, HSP. She recounted staying with Brown in her letter to him of Oct. 3, 1801. Moses Brown Papers, RIHS.

31. Mifflin to Jonathan Thomas and Joel Swain, Feb. 25, 1804, in PYMIC, Box 3, f6, QCHC.

32. Anthony F. C. Wallace, *The Death and Rebirth of the Seneca* (New York: Knopf, 1970), 217–20. The Indian Committee was built on the Quakers' Friendly Association for Regaining and Preserving Peace with the Indians by Pacific Measures established during the Seven Years' War but dormant for several decades. Indian affairs became John Parrish's consuming interest, beginning with a long trip to Muskingum in 1773 and others to Newtown Point Council in 1791, the Lower Sandusky in 1793, and the peace and friendship Canandaigua treaty negotiations between the Iroquois Six Nations and the United States in 1794. Jacob Lindley, William Savery, and James Emlen were also delegates to Canandaigua. Mifflin and three other members of the 1790 delegation to Congress had met for dinner and hours of dialogue with nine Oneida chiefs, who poured out laments of discouragement and impoverishment, John Pemberton to James Pemberton, Feb. 16, 1790, *DHFFC*, 18:549–51.

33. Warner Mifflin, Ann's brother James Emlen, and close friends Lindley and Parrish had all been appointed to the Indian Committee. Warner was among the lobbyists sent to advise the Washington administration of their plan. *A Brief Account of the Proceedings of the Committee Appointed in the Year 1795 by the Yearly Meeting of Friends . . . for Promoting the Improvement and Gradual Civilization of the Indian Natives* (Philadelphia: Kimber, Conrad, and Co., 1805). For Mifflin's role, see Robert S. Cox, "Supper and Celibacy: Quaker-Seneca Reflexive Missions," in David Curtis Skaggs and Larry L. Nelson, eds., *The Sixty Years' War for the Great Lakes, 1754–1814* (East Lansing: Michigan State University Press, 2001), 252. Historians have energetically discussed Quaker motives regarding their involvement in Indian affairs after the Revolution. For some, in taking up the cause of native peoples Quakers found "a means of reconstituting a vestige of social and political power, of establishing a formal role for themselves and their Society in the new American public sphere, and at the same time, finding a way to further revitalize their Society." Cox, "Supper and Celibacy," 250; for less status-driven treatments see Anthony F. C. Wallace, *Death and Rebirth of the Seneca*, 217–27, and Matthew Dennis, *Seneca Possessed: Indians, Witchcraft, and Power in the Early American Republic* (Philadelphia: University of Pennsylvania Press, 2010), 122–28, who sees deeply ingrained "humanitarian impulses" at work.

34. "Relation of a visit made to the Indians in 1802 by H[enry] Kirkbride and A[nn] Mifflin with other friends in the course of their journey to Upper Canada with some observations on their origin, etc." Logan-Fisher-Fox Papers, Box 11, HSP. In her fifteen-page account of the trip, Mifflin made many ethnographic observations of the native people, all of which convinced her they "are of the stock of Abraham." For two recent accounts of the travails of the Brotherton and Stockbridge refugees in Oneida country, swamped by inrushing whites intent on driving them west, see David J. Silverman, *Red Brethren: The Brothertown and Stockbridge Indians and the Problem of Race in Early America* (Ithaca, N.Y.: Cornell University Press, 2010); and Brad E. Jarvis, *The Brothertown Nation of Indians: Land Ownership and Nationalism in Early America, 1740–1840*

(Lincoln: University of Nebraska Press, 2010). Neither book discusses the embassy of Ann Mifflin and her fellow Friends in 1802.

35. Cox, "Supper and Celibacy," 261–63 on the double nature of the Quaker missionaries sent out by the Indian Committee. Ann Mifflin's traveling certificates were approved by the Arch Street Men's meeting. AMMM, June 25 and July 30, 1802.

36. Dennis, *Seneca Possessed*, 119–22; Jill Kinney, "Letters, Pen, and Tilling the Field: Quaker Schools Among the Seneca Indians on the Allegany River, 1798–1852," Ph.D. dissertation, University of Rochester, 2009, ch. 1.

37. Wallace, *Death and Rebirth*, 203–4 describes the whites she saw along the way as "a peculiarly dilapidated and discouraged brand of European culture brought by hopeful speculators, by hungry farmers fleeing the cold and rocky hillsides of New England, and by hard-drinking Scotch-Irish weavers driven from Ulster by high taxes and the new weaving machines," whose brand of civilization compared unfavorably with that of the Seneca.

38. "Account of a visit made by Penrose Wiley, John Letchworth, Anne Mifflin, Mary Bell & Co. to the Seneca Indians, settled on Allegany River," Oct. 1803, Logan-Fisher-Fox Collection, Ser. 4, Box 2A.

39. The trip to the Allegany reservation is described in George Snyderman, "Halliday Jackson's Journal of a Visit Paid to the Indians of New York (1806)," *American Philosophical Society Proceedings*, 101, 6 (1957): 569–70; Ann Mifflin, Journal of Visit to Senecas, October 1803, HSP.

40. Wallace, *Death and Rebirth*, 208.

41. Mifflin to Jonathan Thomas and Joel Swain, Feb. 25, 1804, PYMIC, Box 3, f6. Mifflin recounted her meetings with Handsome Lake and Cornplanter.

42. Just as they had for generations, native people chose selectively from what even the best intentioned white missionaries offered; in this case they accepted some instruction, such as in animal husbandry, while resisting other recommendations such as the private ownership of land. As for gender work reallocation, most Seneca women resisted giving up the power and status they enjoyed as key agriculturalists. Dennis, *Seneca Possessed*, 134–37, 167–78; see also David Swatzler, *A Friend Among the Senecas: The Quaker Mission to Cornplanter's People* (Mechanicsburg, Pa.: Stackpole, 2000).

43. In 1802, Ann had shown interest in Warner's lifetime cause. When the English traveling minister Dorothy Ripley passed through Philadelphia on her way to preach antislavery in the South, she stayed for a week with Ann, finding the widow eager to introduce her to city Friends. *The Extraordinary Conversion and Religious Experience of Dorothy Ripley . . . with Her First Voyage and Travels in America* (New York: G. and R. Waite, 1810), 61–62, 66.

44. In his letter to Jefferson, Dec. 25, 1810, Jefferson Papers, LC, available on Founders Online, John Lynch related that Ann broached her plan in about 1805 with London-based William Dillwyn, the key figure in cross-Atlantic Quaker abolitionist communications, and with his aging cousin James Pemberton in Philadelphia, longtime president of the Pennsylvania Abolition Society. Dillwyn had talked with Granville Sharp, and, if Ann was correct, it was her idea that seeded the London-based African Institution, founded in 1807 to rescue the failing Sierra Leone experiment. Ann's discussion of this with Dillwyn's daughter and her husband is described in Samuel and Susanna [Dillwyn] Emlen to William Dillwyn, Dec. 30, 1806, Emlen and Dillwyn Papers, Box 5, f17, LCP.

45. Mifflin to Paul Cuffe, Feb. 2, 1811, Miscellaneous Manuscript Collection, FHLSC; Lamont Thomas, *Rise to Be a People: A Biography of Paul Cuffe* (Urbana: University of Illinois Press, 1986),

35–36, 59, 77, 90, 117, 130n18, 133n15, 139–40n9 for Mifflin's frequent contacts with Cuffe. Thomas sees Ann Mifflin as "an important figure in Paul Cuffe's future as an African civilizer" (128n35). Cuffe undertook such a mission in 1811. Karen Younger, "Africa Stretches Forth Her Hands unto You: Female Colonization Supporters in the Antebellum U.S.," Ph.D. dissertation, Pennsylvania State University, 2006, opens her dissertation with Ann Mifflin's lobbying effort in Maryland and Virginia in 1810.

46. Lynch to Thomas Jefferson, Dec. 25, 1810, Founders Online.

47. Mifflin combined her trip promoting her colonization scheme with meetings with the North Carolina Yearly Meeting and others at the Western Quarterly Meeting in Isle of Wight County and Campbell County, Va. PWMMM, 1805–1814, 240–41, 264–65, 271 for endorsements for this traveling ministry.

48. Mifflin to Ann Emlen, Sept. 18, 30, 1810, Emlen Family Papers, Box 2. The American Colonization Society is treated in P. J. Staudenraus, *The American Colonization Movement, 1816–1865* (New York: Columbia University Press, 1961), and Douglas R. Egerton, "'Its Origin Is Not a Little Curious': A New Look at the American Colonization Society," *Journal of the Early Republic* 5 (1985): 463–80.

49. John Lynch to Thomas Jefferson, Dec. 25, 1810; Jefferson to Lynch, Jan. 21, 1811, Founders Online.

50. The will, discussed below, is in Will Book #20, recorded May 20, 1848, Philadelphia City Archives. Hilda Justice cited Ann Mifflin's will but gave only a hint of its contents, perhaps because it revealed more than she wished to divulge about the ill-feeling between Ann and her stepchildren. Justice, *Mifflin*, 228.

51. *An Account of the Origins, Progress, and Present Condition of the Philadelphia Society for the Establishment and Support of Charity Schools . . .* (Philadelphia, 1831), 57. Mifflin was appointed to the electing committee, perhaps through the recommendation of Caleb Emlen, his mother's brother, who was one of the founders.

52. Lemuel Mifflin to William Jackson, July 19, 1812, Jackson-Conrad Family Papers, RG 5/217, FHLSC.

53. Lloyd Mifflin to Joseph Mifflin, Jr., Nov. 6, 1813, Mifflin Family Papers, MS 32, Box 3, folder 3, FMCSC. Lloyd Mifflin, later to become a notable literary figure, wrote to his brother that Samuel "is acknowledged to be in a state of derangement—the symptoms occasionally varying, sometimes violent and sometimes more moderate . . . since his first attack."

54. Mifflin to Jefferson ca. Sept. 26, 1814; ca. Sept. 27, 1814, Jefferson Papers, LC, available at Founders Online. Mifflin spelled out that his father had married the daughter of Joseph Galloway's only sister.

55. Lemuel Mifflin Administrator with the will annexed to the estate of Ann Mifflin, April 12, 1815, Book L, folio 244, Philadelphia City Archives. For Dr. Samuel Mifflin, see John J. Jordan, *Colonial and Revolutionary Families of Pennsylvania* (New York: Lewis Publishing, 1911), 194.

56. Mifflin to Jackson, Jan. 10, 1808; April 29, 1808 and undated letter, probably 1809; Jackson-Conrad Family Papers, FHLSC.

57. All eight founders, including Roberts Vaux, Reuben Haines, and Samuel Lewis, were not yet twenty-one. Mifflin was listed as secretary of the Philadelphia Hose Company in 1810–1811, *Historical Sketches of the Formation and Founders of the Philadelphia Hose Company . . .* (Philadelphia: Philadelphia Hose Co., 1854), 62; a picture of "the original hose carriage" is on p. 39. This was the first volunteer fire company using the newfangled "hose carriage" engineered by the

redoubtable Patrick Lyon, fabled in history for his false imprisonment for bank robbery in the midst of the 1798 yellow fever epidemic.

58. Mifflin to Jackson, n.d. but in 1811; Feb. 19, 20, 1812, and Aug. 6, 1812, Jackson-Conrad Family Papers. FHLSC. In the letter of Aug. 6, Mifflin exclaimed, "I have done with this city. I have from this moment resigned my citizenship and am determined never to return except as a transient visitor." The origin of Samuel and Lemuel's alienation from the Society of Friends is hidden from history. Lemuel had already convinced his mother to invest substantial sums in Ohio land. In her will of 1811, she bequeathed 477 acres of unimproved land and two lots in Frankford, Ohio, to Samuel and 480 acres of land and a lot in Muskingum County to Lemuel.

59. John Hunt Diary, Sept. 22, 1812, reported the contents of Lemuel's letter to his mother. FHLSC.

60. *Pennsylvania Archives*, 6th Ser., vol. 8 (Harrisburg, 1907), 431; vol. 9 (Harrisburg, 1907), 154. Payroll records show enlistment from Aug. 27, 1814 to Jan. 1, 1815; David Bowen, *A History of Philadelphia . . . with an Historical Account of the Military Operations of the Late War in 1812, 1813, 1814* (Philadelphia, 1839), 48; *A Brief History of the Military Operations on the Delaware during the Late War . . . with Muster-Rolls of the Several Volunteer Corps* (Philadelphia, 1820).

61. PMMMM, 1814–15, Jan. 5, 1815.

62. John Hunt Diary, April 17, May 26, 1815.

63. Aside from the Ohio lands she left to her sons, Ann bequeathed them many other properties and ground rents in Philadelphia and Darby, along with bonds and cash.

64. *Reports of Cases Adjudged in the Supreme Court of Pennsylvania*, ed. Thomas Sergeant and William Rawle, vol. 6 (Philadelphia, 1872), 460–61.

65. Philadelphia Monthly Meeting Grave Books, 1824–27, 5; PMM Arch Street Burial Records, 1820–1872, 24, where Lemuel's death was recorded as Aug. 8, 1824, noting he was not a member, Ancestry.com. Philadelphia Monthly Meeting Death Notices, FHLSC. His papers include portions of his accounts for his dry goods store. In his will he left $3,000 to his uncle Dr. Samuel Emlen and a substantial part of his estate to his half-sister Sarah Mifflin Neall, who had helped raise him in Kent County and Philadelphia. Lemuel Mifflin Papers, HSP.

66. Legislative Petitions, Accession #10381603 and 10381713; Essah, *A House Divided*, 121–23. The Delaware Abolition Society, of which Mifflin was not a member, coordinated the petition campaign. The society's records, after its revival in the early nineteenth century, show no involvement of Mifflin's sons. Minutes of their meetings are at the Historical Society of Pennsylvania and the Delaware Historical Society.

67. Darby Monthly Meeting Minutes, 1828–1831, 3 reporting on "names brought forward from Murtherkill Preparative Meeting" of members "going off in the separation." Accessed on Ancestry.com, Jan. 6, 2016. The Hicksite Separation of 1827–1828, led by Elias Hicks, badly fractured the Society of Friends, with an impasse on theological and political issues.

68. Dee Andrews, "Reconsidering the First Emancipation: Evidence from the Pennsylvania Abolition Society Correspondence, 1785–1810," in Nicholas Canny, Joseph E. Illick, Gary B. Nash, and William Pencak, *Empire, Society and Labor: Essays in Honor of Richard S. Dunn, Pennsylvania History 64*, Special Supplemental Issue (Summer 1997): 230–31; and Carol Wilson, *Freedom at Risk: The Kidnapping of Free Blacks in America, 1780–1865* (Lexington: University Press of Kentucky, 1994), 95–96. Wilson confuses Warner Mifflin, Jr., with his father.

69. Warner's other half-sisters married within the Eastern Shore Quaker orbit but with much less abolitionist intensity. In 1793, Elizabeth Mifflin (1769–1829?) married the upstanding Samuel

Howell (1755–1806), to whom Warner entrusted many of his affairs. Eyre Mifflin (1774–1802) died only fourteen months after her marriage to Thomas Berry, one of Cecil County, Maryland's leading Quaker antislavery activists, and four months after giving birth to a daughter. Rebecca Mifflin (1777–1804?), Warner's youngest half-sister, tangled the already complicated Mifflin bloodlines by marrying Joseph Galloway Rowland, whose mother, Ann Johns Rowland, was the sister of Warner's first wife. Proudly ignoring the ignominy of her uncle Joseph Galloway, Warner's sister-in-law had named her first son after Philadelphia's infamous Loyalist. This was one branch of the Mifflin tree that bore no abolitionist fruit, for Joseph Galloway Rowland, Quaker-turned-Methodist, became a Kent County banker, investor, and state jurist. J. Thomas Scharf, *History of Delaware, 1609–1888*, 2 vols. (Philadelphia: L. J. Richards, 1888; repr. Delmarva Roots, 2001), 1:310; 2:740, 1109, 1134, 1160.

70. However, as noted in Chapter 3, Jonathan Hunn (1729–1792), the patriarch, had to be cudgeled by Warner to free his slaves and pay them reparations.

71. Will of Daniel Mifflin, in Justice, *Mifflin*, 221. Mary Mifflin Hunn's death came at age twenty-five, four months after delivering a daughter named Ann. Daniel, her firstborn, died at age two. Ann Mifflin Hunn would thicken the Mifflin-Hunn connections when she married Samuel Mifflin, a second cousin.

72. Todd A. Herring, "Kidnapped and Sold in Natchez: The Ordeal of Aaron Cooper, a Free Black Man," *Journal of Mississippi History* 60 (1998): 341–53; Robin Krawitz, Director of the Historic Preservation Program at Delaware State University, drew my attention to this case and has been exceedingly generous in sharing her years of research on the Hunn family, including the interrogatories in the Cooper case from the Natchez Historic Foundation.

73. "Recollections of the Old Home and of Her Childhood by our Grandmother Lydia J. Sharpless Hunn," 1893, typescript in possession of Robin Krawitz. *The Historical and Biographical Encyclopedia of Delaware* (Wilmington, Del.: Aldine, 1882), described Ezekiel Hunn as "a great abolitionist [who] assisted many poor fugitives from the house of bondage."

74. The notorious Patty Cannon, who ran a ring of man-stealers and slave agents in the late 1820s along the Delaware-Maryland border, takes center stage in this historical novel, while the Hunns, and to a lesser extent Warner Mifflin's descendants, hover in the wings as conductors of the Underground Railroad.

75. The Murderkill Meeting was renamed the Camden Monthly Meeting in 1806, when the meeting moved from its rural location south of Dover into the town of Camden. Jonathan Hunn gave the land for the construction of the new meetinghouse. He was appointed a delegate to the Southern Quarterly Meeting for most of the 1850s, was appointed a minister by the Southern Quarterly Meeting in 1854, and served as Clerk of the Camden Monthly Meeting from 1854 to 1856.

76. Hunn related this incident from Beaumont, South Carolina, to William Still in 1871 for the black Philadelphian's compendium of stories of the Underground Railroad, published a year later as *The Underground Railroad* (Philadelphia: Porter & Coates, 1872), 715–19; in 1970 reprint, see 649–50, 741–45. For treatment of the Delaware Underground Railroad network of escape routes and individual participants, largely Quakers, see William J. Switala, *The Underground Railroad in Delaware, Maryland, and West Virginia* (Mechanicsburg, Pa.: Stackpole, 2004).

77. Hunn, "Recollections of the Old Home" for verbal exchange between Taney and Hunn. The two damage suits were *Turner v. Hunn* and *Glanding v. Hunn*, 1848. Though Samuel Burris escaped charges for rescuing the Hawkins family, two years later his role as an Underground

Railroad conductor brought arrest, conviction, and a sentence to be sold on the auction block into slavery in Dover for seven years. Burris stood stolidly as the hammer fell at $500, with an unknown trader holding the winning bid. Then John Hunn stepped forward to whisper in his ear that he had been purchased with "abolition gold." Hunn and Thomas Garrett had enlisted Wilmington Quaker Isaac S. Flint to pose as a slave trader, funded by the Pennsylvania Abolition Society to snatch the man out of the jaws of enslavement.

78. John Hunn to Wilbur Siebert, Aug. 16, 1893, Wilbur H. Siebert Collection, Ohio Historical Society, Columbus, quoted in Eric Foner, *Gateway to Freedom: The Hidden History of the Underground Railroad* (New York: Norton, 2015), 156.

79. William T. Kelly, "The Underground Railroad in the Eastern Shore of Maryland and Delaware," accessed online at www.swarthmore.edu/library/friends/URR_maryland_kelley. htm, January 6, 2016. As Kelly related, a Quaker whose home Hunn frequented remembered "his voice was of a rich, mellow accent . . . and his thrusts into creeds, hirelings, and slave-holding oppression were keen and searching, and when wrapped in a prophetic vision, as he saw in the future abolition of slavery . . . he was as fearless as a lion."

80. Still, *Underground Railroad*, 748. A year before he died, Hunn responded to William Still that he was "Superintendent of the U.G.R.R. from Wilmington down the Peninsula." Still memorialized him as a "freedom-loving, earnest, and whole-souled Quaker abolitionist" who "was well-known to the colored people far and near and was especially sought . . . as a friend who would never fail to assist as far as possible in every time of need." For more on Hunn in Port Royal, see Willie Lee Rose, *Rehearsal for Reconstruction: The Port Royal Experiment* (New York: Bobbs-Merrill, 1964), 78–79, 288, 366–67, 396; Rose calls the Hunns, father and daughter, and Charlotte Forten "unsurpassed in dedication, talent, and tenacity" (79).

81. Elizabeth died in December 1807, when Ann Mifflin was with her in Little Creek Hundred. Ann to her mother, Dec. 18, 1807, Emlen Family Papers, HSP.

82. "Historic Woodburn—The Governor's House in Delaware," *Daughters of the American Revolution Magazine* (August–September 1973). The Georgian-style Woodburn, built about 1790 by one of Warner Mifflin's collateral kinsmen, fronted the St. Jones River. According to family legend, this provided the opportunity to dig a tunnel to escort slaves fleeing northward toward Smyrna, Odessa, and Middletown and then across the Delaware River to New Jersey. Contemporary research has not confirmed this family story.

83. Kenneth Carroll, *Quakerism on the Eastern Shore* (Baltimore: Maryland Historical Society, 1970), 139–42, 182.

84. Ann Mifflin sent the testimony to Moses Brown, Oct. 3, 1801, as cited above; it was inserted in the Raisin family Bible—*The New Testament of Our Lord and Saviour Jesus Christ* (Trenton, N.J.: Isaac Collins, 1791), Bible Collection, Swarthmore, FHLSC. Chris Densmore drew my attention to this Bible with its poignant testimonial.

85. Ibid. Her husband continued the work of liberating slaves and visiting the families of freed blacks on the west side of the Eastern Shore peninsula. He visited the Virginia Yearly Meeting with Warner's widow the year after his wife's death. Carroll, *Quakerism on the Eastern Shore*, 141–42, 182.

86. DCMMM, Nov. 9, 1799.

87. Ten Mifflins are listed on the marriage certificate, along with many other relations; the marriage certificate is in Justice, *Mifflin*, 136–37.

88. Whittier, "Daniel Neall," in *The Works of John Greenleaf Whittier*, 3 vols. (Boston: Houghton, Mifflin, 1892), 3:123–24. Beverly Tomek's *Pennsylvania Hall: A "Legal Lynching" in the Shadow*

*of the Liberty Bell* (New York: Oxford University Press, 2014) treats the incident at length. Whittier had moved to Philadelphia to become the editor of the abolitionist *Pennsylvania Freeman*.

89. The fullest account of Elizabeth Johns Neall Gay is in Don Papson and Tom Calarco, *Secret Lives of the Underground Railroad in New York City: Sydney Howard Gay, Louis Napoleon, and the Record of Fugitives* (Jefferson, N.C.: McFarland, 2015). The marriage, on Nov. 7, 1845, was at the Neall home in Philadelphia.

90. Elizabeth Neall to Elizabeth Whittier, Aug. 17, 1841, Daniel Neall Papers, FHLSC, quoted in Papson and Calarco, *Secret Lives*, 32.

91. Elizabeth Neall to Elizabeth Pease, June 18, 1842, Sydney Howard Gay Papers, Rare Book and Manuscript Library, Columbia University, quoted in Papson and Calarco, *Secret Lives*, 32.

92. Gay was not a Friend, so the out-of-meeting marriage, at first opposed by her father (who finally relented), cost Elizabeth her Quaker membership. Gay's description of his wife is from Willcox, "A Gay Life," quoted in Papson and Calarco, *Secret Lives*, 31.

93. Foner, *Gateway to Freedom* features Sydney Howard Gay as the pivotal figure in New York City's Underground Railroad activities. For Elizabeth Johns Neall Gay's antislavery bazaar work, 188–89 and. Papson and Calarco, *Secret Lives*, 96, 206–7, 213; and Julie Roy Jeffrey, *The Great Silent Army of Abolitionism* (Chapel Hill: University of North Carolina Press, 1998), passim. Elizabeth worked for antislavery fairs in Boston, New York, and Philadelphia, and in 1857 joined Abigail Hopper Gibbons, daughter of Philadelphia's Isaac Hopper, to co-found the Anti-Slavery Fair Association, an important financial supporter of the American Anti-Slavery Society.

94. Keeping the legacy of her grandfather and mother alive, Sydney and Elizabeth Johns Neall Gay named their second child Sarah Mifflin Gay, whose knowledge of her grandfather's history led her to write an account of him in the early twentieth century. Sarah Mifflin Gay, "A Biographical Note on Warner Mifflin," in Justice, *Mifflin*, 38–40.

95. The School for Horticulture is now the Ambler campus of Temple University. I have not been able to find Hilda Justice's papers, which likely would yield further information on Warner Mifflin's life.

96. For the Quaker communities at Pyrmont and Minden, see Francis R. Taylor, *The Life of William Savery of Philadelphia, 1750–1804* (New York: Macmillan, 1925), ch. 16–17. News of Pemberton's death at Pyrmont reached Philadelphia in May 1795. *Drinker Diary*, May 6, 1795 (1:677).

97. Amelia Mott Gummere translated Scenes 1–4 and 10–11, summarizing Scenes 5–9, in *PMHB*, 29 (1905), 439–50. The play was never staged in the U.S., though many of Kotzebue's plays were popular in seaboard cities. For Quaker influence in Russia and Prussia, see Sarah Crabtree, *Holy Nation: The Transatlantic Quaker Ministry in an Age of Revolution* (Chicago: University of Chicago Press, 2015), 19, 34–35, 103, 112, 151, 158, 171–72; Hans Albrecht, "The Meeting House at Bad Pyrmont," *Bulletin of the Friends Historical Society* 25 (1936): 62–73; and Richenda Scott, *Quakers in Russia* (London: M. Joseph, 1964). My thanks to Jenna Gibbs for tracing notices of theater appearances in Germany and Austria.

98. RG26, Records of the Department of State, Corporation Bureau, Charter Books, vol. 2 (1815–19), Pennsylvania State Archives, Harrisburg.

99. *Colored American*, Jan. 20, 1838.

100. *Friends Miscellany* 2 (1832) 328–33; 5 (1834), 193–222. Justice, *Mifflin*, 74, recycled part of this under "George Washington and Warner Mifflin"; Mott, *Biographical Sketches*, 2nd ed. (New York: Mahlon Day, 1837), 123–27. Mott's *Sketches* went through many editions over subsequent decades.

101. *The Friend* 17 (1844): 135.

102. In a rare remembrance of him, *The National Era*, April 22, 1847, called Mifflin one of the "unflinching champions of freedom" in its essay on "Quaker Slaveholding and How It Was Abolished." Today, the Society of Friends counts fewer than 400,000 adult members, about half of them living outside the United States.

103. I have described how schoolbook readers and the public at large for a century after the Civil War would have been clueless about Quaker leadership in the abolition movement in "The Hidden Story of Quakers and Slavery," Carey and Plank, eds., *Quakers and Abolition*, 209–24. Late nineteenth-century multi-volume histories of the United States, such as those by Edward Channing, John Fiske, and Justin Winsor had nothing to say about Mifflin, or for that matter, about Lay, Woolman, Benezet, and other Quakers.

104. Isaac Sharpless, *History of Quaker Government in Pennsylvania*, 2 vols. (Philadelphia: T. S. Leach, 1898–99), 2:250–51. Mifflin's candle flickered briefly in the 1930s when the *Dictionary of American Biography*, sponsored by the American Council of Learned Societies, distilled three centuries of the American past into thousands of biographical essays, including one on Warner Mifflin. *Dictionary of American Biography*, 20 vols. (New York, Scribner's Sons, 1926–1937). In 1999, the *American National Biography*, intent on giving due credit to minorities, women, and post-World War II luminaries, scratched Mifflin from its total of 17,400 entries. *American National Biography*, 20 vols. (New York: Oxford University Press, 1999; Supplement vol. 2002).

### Appendix 1. Crèvecoeur and Mifflin

1. A good entry into the massive literature on Crèvecoeur's *Letters from an American Farmer* is Norman S. Grabo, "Crèvecoeur's America: Beginning the World Anew," *William and Mary Quarterly* 3rd ser. 48 (1991): 159–72. Crèvecoeur's *Letters* was first published in the United States by Mathew Carey in Philadelphia in 1793, the year of the devastating yellow fever epidemic and in France the year of terror.

2. Marie-Jeanne Rossignol, "Jacques-Pierre Brissot and the Fate of Atlantic Antislavery During the Age of Revolutionary Wars," in Richard Bessel et al., eds., *War, Empire and Slavery, 1770–1830* (London: Palgrave Macmillan, 2010), 139–56; Rossignol, "The Quaker Antislavery Commitment and How It Revolutionized French Antislavery Through the Crèvecoeur-Brissot Friendship, 1782–1789," in Brycchan Carey and Geoffrey Plank, eds., *Quakers and Abolition* (Urbana: University of Illinois Press, 2014), 180–93. A century ago, Crèvecoeur's first English language biographer took note of the Frenchman's mention of "Walter Mifflin" in the 1784 Paris edition of *Lettres*. Julia Post Mitchell, *St. Jean de Crèvecoeur* (New York: Columbia University Press, 1916), 26, 76. Mitchell did not identify Mifflin or inquire into the authenticity of their meetings. Neither did Edith Philips in *The Good Quaker in French Legend* (Philadelphia: University of Pennsylvania Press, 1932) after mentioning Crèvecoeur's celebration of "Walter Mifflin" (111–13); nor did Howard C. Rice, *Le cultivateur américain: Étude sur l'oeuvre de Saint John de Crèvecoeur* (Paris, 1932; Geneva imprint 1978), 114, 122–23 for notices of Crèvecoeur's material on Mifflin.

3. For this brief account of Crèvecoeur's early life in North America and England, I have followed Gay Wilson Allen and Roger Asselineau, *St. John de Crèvecoeur: The Life of an American Farmer* (New York: Viking, 1987), chs. 1–5. The English publishers were Thomas Davies and Lockyer Davis.

4. For Crèvecoeur's concluding chapters in *American Farmer* on slavery in the southern colonies and the account of the grisly torture of the slave as an imaginative rather than an actually witnessed performance, see Thomas Philbrick, *St. John de Crèvecoeur* (New York: Twayne, 1970), 45–48. Reading the London 1782 *Letters* from "an antislavery angle," Rossignol shows other passages where Crèvecoeur evidenced antislavery sentiments. "The Quaker Antislavery Commitment," 180–85.

5. Crèvecoeur explained that while on the road to Lancaster, Pennsylvania, he was invited by a new acquaintance to travel to Kent County, Delaware, "to pass some time in the house of Mr. Walter [Warner] Mifflin." *Lettres d'un cultivateur américain* (Paris, 1784), x–xxii. By his own account, Mifflin freed twenty-seven slaves.

6. Deep into the 1784 French edition, Crèvecoeur included sixteen pages of dialogue between Mifflin and the warring commanding generals. Ibid., 182–98.

7. Manuscript Travel Book of Willliam Roberts, Galloway Family Papers, Library of Congress.

8. William Roberts was domiciled in London from December 28, 1780, to June 28, 1782. Roberts Travel Book. Crèvecoeur was in London from about October 17, 1780, to August 1, 1781. Philbrick, *St. John de Crèvecoeur*, 27. This is when the Frenchman secured publication of *Letters from an American Farmer* with Davies and Davis, the London publishers. At no other time were the two in the same city where they could have engaged with each other.

9. Robert Darnton and Daniel Roche, eds., *Revolution in Print: The Press in France, 1775–1800* (Berkeley: University of California Press, 1989), 148. With Mifflin's name now before the French reading public, a spirited defense of slavery appeared in *Mercure de France* three months later. While commending Mifflin's humanitarian actions—"it is an humane act that merits praise when the circumstances authorize it"—the anonymous author insisted that slavery was "legitimate under the laws of Christianity, which are neither contrary to the rights of Reason nor those of Nature." Aaron Freeman provided a translation of this long defense of slavery. The material on Mifflin did not include the peace mission to Generals Howe and Washington.

10. *Lettres d'un cultivateur américain*, nearly twice as long as *Letters from an American Farmer*, has never been translated into English except for the pages on Mifflin that Hilda Justice, in *Life and Ancestry of Warner Mifflin: Patriot—Philanthropist—Humanitarian* (Philadelphia: Ferris & Leach, 1905) took from the 1787 edition.

11. The book's dedication to the Marquis de Lafayette was another indication of Crèvecoeur's enlistment into the ranks of the Atlantic-wide antislavery campaigners. After serving as one of Washington's treasured generals and becoming a virtual surrogate son of the childless Continental Army leader, Lafayette had proposed to Washington that they free their slaves and settle them on Lafayette's plantation in French Guiana as free yeoman farmers.

12. After a number of years in London and its environs, after earning law credentials at the Middle Temple, and marrying the only daughter of Philadelphia Loyalist Joseph Galloway, Roberts cranked out a play that was noted in a literary journal but never staged. He became an amateur artist of Virginia's Natural Bridge and Harper's Ferry, paintings that captivated Jefferson, who purchased them after Roberts visited him during the presidency of the Sage of Monticello.

13. For example, Allen and Asselineau, *Crèvecoeur*, 72–75.

14. In his letter to Jefferson in 1803, Roberts reminded him that Crèvecoeur had introduced them to each other in London. This must have been between March 12 and April 26, the only time Jefferson stayed in the British metropolis. Roberts to Jefferson, July 24, 1803, *Papers of Jefferson*, 41:111–12. In his Travel Book Roberts noted that he had dinner at Monticello the next day. After

returning to the United States during Jefferson's first presidential term, estranged from his wife, Roberts traveled extensively and became a talented painter. He was in Charlottesville when he wrote this letter to Jefferson, hoping to sell him his landscapes of the Natural Bridge and Harper's Ferry at the junction of the Potomac and Shenandoah rivers. Jefferson acquired two of his oil paintings as well as engravings made from them. See Barbara C. Batson, "Virginia Landscapes by William Roberts," *Journal of Early Southern Decorative Arts* 10 (1984): 35–48. Batson and other art historians have been unaware of his background.

# Index

# Acknowledgments

The origins of this book go back to the 1980s, when I stumbled upon *The Defence of Warner Mifflin Against Aspersions cast on him on Account of his endeavours to promote Righteousness, Mercy, and Peace among Mankind* (1793), which alerted me to the obscurity in which this seemingly important Kent County, Delaware Quaker had languished for several centuries. A note on him remained tucked in a file cabinet for years as other projects occupied me. Then, out of the blue, came an inquiry from Sue Kozel four years ago about writing an introduction for a book of new essays that she and Maurice Jackson, author of a stirring biography on Anthony Benezet, were putting together on Quaker abolitionists and their friends. My counter-offer was to write an essay on Warner Mifflin, to which Kozol and Jackson agreed.

Thinking that it might be a stretch to find sufficient material to rescue Mifflin from historical amnesia, I was astounded to find that he had been hidden in plain sight—that is, to be found in the correspondence of founding fathers, in the newspapers of the revolutionary era, in his other essays published in Philadelphia, and in his extensive correspondence strewn across a dozen repositories stretching from Massachusetts to California. Thus began a three-year effort to provide a full biography of the descendant of one of the founding families of William Penn's Holy Experiment in Pennsylvania. And so my first debt is to Sue Kozol and Maurice Jackson for the invitation that launched me on this book project.

A book project is only as good as the opportunity to publish it. I was fortunate that Bob Lockhart, History Editor at the University of Pennsylvania Press, expressed an interest in it and provided important feedback over several years of bringing this project to completion. The support of Dan Richter, Director of the McNeil Center for Early American Studies at the University of Pennsylvania, brought me into the fold of the book series on Early Atlantic History. To Lockhart and Richter I am indebted for this initial endorsement and encouragement.

Then the moment arrives when a manuscript must pass muster with editors, referees, and editorial board members of a university press. For sympathetic and incisive readings, along with critically important corrections and suggestions for improvement, I thank Dan Richter, Jean R. Soderlund, David Waldstreicher, and Mike Zuckerman. Responding to their deep knowledge of politics, statecraft, religion, race relations, gender, and popular culture in the age of democratic revolutions obliged me to rethink and clarify many passages of what I had submitted in draft form. The book is all the better for their collegial criticism. Two friends of many years, Emma Lapsansky-Werner and Marcus Rediker, heartened me with their support and also provided astute advice on revisions. So did a new friend, Alec Dun. And for reading a draft of the introduction to the book, I thank Sara Melzer and Ruth Sabean.

Jefferson said famously that he could not live without books. Like most of my colleagues, I cannot live without librarians, curators, and archivists. The greatest troves of Warner Mifflin material are at the Historical Society of Pennsylvania (HSP), the Friends Historical Library at Swarthmore College (FHLSC), and the Friends Collection at Haverford College (FCHC). The staff at HSP were tireless in bringing me materials; at FHLSC, Chris Densmore and Patricia O'Donnell led me to deeply buried materials; and Ann Upton, Mary Crauderueff, Sarah Horowitz, and other staff members at FCHC faithfully responded to my requests. Jim Green at the Library Company of Philadelphia was, as always, my go-to person on matters of printed materials, and the talented staff there made my visits profitable and pleasurable. At Franklin and Marshall College, where the voluminous Mifflin Family Papers are housed; at the William Clements Library at the University of Michigan; the Delaware Public Archives; the Delaware Historical Society; Special Collections at the University of Delaware; the Henry Huntington Library; Columbia University, where Eric Foner provided assistance; the Rhode Island Historical Society; and the Massachusetts Historical Society I found indispensable assistance. The "Mapping West Philadelphia" website constructed by Jim Duffield at the University of Pennsylvania Archives and Billy G. Smith's "Mapping Early Philadelphia" project provided data that helped me plot Mifflin's sojourning in Philadelphia and connect him with his circle of friends. Chuck di Giacomantonio and Matthew Fleissig, his intern at the Documentary History of the First Federal Congress project, also helped with providing copies of the Galloway Papers at Library of Congress.

At the Young Research Library at UCLA, my home base of operations for fifty years in Los Angeles, I found all the assistance I needed from expert librarians and bibliographers, including Marta Brunner and Nina Mamikumian. Also at UCLA, two graduate students, Aaron Freeman and Bethany Shiffman, helped me with translations of French materials. Joan Waugh and Carla Pestana, my colleagues in the Department of History, gave sage advice on parts of the manuscript. Miles Stanley, an honors graduate of UCLA's History Department, has answered every call as my Research Assistant.

In Delaware, Robin L. Krawitz at Delaware State University provided me with important materials on Mifflin family members and descendants. Introducing me to Mike McDowell provided massive and unexpected rewards. A local historian operating from his home in Newark, Delaware, McDowell has been hunting down Mifflin materials for many years while transcribing letters where age and crabbed handwriting have made reading them difficult. Without Mike's generosity in sharing materials and without hundreds of email exchanges about Warner Mifflin and his struggle for a better United States, this book would have been a pale version of its present form. In Delaware, I also had important assistance from the staff at the Delaware Public Archives in Dover and from Mike Richards, keeper of the flame for local Quaker history in Kent County, Delaware.

Living across the country from my sources in Pennsylvania and Delaware, I obtained the research assistance of graduate students who could ferret out, transcribe, and provide digital copies of materials that I had not been able to consult on my research trips. Kristin Tremper at Lehigh University and Spencer Wells at the University of Virginia were essential to this, especially poring through Quaker meeting records where Warner Mifflin's footprints were frequently found. Nic Wood, whose work on antislavery politics in the Early Republic intersects with my study of Mifflin, has been exceedingly generous in alerting me to sources I might have never found while providing me with digital copies of invaluable materials from Quaker meeting records and collections at Haverford College. After several years of email exchanges and meetings in Philadelphia about our common interests, Wood read a draft of the manuscript and offered important suggestions. I am not sure if scholars working on Quaker materials are unusually generous in sharing materials, but this has been my experience in writing this book.

At the University of Pennsylvania Press, I have benefited from the guiding hands of managing editors Alison Anderson and Noreen O'Connor-Abel.

Sister Mary Jean, CSM, ably copyedited the manuscript. The maps were constructed by Paul Dangel.

In research visits to Philadelphia, Vern and Betsy Stanton and Peter and Gail Hearn have provided bed, breakfast, libation, and lively conversation. Friends for many decades, they made life comfortable for this wandering scholar. Also David Maxey and Mike Churchman graciously listened to my rambling thoughts on Mifflin.